Extra Virgin

Extra Virgin

ANNIE HAWES

PENGUIN BOOKS

PENGUIN BOOKS

Published by the Penguin Group
Penguin Books Ltd, 80 Strand, London WC2R 0RL, England
Penguin Putnam Inc., 375 Hudson Street, New York, New York 10014, USA
Penguin Books Australia Ltd, Ringwood, Victoria, Australia
Penguin Books Canada Ltd, 10 Alcorn Avenue, Toronto, Ontario, Canada M4V 3B2
Penguin Books India (P) Ltd, 11 Community Centre, Panchsheel Park, New Delhi – 110 017, India
Penguin Books (NZ) Ltd, Cnr Rosedale and Airborne Roads, Albany, Auckland, New Zealand
Penguin Books (South Africa) (Pty) Ltd, 24 Sturdee Avenue, Rosebank 2196 South Africa

Penguin Books Ltd, Registered Offices: 80 Strand, London WC2R 0RL, England

www.penguin.com

Published in Penguin Books 2001
17

Set in 10.5/12.5 pt Monotype Dante
Typeset by Rowland Phototypesetting Ltd,
Bury St Edmunds, Suffolk
Printed in England by Clays Ltd, St Ives plc

for Joe Boatman
and everyone who misses her

Acknowledgements

Special thanks to the families Arcà, de Giglio and Filiberto; and to all in the Diano valley who have so diligently kept me abreast of agricultural imperatives and local news. To Martin Lee for getting me started and my brother James for keeping me going; to Carmel Turner and Christina Weir for putting me on the right track; to Lucie Mathiszig, Lesley Katon, Terry Maguire and Martin Brolly, without whom anything might have happened . . . and of course to my lovely sister, without whom nothing might have happened. Lastly to Joe Walsh, Stefan Knight, Tom Brown and Ciccio de Giglio for putting up with the scribbler in the attic for so long.

Prologue

Hearing the racket from above, Franco wades through his pile of prunings and peers up through the trailing branches. A pair of foreign females, skin so white it's blinding in the glare of the sun, are messing about outside Pompeo's old place a few terraces uphill, shouting and giggling. Their upper arms are shamelessly bare. On their feet, absurdly, they have some sort of men's working boots. One of them has found the broken shutter, looks like she's about to climb in through it; the other is eating handfuls of cherries off the old tree by the door. Pompeo may not have used the place for years, but still, a bit of respect . . .

Now the first one's inside, opening an upstairs window; she's leaning out and shrieking happily to her greedy friend below, pointing to the sea down at the foot of the valley. Both of them in transports of delight. Franco rakes up the last few branches with his billhook, pauses to stroke his moustache thoughtfully. Should he approach them right away? Maybe not. He scrambles down the half-collapsed terrace wall, heaving the pile of branches before him, towards the far end of his land where Iolanda is piling up the greenery ready to burn – only way to keep the olive-fly at bay. She'll be cooking lunch over the embers. Nothing like a good fresh horse steak done over green olivewood: nothing like it.

You can still hear them from right down here – singing now, and banging out the rhythm on something metallic. Pompeo's old well bucket by the sound of it. A burst of mad laughter. Still, madness isn't a drawback. Not at all. The Milanesi who've taken over the old stable at the head of the valley, and who think they can farm chickens up there, are certainly mad. So is the bearded German fixing up the abandoned olive mill down in the damp riverbed, turning the old millstone into a table, flagstones into seats. An artist. Franco shudders at the thought of the dampness in the bones, the risk of *emorroidi* from sitting on those cold stone benches.

His wife, busy stripping the leaves off the stuff worth keeping for winter firewood, looks up as he delivers the tangled pile of branches, observes the calculating look on his face. Found some more of your *stranieri*, then, she says. Invite them down for lunch, why don't you?

Franco, unsure if this is irony, taps slowly and magnificently with a horny forefinger at a point just below his left eyeball: the sign for crafty intelligence, *furbizia*. First he will prepare the ground, sound out Pompeo. These must be Patrucco's English girls come for the season. They'll be putting up at the bar in the village; where else could they be staying? No trouble to find them when he's good and ready.

I

Glamour, we soon spotted, was not the outstanding feature of the village of Diano San Pietro. As far as the crusty olive-farming inhabitants of this crumbling backwater were concerned, the Riviera, a mere two miles away, might as well be on another planet. Down on the coast, Diano Marina has palm-shaded piazzas and an elegant marble-paved promenade along a wide blue sandy bay. Diano San Pietro, on the other hand, straggles up the steep foothills of the Mediterranean hinterland, its warped green shutters leaning into decrepit cobbled alleys overrun with leathery old men on erratic Vespas who call irately upon the Madonna as they narrowly miss mowing you down; with yowling feral cats and rusty tin cans full of improbably healthy geraniums.

The lodgings in which we are doomed to spend the next ten weeks – in the hands of Luigi, walrus-moustached landlord of the village's only hostelry and liveliest spot in town – have turned out to be a tiny pair of echoing tiled rooms above a barful of peasants who take thriftily to their beds at about ten-thirty. Our own beds are made of some kind of weird hammocky chainmail that droops horribly under your mattress, squeaks and gibbers at your slightest movement, and are only yards from the village campanile, whose great wheezing bell rings each and every hour, each and every half-hour, shaking the whole building to its roots. Only a masochist, or someone who was born and bred here and had been heaving sacks of olives since daybreak, would try getting to sleep before the midnight-thirty extravaganza was over. Twelve long-drawn-out gut-vibrating bongs and, after a short pause, a rusty, breathless bing. One a.m. is music to our ears.

Down by the sea Diano Marina folk have consorted openly with visiting strangers ever since the elegant days of Wintering on the Riviera. No terrible retribution seems to have fallen upon them: in fact a century or so of this wanton behaviour has left them looking

3

rather sleek and prosperous. Up on the hillside though, the grimly fascinating folk of Diano San Pietro prefer to meet the eccentric behaviour of strangers with a united front of appalled incomprehension. In San Pietro a woman does not wear shorts and a T-shirt. Not unless she wants to face a barful of seriously quelling looks over her cappuccino. No: she wears an apron, a calf-length tube, ankle socks and slippers. Her menfolk go for the faded blue trouser held up with string, the aged singlet vest which is not removed in the midday heat – certainly not, we're not in Diano Marina here – but rolled up sausagewise into a stylish underarm sweatband, leaving the nipple area modestly covered while the solid pasta-filled midriff is exposed to the pleasantly cooling effect of any chance bit of *aria* that may waft by. Naturally, a large and well-worn handkerchief always protects the head during daylight hours; knotted at the corners for men, tied at the nape for ladies. Our slinky holiday gear languishes in our bags, untouched.

Still, since barefaced lying has brought me here, board and lodging paid for, wages (barring detection as an impostor) in the offing, there is perhaps a certain poetic justice in the severe lack, in my immediate vicinity, of bright cosmopolitan life, of frivolity of any kind or, indeed, of anyone under forty apart from the occasional babe-in-arms. Maybe also in the fact that my ten-week stay in Diano San Pietro will end up stretching on into infinity.

Ten weeks' work on the Italian Riviera, board and lodging included, my sister had said, waving the job description at me. Mediterranean fleshpots, sparkling seas, bronzed suitors with unbearably sexy accents, wild nightlife . . . Why didn't I come too?

What about the bit about being able to graft roses to commercial standard, I asked, examining the document. Was this not of some importance to my putative employer? Would I not find it hard to conceal my ignorance of such matters? Of course I wouldn't, said Lucy. Not with her at my side to coach and camouflage.

After a long and gloomy winter of angst and form-filling I'd firmly established that I had absolutely no chance of getting a loan to buy the home of my dreams. I was, I now knew, a Bad Risk. The sister was doing her best to save me from despair. Enough lurking in the London gloom, skidding home exhausted through greasy city dark and drizzle. What did I care about a career? Or real estate, for that matter? Freelance horticulture would do very nicely. So here I am, middle of February, in Italy and ready to graft. San Pietro may correspond hardly at all to any idea I have previously formed of the Italian Riviera, but it is undeniably a great improvement on London. No more miserly damp horizons stopping twenty feet away at the nearest office block. Here they stretch up into the misty foothills of the Maritime Alps on the one hand, down into the intense blue vastness of the Mediterranean on the other. The sun shines warmly even at this unlikely time of year; the sky is blue; and I am seeing plenty of both.

Moreover, the Board makes up twice over for any small defects in the Lodging chosen for us by our boss to be, Signor Patrucco, whose rose nurseries lie a couple of hundred yards down the road, just past the olive mill. In under a week the lugubrious Luigi and his statuesque wife Maria have transformed us from just-give-us-a-sandwich philistines into budding gourmets, agog to meet whatever they'll be putting on our plates tonight. Or more accurately, into budding connoisseurs of antipasti. It has taken us some time to learn that you're meant to start with a few of these delectable antipasti things, then move on to your *primo piatto* of pasta. Next, the focal point of the meal: your *secondo piatto* of meat and vegetables or salad. Followed, if you want, by fruit or cheese. This, to locals, is so obvious that it needs no explaining: just part of the bedrock of civilization. But with no menu, no ordering, only Maria or ten-year-old Stefano, her son, appearing with serving-dish after serving-dish of delicious stuff and doling it on to your plate unless you told them not to, how were we going to work all that out? Conceptually challenged, we saw only a deliciously haphazard abundance, tried a bit of everything – or two bits of particularly good stuff, when the dish did its second round – and stopped, naturally, when we were full up. Usually before we'd even got on to the pasta course, and only, as far as our hosts were concerned, a third of the way through our meal. Causing immense consternation all round.

Maria mills in and out of the kitchen, serving course after course, neatening and tidying, prodding and petting us and the dozen men she feeds every evening, dour hanky-headed folk who, like us, have somehow found themselves short of the womenfolk you need to fix you a decent twenty-course dinner of an evening. Our fellow-diners sit in twos and threes commiserating with one another *sotto voce*, only livening up when we, or any other *stranieri* who happen to be about the place, do something particularly bizarre.

Have some stuffed zucchini flowers, says Maria. A tiny pie filled with broccoli? A few *frisceüi* of borage leaves in crispy batter? Now, oven-roasted baby onions, stripy-grilled slivers of peppers and aubergines with a dash of Maria's anchovy laden *bagna cauda*. A couple of fat slices of rich red tomato under a big dollop of pesto – the oil from Luigi's own trees, the basil from the vegetable patch round the back. Some little squares of fresh herby cheese tart?

How would you guess that all this was just a starter? We know it now, thanks to Luigi, whose training in abstract thinking (he is San Pietro's answer to Antonio Gramsci) alerted him to the fact that our eccentric eating behaviour was not due to a wilful refusal to conform, but to the lack of a whole framework of reference. We have much to learn. Tonight we obligingly horrify everyone by putting salad on the plate with our pasta. Salad, of course, is not eaten with the pasta. Salad comes afterwards. It could easily, Maria explains, snatching it back off again with her serving tongs, make the pasta curdle in your stomach. A lot of wise noddings and a chorus of *Ah, sì, sì*'s rise from the surrounding hoary heads, confirming her words. (Nowadays, with years of experience, we know that you can get around this annoying convention by casually spearing bits of salad out of the bowl as you eat your pasta – the important thing is not to put it on your plate.) Next, as if the salad offence wasn't enough, we give in at the end of the pasta course. No *secondo*? Again? Can't we even fit in a taste of the great sizzling piles of meat that have now appeared? The *secondo* is the whole point of the meal!

No, we can't. Maria is most put out. Unfair, since it's at least partly her fault; she's so entertained by our antipasti addiction that she can't help egging us on to try more and more of her tasty titbits. Still, at least we've made it past the pasta course tonight before falling by the wayside. Our hosts are on our case, and have, they say, great faith in our potential. We will need all our strength, according to them, to deal with the monster Patrucco, our employer-to-be. By the end of our first week's work, we will be begging for seconds.

Our attempts to join in sociably with the chat in the bar using our halting Italian haven't so far been a great success. The taciturn and weatherbeaten card-players who more or less live in this bar, only abandoning it momentarily for home at mealtimes and returning within the hour for the obligatory immensely strong teaspoon-sized espresso, chat away to one another in dialect, not Italian, as they cut, deal and shuffle. We may as well be speaking a foreign language. No: we really are speaking a foreign language. Official Italian is for uncomfortable and probably expensive dealings with policemen, tax-collectors and their ilk, and though everyone here can understand the language perfectly well, actually to speak it out loud in front of your cronies, who are bound to snigger and cackle as you do so, is another matter entirely. It is embarrassing for our poor victims, and utterly disrupts the cosy downhome atmosphere. If we're in luck, someone will make the odd one-sentence contribution in the national tongue for our benefit. Mostly, though, they cunningly evade this ordeal by determinedly avoiding our eye.

Ligurian, a tongue somewhere between Italian and Provençal French, is what the hanky-on-the-head folk speak for sociability, gossip and pleasure. Work, for example, is called *travaio*, not *lavoro*, round here. Not too surprising, since Liguria lies between Tuscany and the South of France, filling the mysterious gap which has existed till now in my mental map of this part of the world: a narrow strip of rugged stony foothills thirty or forty miles wide that stretches lengthwise on down the coast past Genoa, widthwise from the seashore to the high Alps of the Piedmont. We are right up at the French end, in the Province of Imperia; a province whose every scrap of steep hillside is terraced to within an inch of its life, and whose every scrap of terrace is packed to bursting with olive trees. And February has turned out, surprisingly to us novices, to be the height of the olive harvest in these parts. A topic which, when we raise it in the bar, is a big hit: so much so that one of the more daring card-players is moved to speak to us voluntarily, and in something quite like Italian.

The days when a hundred trees meant security for you and your family have gone, he announces, fixing us with a doomladen eye from under his grimy knotted headgear. Once upon a time five hundred was the sign of a rich man. A thousand and you were made. But no longer. The price of olives is so low that most of the harvest is being left to fall off the trees and rot. For the third year running.

A ragged chorus of grim *Ah, si, si*'s from a barful of hankied heads backs him up. Positively Cold Comfort Farm. We gather from the unusually animated debate that follows – not too easy to keep up with, alas, because in the excitement people tend to forget our presence and meander off into dialect – that only the mad optimists among the *contadini* of San Pietro are pruning and ploughing, husbanding their resources for next spring, convinced that better times are just around the corner. Waste of energy, say the doom-merchants. It takes eight years of neglect for an olive tree to dry out and end up barren for ever. Harvest and be damned. Plenty of time yet. Do your chickens, your vegetable garden, leave the trees to their own devices. You may as well come to the bar for a game of *scopa* instead.

How come, we wonder, if there's no money to be made from the stuff, the bar is always packed solid at six-thirty in the morning with horny-handed folk taking their breakfast espressos before rushing busily off to get on with Important Olive Work? Best not to ask. Probably olive farmers just enjoy a bit of wailing and teeth-gnashing of an evening.

The only customer left in the Café of Doom, now that the dawn espresso rush-hour is over, is one extremely senior citizen who is standing at the bar over a nice breakfast glass of wine, communing in companionable silence with Luigi. We are sitting in the farthest corner by the window as usual, busy decoding the bar's copy of *l'Unità*, the Communist daily, with the help of Maria, who has come out of her kitchen to keep us company while she shells her broad beans. Despite the total collapse of the olive-oil market, tiny three-wheeled trucks are buzzing to and fro past the window as usual, some heading off up to the groves to get in the crop, others hairpin-bending down from the hills above the village, already full of bulging greasy sacks of olives, their suspensions groaning under the weight as they round the tight bend in front of the bar and make for the olive-oil mill. You can just see the mill from here, a hundred-odd yards down the dirt-track that runs alongside the river, the back road to Diano Marina. It looks as old as the hills, four foot thick walls and low arched porticoes, crouching plump and turreted over the riverbed. A three-wheeler edges out of the yard, grinds slowly past us, heading back up the hill, loaded down with the new, thick, golden-green oil in its great straw-padded glass demijohns. It all looks fine to us, positively picturesque. Now there aren't any olive farmers left in here to be offended, I ask Maria why everyone says their olive oil is worthless, and still does all this work to harvest and press it.

Maria gives me an old-fashioned look. Worth nothing if you tried to sell it, she says, but it would still cost money to buy, wouldn't it? A year's worth of olive oil doesn't come cheap, does it?

No, we agree, doubtfully, we suppose it doesn't. A year's worth of olive oil . . . not a familiar concept. It certainly wouldn't amount to a truckload in our case. Early eighties orthodoxy in our own land still has it that the oil of the sunflower, polyunsaturated, is the thing for health and longevity. Olive oil is something that lurks exotically on the shelves of delicatessens and Cypriot corner shops, nice but probably as bad for you as butter, and anyway only used in the occasional Fancy Foreign Dish. Or lives in tiny bottles on the skin-care counters of chemists' shops: Olive Oil BP, stuff you rub into babies' scalps. Or something.

Anyway, here is the explanation. Every household is pressing its own year's supply, enough for a litre or two a week till next harvest. They'll be tucking the demijohns away in their storerooms, decanting them bottle by bottle for their own kitchens.

Money saved, maybe, contributes Luigi from behind his bar, but nothing earned. That's the tragedy. The good wholesome oil pressed in San Pietro this year will never so much as see the market. He doesn't know what it's like in England, he says, but here in Italy the so-called olive oil they sell in shops is rubbish – no one in their right mind would let the stuff anywhere near them. Processed in a factory, filtered till it has no taste left, years old likely as not. And made out of cheap nasty olives full of acidity in the first place. Then people wonder why city folk are turning to that seed-oil stuff. (The sister gives me a quick prod under the table – yes, that's us.) It's not just to save a few lire – it's because they've forgotten what real olive oil tastes like, that's why.

Euh! says the old man, moved (it seems) to despair at this vision of a world deprived of the flavour of fresh-milled olive oil. Luigi abandons his enquiries into the Olive Oil of England, and launches instead into an impassioned speech on the topic of Poisonous Olive Oil and the Evils of Capitalism, which, though his aged friend seems to appreciate it a lot – he's nodding away like mad, at any rate – we can't follow at all. We try for a quiet précis from Maria, who just rolls her eyeballs skywards and sighs. Apparently she's heard it all before.

She gathers up her colanders in protest and sets off for her kitchens, pausing to promise us a treat of raw broad beans and salami among tonight's antipasti; and is shocked to discover that in England we don't ever, so far as either of us knows, eat our broad beans raw with salami. *Madonna!* Did you hear that, Luigi?

No, he didn't. He's much too busy, thank God.

Maria off in the kitchens; Luigi deep in passionate debate. Good moment to try for a third coffee. I quickly order one, hoping Luigi is on automatic and won't notice. He turns to the espresso machine and puts the cups ready under it like a lamb, going right on talking; it looks like we're going to get away with it. No. Something about the slow-motion way our cups are going down on the bar, the worried look in the big Saint Bernard eyes, warns us that our host is about to remind us yet again of the danger of drinking any more coffees before lunch. I dash to the bar, grab the cups with a quick *Grazie*, and beetle off back to our table in the corner before he can get up to speed.

We already know, of course, that an extra coffee might easily close our stomachs, preventing us from ingesting enough of our lunch to survive the afternoon. We have been warned of this possibility several times, by several people. Even the most monosyllabic of card-players is moved to speech when it comes to matters imperilling the stomach. The trouble is, though, that the coffees here are so small. They may be ferociously strong, but you only get a couple of sips to a cup. Most people don't even bother to sit down to drink one – just stand at the bar and knock it back as if it were medicine. Which I suppose, at this strength, it is. Then they have a glass of water to quench their thirst. Hard on us English used to having the water and the coffee in the same cup, a nice long hot drink. In theory, the solution is simple: just ask for extra water in your cup. Chance would be a fine thing. Or *magari* as they say round here, reducing that cumbersome phrase to one elegant word. Not only is the cup no bigger than a generous eggcup anyway, but a proper coffee only comes a third of the way up it. Luigi and Maria are constitutionally unable to fill it to the top. Every fibre of their being tells them to turn that Gaggia tap to 'Off' at the third-of-the-way-up mark. They can't ruin a good espresso like this. Screwing their courage to the sticking point, they get it to halfway, and that's their limit. Unless, that is, you're prepared to stand right over them, exhorting and cajoling. Don't turn it off, really, yes really, just a bit more . . . Rather than keep going through this major drama, we accept the half-full version and then have another one. Or another two, when we can swing it. I am pleased to relate that so far, probably thanks to years of rigorous training in our own less delicate land, our stomachs have successfully resisted closure.

The World of the Rose, by contrast to that of the Olive, turns out to be quite startlingly cheerful. Introducing us to our workplace, Signor Patrucco, a fearlessly fluent Italian speaker, takes us round to inspect the premises, beaming and bouncing. To judge by his happy air of smug prosperity and bulging embonpoint, he is doing very nicely. Even better, he seems to have no intention of demanding an on-the-spot display of our grafting skills. Lucy has shown me once in England on a real rosebush, and a couple of times on various old twigs since, but I am not confident that I would come across as much of an expert as yet; not under the critical eye of an employer.

We visit the office first – more of a recycled greenhouse floating in a sea of mud, it has to be said – to be introduced to Caterina who works in there. Amazing! Not only female, but definitely youthful: about our own age. Not a hanky or bit of string about her person;

just ordinary jeans and a T-shirt. A recognizable type of person at last. Caterina is, she says, from Diano Marina. That explains it. She kisses us on both cheeks, smiles and chats happily, makes faces about her boss behind his back. Not only a town girl, but evidently a kindred spirit.

Now, off to our zone of operations. Signor Patrucco's huge flat tract of alluvial plain sits alongside the riverbed just down past the olive mill, covered with acre upon acre of ramshackle wood-framed greenhouses the size of tennis courts, their glass whitewashed against the sun. Between the greenhouses sit equally large rosebeds, open ploughed-up areas stubbly with rows and rows of ferociously pruned-back rose-stumps. This dusty, clod-filled and seriously un-romantic plot of land turns out to be the unlikely source of those individually wrapped red roses that are touted around London's West End every night. These are what we will, in a sense, be creating for the next couple of months, mating the new stem buds with the innocent species rootstock where they will breed like some collection of outlandish parasites until, in a month or two, they will be setting off weekly in great refrigerated lorries to harass the diners and dancers of Europe's great metropolises. I find it hard to believe that fate is not playing some ironic trick on me. Is there not, I ask my sister, a faint yet horrible resonance in this rose business of the more repellent aspects of London that we have travelled so far to escape? No there isn't, says Lucy. Stop being morbid.

As it turns out, luckily for me, Signor Patrucco is off the site most of the time, busy bulging about in his office. He has taken out a patent on one of his roses, which he has called – sign of the times – 'Dallas'; a business move that has turned out to be most lucrative, but which is creating a lot of paperwork. So with my sister to cover for me I am able to muddle my way through the wax and string of my new career as slowly and incompetently as I like, with little fear of detection. At last, after a fortnight of fudging, fumbling, and occasionally slicing my thumb to the bone, I really do know how to graft a rose.

Mr Patrucco may be proud of us, but the same cannot be said, alas, for the denizens of Luigi and Maria's bar. Back at base, of an evening, the older men, the village Godfathers, do their best to set the tone. They are not pleased with our presence. We have burst in on them, sponsored by the evil Patrucco, from another world; one that, as far as they can see, will be satisfied with nothing less than the destruction of their own.

Patrucco has offended them by importing his absurd Roses into the sensible world of the Olive. Think of good nutritious olive oil going to the wall, while foolish nosegays can earn you a fortune! People going hungry in the world, too. Worse still is Patrucco's lack of community spirit. Patrucco's pockets are filling while everyone else's are emptying, but does he give some local lad a chance? No. He parrot-talks about profit margins and suchlike, employs a girl in the office – a girl, mark you, from Diano Marina – and takes on seasonal, casual labour. Then foreign casual labour: last year, we hear, it was two long-haired Dutch youths. Now, adding insult to injury, not just foreigners, but females. Sternly rustling the bar's much-thumbed copies of *l'Unità*, these powers in the land concede us the obligatory politenesses of '*Buon giorno*' and '*Buona sera*' as we come or go, and not a jot more.

They silently watch our toings and froings, our immodestly bare upper arms, our nocturnal visits to Diano Marina, cradle of shiftlessness, drugs and degeneracy, a place where people shamelessly dance without partners. No doubt they have their suspicions about our seed-oil eating past as well. The younger men, the under-fifties, avoid our eyes even more than usual when these brooding presences are enthroned in their corner of the bar. Which they are most evenings till nine-thirty or so.

On Saturday nights, party nights, the company stays late in the echoing vaulted bar. The old men, when they've drunk enough black wine, start to sing terrible sad songs. They stand in a tight circle, heads uncovered for once, arms round one another's shoulders, backs turned to the company, and close-harmonize with their eyes closed, voices thick with emotion: songs of dark satanic mills sucking the lifeblood from the countryside, of deserted villages and abandoned olive groves, of tradition dying out and family ties withering away, of the city-hardened hearts of ungrateful offspring, of a lifetime's heroic struggle to wrench a living from this hard stony land all shrunk to nothing, to pain and pointlessness . . .

We, of course, won't understand the lyrics of these old favourites for some time yet; they are in deepest dialect, and we'd be hard put to understand them in plain Italian. How could we guess that we are the incarnation of the bleak future they're so depressed about? We love the singing, so sad it gives you gooseflesh: no mistaking the tragedy and despair. How has our own country come to be so culturally deprived? we ask one another. Why have we ended up with morris dancing instead of this? And, although the assembled company shows no sign of being especially keen for our approval – rather the contrary, if anything – we always, in our mad foreign way, call enthusiastically for an encore.

2

Diano Marina is the obvious refuge from the brain-wrenching complexities of village life. Here, refreshingly, we are objects of interest to no one, no longer weirdly foreign but generic strangers in a town used to *stranieri*. Or is it Diano Marina that's less foreign, more like Italy's public image? At any rate down there by the sea we have less of that feeling of living in one of those crossword puzzles where you have to work out the grid as well as the answers. Today we decide to take advantage of our three-and-a-half-hour Italian lunchbreak, and rest our brains from the mysteries of peasant social relations, by going swimming in Diano's wide sandy bay.

Although it is only March the sun is shining, the sky is a cloudless blue, the temperature baking hot. In England, this would be a scarcely to be dreamed of summer's day. We set off on foot along the flat river road from San Pietro in high spirits, with costumes, lilos, bottles of a strange local lemonade called *gasosa* – or, in dialect, *gazüa* – and a bag of fresh rolls from Ulisse the baker. Arriving in Diano Marina twenty minutes later, we detour to the town's *rosticceria* to buy a mouth-watering spit-roasted chicken filled with herbs which (such is the power of horticulture in this part of the world) is cut up neatly for us with a pair of secateurs, and sprayed from a plant spray with aromatic white wine, before being wrapped in silver foil.

We have the beach all to ourselves: nodding palm trees, gently lapping waves, warm sun, soft sand, mouthwatering picnic. Idyllic. But the people of Diano Marina, models of moderation though they may be compared to their neighbours in San Pietro, turn out to have one fatal flaw: their conviction that to immerse yourself in the Mediterranean outside the months of July and August is to court certain death. Seawater at the wrong time of year is even worse for your health than coffee at the wrong time of day, and the beach is only deserted because, as far as the citizens of Diano are concerned, if you put so much as a toe into the water before June you are certain to die within the week from exposure or pneumonia or both. Since almost the entire length of the bay is bordered by the wide paved walkway with its strip of palms, and is a favourite spot for the after-lunch digestive stroll, our suicide bid is highly visible. The people of Diano Marina may not actually know us personally; but, of course, you don't need to know someone personally to feel morally obliged to stop them killing themselves.

What we had in mind was stress-free sensuous relaxation: instead we find that we are putting on a cabaret show. Not content with inducing bad self-consciousness about plumpness, pallidness, finger-licking chicken-eating manners, swimming style and suchlike, our public-spirited spectators are waiting agog to leap on us, as soon as we leave the relative privacy of the water, with dire health warnings and their own personal recipes for survival after unseasonable immersion, mostly involving grappa. One kindly middle-aged lady in startling green eyeshadow and a seasonable fur jacket even braves the damp and life-threatening sands, coming right down to the water's edge, heedless of her own safety, to call us back from our watery grave. She listens to our foreign ravings about swimming habits in our own land, the freezing North Sea, the lukewarm weather, the windswept beaches, with the patient indulgence usually reserved for the mentally ill. Once we have done, she gently explains to us all over again the perils we face in the Mediterranean on a sunny March day.

We boldly put on another couple of these two-woman shows, hoping that people will get bored and leave us alone once they've noticed that, thanks to our stout Northern constitutions, we are still hale and hearty in spite of repeated immersion. But we are given no quarter, and after various ever-more-agitated encounters with our well-wisher in the fur jacket and her fellows, we give up flying in the face of this central tenet of the local faith. It is impossible to go on stoically sunbathing when all around you are wrapped in layer upon layer of winter wear and fussing about draughts. We too will have to wait for official summertime. We will abandon the sea and take to the hills for our recreation.

Henceforth we energetically and sweatily follow the steep, pester-free cobbled muletracks leading uphill and inland from San Pietro, where we potter about the olive groves nosily inspecting local agriculture, marvelling over the enormous numbers of lovely old farm buildings lying abandoned and semi-derelict around the hillsides, over the ancient igloo-shaped stone roundhouses which are dotted about the place in various states of decay, and whose design, we're told, hasn't changed since prehistory: strange to look at one and not know if it's BC or AD, maybe only fifty years old.

Hardly have we adopted this new inland exploration plan when, much to our surprise, we make a friend. And, incidentally, meet our home to be.

We have finally made it to the top of the village, following the heroically steep and straight-as-a-die cobbled alley that climbs onwards and upwards, tunnelling through the various neighbourhoods of San Pietro – the *frazioni* Gionetti, Ughi, Colla – and crossing the toings and froings of the long-winded, hairpin-bending road half a dozen times as it does so. We are high enough to see the sea again, up where the village ends and the serious olive groves start, when Domenico appears bearing down on us, hanky on head, in a huge rusty tip-up truck. We stop and wait for the lorry to cross our path. But, grinding and squealing, it comes to a halt before us, blocking our way.

Patrucco's girls! Mount! cries its tiny driver cheerily. We recognize one of the smallest and quietest of the bar's leathery habitués, one whose fellow card-players enjoy tormenting him of an evening with humorous sallies concerning – as far as we can tell through the linguistic haze – his rampant sexuality.

We clamber in. What else can we do? This is the first friendly gesture we've been offered. Moreover we've grasped, thanks to our own acuity and the hints and tips section of our *Blue Guide to Northern Italy*, that the concept of the recreational walk hardly exists in these parts: its nearest equivalent, the *passeggiata*, implies something much more like a promenade to and fro in the village square after dinner. Of course our guide is an heirloom, thirty-odd years out of date, but it seems things haven't changed overmuch here since the 1950s. Maria has already exhibited signs of perplexity over our aimless walking behaviour. Do we need something? Can't she get it for us? Where are we going?

Caught red-handed roaming so far afield, right on the very boundaries of the village, we feel that turning down a lift might seem either mad or rude. Keen to avoid creating either impression, well aware that we are already borderline cases, we swiftly change our plans.

Our small and bristling-moustached benefactor luckily shows no curiosity about our intended destination. He is giving us a ride, he announces, to the top of the ridge. Silence falls. Having so boldly got us on board, he seems to have been overcome with shyness. Unless it's the language problem? A bit of gentle prodding elicits that he speaks perfectly good Italian – better than ours, at any rate – and that the load we are carrying is the amalgamated garbage of all the villages and hamlets on this side of the Diano valley. As well as owning (naturally) a respectable number of olive trees, Domenico is in charge of the valley's rubbish disposal. We're off to dispose of it now.

Sympathy having been established, Domenico spends the next five minutes in morbidly intense speculation about how much more per kilo Patrucco will be getting for his useless roses than a good honest olive farmer gets for his fine and nutritious crop. He is certain that we must have some insight into this matter, and our ignorance is a great disappointment to him. But there it is: we have never, so far, thought of roses in terms of their net weight. I offer, foolishly perhaps, to let him know as soon as we've wormed the information out of Patrucco.

Brava! Brava! he says, giving me a conspiratorial pat on the knee. I realize, too late to back out, that I have heedlessly taken sides in some as-yet-uncomprehended battle between the Olive and the Rose. Further conversation becomes impossible as the asphalt ends abruptly and we begin, with much first-gear roaring, grinding and jolting, to breast a series of scarily steep hairpin bends out of the olive terraces and on to wild broom-clad mountainside. Ten minutes of this, and we stop, shaken and deafened, at the top of a ridge mysteriously wreathed in smoke and fumes.

Eccoci! Here we are! announces our chauffeur gaily. Are we? We don't seem to be anywhere in particular. This is a bit of mountainside like all the rest. No buildings, no machinery, nothing at all reminiscent of a rubbish-disposal plant. We stagger down from our seats; Domenico stays in the lorry battling with its controls. What is all this smoke? Is there a forest fire? Lucy and I peer cautiously over the shrubby vegetation to the landward side of the ridge. And a hundred feet below us is a scene from hell: a stinking slow-burning virtually vertical cascade of a dump. Around its black and smoking heart the whole side of the hill is a seething chaotic mess. The odd fragment of charred fridge or washing-machine, half buried under years of carbonized household waste, rotted cardboard boxes, tangles of mattress springs, peer out here and there from amongst fire-reddened rocks, while limp curls of half-hearted smoke rise from the remnants of tables, rabbit-hutches, bits of sofa and iron bedsteads which stick out at unlikely and vertigo-inducing angles from the occasional clump of broom or juniper or gorse.

Clearly the people of San Pietro have not yet got to grips with the non-biodegradability of modern rubbish. We watch open-mouthed as Domenico manoeuvres his decrepit machine back and forth on the narrow rock-strewn road until its rear wheels are balanced on the brink of the precipice. Then, at a casual flip of a lever, nine villages-worth of garbage plummets crashing off the ridge. We gaze with new respect at our driver. Hard to believe that such a small, shy, innocuous person, impressive though his moustache may be, could be the single-handed author of this gigantic natural disaster. The job well done, he fishes a squashed packet of cigarettes from his breast pocket and a bottle of wine from somewhere below his seat, deep within the chassis of the lorry.

Un po di riposo, he announces, lighting up and settling down to repose himself on a handy rock, gesturing hospitably towards another smaller pair of rocks for us to follow suit. We sit down obediently. He has only the one glass, which he is now wiping out on his vest-tails. We will share that, and he will drink from the bottle. I try to read what's left of the scuffed and greasy label.

Colli Pia . . . something, it says. Impossible to make out. Is it from round here? Domenico lifts the bottle up and looks at the label, vaguely surprised by its presence. *Colli* what? No, no, this is his own stuff, *vino d'uva*, wine made of grapes.

Are there places where they don't make it out of grapes, then?

Domenico laughs uproariously at this. Apparently I've made a great joke. Still chuckling to himself, he twists the screwtop off and performs a violent wrist-flicking movement with the bottle, momentarily giving us the impression that it too is being hurled off down the hillside. No: he has just sent the first inch or two of the wine flying out over the valley. My capacity for amazement exhausted, I gaze on and ask nothing. The sister has more stamina. Is the top bit no good, then? she asks.

No, that was only olive oil, not wine, says Domenico, pouring out our glass, on whose surface, confirming his words, the odd flattened globule floats greasily.

Saves wasting time with corks, he adds. Seal it with a dash of oil instead.

We accept a cigarette and settle in for a chat, sipping at our wine made of grapes and complimenting its maker. Delicious. Here on the seaward side, vague through the sun-haze, a vista of silver-green olive terraces dotted with cream and ochre hilltop villages stretches down to the azure bay of Diano. No hint of the horror at our backs, the black choking smoke from the rubbish down the other side of the ridge. Domenico, outlined against the sky, elbows on knees, puffs away at the Superking cupped in his hand, serenely undisturbed by the occasional small but ferocious explosion as an aerosol can from our load finds its way into the heat and blows up down the scree behind us.

Ah, sì, sì, he says, exhaling with a deep sigh. He, unlike many people in San Pietro, knows quite a bit about foreigners. He has even visited foreign lands. His first son left home almost a decade ago, married a Dutch girl and set up a hairdressing salon in The Hague. His daughter, must be about our age, is a nurse in Buffalo, New York.

In America? we say in chorus, somewhat taken aback, brains working overtime at reinventing what we now see are absurdly inadequate stereotypes of Italian hairdressers and Italian-American nurses. Why do they not include very small vest-and-hanky-clad olive-farming fathers?

Yes, says Domenico patiently, New York, United States. He hasn't been there, it's too far and his wife Antonietta is scared of flying. But he went to Holland a couple of years ago, for a whole six weeks.

How was that? we ask.

A long pursed-lipped pause while Domenico considers Holland. He lost five kilos in those six weeks, he says. He was very impressed by the land – all that *pianura*, that flatness. But what use is good land if you don't grow decent food on it? Which they don't. Everything tastes of nothing. Worse still, you never get any bread with your meals. Unless you ask for it, that is, which he didn't like to do in case the daughter-in-law took offence. Not more than a couple of times, anyway, he adds darkly.

Like England, I say. That's how we eat. It's not too bad once you're used to it.

Domenico shudders. He has seen enough of Holland. Nowadays they see their son just once a year, when he comes down to collect his share of the olive oil. To think how he and Antonietta scrimped and saved, wore themselves out to buy up their few extra plots of land, a few more olive trees, give their kids a bit of security! For what? No security there any more. No kids either. Their grandson hardly speaks a word of Italian, never mind Ligurian. What does he care about a few dozen olive trees up some foreign hill? Nothing. And who knows what his mother does with all that good oil? She certainly doesn't use it in her cooking: not as far as Domenico could tell. But that's life these days.

Sounds terrible, we say, on cue. But he said that was his first son – what's happened to the second?

Nothing yet, says Domenico, not sounding much cheered by the fact. He's only a baby. Suddenly, at forty-six, his wife found herself pregnant again, and Maurizio was born three months ago. (Aha! Here is the explanation for all those jokes in the bar.) He knows it is the *destino* that has sent him Maurizio. But destiny knows nothing of fair play. He and Antonietta were looking forward to a peaceful middle age and a bit of spare cash for a change. *Magari!* (Chance would be a fine thing!) Luigi and his Communists are right: sweat blood to bring up your kids, feed them, clothe them, educate them – and send them off as a free gift to America or Germany or somewhere. Or Milan and Turin, come to that. No justice in it. Maurizio will go like the others.

He was born hating the land – screamed his head off the whole time they were getting this year's crop in. The right sort of baby would have lain quietly watching the sky through the branches, let you get on with the job. Domenico is *disperato*. There is no longer any tranquillity in his home, he says. And in the bar, he adds with a small sidewise grin, he gets no peace either.

We part soulmates. Domenico, with a grasp of local customs infinitely superior to anything the Blue Guide can tell us, is unperturbed by our desire to walk back down the muletrack from here instead of riding in his lorry. Domenico has known all along, of course, that we were off hunting and gathering, foraging for food. Walking about villages may be distinctly odd behaviour, but walking about hillsides, we see now, is fine. There should still be some wild asparagus left, he says, though we'll have to get well off the path to find a decent amount. We'll find no *funghi* though, except maybe a few oyster-mushrooms on some treetrunk – we're too close to the village. As for snails, no chance. We'll have to wait till next time it rains. Domenico provides us with the carrier bag we have unaccountably forgotten to bring with us – never mind, he has plenty in his wine-cache under the driver's seat – and roars off, raising a hand in salutation. No, we won't forget about the price of roses . . .

We wander off down the muletrack, detouring along the groves every now and then to see if we can spot some asparagus – the only item on Domenico's menu we feel at all comfortable with. Snails, definitely not. Mushrooms maybe, but we wouldn't trust ourselves to recognize an oyster-mushroom. As it turns out, we can't trust ourselves to recognize wild asparagus either. We prod hopefully about against terrace walls, by the roots of olive trees, but find nothing at all asparagus-like. Nobody around to ask, either. The hills are deserted this high up, it seems, though we can hear the odd voice of peasants a-peasanting on the terraces below. We do, however, come across our best abandoned house so far: not a two-roomed stone bothy, one up, one down, like a lot of the hillside *rustici* we've come across, but double-size, a proper cottage, with a kind of huge vaulted alcove built out from one side where some enterprising peasant architect has incorporated one of the ancient roundhouses into its walls. The real-estate yearnings I thought I'd put so firmly behind me surface again, double strength. How could anyone leave such a lovely place to go to rack and ruin? It looks as if no one has been near it for decades, its lands untended and its olive trees unkempt. I want it very badly. It ought to be mine. Two big lemon trees, a lovely little cobbled area on the higher terrace by the upstairs door, shaded by a ramshackle bit of tiled roof; by the lower door a small cherry tree which, thanks to the weird semi-tropical climate in these parts, is already fruiting at this unlikely time of year. We gather and guzzle. Delicious, though not exactly the wild mountain provender we were supposed to be after. The sister being fully occupied with the cherries, I go off for a tour of inspection, find a window whose olive-plank shutter is hanging off its hinges half-open, and naturally, with nobody around to know or care, can't resist climbing inside to check out the facilities . . .

Did I say there was nobody around? Did I call these hillsides pester-free? If we are still here all these years later, that lady in the green eyeshadow and her fellow devotees at the altar of Italian health are to blame. Preventing us, as they did, from lounging innocently by the sea of an afternoon on that wide sandy beach – a beach free of cunning peasants and their machinations – they drove us instead straight into the waiting arms of a certain Franco, otherwise known as 'Il Coltello': Frank the Knife, local property speculator extraordinaire. Who has spotted us now; and will soon be hot on our trail.

Follow the wide and shallow riverbed a little way up the valley from Patrucco's business premises till it comes out on the other side of San Pietro, and you find a rambling shed-festooned house with a roof-high hammer and sickle daubed on its side wall in what must once have been blood-red, nowadays weathered to a tasteful dusky orange. Its owner, Giacò, is a large, loud and laughing person who augments his dwindling olive-income by dealing in second-hand goods, his home surrounded by chaotic heaps of irresistibly fascinating ancient hardware, a junkyard terrain stretching a good quarter of a mile among the tall clumps of wild cane and the smooth pale stones of the dried-up banks of the river. Not really a river, in fact, but a *torrente*, which means that it is almost completely dry for most of the year, just a trickle amongst the pebbles, and only fills up when there's a big storm, or when the snows melt somewhere high in the hills. We are getting everybody's gifts from Italy here at Giacò's: strangely shaped ancient espresso pots, fat round-bellied saucepans with Bakelite handles, pre-war fashion catalogues, earthenware tureens for *pasta al forno*, intriguing twiddly glass light fittings from the 1950s. Most of which will never see England. Destiny has other plans for them.

Intimacy between us and Giacò has grown rapidly, thanks to our frequent lunchtime visits as we work our way slowly and methodically through these delights; and to his sympathy for our plight as exploited migrant workers oppressed by the heartless profiteer, Patrucco. It has even reached the point where we get invited out of the heat into his cool, dark stone-flagged kitchen once we've selected our bargains of the day, to be given various wines, grappas, types of olive marinade to try; or give our opinion on the merits of goat cheeses made respectively by his sister and his mother. Today we check out a remarkable bottle of whisky which Giacò bought last night from a Moroccan travelling salesman at a most reasonable price; a whisky bottled, according to its label, in the Highlands of Scotland, and going under the long-established name of Crazy Glen.

Seeing us arriving for yet another exhaustive investigation of his wares, Giacò comes puttering alongside us through his rubble-strewn terrain seated casually sidesaddle on his aged Vespa, his several rolls of grizzled chin unshaven, wearing the usual San Pietro tattered vest and – Giacò is a bit of a rebel – men's legs here usually remain firmly under cover – a pair of battered army surplus shorts. Dismounting when we've selected the area we'll be concentrating on today, he takes a seat in a shady spot and looks on with sharp-eyed bristly benevolence while we sort through the mounds of kitchen-ware cunningly concealed amongst stacks of old doors and windows, under reclaimed rooftiles, behind piles of those iron-and-chainmail bed bases dating from the days when the average height of an Italian must have been about five feet.

Giacò chats on, plying us with sips of his lethal homemade grappa, with tales of his life and times, of his wartime Partisan deeds and the collapse of his marriage, apparently utterly absorbed in his stories, casually announcing a price every now and then off the top of his head with hardly an interruption to his flow. Nazi reprisal killings in the piazza of San Pietro . . . his best mate's grandad about to be shot . . . the Nazis were fools – five thousand lire – new lads would flock to join the Partisans after every reprisal . . . We even know all about Giacò's wife running off with the bus driver to Venezuela, and how the bus driver's wife blamed Giacò for not keeping his own wife satisfied, and how he was scared that this might be true and so never found the heart to try courting again . . .

So, of course, when we bump into Giacò back at Luigi's bar taking his before-dinner *aperitivo*, we say *Ciao* to him and ask how business is doing. Not the right move at all. The cheery, talkative Giacò of the junkyard, he who has shared his cheese, his whisky and his innermost secrets with us, shrinks to a hunted shadow of his former self, casting around wildly for some means of escape. Muttering something inaudible he leaps from his bar stool with an agility startling in one so large and shapeless, and makes for the safety of the card tables.

Is mateyness with females in the bar not done? Can't be that, there are always a couple of overall-clad women in here, shouting in dialect, cackling and card-playing with the best of them. They're at the next table to Giacò now. Soon though Domenico does a runner on us in a strangely similar fashion. We spot our tiny friend at his after-dinner espresso and *digestivo*, bounce up to him and sit down at his table, looking forward to a chat about rubbish disposal technology and the price of roses and the wife and the baby and whether its attitude to olive trees might be said to be improving, and suchlike. A pair of white-haired Godfathers are looking on beadily from the Methuselah corner: Domenico glances over at them, opens and shuts his mouth a few times, turns tail and shoots into the loo, whence he emerges shamefaced some time later to scuttle straight out of the bar and off into the starry night.

Next time we pass Giacò's yard, we try haltingly to apologize for whatever it was, hoping for a clue. *Mah!* How could we have offended him, whatever are we talking about? he says, getting out the Crazy Glen and settling down for a cosy chat. We retire to our beds some hours later, weaving horribly, much better informed about the history of the local Partisans and the struggle against Nazifascist Barbarism, but otherwise utterly unenlightened.

How to account for the apparently random mood-swings of these olive-farming folk? Away from the bar the men of San Pietro will lay down their ferocious sharp sickles and roaring chainsaws to press swigs of wine on us from the bottle-in-a-sack they all keep handy in the hollow of a nearby treetrunk, bare their hearts to us about their joys and woes, their love lives, their worries about aged parents or wayward children, their secret desires to dump everything and run away to Paris, as if we were their long-lost sisters. Or their therapists. In the bar, though, they determinedly blank us.

Maybe, I suggest to my sister, the essential feature of the relationship is that we aren't really part of their lives, so they can say what they want, about anything, like people do with their analysts. But by the same token, in the eyes of the village, a therapeutic distance must be maintained: glowering must prevail. Why shouldn't the menfolk of ancient olive-farming cultures have developed, over the aeons, the habit of using any strange females who happen to pass through their villages as unpaid therapists? Seems quite likely to me. Peasants are, after all, famous for their thrifty ways.

3

Buon giorno, we say as custom dictates, upon entering the bar on this fateful day. But, for the third day running, we take care to say it in a most abstract and general manner, avoiding making eye contact with anyone for more than a second. There will be no more of those thoughtless displays of public sociability. We have realized that the card-playing and man-frequenting women in here are always, and only, the same two women, and now that our grasp of the local dress code is firming up, it has been borne in upon us that they are in fact women who dress up as men. A pair of eccentrics, no less. Who knows what they have gone through to get themselves accepted as honorary card-players by the Methuselah gang? Outrageous of us to expect preferential treatment so early in our San Pietro careers.

'*Giorno*, the men and the two eccentrics mutter in reply. The multicoloured plastic strands of the fly-curtain flap heavily behind us. Our eyes slowly adjust to the gloom within as we make our way to the bar. Giacò is there waiting to be served, bleary-eyed and unshaven, hanky on head. He does, it is true, edge slightly away from us. But it is an almost imperceptible edge; and as it becomes clear that we aren't planning to address any further remarks to him, a certain rigidity about his spine seems to melt. We ask Luigi for two coffees. Things have gone well with Giacò; how will we fare with Domenico? He is over in the corner by the vine-tangled window overlooking the olive mill and the river, apparently engrossed in *l'Unità*, blue-black moustache bristling as usual, the usual shrunken and shapeless vest covering his stringy mahogany torso. We let our eyes flick, just for a second, in his direction. He gives us a minuscule nod of recognition. Lucy and I return the brisk, casual jerk of the head we've been practising – more of a tic, really – and swiftly look away. Perfect. We've cracked it. At last we are behaving normally.

Giacò, finishing his glass of wine, gives a faint nod-and-a-grunt in our direction, publicly admitting to knowing who we are. A triumph! Luigi finishes the battle with his cranky hissing espresso machine and turns to plonk our cups on the bar. We head for our corner table, Giacò for the knot of men already shuffling the tarot-like cards they use for their interminable games, cards whose mystical symbols – curved scimitars, fat-bellied urns, golden coins – give you the impression that you're looking, not at a roomful of gossip and gambling addicts, but at a bunch of horny handed fortune-tellers bent over their muttered predictions.

The card-players call Domenico over; hasn't he finished the paper yet? Ribald remarks about his lack of energy. What has he been up to all night? Hasn't he let his wife get any sleep – again? Uproarious laughter from the card table; lots more humour in dialect, incomprehensible to us. Domenico mutters some blasphemy that involves the Madonna and (I think) a pig: 'Porca Madonna'.

We are still busy behaving normally, glowering poker-faced into our coffee cups and giving no sign of fathoming this arcane men's talk, when an unfamiliar figure bursts in through the fly-curtain trailing sunlight, buon giorno-ing cheerily all round and not, frankly, getting an overwhelming response. Flouting all convention and decency, this free spirit has his hanky tied rakishly round his neck, cowboy style, not knotted on his head. He wears brown corduroys with braces, and a bright yellow waistcoat.

Under a natty straw trilby we meet a laughter-line-furrowed walnut of a face, drooping grey moustache, bright blue sparrow-eyes whose lightness is startling against the weathered skin, greying slicked-back hair, and a strong aura of mischief. The dashing stranger leans chirpily on the bar and orders a glass of black wine, speaking in dialect. He certainly isn't a foreigner then – not even one from Milan or Turin. Luigi reaches unenthusiastically for the wine-bottle. Now, startlingly, the newcomer steps over and introduces himself to us. He is Franco, our paths have already crossed, he says. Salve.

Our grasp of reality weakened by our recent intensive course in peasant respectability, we are almost as appalled as the rest of the clientele at this Franco's extraordinary free-and-easy behaviour. Luigi, to judge by the lack of eye contact and the heavy way the chunky wineglass hits the counter, disapproves mightily. The apparition goes on carelessly ignoring the iron rules of social inter-course we have been at such pains to unravel; now he is asking our names and shaking our hands, brazenly talking Italian. The shockwaves reverberate round the bar.

Are we on holiday here?

No, we say, we are working.

Ah, we're Patrucco's girls! What fine taste in women Patrucco has!

We roll our eyeballs. Luigi, politically correct in this as in other matters thanks to his extensive reading of *l'Unità*, snorts something in dialect. Franco continues blithely in Italian. Where are we from – England? We agree that we are.

His nephew brought home an English girlfriend last summer, he tells us. She wore her hair messy like ours, and T-shirts with holes in them. Franco didn't mind. Unlike a lot of people round here, he announces with a casual gleam over his shoulder, he has no problem with *stranieri*. And he pulls up a chair and sits down nonchalantly at our table, knocking back his wine with noisy gusto. The glass empty, he leans round to dump it back on the bar, tips his hat on to the back of his head, whisks the handkerchief off his neck, mops his brow with it, and leans forward sighing happily, elbows on knees, ready to commune.

How are we supposed to stick to the rules when locals go around breaking them at will? Nobody is actually staring openly at us, but the feeling of every ear in the bar being pricked in our direction is unnerving. We suddenly know exactly how our own victims must have felt when we assaulted them in public with unsolicited friendliness.

We are at a loss to place this Franco. His style is certainly not that of Giacò's card-playing cronies, who are busy studiously ignoring us. Nor is it that of cosmopolitan Diano Marina. Franco is no ordinary olive farmer, but some as yet unknown variety of country person.

Gaily addressing Luigi, who is regarding him with a fixed and sceptical eye, Franco calls for another glass of wine. No, he doesn't always want to just see the same old faces, he says, knocking back a good half of it in a single gulp and giving his moustache a quick wipe with the back of a callused hand. This place needs new blood. Quite a few *stranieri* are moving in round here these days, did we know that? Getting themselves holiday homes so they don't waste their money on hotels every summer? No, we say, beginning to suspect our forward new friend of some hidden agenda, we don't. We haven't met any *stranieri* except the odd Milanese passing through.

Ah, says Franco, that will be the Mad Milanese who's moved in at the top of the valley. Comes through the village on one of those new-fangled mini-tractors with a trailer, brand-new, a load of eggs on the back of it? He will find that people round here use three-wheeled trucks for a reason. One day that affair will hit a rock and tip right over. Probably with a full load of eggs. *Ah, sì sì.* (A longish pause here while Franco savours to the full this salutary scenario.)

No, we say, we just meant the tourists who appear in here every now and then, looking for a meal.

Have we met the German with the mill by Moltedo, then? Or the other foreigner, the one from Rome who is doing up the old *rustico* on the ridge above the Colla? Franco has, it seems, helped all of them, the Mad Milanese, the German and the Roman, with their house purchases. He could help us, too, he adds with calculated innocence, if we were interested in buying something in these valleys.

No, we say, we don't even have a first home, never mind buying a second one. We're just here to work.

Franco caresses his moustache thoughtfully, preparing his coup. I only ask, he says, leaning forward and lowering his voice confidentially, because I saw you the other day, up there in the hills, inspecting properties. The house with the cherry tree . . . You seemed to be interested in that place all right. He intensifies the knowing look, tapping a forefinger meaningfully just below his left eye.

I can feel myself going red. Lucy is kicking me under the table; she told me not to go inside. This is our second encounter with the omniscience of villagers in these parts, the second time I've got us into trouble. No matter how much you feel you're in the middle of nowhere round here, completely unobserved, you're sure to come across someone who saw exactly what you were up to – or who knows someone else who did. Never do anything you don't want noised all over the Province of Imperia; especially picking up objects which seem to be thrown away by the side of the road. These will be someone's prized possessions, with some aged aunt or uncle watching over them from a nearby green-shuttered window or leafy treetop, who will rush out at you from an apparently empty hillside to give you a stern ticking-off. This was my fate over a long stick idly picked up one afternoon as I rounded a hairpin bend. It was, as I ought to have guessed, part of an important and useful set of sticks for supporting runner beans, the rest of which were being sensibly if inexplicably stored elsewhere. I was accused of wanton thievery over the stick; this latest episode will be breaking and entering or something.

You got in through the window, says Franco, who seems to be enjoying my discomfiture immensely, and went upstairs and opened the shutters. And you, he adds with great glee and more tapping under the eye – addressing his remarks, thank God, to Lucy – you liked the cherries outside the door so much you stripped the tree naked!

In spite of the gleam in his eye, we start apologizing wildly. The place looked abandoned, we thought no one would mind . . .

Franco, with delighted insincerity, hopes Lucy didn't get a problem with the *digestione* that night; those were Morello cherries, *amarene*, and no one in their right mind would eat more than a handful of them raw, unless perhaps to aid the stomach after a particularly heavy meal . . . He looks searchingly at her, checking for long-term symptoms. No, says Lucy. No problems.

Ah, says Franco, you Northern peoples! Digestions of iron! Constitutions of steel! Anyway, he goes on, demonstrating those socially irresponsible tendencies we will come to know so well, it wasn't his land or his tree so we needn't worry. The house we were inspecting with such appreciation belongs, in fact, to an uncle of his old friend Bacalè, who by chance is sitting over there, he says, waving airily in the direction of Giacò's card table; and the unfortunate Bacalè, a large lumpy man wearing the regulation potato-head hanky, set off by an egg- and wine-stained vest with a forest of grey straggly hairs sprouting from its neck and armholes, is dragged over to make our acquaintance.

We shake a damp hand; Bacalè avoids our eyes. Though hardly a head turns, all attention is upon him, and many packs of cards shuffle apprehensively on his behalf. Lucy and I still aren't sure that all this isn't designed to make us grovel some more about burglary or cherry-thieving, and brace ourselves to apologize anew. But this is not what Franco has in mind at all.

Is it not true, Bacalè, he says, that Old Uncle Pompeo can no longer keep up all the plots he holds, scattered about the valleys as they are? Might he not be pleased to get rid of one of his furthest-flung *terreni*, in which these two charming *signorine* are interested? Bacalè, still avoiding our eyes, seems to be agreeing in dialect that this is probably the case.

We should meet with him up there one evening, this weekend maybe, Franco goes on breezily, we'll light a fire and cook dinner *alla brace* under the olives, and both parties can get to know one another . . .

Don't be ridiculous, we say, boldly ordering another coffee now all this company protects us from comment by Luigi. We would be wasting the poor man's time, we say. We can't afford to go buying property on the Italian Riviera.

Not to worry! says Franco. He will negotiate a price for us. It will be very reasonable. He knows we like the place.

The point is, we say wistfully, not whether we like it, but that we don't have the money. Franco leans forward till his eyes are only inches from ours, speaking so low that his moustachios hardly move. Five million lire, give or take a few thousand, that should probably do it.

Five million . . . Slowly it dawns on us that the sum in question is not much more than two thousand pounds. Even we could raise that amount! We look at one another with a wild surmise.

Our second coffee arrives at this moment, a fact pointedly announced by Luigi as he delivers it. Franco may be prepared to fly in the face of social convention in many ways; but he has certainly not risen above his nation's rules and regulations surrounding caffeine. The idea of a second coffee – thank you, Luigi – before lunch is so appalling that it is momentarily more important even than salesmanship.

Two espressos! Before eating! And another one, of course, after lunch . . . That will be three. What about our stomachs? Our nerves? Will we sleep tonight? Why don't we have a good healthy glass of wine instead? Or at least let Franco get the coffee corrected for us?

How exhausting is this country? Everybody is so determined to save your life, and so full of fixed ideas. It is, for example, pointless to say that we might not have another coffee after lunch. As far as anyone within many hundreds of miles is concerned, the one after lunch is obligatory: civilization will crack, chaos break out, if you turn it down. How do they think our Island Race has survived all these centuries without their advice?

And no, we certainly don't want our coffees corrected. We have already been introduced to this bizarre solution to the eternal Italian coffee problem: we won't be falling for it again. Not before the sun's over the yardarm, at any rate. The *caffè corretto* means simply that you drink the same cup of coffee you were originally planning to have, but with a small dose of stiff liquor added to it. The alcohol will counteract all the harmful effects of the caffeine. More than happy, as always, to comply with local custom if only anyone will tell us what it is, we agreed one lunchtime to a dollop of brandy in our coffees. (Grappa, naturally, is the traditional coffee corrective, but there are moments when the British liver quails at the very thought of that ferocious stuff.) The correction cheered Luigi, but had the direst consequences on the rest of our afternoon, turning the four hours bent over rosebushes, wax and bits of string under hot sunshine into endless torture.

Franco has seen us swallow his two-thousand-pounds bait; now he switches on to full power, ignoring our feeble protestations. Only three kilometres up from the village – six terraces, fifty good well-kept olive trees, a small but perfect vineyard, fine well with plenty of water, vegetable patch, house sturdy and stone-built, roof intact, *and* a spare roundhouse we can easily build back up and use as a *cantina* . . . Enough trees to make a couple of hundred litres of oil in a decent year, easily enough for us and all our family . . . He's sure we could sort something out with Pompeo, we can probably pay in two or three instalments if we don't have all the cash here and now . . . cheap at the price. Of course we can afford it! We'd only have to put down 20 per cent of the price to keep the offer open . . . and haven't we just got our month's wages off Patrucco?

(How on earth does he know that? He's right, of course.)

Bacalè, who has edged off during the coffee confusion, is called back, still shuffling and shifty eyed. Intense negotiations proceed in dialect.

Aposto! Sorted! says Franco, with a decisiveness born of years of horse-trading. We are meeting Pompeo up there on Sunday evening for dinner *alla brace*. We are not to preoccupy ourselves about the food – Franco, it goes without saying, will organize everything.

As we trudge up and down our rows of roses, slicing, slotting, waxing and winding, we half-convince ourselves that we must have misunderstood the price. We must have missed off a nought – or even two. You couldn't possibly get anywhere to live for just two grand. Mistaking prices is easily done in lire, everything is so riddled with zeros. The tiniest item such as a single boiled sweet, for example, costs a hundred of the things. Our familiarity with the price of individual boiled sweets may seem surprising; but at this time Italy is going through a small-change crisis, and boiled sweets often replace coins as a medium of exchange. When you go shopping your change can easily be, for example, two one-thousand-lira notes and three boiled sweets. The Japanese, it is rumoured, are stealing hundred-lire coins by the shipload to use them in watch manufacture. If you take your Japanese watch to pieces – a thing most people are strangely reluctant to do – you will very likely find built into its casing one of the coins whose lack is so sorely felt in this country. This rumour is perhaps, like so much we will hear in San Pietro over the years, not entirely true.

We ask Caterina-in-the-office, our ally. Does she think we've missed off a nought? Does she think Franco is up to something? Does she have any idea why he is immune to the no-speaking-to-us-in-public rule, or why he dresses so differently from everyone else in San Pietro?

Not only does she have no idea, being, as she points out, from

Diano Marina and therefore of a different breed, but she thinks the whole idea is deranged. It's bad enough, she says, coming to San Pietro to work among a bunch of crusty old *contadini*: why on earth would we want to live here as well? And as for an isolated house way up in the hills, we must be mad! A *rustico* is only for staying in at busy times in the farming year; nobody's lived in one full time for centuries, not unless they had no choice. Silly idea. Why don't we come out with her and her mates tonight and forget all about it?

4

Logically, Luigi is the man to talk to about the renegade Franco and his proposal. Luigi has taken to sitting chatting with us whenever he has a quiet moment. He has educated himself in defiance of the class system that would keep him down; and he is still busy researching. Why, he wants to know, has the British aristocracy bred so many radicals? Is there any connection between the Labour Party and socialism? What is our attitude towards the Irish struggle for national liberation? He registers every halting syllable of our attempts to do justice to his heavyweight topics in our make-it-up-as-you-go-along Italian, fixing us with his mournful eyes. Frivolity and ignorance are not in order. My momentary lapse in a session entitled, I think, The Influence of the English Romantics on Tourism in Italy (I speculated that Lord Byron, among others known to be fond of the place, might be buried somewhere in Italy) almost put an end to our budding friendship. Luigi's horror was such that he had to rise momentarily from his seat. Did I not know, he exclaimed, clutching at the table for support, that Byron had died fighting for the liberation of the Greek people? I was mortified.

Dare we bring up the topic of Franco? Perhaps not. Not only is Luigi the only man in San Pietro who doesn't enjoy a good gossip, but it is obvious that there is no love lost between him and Franco the Mystery Peasant. We will start, we decide, by getting Maria on her own.

Easier said than done. Maria is much too busy setting tables and ministering to her cauldrons. Which Franco do we mean? She'll be with us in a minute. Pasta with potatoes tonight, she adds, followed by liver and sausage. Sounds oddly English. Obviously we'll just have to wait till after dinner if we want to talk to Maria about anything but food.

As we wait to be called through, two new customers arrive; a pair of weekend holidaymakers straying in from the coast, to judge by the lack of string and knotted hankies about their persons. Yes: their linguistic handicap gives them away. They are addressing Luigi in Italian. And they are ordering sparkling white wine and a dish of olives: the classic pre-dinner *aperitivo*. Are they going to try to insinuate themselves into Maria's dining room? Are they, like us only a few weeks ago, innocent of the fact that our hosts will have no truck with the foolish modern notion that the job of a restaurant is to feed casual passers-by on demand? We hope so; and judging by the expectant silence that has fallen among the assembled card-players, so does the rest of the company.

Lured by the clatter of knives and forks, the low hum of com-panionable eating-chat, the mouth-watering cooking smells, every now and then a bunch of these ignorant strangers will walk confi-dently in thinking they have found the delightful country restaurant they were looking for: good peasant food, traditional local dishes, home-grown specialities fresh from the vegetable garden. They're right, of course. Maria is happy to feed anyone who's given her a bit of warning with endless deliciously authentic dishes, in terrifying abundance and with great insistence, as we know to our cost. But the bit of warning is vital.

Maria will tell you that it's simple politeness to give a day's notice if you're expecting to be fed a decent meal. Or a morning at the very least. She has much to say on the topic, and everyone is looking forward to hearing her say it again.

Is it possible, she will ask, that the lives of *stranieri* could be so senseless and chaotic that they are unable to predict from one day to the next where and how they will be eating? Do they have no respect for their hosts, who will have to improvise something shameful from whatever's lying around, and be hindered from demonstrating the full range and virtuosity of their cooking? Unless, of course, they want pasta out of packets, *sugo* made with tinned tomatoes: in which case they have no respect for their own stomachs, and have come to the wrong place. Her poor starving victims will slink out with a flea in their ear, or agree meekly to come back tomorrow with an appointment – having preferably sat down for a civilized chat about what is available, what is in season, and how they like it prepared. Like normal people. A gleeful cackling commentary in dialect will break out the second they are out of the door. Watching persons who think themselves superior losing face, making a *brutta figura* as they call it here, is a national sport: and shamefully, we can't help but look forward, along with the rest of the bar, to witnessing the discomfiture of the strangers.

We have understood by now that we are hardly any more foreign than people from other parts of Italy; they also count as *stranieri*, can't speak the local tongue either, and are easily as glower-worthy as us. People from Milan or Turin, or any of the other towns and cities of the rich high plains to the north, are not just *stranieri* but Plainsfolk into the bargain, *'gente de pianüa'* in dialect. Said in the right tones of withering scorn, this phrase conveys everything a hardworking hill-farmer locked in constant struggle with deluge and drought, with collapsing terrace walls and recalcitrant olive trees, might wish to say about rich lazy good-for-nothings who live a life of ease messing about in offices or factories, or farming that flat fertile land where you hardly have to lift a hoe. People, in fact, who have never done a day's hard graft in their lives. Furthermore, among the crops that grow so smugly and effortlessly up there on the plains you will find – yes – hectare upon hectare of sunflowers. It is some slight consolation to our olive-farming hosts in San Pietro that it is always cold, rainy and foggy on the *pianüa*, and its inhabitants have to travel all the way down here to catch the odd ray of sunshine. But not that much of a consolation: evidently, they can afford their travel.

Yes! The poor sap of a Plainsman in the stylish suede jacket is asking Luigi about dinner. They will have to ask his wife, says Luigi, playing to the gallery. Simple country folk outwit smug city slickers. Alas, just as Maria arrives, wiping her hands in a businesslike manner on her apron, and the entertainment is about to begin, little Stefano appears to call us privileged guests away to the dining room. There is a small amount of satisfaction to be got from showing off our easy access to Maria's domain, and we make a majestic exit. But we're missing the fun: we can only just hear Maria's voice from in here.

The strangers? asks one of our hanky-headed companions, already grinning in anticipation, when she appears to take over the doling out of the ten thousand antipasti.

Coming back tomorrow for lunch, of course, replies Maria briskly.

Tonight we get a short training session in the use of a bowl of hot *bagna cauda*. Pick an item from the pile of crunchy raw vegetables cut into sticks; dip it into the bowl, shovelling up as much of the garlic-and-anchovy-laden stuff as you can. Now, straight into the mouth! Well done! We do our usual transports of delight routine. Turning to the floor, Maria wonders aloud what on earth people *do* eat in England.

What has been billed as potato pasta turns out not to be so English after all: a most pleasing mixture of fresh green beans, pasta, and chunks of potato spiced up with tons of basil-loaded pesto and fresh Parmesan. *Pasta alla Genovese*, says Maria. I am surprised to meet the potato in what, judging by its name, must be a traditional local dish. Until, that is, my erudite sister points out that Christopher Columbus was from Genoa, capital city of Liguria. The potato will have arrived here, likely enough, before it ever saw England. Now I come to think of it the tomato is from South America too. What on earth did Italians eat, I might ask Maria, before the tomato?

She is doing a second round with the refilled pasta dish: surely somebody wants some? We hesitate and are lost. Just a taste! She swings into generous action with the serving tongs. Double *primo piatto*; what have we come to? Next a dish piled high with fat spicy sausages and wafer-thin slices of crispy liver; we accept with alacrity. New information: the reason liver crops up regularly on a Tuesday here is that the village butcher does his butchering on a Tuesday. No one here would dream of eating liver that was even a day old. Alarming to think how much dodgy liver we must have consumed in our lives so far. Maria can't tell us exactly what old liver does to you; she doesn't know anyone who's ever eaten any, she says, and she certainly wouldn't dream of eating it herself. How should she know?

Once we've got her to sit down and she's worked out which Franco it is, there's no holding Maria back. Franco, as we'd feared, doesn't have much of a reputation to lose by hobnobbing with strange women. We should watch out; he's bound to be up to something. Most of his land is miles away up at the head of the valley, well past where olive groves and civilization end and the wild pines and scrub oak trees take over, where cultivation stops and the bare white bones of the mountain begin to show. His beasts are pastured up on the high pre-Alpine meadows and unlike the silent majority of the village, rooted to the spot, he is always on the road, travelling hither and thither to livestock fairs, wandering right out of the province, over the mountain passes to the grassy uplands where Liguria meets France and the Piedmont. He may have a few hundred olive plants, like a respectable man, but his horse and cattle breeding put him beyond the pale; he is known for a wheeler and dealer, hanging out with the Lord knows who, eye to the main chance; haven't we noticed how seldom he comes in here?

We have not so far thought of using the regularity of visits to this bar as an index of social responsibility; but we have, indeed, only seen Franco set foot in here that one time. Looked at in this light, his behaviour leaves a lot to be desired.

And what will Luigi the Wise have to say about Franco? Hardly a word. Eventually we drag a reluctant opinion out of him, blood from a stone. He does not think that Franco is a very responsible person, though underneath it all his heart is not bad; and he drinks too much. Unfortunately, this does not make him any less astute. He is bound to be making a few lire for himself on any deal we make with Pompeo – in fact, he is already entitled to ten per cent by law for introducing buyer to seller. Which, of course, he made sure to do in front of a good twenty witnesses . . .

Maria does her best to liven up proceedings. Does Luigi remember all the trouble that time Franco rode his horse right inside the Bar Sito down on the seafront in Diano Marina and let it mess on the floor in front of all the tourists? To punish Federico the bar-owner's son for daring to try to date his beloved only sister, Silvana?

Luigi refuses the bait. Yes, he pronounces. Irresponsible. That's what I said.

And that's our lot. Time to move on to the Principles of the Matter. For years now, Luigi tells us, the only possible targets for unloading a few hectares of profitless olive grove have been the occasional family of ignorant landless peasants migrating up here from the poverty stricken South, from Sicily and Calabria. Once upon a time there were loads of them, unskilled labour, poor saps coming to tunnel through mountains, viaduct over valleys, build the motorways linking North to South, Italy to the rest of Europe. Where they came from, to own your own *campagna*, your own bit of land, was everybody's dream, a golden vision of permanent security. That's why they're called – though not to their faces, of course – *terroni*: land-folk, dirt-grubbers, clodhoppers.

The *terroni* would jump at the chance to buy, hock themselves up to the eyeballs if necessary. Luigi is sorry to say that they often paid well over the odds for their plots, a lot more than a Ligurian would have. The slow death of the olive-oil market meant nothing to the Southerners. For them the land was just an insurance policy against finished motorways and joblessness, a way to be sure of feeding their families. With a year's worth of olive oil and a vegetable plot, a few chickens maybe, at least you won't starve.

So after their day's work on the soaring pillars of the motorways, monumental reinforced concrete, throbbing power tools, roaring pneumatic drills, the quixotic *terroni* would trudge off up into the hills to the other end of history and work on by paraffin lamps with the sickles, shovels and hoes of the dirt-grubbing past, rebuilding the terrace walls stone on stone, clearing the old wells half-choked with mud and weeds, freeing the vegetable gardens from decades of rampaging brambles, pruning sickly olive trees back to life and fruit. Often as not with their stoical wives and scruffy kids working alongside them. Once upon a time Ligurians would laugh at them for ignorant backward folk, says Luigi. Now look. Everyone's reduced to the same sorry state: subsistence farming, or give up the land.

Franco, we gather, made a few bob brokering for the *terroni*; but the supply has more or less dried up. These days not even the Southerners want San Pietro land. Us Northerners may as well take over.

Caterina and the rest of her *compagnia* – Gianni, Paletta, Bruno, Ciccio, Barbara, Anna, a good dozen of them and far too many names to remember – are in their usual after-dinner spot outside the Bàr Sito in the thick of the evening traffic on Diano Marina's main sea road, the Via Aurelia. We take our seats with them, unprotesting among the noise and the fumes. We've given up trying to persuade them to sit on the other terrace over the road by the sea, nicely shielded from the traffic by a thicket of lush palms. Only tourists sit over there. Caterina and friends come to the bar at this hour, we now understand, on purpose to watch – or rather, to participate in – the traffic. Which is not, after all, an undifferentiated mass of racket and pollution but a fascinating concatenation of friends and enemies, acquaintances, relations and neighbours going about their interesting and newsworthy business. Cars stop, blocking their side of the road while the drivers chat and everyone else hoots and shouts; messages are passed, news is swapped, go-betweens roar to and fro on mopeds and bikes, everyone catches up on the day's events and arranges the evening's entertainment. Hissing blue buses pull in with the latest bulletin from Imperia or Albenga, San Remo or Savona; scandal is talked, gossip exchanged. There's nothing going on over the road, meanwhile, but a bunch of boringly generic tourists who provide hardly any scope for speculation; and some palm trees, and the sea. Why leave the action-packed roadside to go and stare at a bunch of unknown foreigners and a few waves? Who knows what you might miss?

In any case, the service is terrible over there. The waiters can only get to you by trekking back and forth through the unpredictable traffic across a seriously ineffective zebra crossing. And they too, at this quiet time of year, find it hard to take an interest in tourists. Once we've realized that you have to pay almost double for the privilege of sitting by the sea, we are embarrassed ever to have suggested such a thing. And truth to tell, after only a few weeks' training we too have got to know enough faces and stories to be as keen as everyone else to get the latest update: we're already thoroughly hooked on this heady combination of soap opera and regional news bulletin, spiced up with a good lungful of carbon monoxide.

Allora, says Caterina, surely you're not going ahead with that absurd hovel-in-the-hills plan? Recount!

Proud to come up with some good gossip of our own at last, we pass on the news about our wonderful offer. But the response is not what we expected at all: everyone is more disturbed than delighted. It isn't just Caterina who thinks our idea of living in a *rustico* is utterly deranged. None of them can imagine how we could think the idea was remotely attractive. And not because they are townsfolk, as we immediately assume. We are surprised to discover that almost all of them have a family *campagna* or two somewhere up in the hills, with some retired or unemployed relative working it; and though you'd never guess it to see them so elegant and hanky-free, most of them join in the grape harvesting and the winemaking, the tomato-bottling event in September with the fires going on day and night; the olive harvest is fine too, in the first sunshine of the year . . .

But it is only on these great social occasions that they like the countryside, when the fields are full of folk. None of them can get their heads round our idea of a country idyll, where you live in a house on your land, your vegetable patch outside the kitchen door, your fields (or, as it were, groves) visible from your windows, nothing but nature all around you. Here in Liguria, you live in a town or village, travel to work on your land as if it was a job. The idea of living alone and isolated up in the country is horrible, and totally foreign to them. English, in fact.

On top of this, not a few of them have an alternative idyll where they escape the tedium of small-town Italy and run to London where the streets are paved with famous musicians and you metamorphose on the spot into Cool Incarnate. Why would we want to move the opposite way? Inexplicable. We should come out for a dance, forget all about it. All right.

We go, we dance, but we cannot forget.

Back at Luigi's we sit in our cosy corner with a nightcap, alternately trying to follow the TV news and mulling over the house-in-the-hills business while we wait for the midnight-thirty earthquake to happen. The last few card-players are packing up, knocking back the dregs of their *digestivi*.

A bold move, I say to the sister. Sidestep all this what kind of life are you trying to have business with a throw of the dice: arbitrarily set one fixed term to it. Attach yourself to a certain shack up a certain hill near a certain village, and then see what you can make of it. It would certainly eliminate vast swathes of the paralysingly endless possibilities in life.

43

And no mortgage. The idea of a fixed home, a home anywhere, which I don't have to spend the rest of my life atoning for – even if it is a very long walk to the Central Line – is irresistible. And this is a seriously beautiful home, short though it may be on mod cons. We could just camp in it to start with, slowly civilize it as we got bits of cash together. We could do lots of the work ourselves.

The sister is not sure. Maybe I'm not either. We look round at the late night remnants of wine-laden peasantry trickling homewards out of the bar, stopping in a huddle just outside the door to count out crumpled handfuls of grubby thousand-lire notes. Maybe, after all, you can limit your possibilities too far?

5

Up at the head of the valley one morning, a year or so before our arrival in San Pietro, a certain horny-handed innovator stood leaning on the gate of the muddy yard outside his calving shed, contemplating the plume of smoke from the rubbish dump a couple of miles downhill, the depressing vista of ever-increasing numbers of abandoned olive groves, and the ruin of his neighbours' fortunes. And worst of all, the absence of any bright idea which might turn the situation to some advantage.

Franco's conceptual leap, he will confide to us one day in a hillside therapy session, was brought about by a new breed of tourist: the hill-walking German backpacker. There might be nowhere near enough lowly *terroni* to take up all the slack in the wasted hills above San Pietro. But thanks to the lovely new motorways the *terroni* had built, here came the harbingers of the future: bare-legged and be-sandalled young tourists, beetroot headed from their senseless rucksack-laden trampings about the hillsides under the baking sun. Franco, from his strategic gateposts, watched the blond apparitions heading energetically up through the olive groves towards him, out on to the high pastures, and finally right into his yard, waving their map and asking directions, radiating cheery goodfellowship. Blessedly unburdened by any depressing grasp of the local economy, they raved on happily about the beauty of his miserable landscape.

Bello, bello, they said in their pidgin Italian, waving their arms delightedly at the scene of decay and dilapidation all around them. What a pity, they said, pointing at the half-ruined *rustico* in the crook of the valley just below them, on the edge of the olive belt. Such a lovely old building, such a beautiful spot, with such a wonderful view, going to rack and ruin! Was it Franco's? Was it for sale?

Franco, as it happened, could remember the place bustling with busyness, with wives and children, olive-harvesting, tomato-bottling, cheesemaking. This *rustico*, like many others, had been left to rot well before the olive market shrank beyond recognition. Once the motor had replaced the mule, you could easily nip to and fro from your village home to your groves in half an hour; get on with the cash-crop, the olives, and dump the rest. No need to stay over now, no point bringing the family up here. And now look: no cash-crop either. Even the olives were no use. Nothing left but a view for *stranieri* to enjoy. Did Franco perhaps hum a few sad bars of one of those Death of the Old Way of Life songs at this point? Probably not: after all, this was a happy day. Inspiration had struck . . .

No peasant, Franco said to himself later as he mulled over this interesting encounter, would ever buy a piece of land unless it would contribute to his resources. But then no peasant would do any of the other things tourists did. These days all sorts of mad thriftless folk were rushing down the motorways to throng the coastal strip. Down in Diano Marina they wilfully exposed themselves half-naked to the midday sun instead of finding a nice bit of shade to relax in like normal people. On the promenade in Diano Marina, he happened to know, they paid three times the San Pietro rate for a cappuccino. They trudged for hours through steep olive groves, it now appeared, with nothing more useful in mind than to admire the same seaside from a different angle. Some of them, he'd heard, had bought up abandoned houses in the half-empty villages inland: places they used for just a few weeks of the year, not homes to live in. And a *rustico* was specifically built for staying in part-time. If they found this miserable dying landscape so attractive, maybe they would like to have a bit of it for their very own. Who could say whether they might not want olive groves you couldn't make a profit from? Had anyone asked them? It would be money for old rope. Franco girded his loins and set off to seek out land-hungry *turisti*. An empire was about to be born.

Keen to make sure we don't miss our appointment with Pompeo and nephew, Franco comes to collect us from Patrucco's after work, driving up with a flourish in his Ape, the modern peasant's beast of burden, an unlikely looking three-wheeled contraption which is really a kind of Vespa. A *vespa* is a wasp; so logically this chunkier, buzzier, harder-working version, with a cart built on to the back and a tiny carapace over the driver, is an *ape*, a bee.

The latest Apes have developed a wee steering wheel, but Franco's ancient model still has handlebars in the cab. Only room for one inside, too, so we leave Patrucco's in the truck-bed of this glamorous vehicle, waving nonchalantly to Caterina-in-the-office, jolting through the knot of rose-lorry drivers hanging round outside the gates, who cheer us rousingly on our way. A couple of hairpin bends later we stop to collect Franco's wife, Iolanda, from their house halfway up the village. At a hoot from her husband's Ape she appears in her apron, clutching a large white knotted cloth full of huge ripe tomatoes, a great bunch of basil making that overpowering per-fumey mouth-watering smell, and a bulging carrier bag. Iolanda, Iole for short, is tiny, lively, bright-brown-eyed. And she can't believe her husband is planning to take us all the way up that bumpy road in the back of the Ape. Shouldn't he get the truck out? Is he sure we'll be OK? Yes, says Franco firmly. We'll love it. Iole looks doubtful, but gives way to her husband's superior knowledge of the eccentricities of *stranieri*. She hands us the carrier, apologizing for the frugal fare. Franco, she says, feinting a slap at him, has only just told her that we were eating up in the hills. Lucky she always has something put aside, what with the cattle and the horses, not to mention the basil plantation to worry about and the cheese to make and the olives still not finished pruning – Franco is more at home in the hills anyway than down here, you never know when he'll turn up – but if she'd known there were guests . . . Still talking, she squeezes herself impro-bably into the tiny cab somewhere under her husband's right armpit.

Franco puts the Ape into gear. As we're moving off he hollers out, 'Te!' – Here, You! – at which signal a hitherto unnoticed large hairy dog leaps off the terrace above and lands slavering in our midst, causing panic amongst the foreigners. Iole, watching through the rear porthole, has a fit of giggles. Once we and the dog have got our many and various limbs sorted out, I have a quick nose in the carrier bag. Several yards of sausage all in one long meaty garlicky loop, a whole cheese, four large red peppers and a huge flat round loaf. As usual in this country, no fear of going hungry.

Lucy and I have always gone through the village on foot, up the cobbled mule path, which has a step in it every couple of yards, steps being no more problem to a mule than to a human. The road we now shoot skittishly off along must have been bulldozed for Apes as the mule was phased out. The only logic it follows is that of the deepest promptings of the peasant heart: never give up a decent bit of land if you can help it. It curvettes eccentrically round outbuildings, skirts vegetable gardens, cuts through lemon groves, squeezes between olive trees, weaving crazily back and forth across the muletrack, into and out of the village, hairpin-bending to over-come the steepness. Seven – or was it eight? – zigzag crossings turn the few hundred yards up to where we first met Domenico into something more like two miles.

Once the tarmac stops, we soon see why ours is not a customary seat for ladies. The Ape lurches wildly from rock to rock, and has the most vestigial suspension. We have to cling to its low metal sides so as not to fly bodily out every time we hurtle over a bump or lurch down a crevasse. The dog, intriguingly, manages to stay on its feet the whole way, using some sophisticated canine no-paws internal suspension system. Up past the smouldering dump we ride, and back into olive country again. New light is thrown on Franco's pessimistic predictions for the Mad Milanese's egg-trailer. It is hard to believe that any good could come of a business operation involving eggs up this hill, whatever the means of transport.

Now, as we round each perilous hairpin bend we get a breath-taking view over the tops of the trees down hundreds of hair-raising feet to the riverbed below and the vibrantly blue sea beyond; and abso-lutely nothing at all to stop you plunging straight off to your doom except this tiny Vespa motor, grinding horribly as it changes down a gear, pauses heartstoppingly, and churns its laborious way on up.

We catch the occasional glimpse of our safe, friendly muletrack, crossing this alarming road and vanishing off across country again, cosy in the olive trees, heading straight as a die for our destination; it's all we can do not to jump out and finish the trip on foot. The sky is starting to go pink and streaky across the valley. Not long till sunset. The bothy of our dreams may be only three kilometres up the old pathway, but it's more like six by this modern route.

Finally we round the twelfth of the tight bends that we will one day know so well that we have trouble imagining what visiting friends find so scary about them. Here another Ape is parked, this one in eggshell blue and even more rattletrap-looking than Franco's. On its bonnet someone has painted the word TURBO in dribbly orange. Bacalè's machine. The dog leaps out as Franco gets on with the ninety manoeuvres required to park anywhere in these valleys, and we clamber after it wobbly-kneed, exhausted yet elated by our turbulent Ape-ride.

Are we sure we're all right? asks Iole, looking reproachfully at her husband as she struggles out of the cab. We are. We've enjoyed ourselves immensely. Franco knows his onions. Off down the path to meet our doom.

Bacalè and Uncle Pompeo, turbo-Ape riders, are waiting for us on the grassy cobbled patch outside the house, a hysterical pink and orange sunset going on all around them. No soppy bench for them; they have moved a pair of manly rocks on to the patio under the dangerous cherry tree, and are sitting surrounded by sickles, machetes and the obligatory old sacks. They have thrown the doors and window shutters wide open to the warm evening air, and picked a large pile of lemons from the two trees by the side of the house, which lies on one of their sacks; next to it, resting miserably on a small crumpled paper bag, is, we see guiltily, a tiny pile of *amarene*.

They have seized the chance to do a bit of property enhancing; the terraces have lost that wilderness look they had last time we were here, and are newly lawn-like, while a great mound of grass and weed cuttings is piled beside them on the cobbles, next to the pile of olive prunings for the bonfire. Every now and then one of them idly throws an armful of greenery from the mound on to the fire, producing a great column of thick white smoke. Bacalè, only marginally more chatty than he was the first time we met him in the Sulking Café, gets up and drags our bench round, while we are introduced to his uncle; a man almost as short as Domenico but much more stockily built, with a brush of thick white hair, startlingly black brows, and designer stubble in iron-grey. The sprightly if seriously wrinkly Pompeo couldn't be more different from his low-energy nephew, who is now lumpily starting to unpack the supper stuff on to a particularly greasy and repellent-looking sack.

Iole snatches it from him and replaces it with her crisp white cloth. We'd like to help, but in these unfamiliar surroundings can't work out what might be useful.

We settle down on the seat and receive our wine rations in paper cups provided by Iole, while Pompeo checks out our background and credentials. Pompeo is almost a generation older than the others though, and not bilingual like them; he has to concentrate hard to speak Italian, and disconcertingly wanders off into dialect whenever his eye strays on to Franco, Iole or Bacalè. And our own foreign accents and mistake-riddled speech are the last straw for Pompeo. We are all but incomprehensible.

We do our level best to answer his questions, while he peers hopefully at us, brows furrowed with intense concentration. Each time we finish speaking there is a long pause while he thinks our gibberish over slowly and carefully just in case he can extract some shred of meaning from it; nine times out of ten he ends up turning in despair to Iole or Franco for an explanation of whatever it was in good Ligurian. For some reason he seems to think that we're going to chop down the olive trees.

No, we say, we love them, they're beautiful, of course we're not going to chop them down.

What did they say? Iole translates for him. Pompeo does not look any less worried. He is half-convinced, did we but know it, that we are planning to plant some new and outlandish crop – something like Patrucco's roses, but needing less water – which will enable us to make a fortune up here, and whose identity we are craftily concealing until after the transaction is done.

He would like to sell this piece of land; the price Franco has mentioned is an unexpectedly good one. But he would not like to be made a fool of. He stares deep into our eyes; we certainly have an air of innocent incompetence. But as far as he is concerned, beauty in an olive tree is a function of how well it has been pruned and looked after; a matter intimately linked to how many kilos of oil it will produce next year. He hasn't pruned them for the last four years; it wasn't worth his while. Why have we said his trees are beautiful?

You're not going to replant the place with something else, then? he asks.

Of course not, we say, mystified.

Pompeo can see at a glance that we are not a pair of Calabrian subsistence farmers wanting a cash-free supply of oil for our families. Perhaps we are merely the ignorant agents of our menfolk who have put us up to this purchase, and are using our innocence as a crafty front?

What about your husbands, he asks, after a longish pause. Do they have a lot of land? Are they farmers? Where are they?

Nowhere, we say, we aren't married.

Pompeo understands this without Iole's help; it does not seem to reassure him. The impressive eyebrows sink another few millimetres.

Franco explains with a flourish of international savoir faire that English men are cold fish, wouldn't know a Fine Figure of a woman if . . . etcetera. But Pompeo doesn't want jollity and innuendo: this is serious business. He tries asking what our father does for a living; maybe this will give him a clue.

An electrical engineer, we say.

Not a *contadino*, a peasant farmer, then?

No.

Have we got any brothers?

Yes, three, but they're not *contadini* either. Pompeo seems positively downcast by this news. Obviously he can't ask us straight out why on earth we want to buy a piece of utterly valueless land without cutting his own throat. He tries another tack.

What do people grow in your country, then? he asks.

Well, we say, potatoes, we suppose. Or wheat. Or sheep.

Pompeo looks at us sharply. You won't do much with sheep and potatoes up here, he says.

We are beginning to wonder whether we're not going to be offered the place unless we can produce some olive-farming credentials. Maybe he has a sentimental attachment to his land, wants to make sure it's in good hands? We would love to learn all about olive growing, we say. If we bought the place, we certainly wouldn't leave the trees to dry up unpruned, or cut them down, or anything, he needn't worry about that. This is clearly not the correct response either. What is all this about our family, then? we wonder. Is it just that he can't believe women could be in a position to make a deal with him? Does he want our menfolk to negotiate with? We try asking Iole this.

He's old, he's old, *e vecchio, vecchio*, she tells us through peals of laughter. She gives Pompeo a short lecture in dialect, which we decide is about the advances made in the legal rights of women since Pompeo last considered the matter. With hindsight I see that it must equally have concerned the importance of not looking gift horses in the mouth, and the pottiness of the inscrutable foreigner, female or otherwise, in the matter of land-use. She finally gets him to join in the hilarity, looking a bit sheepish, and makes us all shake hands. He goes on giving us perplexed glances every now and then from under the eyebrows, though. Whatever Iole may say, it is obvious that we are not being entirely straightforward about our motives for buying the place. Who knows what we are really up to?

Franco is the only one who has fathomed the depths of the profound misunderstanding going on here. Pompeo is selling fifty olive trees and a piece of arable land which just happens to have a useless rustic building on it; he doesn't even store his tools in it any more since the rumoured maraudings of evil biker junkies, *drogati*, from Milan and Turin, who will steal anything movable to sell for heroin. We, on the other hand, are buying a lovely rustic dwelling with a large garden which just happens to contain fifty olive trees. Franco certainly has no interest in resolving this mutual incomprehension – the more unaccountable and mysterious is his selling-power, the more locals will put themselves in his capable hands, and the more percentages for him.

Bacalè has silently subsided on to his rock; Franco is prodding at the fire. Almost ready, he says, changing the subject with some relief. Prepare the sausages!

Time for our first Ligurian outdoor cookery lesson. Bacalè has cut a handful of rosemary and thyme twigs from the bushes at the edge of the terrace, which are lying neatly on his uncle's sack by the lemons. Our hosts have to show us several times how you twist off a foot or so of sausage, roll it into a snail, and skewer it flat with one of these herb sticks.

We battle with our lengths of sausage, which insist on unravelling as we try to get the bendy twigs through each layer of the whorl; either the twig snaps, or the whole thing disintegrates completely. Everyone else has theirs done in seconds. As mine escapes for the third time, one end trailing on the ground, Iole indulgently gives me her apron to put across my knees and protect my dinner from the alarmingly large amount of leaf debris it is collecting. Franco the diplomat pretends to be too busy with the fire to notice our difficulties, but Pompeo and his nephew can't help giving us the odd sidelong glance; they are undoubtedly concluding that our unmarried state may not be unconnected with our culinary incompetence.

How do we cook sausages in England, then? We try to describe the truncated form and uncurlable rigidity of the British sausage – only to be laughed at uproariously. What we are describing are clearly salami. The second glass of wine improves our sausage-spearing dramatically. It must just have been nerves. A sharp, stabbing motion is the way to do it. And stick to rosemary. The thyme twigs are knobbly and snap at the joints easily, while rosemary is lovely and straight and skewer-like. Sadly, we will discover later that the thyme ones are just that touch more delicious. The grill is an old oven shelf, now red-hot, which Pompeo has brought from some murky corner inside the house and balanced over the fire on four small rocks. I seize the chance to be helpful at last, and begin loading the sausages on to it. Consternation breaks out.

Not yet! Not while there are still flames! cries Iole, snatching them back off by their skewers. You have to wait until there is nothing left but *la brace*, the embers. She thinks it's hilarious, but we can see this episode has confirmed Bacalè, at least, in his diagnosis.

Amazing, the English digestion, says Franco; you even eat your food carbonized.

We go for a quick inspection inside the house as the moon rises and we wait for the perfect *brace* to finish forming. Pompeo thinks he's got some real glasses in there. I know just which glasses he means; they are ancient curvaceous chunky lovely things, and at this moment I am eternally grateful to whatever power (probably Lucy) prevented me from pinching them the other day, sure that no one would ever miss them.

First we check out the one huge room downstairs, its back wall built into the earth, the beasts' byres still standing, olive-wood pegs and iron rings built right into the drystone wall for tethers so the animals couldn't have got away without pulling the whole house down with them. Not easily done, when the walls are a good four feet thick. The upstairs room is even larger, built back on to the terrace above; some old chairs, a built-in corner cupboard from which Pompeo extracts the glasses and a couple of large earthenware bowls. A huge table made of thick olive-wood planks that weighs a ton takes up the centre of the room, and there is an ancient cast-iron wood stove in one corner, its chimney tube hugely and unnecessarily long, stretching right across the room at just-above-head height.

Pompeo sees me prod incredulously at this tubery. It works like central heating tubes, he explains; it is his own design, saves heat and firewood. The warmth stays in the room instead of flying up the chimney.

And what, I ask, are all these long hooks dangling from the beams with weird flat round plates of slate halfway down their length?

Mice, says Pompeo mysteriously. I think I must have misheard him; how would you catch a mouse with that? I hover uncomprehending, not wanting to be laughed at again. Pompeo does a small bit of mouse-mime for me and I get it. You hang your salami or bag of bread or whatever from the hook; and even if the place is riddled with mice they won't be able to get at it unless they can walk upside down on a smooth surface like flies. Which they can't.

I'm a sucker for odd bits of ancient technology like this; I want to move in immediately just so I can hang a salami on one of those hooks and gloat as desperate mice contort themselves trying to get round the slate. There is no getting away from it: we have to buy this place. I'm sold.

6

Built into the back wall next to the gigantic stone-age alcove is the only modern convenience in our dream home: a strangely elementary bit of plumbing – a huge sculpted marble sink (and draining-board) with no taps to feed it; a piece of hosepipe leads from its plughole out under the door and on to the roots of the cherry tree. There is an old cork for a plug, and a bucket to fill it with water from the well. Pompeo is very proud of this sink; his dad pinched it from a disused church during the war, he tells us, a church whose priests ran away as soon as the Germans invaded. Better us than *cretini* of priests who leave their flock in the lurch, says Pompeo; and asks Franco to ask us if we've seen the two forks painted on the side of the Church of the Madonna of the Snows at the Colla, right at the top of the village?

We have; or rather, we've seen a mysterious graffito in palest green, ten feet tall, of two objects which we thought were meant to be rakes, or possibly afro-combs. Some type of agricultural implement? We couldn't guess what their portraits might be doing on the side of a church.

Forks! For eating! To show that the church is only interested in lining its own stomach, not in the welfare of its flock! says Pompeo excitedly. He painted those himself, he says, with some other partisans during the war. Didn't we get it?

Well, no, say I, apologetically. In fact, even if we'd recognized the implement I doubt we would have got the point . . .

Ah, says Pompeo, but in those days it was easy to understand. Lots of people couldn't read, so they had to be more intelligent, he adds, rudely. The church has tried painting over them, lots of times, but they always show through again in the end! Of course they do. Nothing's changed, has it? *Euh!!*

(A long-drawn-out *Euh!* accompanied by slow, wise nodding, which is how Pompeo is delivering it, means in Liguria something like 'I told you so all along'. Minus the nodding, and depending on the tone of voice it's uttered in, it can convey anything from 'Yes, of course' to dismay, shock and amazement.)

All very solid, says Franco, prodding at the roof with the handle of his sickle, studiously ignoring Pompeo's irreligious remarks. He dislodges a tile, hooks it deftly back into position with the point of the implement. No cracks in the walls – nothing you can't sort out with a bucket of *calce*.

Lucy looks at me. I'm supposed to be the linguist. *Calce*? I don't know. Calcium? Chalk, maybe? It's a mystery to me, too. Franco and Pompeo get engrossed in dialect building-talk. Lucy and I wander off back to the fire and Iole. By now the sunset has calmed down and the yard is bathed in moonlight so bright it makes shadows. The fire has achieved the correct format, and a delicious perfume is rising from the sausages. Iole has also put the red peppers on to roast before retreating to the cool of the bench.

What is this *calce* they're talking about, I ask, what do you do with it?

Well . . . it's a kind of white powder, it burns your skin if you're not careful . . .

Burns your skin! Can it be lime, we wonder, visions of mass murderers and plague pits rising before us.

It disinfects everything, fills up the cracks, kills the insects, says Franco, returning. You make paint with it, just mix it up in a bucket with water.

Lime! That must be what it is. We think we may have heard of limewash, something like whitewash. But why does the house need disinfecting? I ask, nervously.

Nobody takes this up. The need for disinfection is too obvious. Here in Liguria you are surrounded by life-threatening terrors. Infection is as one with draughts and dampness and sea-bathing out of season and the awful things that will happen to your digestion if you don't eat your food in the right order.

It comes out better if you add a litre of milk though, or a kilo of glue, says Iole. To stop it making dust that comes off on your clothes when you lean against the wall.

You can if you want, says Franco, his tone implying that this is namby-pamby women's stuff.

And if you don't want your walls white, Mariuccia at the shop has little bottles of colour you can add to it.

Franco tells his wife rather pointedly that there is no need for us to know these things. He personally will be organizing the work needed to make the place habitable and it will be done by professionals. We will of course want the rooftiles taken off and the roof re-lined with wood instead of the crumbly cane it has at the moment; we will want proper doors with frames, and windows with glass, and probably an extension built for a bathroom. This will involve not only his skills in Adjusting, but in tricky negotiations over building-permits with the Comune, the Town Hall.

We will later discover that this word he is using – *aggiustare* – sounds like 'adjust' and is about right for the level of home improvements we have in mind – actually covers anything from a lick of paint to knocking the whole lot down and starting over. '*Giusto*' means 'right'; *aggiustare* is just 'getting it right'.

We conceal, for the moment, our complete lack of intention to spend more than a negligible amount of money on our Adjusting, most of which we will be doing ourselves. If we ever do end up living here, it'll have to be on a shoestring. Forget the Country Ladies. Bonfires and buckets at the well, sickles and axes. Ferrets and shotguns even? Wild frontierswomen: could be good.

Now off to check out the water supply before we eat. Pompeo and Bacalè's clearing didn't extend this far from the house, and Franco brings one of the sickles, laying about him as we go at the knee-high vegetation all around us. Wildflowers fall before him in their thousands in the moonlight. The wells are down three high terraces from the house in a rock grotto full of ferns surrounded by clumps of wild iris, through the other side of a tiny vineyard which has been almost choked to death by creeping Old Man's Beard. The four olive terraces down below and to the right of here are Franco's, he tells us. (Ah! So that's how he spied us up here!) And so is the adjoining bit of land just below the wells; it used to be his vegetable garden. Fine piece of land, good and fertile, as we'll find out when we replant our own *orto* on this terrace. Franco's not using his own plot just at the moment though.

We can see that; it consists, as far as we can tell, of two terraces of rampaging brambles with three depressed apple trees just showing their heads above the tangle. Pompeo tells Franco to tell us that he had a fine vegetable garden down on this well-terrace, too, in his younger days, and the ground has all been cleared of rocks. There are still some artichoke plants going strong over there, he says, waving towards the far corner of the terrace, which appears to have been invaded by a clump of giant thistles since he last inspected it closely.

At first sight we aren't at all impressed by the main well; it's just a stone-edged circular hole in the ground, no wall round it or even a lid on it. A selection of grass seeds, drowned insects and bloated snails float on its surface. When Franco lights a match inside its mouth, though, we see it's beautiful: shaped like a giant Grecian urn sunk under the ground, very wide and curved at the bottom, narrow at the neck, and only about fifteen feet deep. It's built into a natural spring, Pompeo says, it doesn't need to be deeper than this. Franco shows us the second well, a square muddy hole open on one side so animals can get at it to drink: this, he says, is as deep as the other well, and just needs clearing out.

Both of them full to the brim and it hasn't rained since January, says Pompeo proudly, but as city girls born and bred we've no idea what a vital resource we're being shown. We've never met a house without water; we've never had reason to consider how impossible a home would be without it.

Seeing there are two wells here, Franco says, he may as well reserve one of them for himself if we don't mind. If we decide to buy that is. Plenty of water for all, anyway. Who knows if he may not want to reactivate the vegetable garden, or need water for his beasts one day?

Unfortunately for us, *Jean de Florette* has not yet been filmed: and without giving it a second thought, we agree to give up the rights to half our water supply, no problem. We are however slightly worried when we see Pompeo simply crouch down and dip the salad bowl straight into the first, beautiful well amongst the decomposing snails to rinse it.

Is it cleanable? we ask Franco, is the water drinkable?

Pompeo proudly demonstrates how pure it is by taking a great swig of it out of his newly rinsed salad bowl. The dog joins him, ignoring the special Well for Animals and just lapping it straight out of the human well. We will definitely make it a lid.

Of course it is; pure as a mountain spring, says Franco, no hint of irony. Just throw a bucket of lime down it and wait two or three days, that'll get rid of any dirt down there.

Lime again! We'd established it in our minds as a kind of cross between insecticide and whitewash; now it's a water purifier too. Neither of us has a clue about lime. Where do you get it? What does it look like? Is it really the stuff people in thrillers use to get rid of bodies? If so, do we want to drink water with it in? We'll save all this till later. We've had too much wine to care just now.

You can tell how good and fertile the land still is by the height of the *erba*, the weeds, says Pompeo, waving at a bank of narcissi, a few unnaturally perfect blue irises, and few dozen gladioli-like pink things. Hard to believe these beauties are nothing but wild weeds round here. Franco takes a slash at them with his sickle, remarking that the land is very dirty – *sporco, molto sporco*, he repeats in tones of disgust, as a swathe of wildflowers falls under his blade. We can't help but pick them up, dirt though they may be.

Bisogna pulire! Cleaning is necessary! says Franco. It wouldn't take much to sort it out, though, he goes on, just a couple of days' work with a sickle.

Euh! You could do it in an afternoon with a decent brushcutter, says Pompeo.

Magari, says Franco pessimistically.

Pompeo shakes his head sadly at this Luddism in one so young. He has just got himself a good petrol-driven brushcutter, he says, a *decespugliatore*; if he has time, he'll come up and clear the land properly for us.

Perhaps we could just borrow it ourselves, we ask, fearing for the safety of all those amazing flowers. But no, we couldn't. It's too heavy for a woman to use. This from a man who's about two feet shorter than us. We're too busy trying not to draw attention to our soppy bouquets to argue. We may do less Cleaning than they think, though, as well as less Adjusting, if the place is ever ours.

A ludicrously huge moon is looming above our heads as we head back to house and sausages. Iole loves our bouquets. Relieved that not everybody round here is a philistine, we give her all the irises.

Pompeo passes round the bread: each of us carves a thick slice off it with Franco's jackknife, and he dishes a fragrant sausage on to it as if it were a plate. There is no sign of a fork but the twiggy skewers make up for it. They don't just add savour, but give you something to hold on to so as not to burn your fingers on sizzling hot sausages. How wise these peasants are!

The other men turn out to have their own jackknives too, which they produce from their pockets to slice and spear bits of meat; women, it seems, just use their fingers.

Now the dog appears, smelling sausage and eager to join in. It doesn't seem to have a name at all, it's always just called 'Te!'

Iole tells us it's already eaten a huge bowl of pasta down at the house and isn't hungry, only greedy. Pasta! We keep our lips tightly buttoned. And rightly so: pasta is a completely normal thing for dogs to eat in Italy. Pet shops sell the stuff, *pasta per cani*, in huge sacks and the dog-owner religiously boils up a portion every night.

Lucy and I pick up a tomato each. I put mine, whole, to my lips, ready to take a bite. I've done it again: the assembled company is horrified. Maria's lessons have not got as far as outdoor eating etiquette yet. Firstly, tomatoes are inedible unless cut up and dosed with salt and olive oil. Franco produces the oil from another nearby sack – or is it the same one? – in a two litre bottle. Secondly, you don't eat salad items with the sausage, but after it. We should have guessed that.

Fortunately, it is OK to eat the roasted peppers as a *contorno* with the sausage. They look burnt to a cinder to us, all shiny and completely black. Just like English cooking, I say to Franco, who at first takes this at face value, then goes into gales of laughter and back-slapping. Iole whisks the peppers off the grill with a twig, neatly removes the blackened skin with Franco's knife to reveal the olive-wood-smoked red flesh: delicious. So are the sausages; so is the bread. We wash the lot down with copious quantities of wine. Bacalè tells us that this is wine made of grapes, *vino d'uva*, which he has made himself. Why, we ask, do you all call it *vino d'uva*?

Obvious. It is called this to distinguish it from the stuff sold in shops, which is made out of only the good Lord knows what.

A quiet munching and slurping period over, the sausage eaten down to the last crumb; time for the salad. Pompeo has vaguely dusted out a bowl with one of the sacks. My sister starts to slice the tomatoes into it. Iole, squeaking with horror, whisks tomato and knife out of her hands.

Like this, *così*, she says, doing something with the tomato in the palm of her hand, knife flying at the speed of light. In seconds three huge tomatoes are down, and the bowl filled with juicy chunks. Chunks, not slices. Bacalè applies the olive oil, Iole the salt. Franco rips up the basil leaves and throws them in too. Undeterred by my sister's fate, I boldly pick up one of the lemons and cut it in half to go in the dressing. In the nick of time, Franco snatches it away from me. It had slipped my mind that of course you don't put lemon on a tomato salad. Lemon, as you are no doubt aware, is only for salads with leaves in them. Tomatoes have enough *acidità* of their own.

Worn out with our own ignorance, we give up trying to be helpful and collapse into passivity again. How do you eat a salad with no fork, anyway? Easy: dip a piece of bread into the bowl to sop up some of the juice, catching a bit of tomato on it as you go. We follow suit. It dawns on us that the older folk here grew up in a forkless world; this is why Pompeo's painted ones on the church look so oddly agricultural. Forks must have been luxury items. He'd hardly ever seen one.

In spite of our tyrannical hosts, we're already in love with the house and the herb bushes and the view and the sunset and the sausages and the grapevine arbour down by the well, not to mention the two lemon trees and of course the morello cherry. And Iole who made the voluptuous fresh cheese we are now eating, and will show us how to do it any Wednesday, whenever we feel like popping in. And Franco beaming and gleaming, flushed with wine, hat pushed right back on his head again, who has offered to take us up with him one of these days right to the top of the mountain where he keeps his beasts. You can see right over into the Piedmont from there, he says. And the olive trees all twisty and gnarled in the moonlight, looking like the fairy woodlands of our kiddy books. And the tale of Pompeo's great-grandad who built the house himself, recycling the stone from two roundhouses that had been here since the dawn of time, since the great-grandad's great-grandad at least, and who knew the importance of facing house, doors and windows the right way so as to get the moonlight and save on candles . . . Though in those days, says Pompeo, it wasn't candles, you got some olive oil in a dish and laid a wick in it – a bit of string or rag – and that was how you made your light.

Even the graceless Bacalè, now we know he made the wine with his own hands (best not to think about the feet), and now he has begun to look us in the eye, has developed something akin to a loveable glow. Pompeo himself has unbent so far as to offer to show us how to get the olive trees back into working order, and is now busy explaining the use of that wonderful piece of modern technology, the nylon olive net, which will quadruple our harvesting speed. We can't understand a lot of the words, but he's miming it all anyway – he's up a tree beating it with a stick, the olives fall, he's down on the ground scrabbling for them one by one . . . he's exhausted, has a terrible backache . . . but look! The net has arrived to save us! We spread it on the ground, pinning it together round the treetrunks. (How do you say nails? Tell them you use nails to pin it.) We batter the trees again, we lift the net by the edges, we heave, and the olives all roll into a pile. We have our crop bundled up into its sacks, on to the back of our Ape and on its way to the mill in a trice. Backs unscathed – no crawling necessary!

Franco, Defender of the Good Old Ways, is busy looking unimpressed. More trouble than it's worth, the nets cost a fortune, it takes a whole day to spread them, they get ripped on brambles . . . a bit of old sheet thrown on the ground is just as good.

Iole tells us, *sotto voce*, that the men have a fine old time up in the trees bashing about with their *bastoni*; scrabbling about after the olives is a woman's job. She can't wait for the day Franco sees sense and gets some proper nets.

The only thing we're a bit worried about is the loo. Is there one?

Pompeo points to a small wooden shed away under the olive trees, level with the house, which seems to be constructed out of a selection of old doors and slatted green shutters.

But where does the sewage go? we ask.

It doesn't, it's an earth closet.

Do you have to empty it, then?

No, it just goes away by itself.

We are perturbed. How, exactly, could it go away? And doesn't it get a bit smelly in the height of summer?

No. Not at all. (Franco again) Strange to relate, you just need a bucket of lime . . .

Pompeo finally grasps that we are actually thinking of living up here, not just farming the land. He is appalled. It is too far from the village, he says, we can't possibly do such a thing!

We are confused; it's only a twenty-minute walk, we say. Franco leaps into the breach, tells him it'll only be for the odd week or two in the summer, a holiday place. We've never said any such thing to Franco, as it happens, but Pompeo is so relieved that we can't contradict him. What is this country-living phobia they've all got round here? Very odd.

Does it get very cold up here in winter or something? we ask. Weather being a topic as dear to the heart of a Ligurian as to any Englishman, this unleashes a torrent of dialect. Pompeo, we gather, once saw snow actually settled on the ground up here, a good inch thick, one January when he was about waist-high. Not something we two Northerners can get seriously worried about.

All right: done. The moment has come. We shake hands and the place is ours for four hundred pounds up front. We can scarcely believe it. We will just stay up the mountain and ignore everybody. We will make the place a paradise, turn into old hippies, outpeasant the peasants. Maybe you can make money out of the wine? And just think of the money we'll save on our year's worth of olive oil! At the very least we will sort the house out, have cheap holidays for the rest of our lives. Could we turn it into an Inn for Displaced English Folk and never have to work again? A snail farm? A Wild-flower Theme Park?

We pack up and start to leave but the thought of Ape-lurching round all those hairpin bends after all that wine with extremely full stomachs is most unattractive. We need peace and quiet. We need to think. After a short but spirited battle, we are permitted to walk back down to San Pietro. Off we go through the moon-bright night along the muletrack now stippled with eerie twisted olive-tree moonshadows. The Ape wends its weary juddering way downhill before us, back and forth across our path, illuminating random, shifting patches of the hillside below, picking out a terrace wall here, a treetrunk there, now in the red of its tail lights, now in the silver of its headlights, until it is just a vague glow through distant branches. At last it vanishes, swallowed up by the warm leafy darkness of the village down below.

It will turn out to be harder to make a living in these parts than we think. Wildflowers are ten a penny round here, and no one knows what a theme park is, or wants to find out. Snail breeding is a non-starter; there's nothing the locals like more than hunting down their own free-range slimy creatures. And the house is way too small for a decent inn. Not that that will stop us putting up any amount of displaced English people over the years. The vineyard isn't up to producing our own year's supply of wine, never mind any to sell, as we'll find out come September. And, of course, nobody wants the olive oil. Not yet, at any rate: not for a good few years. For now, even people born and bred in this valley can't find work round here, and apart from the pruning season at Patrucco's there's no chance at all for us.

Still, this act of folly has knocked a good few of those paralysingly endless possibilities firmly on the head. Once I've installed myself up this hill, I will lock immovably on to the place: home-base at last. Although I may go on for years yo-yoing back and forth to England to re-stock with money – even end up with something vaguely resembling a career there – this place is my fixed point. But I shall leave the English bit out of it. This is, after all, a Ligurian story.

7

What difference does it make to me? Pompeo says gloomily when we ask if we can start using the place before we've officially become its owners. He's not using it for anything, is he, and who knows how long Alberti the lawyer will keep us all hanging around waiting? As far as he's concerned, it's ours already. We remember to ask him the name of the bit of mountain it's on, to avoid further humiliations. Several people have asked us this already and we've had to admit to having no idea. Truth to tell, it hadn't occurred to us that bits of hillside might have names of their own. *Besta*, he says.

Does that mean anything? Of course it doesn't. But we're pronouncing it wrong. It's a dialect word, even if meaningless, and you have to pronounce the 's' very soft, as if you were a bit tipsy. (Have I mentioned that *Ah, sì, sì*, favourite local expression after *Euh!*, is really pronounced *Ah, shi, shi*?)

'*Beshta*,' we say dutifully. The nearest table of card-players cracks up laughing. Have we said it wrong again? No, it's just utterly hilarious to hear us speak dialect. How irritating these old men can be.

There is only a week left to go before we finish at Patrucco's and have to leave Luigi and Maria's. We'll camp in the place for the weekend, we say, while we clean it up. Maria is convinced that all alone up there we are bound to be set upon and murdered by the Milanese biker *drogati*. Make sure to keep a sickle at least upstairs with you, says Maria, and check that Pompeo hasn't left any tools lying about outside, anything they might use as a weapon. She has loaded us down with tons of home cooking, including a whole spinach tart, two-feet across, all neatly packed up in paper and foil, with which we will certainly be able to appease any bloodthirsty junkies if we don't manage to scare them off with our antique agricultural implements. We ask if she's got any toothpaste we could take up with us; we've run out. No, says Maria, but she's got plenty of baking soda. Baking soda? We try our best not to snicker at weird peasant ways. In a decade or so, of course, exciting new baking-soda-based toothpastes will appear in our own land; now, the laugh is on us.

Maria, surveying our muddy overalls, scruffy travelling gear and general unkemptness, is suddenly seized with a fit of nostalgia for the beautifully groomed English of her childhood. When she finally gets to look her fill at a pair of real English girls, see what a state they're reduced to!

When she was a kid, she says, in those long-gone days before the war, we English were magical apparitions, lovely ladies with pale, pale skins in floating silken dresses, gentlemen tailored in fabrics impossibly light, promenading out on Diano Marina's seafront – fairy-tale princes and princesses, accompanied by our ethereal delicate children. Children of Maria's own age, but nothing like her; their fair hair always smoothly combed and dressed, their linen snow-white and immaculate, and on their feet tiny, perfect replicas of the impossibly fragile shoes of their parents. Here in San Pietro, says Maria, you didn't get shoes at all till you were grown up enough to need them for work. Then you would get a pair of lumpy lace-up boots made by the village cobbler. You just wanted to stare and stare at those angel children; but it wasn't easily done. There was always some eagle-eyed adult busy protecting them from contamination, keeping off the ragged thieving Italian urchins. Maria and her barefoot friends, trying to creep closer for a better view, would be loudly driven off as soon as they were spotted.

Poor Maria! We are horribly ashamed of our vile forebears. What a revolting bunch.

Maria laughs at our expressions. It was a good game, though. Especially if you got close enough to touch one. You've never seen anyone so terrified! *Mamma mia!* Not just white, but transparent. Scared to death!

Ah. Not so much the tragic victim, then.

Never mind angels, pronounces Luigi. Those English were just the rich, the privileged few. Some features of capitalism are, in fact, progressive. These days even the poor can travel. Our presence here is the proof.

Euh! say I, trying out some of my newly acquired Ligurian.

Ah, si, si, says Luigi, without batting an eyelid.

Luigi contributes a huge bottle of his own *vino d'uva*, not the wine he sells in the bar which he makes from bought grapes, but his special reserve from their own vineyard. We will sleep so soundly after a couple of glasses of this, he tells us with a heavy wink, that we won't even notice the *drogati*. At the last moment, we are not quite sure why, he makes us a present of a pair of binoculars. Something to do with his seeing us as partners in the quest for knowledge, though. We are honoured.

Secretly, thanks to our city upbringing, we are much more scared of marauding peasants than of heroin-addicted *drogati*. We have several times crossed paths with a seriously scary looking man who wanders the hills, cross-eyed, filthy and dribble-stained. He has stopped dead each time we've met him, and stared unnervingly at us in a definitely mad and probably lewd and salacious manner. Hard to tell with those wobbly eyes. Luigi and Maria think, from the description, that it's probably only Franco's intellectually challenged cowherd, wandering down from the top of the mountain because he's often left on his own up there for weeks on end and gets *disperato*. Though they seem sure he's no threat, we don't find this explanation at all comforting. What sort of desperate do they mean, for example?

On the other hand, the only evidence of drug-use we've come across so far has seemed pretty harmless; a roofless *rustico* on an abandoned patch of hillside filled with rows of tiny peat pots, each one containing a fledgling marijuana plant. We couldn't imagine why, in what we ignorantly thought of as the middle of nowhere, the marijuana growers hadn't just planted their crop straight into the earth instead of putting it in pots where they'd have to water it all the time. We are still unacquainted with the eagle eye of the peasant for any unusual and obviously tended vegetation, have no idea how intimately every inch of these hillsides is known, olive land or wilderness, constantly criss-crossed by obsessive hanky-headed hunters and gatherers. The peat pot owners had to be from round here, anyway. How would they have found the place? Nobody, surely, could be biking the 150-odd miles from Milan a couple of times a week to water the things.

We too have got ourselves a pair of bikes: not Milanese biker jobs, but *motorini*, ancient motorized bicycles found for us by Giacò, proper respectable things just like the ones all the San Pietro ladies have, on which they whizz up and down the hairpin bends, be-scarfed and be-aproned blurs of speed, with heavy shopping baskets wedged between their ankles and enormous bundles of unidentifiable greenery bound to the luggage racks over their back wheels. Do we know, asks Giacò when we go to collect our *motorini*, how the first ever motorbikes arrived in these parts?

No, we don't. So Giacò tells us.

They were, it seems, dropped from the skies by compatriots of our own, dangling from parachutes. They came in crates, and were folded in half. The British, who seem to have been busy round here at the end of the war, perhaps supporting the Partisans or perhaps stealing their glory, depending on who you listen to, informed the local peasantry that it was their patriotic duty to recover these crates from among the olive groves where they landed. They were to load these unwieldy objects on to their mules, and bring them down to British HQ. Once people had seen the use of their fascinating contents, though, they began to find it altogether much easier and more entertaining to open the crate, put the bike together, and ride the thing down the hill instead. After a while, naturally, the crates became more and more difficult to track down: a surprising number of them, says Giacò, placing a finger under a rheumy eyeball, were lost among the olives, never to be found at all.

We are already sick of the walk up from San Pietro and back down, which we have naturally done many times since that first evening to make sure the house really exists. We are looking forward immensely to the internal combustion engine, which we hope will solve the problem of the wild variations in the distance between our home-to-be and the village. Sometimes it is so near you can pop up and back, no problem. Sometimes it is ludicrously far from civilization, and we wonder what on earth possessed us to think we could live in it.

We will eventually learn to abandon any notion of using ordinary terrestrial measurements for calculating the distance between our house and the village. Miles or kilometres mean nothing. You have to use a complex equation based on time, not space, to plan any trip on foot in these hills, along with a set of other variables: height of sun, quantity of shade on chosen route, and steepness of ditto; wind speed, muscle tone, how much you've eaten and drunk recently. Distances multiply or shrink exponentially depending on these factors. Going down to Diano San Pietro by the muletrack takes fifteen or twenty minutes: that remains pretty constant. But going up? Anything between twenty minutes and an hour and a half. The muletrack is so steep and steppy that once the sun strikes your heart will explode if you don't stop every fifty yards for a break. The dirt road is less steep, but a psychological disaster with its hairpinning to and fro, back and forth over the way you really want to go. No shade, the sun beating your brains out, an eternity of dry dustiness. Unless you're suffering from those just-arrived-from-England atrophied leg muscles, the cross-country lumpy cobbles win every time, however steep.

Wait till after seven p.m. though, when the sun's going down and the evening sea breeze rising, and magically the muletrack is a pleasant stroll again. Just the one rest halfway by a small pond on a fine double-width bit of muletrack with a sea view, under a particularly large and shady olive tree; a spot evidently used for centuries for this purpose. Where some witty muletrack-repairing San Pietro person with time on his hands has incorporated a central line of white cobblestones into the path, dividing the lanes up, highroad style, to avoid head-on mule crashes.

Our trips to the house have been informative, if hard on the legs. On the first, we have met Franco's Mad Milanese on the way down with his eggs, at the helm of his misguided city person's tractor. (About five years on, we will meet Franco himself driving one of these useless and inappropriate things, spanking new; we will tactfully refrain from commenting on it.) The Milanese stops and bounces at us; we must be the English girls, he has heard that we're going to be neighbours, we must come to him if we need any help, there are many things it is convenient to learn about this place before we get the wool pulled over our eyes by some cunning peasant, he will be happy to give us any advice we need . . . when are our menfolk arriving?

His name is Sergio, he is in his late thirties or early forties, and he looks as if he's just wandered off the set of some Fellini film, tawny and leonine with a compellingly high energy output, carelessly swept-back hair and intense golden-brown eyes. His wife Lilli, perched next to him, also has more than a hint of 1960s Cinecittà about her – aquiline-featured with dark hair pinned up in a complicated structure of backcombed loops, huge almond eyes outlined in something black and shiny which extends dramatically into sharp points a good half-inch beyond their outer edges. Noting our stumbling Italian, she addresses us in perfect French, in case that makes things easier. We must come up and visit them, she will introduce us to Italian food as it ought to be cooked, we must be so tired of crude Ligurian peasant fare . . .

We have also twice met a large red lorry driven at breakneck speed by two gimlet-eyed Heathcliff lookalikes, the only San Pietro residents not over forty or under eighteen we have seen so far. This intriguing pair, all wild dark curls and alluring five o'clock shadows, do not stop to offer us a lift or to find out who we are, unlike everybody else on these roads. They don't even wave or say '*Salve*'. This makes them all the more fascinating, and we can't help but hope that they are unencumbered by wives or girlfriends.

Today, as we set off up the hill riding our new purchases, rattling our way heavily burdened up the boneshaking road, we are rather keen not to meet anybody at all. We wobble about on our bikes a lot, feeling remarkably silly; everyone over the age of ten in this country can ride these things expertly, and somehow it hadn't occurred to us that there was any learning process involved. Their motors are tiny, but you can pedal-assist them when the going gets really tough. With all the weight of our curvaceous espresso pots and our saucepans with Bakelite handles, our pair of roll-up camp beds, Maria's snacks and Luigi's wine, not to mention the binoculars, our *motorini* only just make it round the steeper hairpin bends, even with maximum throttle and fierce and furious pedal-assistance. We are utterly humiliated when, just as we are making a big fuss about a particularly rocky section of road, stalling for no reason and squeaking soppily and generally carrying on like a pair of big girls' blouses, a stony faced old man on a Vespa, with a large dog balanced casually on his footplate, zooms nonchalantly past us, his lip curling (or so it seems to us) with scorn as he skims lightly over the boulders in his path.

Still, after a couple of weeks we'll be resting our feet casually on the chassis, local-style, instead of the pedals. Returning home after dark on two wheels along our rock- and pothole-strewn road will never stop being horrible, though. You can't learn this road, because every winter its configuration changes, one rock covered up, another revealed. The slower you go on your bike, the dimmer your headlight becomes. Speed up and the potholes show up beautifully, but now you're going too fast to swerve and avoid them. Slow down again, and you don't see your obstacle till it's already upon you . . . Sober, we creep along in the gloom trying to remember where the pitfalls are this year; after a couple of drinks we throw caution to the winds and fly boldly over the rocks, brilliantly illuminated and clinging on for dear life. There is obviously no correct method. The trusty *motorino* will bring you safely home, no problem, whatever insults and injuries you heap upon it.

How refreshing it is to breakfast so far away from anxious Italian eyes! After a short battle with the bonfire and Pompeo's oven-shelf-and-rock arrangement – no point lighting the stove indoors, it'll take ages to get hot, then keep the room unpleasantly warm for hours – we have succeeded in making and drinking three whole hissing espresso pots of coffee, one after the other, in perfect peace. Although we can already hear the cries of peasants a-peasanting somewhere not too far away, they have no power at all over us up here in our mountain eyrie. Maybe we'll have a fourth pot, just to prove it. It's a bit nippy out here this early, and we are sitting right by the fire, waiting for the sun to make it over the ridge behind us and hit the house. It arrives at ten o'clock sharp: suddenly it is absurdly warm and the fire positively unpleasant. Time to get on.

We have decided only to domesticate the upstairs for now, the bit that was originally intended for humans. The byre or *cantina* below is earth-floored and will have to have something major done to it. We clean, we scrub, we tidy away enormous amounts of ancient rusty tools to the downstairs room, we make up our camp beds (we have turned down an offer from Giacò of a pair of those chainmail ones: we want no more truck with that sort of nonsense, thank you), remove acres of dangling cobweb from the beams, lung-rendingly carry buckets and buckets of water up from the well. We find some wild narcissi on the way, their perfume so strong you can track them down by it, and collect a huge bunch to freshen our new home. When evening comes the place is looking quite presentable, though we haven't finished cleaning the floor tiles properly. They are pitted and porous with age and seem to have been made by amateurs – odd and irregular, not entirely flat. We haven't been able to face bringing up the half-dozen more bucketsful we'd need to sort them out, and are beginning to think longingly of taps and plumbing.

Our house-to-be is not a place to sit and admire the intricacies of the superior craftsmanship of days gone by. Its builders have made no attempt to disguise or civilize its materials, and you can see exactly how everything was made, and what from: bits of the surrounding landscape. They have simply reordered its already existing elements to suit their own purpose. I suppose that's what all building is when you get down to it; but it's not usually quite this strikingly obvious. You find yourself marvelling at the ingenuity, muscle-power and general heroism of Pompeo's great-grandad and his ilk. Imagine starting to build one of these massive places, with their great thick walls and their load-bearing arches, in the middle of nowhere, no road, no machinery, just an axe, a shovel, a mule, and your own muscle-power. The wild stones and rocks which lie about shapeless and unwieldy all over the hillside have been miraculously transformed – no cutting, no cement – into vertical, level and straight walls with right-angled corners. Walls which have stood for over a century, and show no sign of giving up. The beams supporting the roof are ancestors of the leafy scrub oaks that straggle up the hillside behind the house, where olive land stops and the steep wilderness of oak and pine begins. The marks of the blade the ancient heroes used to chop them down and strip them, the stumps where branches were trimmed off, are still plain to see. There are even bits of their original bark still clinging to them in places.

Inside the house the chinks between the stones have been filled and smoothed with some kind of mortar whose main ingredient is evidently earth. Just getting that together must have been a labour of Hercules; in a bucketful of what appears to be soil up here, as we have already discovered – we have liberated a few rosebushes from Signor Patrucco to start our garden – a good two-thirds will turn out to be stones. Get rid of those, and you'd only have a few cupfuls of friable stuff you could mix up with water and apply to your walls. Once you'd dragged the water all the way up from the well, that is. Exhausting thought. Even the roof was of stone once, though now the middle of it is tiles with just a fringe of stone left around the eaves. The countryside round here is dotted with slate-grey rocks the size of haystacks, standing like prehistoric altars among the olive trees; the remnants of the one which was used to make the original roof of this house – a section broken off and split with fire and water, making thin slabs which were simply overlapped, no cutting involved – still stands gigantic and gap-toothed by the path to the road. Earth, water, fire and stone. We take our hats off to Pompeo's great-grandad.

Eventually, worn out by our cleaning operations, we drag the great heavy table outside and sit at it on Pompeo's bench in the warm evening under the lemon trees, while the sun sets spectacularly as usual behind the digestion-threatening cherry tree. We eat rolls and goat cheese and Maria's stuffed zucchini flowers and her aubergine *frittata*, a kind of cross between a pancake and an omelette, accompanied by Luigi's wine. Then we attack the *torta verde*. We gloat about the house, the food, the view, everything, whilst pondering the strange fact that if we saw a representation of this sunset on a postcard we wouldn't buy it. We would think it was tasteless. Can nature be tasteless? We are overpowered by the wine just as the debate gets interesting. The narcissi turn out to be overpowering too in an enclosed space, their delicious perfume mysteriously transformed into something horribly reminiscent of ancient cats' piss, and we have to put them outside before we can get to sleep. By the end of the night we have discovered a serious drawback to this 100 per cent natural wholemeal organic style of homebuilding; it is indistinguishable, to many of God's creatures, from the wild world to which they belong. We will discover over the next few weeks that our home is an integral part of the local ecosystem. Nameless things rustle and scrattle about in the walls and on the roof, while mosquitoes bite and itch. We don't mind too much for now: they are soon to be our own nameless things, our own mosquitoes, or *zanzare* as the Italians call them so onomato*poet*ically. And tonight we wish them well.

At midday, all the clocks of all the churchtowers of all the villages in the valley are clearly audible from up here at the house as they begin to strike the hour one after another. The complicated folds of the hills somehow bounce and baffle the sound so it's hard to tell which village is doing what. It takes a good fifteen minutes for them all to get midday out of their systems: but how pleasingly romantic are their distant chimings to those of us who have lived with the close-up torture version down at Luigi and Maria's.

From our cobbled patio-thing we can see right down to Diano Marina and the sea. We sit with our map under the lemon trees checking the place out with Luigi's binoculars. The higher villages, at our level and above, have ancient grey onion-domed stone campanile; lower down they go stuccoed and rectangular. From its fat little central hillock in the middle of the valley, Diano Castello, leader of the flock, dominates the view, as it once dominated the valley, from amid the remnants of its feudal castle walls. The barons of the good old days certainly knew their way around when it came to choosing a spot from which to keep their peasantry in the right frame of mind; there is hardly a nook or cranny round here from which you can't see Castello. No skiving *contadino* can have felt safe from its prying eyes. You can even see it from our earth-closet window.

Almost all the villages are called Diano something or other – Borganzo, Serreta, Borello, Arentino: the whole valley, our Blue Guide explains, was consecrated by the Romans to their hunting goddess Diana. Why the sex change? When the Romans arrived, it seems, the wild Liguri already had their own, male hunting god, Bormano. In the interests of imperial unity the Romans – busy building the Via Aurelia at the time so as to reach their more far-flung possessions in the rest of Europe more easily – simply declared Bormano to be, in essence, the same entity as Diana. The Liguri, we gather, quite liked the sound of the new name, but weren't so sure about the girly ending. So when, eventually, the Romans abandoned this section of the Via Aurelia – easier to go by sea as far as Marseilles than to deal with these unruly mountain tribespeople – the Liguri celebrated by giving their god back his masculinity – Diano, not Diana. Honour was so thoroughly satisfied that the name has stuck now for a couple of millennia.

By road the only way to any of these villages is to go seawards right back down to San Pietro, and then turn back up the other side of the valley. We know there must be pathways across country, though. When people used mules, they wouldn't have wasted all that energy. We pore over our map, stare through the binoculars, trying to work out where paths might pass through the groves. I start agitating for an exploratory walk, but Lucy will have none of it. It's midday, it's hot, and if we get lost in all that steepness, which we will, it'll be torture.

She's right, of course. But across the valley from us I can see, nearer than the villages, a tantalizing hamlet that isn't on the map. A dozen ramshackle piled-up houses balanced on one alarmingly tall and narrow arch, which alone seems to be stopping the whole lot collapsing into the ravine below. You couldn't possibly get lost just going there, I say. And it's about the same height as us, no sweating up and down, we can just do a loop round the valley, stay on the one level, even if we don't find a path. The boring sister just gives me an evil look. Mad dog, she says. Can she be addressing me?

I get ready to leave anyway; I shall, I announce, intrepidly explore alone. Following the example of Frank the Knife I take one of Pompeo's sickles with me for clearing the Dirt from any useful muletrack I may come across. And for keeping away any junkies or rampant socially deprived underfed cowherds I may meet. I sling the binoculars round my neck for good measure, and, full of daring and enterprise, set off. Lucy sniggers and settles back with her book in the hammock strung in the shade of the lemon trees.

About three hours and an awful lot of leg scratches later – I have encountered some particularly vicious sloe bushes when an irresistible footpath turned into a goat track and then into nothing at all, by which time it was too late not to go right down into the bottom of the valley, cross the river by a tiny rushing waterfall, and then drag my superheated chest-heaving way back up the other side of the hill – I finally arrive, sweatily scrambling out of a clump of bushes on to a dirt track. A rotund old lady dressed in the usual assortment of tubular garments, with a face like a babushka doll and the obligatory hanky tied over her hair, jumps at the sight of me heaving into the road, tousled and bloody, binoculars flying, clutching my sickle. She is busy piling a bundle of greenstuff as big as herself on to a large piece of sacking. Her sickle, I am pleased to see, matches my own perfectly.

Buongiorno! I say.

Salve! says the old lady, already over the shock and getting on with tying up the corners of her bundle.

In those days I used to think they did it on purpose – whatever salutation you tried, they had to say something else. Trying to work out what time of day you're supposed to swap from *Buon giorno* to *Buonasera* was hopeless; between midday and four in the afternoon, whichever I said, I was sure to be answered with its opposite. Then there are the *salves* and the *ciaos*. How to tell which is which, when and why you're supposed to say one rather than the other? Now more mature, I see that this is quite normal; in my own land, I might say Morning! for example, and the person I address might say All right? or Hello! But the insecurity of a foreign language gives this sort of thing a flavour more of annoying perversity than happy diversity.

Salve, I say grumpily, thinking I'm being corrected.

Straniera? she says; foreigner?

Well, that wasn't too hard to work out. Look at the binoculars. Look at the broiling sun. I'm obviously an Englishwoman.

She clucks over my bleeding ankles and forearms, and beckons me to come with her. *Vieni, vieni*, she says. I don't care what I do as long as it involves sitting down and liquid refreshment. This looks hopeful. She sticks her bundle on her head – does she think we're in Spain or something? I haven't seen anyone doing this sort of thing round here before – and leads me down a steep skiddy stony path round the back of a house and into a courtyard with rushing squawking chickens all over the place: I go over to the low wall at the other end of it, the side facing down into the valley, aiming for the slate seat built into it under a vine-leaf pergola. Leaning over, I see we are balanced directly on top of the tall thin arch arrangement I spotted from the house. I haven't really got lost at all, then. I knew I wouldn't. I also discover that the vine in whose shade I am standing has its roots miles down below in the riverbed. How long must it have taken to get up here? How determined people are to have a grapevine pergola round here! Everyone except Pompeo, that is. Thanks to his and his forebears' negligence ours is the only place without a beautiful shady vine-leaf roof to gloat under in the whole valley – possibly in the whole of Liguria. I look down to the vertiginous depths below the arch to see how on earth they attached it to the rock and wall on its way up. No sign. The perch I'm on looks about as scary as it did from across the valley, and its continued existence even less explicable. Not a scrap of mortar between those huge stones, and the arch below me horribly out of true. The fact that it has clearly been here for a century or three – maybe even longer, they started terracing these hillsides when the olive first arrived here around eleven hundred A D – somehow counts for nothing. In fact, it is so old that it's practically bound to collapse under my weight at this very moment. I back slowly and carefully away from the precipice, avoiding any sudden movements, and sit down instead on the side of the yard nearest the house. We swap names; she is called Erminia. I am called Annie. And where am I going, she wants to know. Nowhere, I say, I was just having a walk – a *passeggiata*.

I receive a most suspicious and disbelieving look for this. Should have said I was looking for mushrooms. Still, I don't look like a potential marauding junkie either, with my respectable sickle and my stylish binoculars, and she doesn't look like a woman who'd be scared of cowherds. I can see her slowly deciding to give me the benefit of the doubt.

I gesticulate and gibber in my daft foreign way, trying to communicate where I've come from, pointing to the other side of the valley. '*Besta*,' I say. No, '*Beshta*.' Great confusion ensues; she only speaks dialect, there are no translators around, and she seems to be insisting that this place, the place where we are now, is Besta. There are, she says, no houses over the other side of the valley. I am momentarily nonplussed. Have I somehow walked in a circle? Are there loads of hamlets balanced on dodgy arches round here? Then I realize that of course Erminia, being a Ligurian, won't think of a *rustico* as a house. A *rustico*, I say, and the penny drops, although I get another of those funny looks. With both of us working hard at the language problem, the mystery is soon unravelled. Both sides of the valley are called Besta: this is (in dialect, naturally) *'Besta de' Ca''*, Besta of the Houses. The hill opposite, where I've come from, is *'Besta de' Fascie'*, Besta of the Strips. *'Fascia'* is the word for a terraced strip of land. Or for a bandage, just to make life more interesting.

Anyway, if names are anything to go by, after all that torture I am in what amounts to virtually the same place I started from. I am appalled. Erminia potters off busily into the house and comes out not with a drink but with a bowl of water for my scratches. A big chunk of slimy looking greenish-grey soap sits in it toad-like on top of a grubby rag. I eye it squeamishly. Another trip indoors, and this time a better result; two glasses and a jug of white wine. Once poured, the stuff turns out to have an overpowering bouquet of rotten eggs. But to a woman with a bad thirst on, this isn't too hard to deal with. I've solved it by the second swig; just make sure to breathe in deeply, well away from the glass, before taking a mouthful. Once the bouquet is eliminated by this method, it tastes fine. Has an egg from one of her chickens somehow fallen into the barrel without her noticing? Comforting myself with the thought that alcohol is a disinfectant, and that she, an aged and presumably wise peasant, is drinking it too, I sup busily away.

Sulphurous stinkiness, I now know, is a common feature of home-made white wines round these parts, and locals seem to think nothing of it – in fact they appear actively to prize it. You will find yourself with some knowledgeable person who is fussing over wines in a restaurant, about exactly which goes with what food; the proprietor will reveal that they have some of this white *vino d'uva* (in recent years, the manoeuvre is always done in *sotto voce* mutterings – the tax people have decreed that any wine not in a bottle with a government sticker on it cannot be sold to the public, so a complicated farce goes on where everyone agrees that it's a free gift in exchange for a large tip), the connoisseur will go on about how we must taste some, and this fart-flavoured stuff will be brought out and send everyone into paroxysms of delight. Mysterious. It has a kick like an ox, though.

I rest, we drink, and Erminia tells me lots of things I mostly can't understand except by deep guesswork. She is starved of company, it seems; once upon a time there were thirty-odd people in this hamlet, but now since her husband died and her son left there is only her and one other family – but they don't count as company because they are from Calabria. I'm not really sure if this is what she's saying though. Maybe no one speaks the same dialect? But then if I can understand her, they must be able to.

What happened to the other Ligurians, anyway? Did some catastrophe happen that drove everyone away? Was it at all connected with subsidence and dodgy arches? Erminia and I end up laughing matily, probably about completely different things, and prodding one another gaily in the ribs. And we move imperceptibly (to me at least) back to the topic of the soap and water. She is very keen for me to clean my wounds with it. I, on the other hand, think it looks a lot dirtier than the thorns on the sloe bushes did, and would rather avoid it if possible. She made the soap herself, she is saying, with her own olive oil. It does smell of olive oil, too. What are all these little scratchy bits in it? I ask. Answer incomprehensible.

I create a diversion by untangling Luigi's binoculars from round my neck; we both have a go with them. Neither of us can find the house, though, even though it has to be there right in front of us on the slopes opposite; perhaps there are too many trees in front of it. In any case, with no landmark but endless olive trees, of which I don't have enough experience as yet to distinguish their separate personalities, I'm not really sure which bit of hillside to focus our energies on. Erminia is so overcome by the way the binoculars bring the distance right up to her nose that she's not much use at all. Look at that branch – I could reach out and touch that! she keeps saying, handing me the binoculars as though this particular branch had somehow imprinted itself on the lenses.

Now we are talking about *conigli*. Got it: coneys. Rabbits. She is telling me what all the greenstuff she was gathering is for. We carry it into the shed where her rabbits live to dole it out, I guess, but she takes me first over into a corner where a small grimy barrel stands with an old sack (of course) over it.

For the soap! she says, whisking off the sack to reveal what seems to be a barrel of damp grey ashes.

From the fire? I say, not knowing how to say ash.

Yes, that's right. Later on you add the oil.

I am finding it hard to connect anything about these ingredients or the general ambience with the notion of getting clean. Much later my Scots granny will confirm that all this was not just an hallucination brought on by heatstroke and sulphurous alcohol; her own granny used to make soap with wood-ash and pig-fat, she says, up in her old Highland home. The Italians got off lightly, then. Think of a soap perfumed with pork scratchings.

The rabbits lounge smugly on their beds of straw. I wish I could join them instead of having to do all this brain exercise, willing myself to understand by osmosis. I think evil jealous thoughts about sisters in hammocks hot steep miles away, and yet so close as the crow flies. Some long pointy leaves have to be picked out of the pile of greenery, or the pets will get stomach problems, apparently. I join in the sorting out, although I have my suspicions that Italian rabbits may be just as unnecessarily neurotic about their diets as their human counterparts. Erminia picks one of them up, a big black-and-white one, and cuddles it; her favourite, she says. She hands it to me to stroke. Beautiful, I try to say, *bello!*

Not *bello*, but *bella!* says my hostess. This Best Rabbit is not only a *femmina*, but is the mother of almost all the others. She seems to be taking it personally, the way people do when you get the sex of their baby wrong. The wine is getting to me horribly. Amongst all the gay chit-chat of rabbits, their foodstuffs and delicate digestions, we suddenly seem to be on thyme, rosemary, garlic . . . a few olives, red wine, a slow oven . . . While I've been playing along with what I thought was sentimental rabbit-lovers' chat, we have actually been running through her favourite recipe for serving up the little fluffy darlings. I am horrified. Probably that was what she liked so much about the rabbit I've just been holding – not its loveable personality at all, but its reproductive and stomach-filling potential.

No. I have some serious brain juggling to do to get to grips with this. Of course you can cherish your wee bunnies at the same time as gloating about how tasty they're going to be. Do I genuinely think you have to hate an animal just because you're planning to eat it? My own culture is obviously the weirder one of the two if I do. The effects of the ferocious beverage make it impossible to get any further with this philosophical problem. Again.

As dusk begins to fall, I totter off homewards, promising to call again soon. Well, not really homewards; I have come by such a tortuous and pathless route that I am bound to get lost on the way back unless I keep to the road. Erminia can't help with the right path, because we still haven't identified which part of the hillside facing us, so tantalizingly near, so unreachable, I am aiming for. Erminia is right. The only sensible thing to do, I have to agree, if I don't want to meet those evil bushes again or break my leg stumbling off a terrace in the half-light, is to go on seawards and downhill to San Pietro. Then, alas, turn back up the other side of the valley for the long steep walk up that darned muletrack.

I am also going to stop off at the Sulking Café and have half-a-dozen espressos first, regardless of public opinion on the matter, or I will never make it alive.

8

Since the Foreign Females have moved into Pompeo's old place, a surprising number of people have decided that it was about time they popped up here to check on how their abandoned bits of grove were doing. The land round here is divided into such tiny parcels that a good dozen people have a terrace or two of olive trees, or rather plants – they all just call them *'piante'*, don't even bother to specify what kind, it's so obvious – right near us. A couple of families have a proper *campagna*, still tended, complete with a well and an *orto*, a vegetable garden. Ours is the highest well, but several others are plumbed in, at various levels and on various terraces, to the *sorgente*, the spring somewhere under our feet. There is, we've discovered, a whole collection of these olive-free *orto* terraces in this bend in the hillside. Most of them going the way of Franco's bramble patch: they're too far from the village to be worth bothering with unless you were already coming up here anyway to do your olives.

A burst of cheery *salve*-ing from down below us, somewhere past the well: not unknown San Pietro sightseers at all, but Domenico and family. We are neighbours now, he shouts; their own *campagna* is just down here. Domenico, sandpaper-chinned, moustache fierce as ever, has the Bad Baby Maurizio in the crook of his arm as they come up the path from the bottom road. We clamber down a few terrace walls to where their *orto* is concealed in one of the snug nooks below, squeezed into the fertile space around their well, eye-bogglingly green amidst the silvery-greys and earth-browns of the olive land around, startlingly tidy and ordered compared to our own swathes of tall scruffily waving weeds and flowers.

He introduces us to Antonietta, plump and curvaceous with crinkly hazel eyes and short wild raven-black curls showing the odd thread of silver. Antonietta is twice as wide as her husband, several inches taller, and makes up for his shyness at least twice over with her huge sociability. She tut-tuts over how Dirty our land is, how much work we've landed ourselves with. Our resolve to keep our wilderness as it is has already begun to weaken: not only has everything grown nearly waist high by now, making it difficult to move around our domain, but it is deeply disturbing to our neighbours, who always comment upon it in this worried manner. We are beginning to feel faintly embarrassed about it, as if it really was dirt, the agricultural equivalent of never hoovering your carpets.

Domenico and Antonietta have come up to collect their olive nets, which have to be put away before Dirt starts to grow up through them and ruins them. We help them shift the great cloudy white rolls piled up against a terrace wall in a corner of their land, and heave them into the back of their Ape parked on the road below. From the cab, Domenico extracts a house-warming two-litre bottle of wine they have brought for us, their own *vino d'uva*, carefully wrapped in an aged carrier bag resting cosily on an old sack.

I don't feel that I've entirely got to the bottom of this *vino d'uva* business. What else might it be made of apart from grapes? I ask. Do Italians have things like parsnip wine or elderberry?

They certainly do not. Domenico and Antonietta have never heard of such a bizarre and revolting idea. Why, when grapes exist, would anyone wish to use such unpromising raw materials? In fact, it is precisely the knowledge that such outlandish ingredients have on occasion been sneakily added to mass-produced wine that has led to people using the phrase 'wine of grapes', rather than just 'wine', to describe the stuff that really is made from grapes, by known humans, using natural processes. Under Mussolini's Fascist regime, Domenico tells us, experiments were even conducted into producing wine entirely without grapes. Why anyone should have bothered to do this in a land stuffed full of vineyards remains a mystery. But it has created a general and lasting paranoia about bought wine, into which the more recent scares about antifreeze, wood alcohol, pesticides, have fed. Nobody in San Pietro would ever dream of buying wine from shops, say our neighbours.

Domenico and Antonietta decide to inspire us to get our noses to the grindstone by giving us a guided tour round their *campagna*. They come up here a couple of times a week, they say, to do some weeding and watering and collect whatever is ready for eating. By their well at the moment is a great dark green clump of *bietole*, spinach-beet, which Antonietta is now busy cutting; she thriftily retrieves the carrier bag in which our bottle of wine arrived and begins to stuff armfuls of leaves into it. She will make ravioli tonight, she says, use the *bietole* to fill them, chopped up with ricotta cheese and garlic. Round here you don't decide what you want to eat first, and then go out and get it: you go to your *orto* first, see what there's a lot of, and base your next few dinners around that.

We have already had a good nose around this vegetable garden, as it happens, though we didn't know whose it was, and have spent some time admiring, and even photographing, the extraordinary marrow frame at the back of the plot. It is a rectangular construction of canes, head high, from which dangle a dozen or so four foot long stripy-green marrows as thick as your arm, jammed ludicrously into recycled ladies' stockings for support. The stockings, full of sexy ladders, are tethered suspenderwise to the framework above, and the vast fleshy weight of the marrows bulges, obscenely deformed, inside them, swelling lewdly, fat and thigh-like, out over the stocking-tops. It looks like the wildest dream of some surreal naughty underwear fetishist.

Our guided tour, however, starts at the other end of the Garden of Eden. We are proudly shown yards and yards of tomatoes growing in serried ranks up pointy cane frames: some of them huge, lobed, almost pear-shaped – *cuore di bue*, ox heart, says Domenico; others round and English style – *tondo liscio*, which means something like 'round smoothie'; and the long oval plum kind you usually meet in tins, which will be minced and bottled in the autumn, says Antonietta, for next year's *sugo*. There are more frames, these ones triangular, with the tallest bushiest green beans we've ever seen; two fig trees, one white, one black, near the well where their roots will find more water; a peach, an apricot and a pear tree up at the drier end; nearby, a dozen big prickly leaved artichoke plants: no, they're not thistles. The down-covered thistle heads are just last year's overblown artichokes. Revelation. Pompeo was right. We do have an artichoke patch.

Not to waste space, rows of stuff that doesn't need too much sun

– at least a dozen varieties of lettuce, rocket, broccoli, spinach, parsley and suchlike – are planted under a melon frame, along with strips of low, bushy peas. Zucchini clamber up to fill the last gaps on the frame, peppers and aubergines and little bushy chillis, *peperoncini*, in full sun around it. Patches of basil for the *pesto*, Liguria's summer staple and most famous export, are squeezed into every gap. Hard to imagine that Franco's bramble patch once looked like this. Or that our scruffy plot will ever achieve such perfection.

Even the canes for making the frames grow here, in a tidy clump by the narrow stone watercourse which carries the overflow from the well. For string you use strands of broom-bush. Talk about self-sufficient. Domenico is demonstrating their use, tying up the tall new top-shoots of the tomatoes as he pinches out the side-shoots. Incredibly, some of the earliest tomatoes, low on the stems, are already turning colour. In March.

By now we have arrived at the marrow-frame end of the *orto*. We can't help catching one another's eye as we are introduced to the bizarre marrow-support system. Antonietta's work, says Domenico hastily. His wife bursts into great gales of laughter. *Non cacciar' niente, che tutto serve per il camino* ('Throw nothing out; everything serves for the fire'), says Antonietta, once she's got over it. Is this remark at all connected with her husband's rubbish-disposal techniques? No, it is how they say 'waste not, want not' where Antonietta comes from.

Is she not from here, then?

No, she says, she came up here from Calabria to work on the olive harvest thirty years ago. And in spite of the Ligurians' reputation for penny-pinching – so stingy that they use confetti for loo-paper, she'd been told back home – not only were the wages here nearly double those in the South, but on her very first job there was Domenico, man of her dreams, up a tree with his *bastone*, beating her branches for her. (Outbreak of naughty laughter.) And he hasn't stopped since.

Her husband grins happily, avoiding our eye, a faint blush appearing beneath the mahogany; somehow we all find ourselves looking over at Maurizio, now lying gurgling happily under an olive tree.

He seems to be a reformed character, I say.

Maybe he'll stay after all, says Domenico proudly.

The olive grove which surrounds their *orto* stands out like a miracle of labour and love against the sad decay all around. Olive country as it should be. As we've explored round San Pietro, we've met so many acres of ramshackle half-collapsed drystone walls, the olive trees messy and half-bald, surrounded by broom-covered sloping scrub, that at first we thought this was normal. As soon as you come across a properly tended bit, though, you realize your mistake. Here there is no sign of the encroaching wilderness. Walls are ramrod straight, terraces firmly horizontal beneath the ancient twisted trees, level strips of velvety green meadow weeded, hoed and sickled to within an inch of their life, Nature regularly beaten back into shape at the first sign of indiscipline. Only the odd patch of violets or clump of wild irises is spared here and there, pressed up right against a wall. The olive trees are meticulously pruned, branches elbowed and angular, bent low under the thick glossy weight of their two-tone leaves.

It's lovely, we say. But what on earth are all the other olive grove owners doing hanging about in the bar playing cards all day long, leaving their land to go to rack and ruin? Is there some terrible province-wide epidemic of gambling addiction? Are they really never going to be able to sell their oil again? Domenico removes his hanky and scratches his head thoughtfully. He himself has another couple of plots, he says, a hundred-odd trees more: he hasn't been near them this last two or three years except to do a bit of Cleaning. What's the point? We should take his advice and cultivate just enough trees to be sure that in the lean years we'll have enough oil; in the fat years, every second or third year usually, you sell off the surplus through the miller. At least, that's the idea. This year the price is so low it costs more in petrol to get your olives to the mill than you get back for the oil. *Ah, sì, sì.* The earth is low – *la terra e bassa.*

The earth is low? I move my gaze vaguely groundwards, trying to work out what he's on about, figurative speech being a bit tricky in a foreign language. Domenico stifles a laugh. A peasant's life is hard, he adds helpfully, bending to mime a hoe and a backache. We will see what he means when we start trying to get our own plot into working order.

Not just our land, but our trees, too, look very messy compared to Domenico and Antonietta's paragons – not entirely neglected, but very hairy and wild, sprouting suckers everywhere. They've still got quite a few olives on them, though, even if most of the crop has already fallen squishily to the ground. They are oddly mottled, neither green nor black but a bit of each. And they taste utterly revolting, so bitter and mouth-shrivelling that you have to spit them out straight away. Is this because they aren't quite ripe yet? Or because they haven't been looked after properly? Have they got some kind of disease?

The olive trees round here are the Taggiasca breed, says Domenico. Zero acidity level. Best oil in Italy. They're meant to be mottled. And bitter is what olives are like, even when they're ripe. Of course they taste horrible raw – no one ever eats olives raw. They have to sit at least forty days in brine, *in salamoia*, before they're edible.

I mentally take my hat off to whatever unbelievably desperate person first discovered the edibility of the olive – I'm sure I would have starved without ever guessing for a moment that the things weren't poisonous.

If we look carefully, says Domenico, we'll see that every fourth or fifth tree on these hillsides is another variety, the Palomba, smaller and more delicate; the cross-fertilizing makes a better fruit.

We do look carefully, very carefully, but still can see no difference: it's all right for people who've had a whole lifetime to get their eye in. Domenico finds our olive blindness hard to credit. After he's shown us the fourth or fifth Palomba we give up and pretend we've got it.

It is urgent, according to Domenico and wife, that we get on with our pruning if we want a decent crop next year. Easier said than done. Something like the way you prune an apple tree in England, we think, judging by Pompeo's cryptic remarks about 'opening up the middle': but we were so distracted by his unusual technique for pointing out which bits of branch we needed to remove, done by hurling illustrative pebbles at them, that we missed rather a lot of what he was actually saying. Though we did grasp that it was vital to slice off all the suckers.

Yes, says Domenico, unless you need to replace a tree that's too ancient to fruit well any more. Then you keep one of its best suckers, leave it to grow. By the time the old tree's had it, the offspring will be ready to crop. Domenico does the pebble-throwing routine in his turn – obviously normal behaviour here, then. This time we manage not to be distracted: we think we've got the idea. Fine. We'll start right away, as soon as we've got ourselves a saw.

Not, says Antonietta, horrified, before we've gathered in all these olives though? We can't just let them go to waste . . . we should pick them now before they all fall of their own accord, get them potted – do some of them oven-roasted with chillis, some cracked and boiled with garlic, some *in salamoia* . . .

We're not entirely sure, we say nonchalantly, that we remember exactly how you make a *salamoia*. We have forgotten that we are dealing with a woman who has been mother-in-law to an ignorant Foreign Female for a good decade. Don't make me laugh, says Antonietta (or words to that effect), you've never prepared an olive in your lives. The first two are, in any case, Southern Italian procedures, which we naturally could know nothing of, being Northern folk ourselves. We should begin with the simple *salamoia*, which goes like this:

First leave your olives for four days under plain water, changing it every day. Now put them in a big jar or pot with just enough cold water to cover them, and add whatever *gusti*, you fancy – thyme, rosemary, bay-leaf, garlic. You can add a chunk of lemon if you like. Olives, being full of oil, will try to float on the surface of the water; you must add just enough salt to make them sink. Too little salt and the top layer will be in contact with the air, making the whole jarful go off instead of pickling nicely. On the other hand, too much salt in an olive is horrible, so you must keep stirring, letting the salt dissolve completely before you check for float-or-sink. Now you lightly cover the jar, nothing airtight, while the olives soak up the brine and the flavours, and lose their bitterness into the water. Forty days and four salt-water changes later your olives are ready for eating – or for sealing in airtight jars to be stored for the rest of the year.

Okay. First we'll pot the olives, then we'll prune. We're beginning to see that the earth is, indeed, a bit on the low side. Still, we'll get our own terraces sorted out, just like this, and never need to go down the hill ever again. Except for the odd yard or two of sausage, maybe. Or could we get ourselves a pig? Go, as you might say, the whole hog?

Paradise complete. All those succulent vegetables burgeoning at your feet, the oil to cook them in dangling above your head, endless chatty passers-by who like nothing more than to share a recipe or two with you . . . and in the crook of the hill, just below us, a large vineyard: you even get the wine to wash it down with.

Is that where your wine comes from, then? asks Lucy, pointing at the vineyard, evidently thinking along the same lines as me. Domenico's brow darkens. Not the right thing to ask. Sadly, it is not theirs. It used to be; they wish it was; it ought to be. They rented it by the three-year period until two years ago, when its old owner died. Then his inheritors decided to sell up. And somebody else, a newcomer to the place, offered a ridiculous amount for it. Much more than them: much more than it was worth. After all the work they'd put into it, they lost it. Worst of all, the sellers were neighbours of theirs down in San Pietro, so-called friends.

What do you expect? says Antonietta, with a sly look at Domenico. Ligurians' only loyalty is to their pockets.

Yes, says Domenico. And the idiot who bought it at that price is a Southerner like you. A *cretino* of a Sicilian.

Antonietta points out the place where their own vineyard really is these days, in the middle distance, snug in an elbow-fold of the next curve but one inland. There are vineyards, in fact, tucked into every possible south-facing elbow of this valley, sucking up the sun, curving rows neatly regimented, stripy brown-and-green patches amongst the silvery-grey of the olive terraces. This new vineyard is another rented one, and they have to go all the way down to San Pietro and back up again to get to it. Still, you can see even from here how well-kept it is, compared with what that fool of a Sicilian's done to theirs . . . see how he has reduced it, how incompetent his weeding, how badly pruned his vines!

I'm sure you can, if you have an eye for that sort of thing. What can we do but agree wholeheartedly?

Their tiny *rustico* at the far end of this model *campagna* has newly added metal bars fitted across its tiny ground-floor windows; its aged olive-plank door, sufficient to deter tramps and thieves when the hillsides were more thickly populated, now leans against its side wall: Domenico has replaced it with a great slab of iron, incongruously cemented into the thick stone walls and sealed with a huge padlock. A defence against *drogati*, he says.

So have these *drogati* actually pinched anything from them?

They're not sure. But they don't keep their olive nets in there any more just in case. Somebody pulled up a good dozen of their onions last summer, says Domenico. Could have been Franco's poor neglected cowherd, though, says Antonietta.

I have been fiddling with the bottle of that respectable and time-honoured drug we have just been given, and now having got it unscrewed I try to do that clever olive oil removing wrist-flick. Hopeless. I shower my sister's T-shirt, dribbling wine all up my arm. Have you actually seen any *drogati*, though, I ask, because we haven't. What do they look like?

But no, they haven't come across any either – though Domenico has heard that some have been spotted recently going around on big bikes, driving hell-for-leather around the valleys, looking positively ferocious.

We are perplexed. We, who undoubtedly have more experience of such matters than Domenico and his comrades, would find it hard to tell whether a person who whizzed past us on a motorbike was, or was not, on drugs. Moreover, we're sure we would have spotted at least one *drogato* by now if there were any – if, that is, we're really talking about heroin addicts from big cities. Even without their bikes, surely they would look rather noticeably different from a resident of San Pietro? Are these drugged city folk masters of disguise? In all our trekkings to and fro up in these hills we have met nobody who wasn't handkerchiefed and overalled and generally immediately identifiable as San Pietro born and bred.

We will begin to see the light when we're told in all seriousness by a bunch of the more hoary card-players down at Luigi's that any young male person wearing an earring is by definition a *drogato*: otherwise they wouldn't wear one, would they? The term *drogato*, though its main meaning is 'addict', or rather 'drugged one', gets applied indiscriminately to any young person who openly breaks the rules of peasant respectability. Frequenting the so-called English Pub in Diano Marina, we soon discover, is another major index of *drogati*-hood. Otherwise they wouldn't go there, would they?

Strange. Nothing much goes on in this pub, although it does hold a mysterious attraction for our Diano Marina friends, who, according to the San Pietro definition, must all be teetering on the brink of addiction. Horrible place, the diametrical opposite of the wide-open and transparently public ordinary Italian piazza bar which we foreigners love: the sister and I do all we can, against great odds, to resist being made to go there by Caterina's Diano *compagnia*. Why do they want to sit in this place which keeps its doors firmly shut, has only one window, done in panes of dimply yellow glass you can't see through, and is dark, gloomy, and airless? Why not sit outside in the pleasant evening breeze on a lovely terrace instead?

We finally learn our lesson when, having won the argument and got the Company to join us for an after-dinner drink on the terrace of the Bar Marabotto in the town centre instead, we witness poor Alberto (aged twenty-six) having to explain to no less than three family members who happen to pass by, the last of them a very perturbed mother, what he is doing here without Anna, to whom he is *affidanzato* . . . ?

He is having a drink with friends, he snaps at the mother. Has she not heard that these days you are actually allowed to have friends of both sexes? Why doesn't everyone leave him alone?

What will Anna's mother think when she hears about it? She asks, going off all hurt and upset.

Who's going to tell her? Why don't you all try minding your own business! Alberto shouts after her, at the end of his tether.

Minutes later he collapses into a puddle of guilt, good Italian son that he is, and has to rush off home to apologize and set things right.

This, our friends point out, is all our fault for making them come here; of course we think it's great, all the traditional Italian stuff, piazza life, open bars, multi-generational *festa* nights. It's fine for us, we're not part of it and its social sanctions have no power over us. For our friends these are the loci of oppression, places where the smallest deviation will be noted, commented upon by the entire community, and traditionally, if you've embarrassed your family badly enough, punished with threats of removing your future livelihood by leaving the land and the *piante* to your sisters. Not much of a threat these days, as luck would have it.

The whole point of the pub is its oddness and foreignness, offputting to all these old-style village judges and town social commentators, who wouldn't dream of going in there. The pub is a hotbed, in fact, of social change: change which (if there was any in the good old days) must have moved at a snail's pace under all that constant surveillance. You wouldn't even have dared nip off to the countryside for a quick snog, riddled as it is even now with hunter-gatherers, *orto*-improvers, bean-stick guardians and olive inspectors: just think what it was like in those more heavily populated times. Piccadilly Circus. You'd be lucky if your snog didn't end in a shotgun wedding.

In the pub, though, lurking far from prying eyes under the traditionally English low vaulted ceiling, until the traditionally English closing time of four a.m., you can enjoy several hours of traditionally English anonymity. Naturally, as far as the older generation are concerned, this modern desire of the young to hide away from their elders is disturbing and inexplicable. Why would you want to hide yourself away unless you were up to something? You are undoubtedly in great danger of turning into a drug-crazed onion-thief.

Just past the church at the Colla, the one dedicated to the Madonna of the Snows and decorated with Pompeo's bizarre approximation of a pair of forks, there is a large round patch of smooth concrete under the trees whose purpose has so far eluded us. Not for parking cars: it has a steep little flight of steps leading up to it on one side, and on the other an abyss. Now we know. It's a dance floor. And suddenly a bar and restaurant has sprung up alongside it in the wide clearing under the olive trees: tables, chairs, strings of coloured lights and all. Under which we find ourselves sitting, as dusk falls, surrounded by thirty or forty other tables of San Pietresi all become unwontedly gay and sociable, shouting and chatting to the strains of a rumpety-pumpety band, all saxophones and accordions. And on the dance floor, doomladen string-and-hanky folk magically transformed. Men we have only seen looking lumpy and shapeless, burdened with agricultural uncertainties, dumpy trudging women always loaded down with those vast piles of shopping or garden produce – now all combed and ironed and natty, metamorphosed into these lively fleet-footed dancing couples, polkaing and mazurkaing and waltzing and flirting the warm night away, light-hearted and light-footed, stepping and half-stepping, forwards, backwards, side to side, trotting, twirling, jigging ... cackling with laughter as a huge fat moon slowly moves from horizon to horizon across the purple-black sky. We watch spellbound for some time, sipping wine and munching olives, before we notice that, disturbingly, the band appears to be resting on nothing, balanced over the abyss to the other side of the dance floor. A quick reconnoitre round the back reveals that they are in fact perched on a wooden platform supported by an immensely complicated scaffolding structure cantilevered out over the precipice. Nothing to worry about, then.

Meanwhile, back against a terrace wall, lit by a tremulous generator, the cooks, a good half-dozen of them, move busily to and fro behind a long trestle table, chopping and stirring, spooning and serving; huge cauldrons bubble, fat hisses, a dozen industrial-sized gas-jets roar bright blue at their backs. You buy a different coloured raffle ticket for each dish you want from a young girl at a little side table, who has a chalked-up list of the night's specialities nailed to the trunk of her olive tree: and you hand the ticket over to the cooks, who are thus saved the bother of handling money. We go over to see what's on offer. At the bottom of the list is something called *zuppa inglese*, English soup. Of course I can't resist getting one of these for my starter, just to see what it is, even though the look I get at the serving-bench – if not the position of this soup right at the bottom of the list after the desserts – should have warned me I was setting myself up for a *brutta figura*.

Am I sure I want it now? I am. A large serving lady, damp with the rush and the heat, kindly tries not to look at me as she hands my order on. A few minutes later, in amongst everyone else's sensible antipasti – vegetable fritters or bowls of broccoli soup or plates of *cundiun*, the local salad of tomato, peppers and olives –

appears a plate filled to overflowing with a rich creamy chocolatey and seriously alcoholic trifle. Yes, it's mine.

English soup! I can't help feeling that it is not entirely fair of the Italians to call it so. True, we English are not a nation of gourmets; but, Italian public opinion to the contrary, we can tell the difference between sweet and savoury. This English-soup calumny, however, is all of a piece with people here insisting that we eat jam with our meat in England – a notion that must stem from some garbled description of roast pork and apple sauce, or maybe beef and chutney? – and is not helped at all by black propaganda such as we found on the back of the packet of so-called cornflakes we bought down in Diano where the illustrated serving suggestions on the back included, I swear, a fried egg balanced on top of the bowl of cereal.

Domenico, accompanied by his wife, catches me as I arrive back at our table with the offending item, to the great entertainment of my evil sister, who is already munching her way happily through her *cundiun* and fresh roll. Needless to say Domenico doesn't bat an eyelid. He already knows all there is to know about vile foreign eating habits. But Antonietta is not about to let my English soup starter pass unnoticed; fifteen tables of San Pietresi are soon rocking with delighted laughter at this confirmation of all they have ever heard about the English. I confound them all by putting the thing firmly to one side, to be eaten later, and nipping back to the ticket girl; a few minutes later I am stuffing myself like a normal person with cuttlefish stew in a rich wine-saturated sauce. When I finally get round to the English soup course, it is fabulous; but I certainly don't let on to the interested spectators that I've never tasted a soup half as good back in my homeland.

That dancing, though! We yearn to join all those people moving in time with one another, bouncing and twirling, laughing and chatting, hardly needing to concentrate at all. What we have until now thought was dancing is, it is blindingly revealed to us as we watch the syncopated San Pietresi swirl round their dance floor, nothing but waggling our arms and legs pointlessly and individual-istically about the place. Whole families take to the dance floor together, the tiniest tots whirled around in the arms of parents or grandparents to get the feel of the thing. Maurizio, in his father's arms, is already jiggling a tiny fist in time to the music. By the time you can toddle you are already deep in advanced footwork training with older brothers and sisters, aunts and uncles, grannies and grandads. Is there any hope for beginners of our advanced age?

Domenico and Antonietta, Franco and Iole, Luigi and Maria; even these last two large and ungainly folk take on a mystical glow of grace and bravura. As the evening wears on and the wine goes down, Luigi and Maria even get up for a tango, strangely unfamiliar when performed not with the wild sexy abandon of its Latin American originators, but with a cheerful Ligurian matter-of-factness. The only bit we can participate in is the gap in the middle of the *festa*, the point at which the band plays a few pop songs and kiddies' favourites to entertain the youth: one of which songs, astonishing in this idyllic olive-grove setting, is the awful 'Birdie Song', known and loved here as the 'Qua Qua'. Now all the real dancers sit down for a good gossip about the children and the price of olives and other matters of importance, while a motley assortment of teen-agers, toddlers and foreigners (us) stand up and jiggle tediously about, racked with anomie. The foreigners are racked, that is; the teenagers and toddlers can already do proper *ballo liscio*, 'smooth dancing', as it is called, if they want to, and are not suffering. They are just at that weird age where they actually want to dance the 'Qua Qua'.

This festivity is officially billed as a *Festa dell'Unità*, a Communist Party party. But – coincidentally? – it falls on the day officially allocated in the church calendar to the Madonna of the Snows, patroness of this neighbourhood, the Colla, topmost *frazione* of San Pietro. As the band struck up at the beginning of the evening, a dozen or so ladies of advanced years were to be seen scooting out of the church sacred to this Madonna's name, straight past Pompeo's painted forks and round into the olive groves to join the queue for godless Communist boar and polenta and a night of pagan dancing. Meanwhile a small beleaguered priest, having done his best for Christianity and abandoned by his flock, snuck off alone in the opposite direction, towards the many hairpin bends that take you to downtown San Pietro. Whose own *Festa dell'Unità*, it will turn out later in the summer, just happens to fall on Saint Peter's day. A cynic might suppose that the Communists were taking a leaf out of the Romans' book, lazily naturalizing already existing deities rather than devoting their energies to uprooting superstition in the interests of progress.

The fascinating pair of young men who drive the red lorry are here too, eating at Franco and Iole's table and, rather disappointingly, showing no signs of dancing. Or perhaps not so disappointingly: we wouldn't be able to dance with them anyway, unless it was to the 'Qua Qua'. Franco calls us over to be introduced: they are his *nipoti*, Carlo and Nicola, who work with him up in the high meadows with the cows and horses. *Nipoti* could be grandsons or nephews; with all the excitement we don't manage to find out which. Franco has interrupted them in mid-flow, busy telling some long tale in dialect which seems to involve horses and police stations. Everyone roars with laughter at the punchline, and Franco insists that they tell it again, in Italian, for our benefit.

Is it a joke? we ask. The three varieties of policeman in this country are a favourite butt for humour – instead of an Englishman, and Irishman and a Scotsman you get a *carabiniere*, a *poliziotto*, and a *finanziere*: the *carabinieri* thick as two short planks, the *polizia* marginally less so, while the *finanzieri* occasionally manage to come up with a streak of low cunning.

Do you know the one about the *poliziotto*, a raw recruit, who is fed up with being sent every morning down the long steep hill to the bottom of town to collect the daily paper for his boss? He decides to buy six at once to save his feet. Second day, all goes well . . . Third day, ditto. But on the fourth day he is called into the boss's office; he edges round the door nervously, sure he's been caught out. But no. 'Take a look at this,' says the Capo, in tears of laughter, waving the paper at his subordinate. 'Two fools of *carabinieri* have had a head-on crash in the very same spot – for the fourth day running!'

Carlo and Nicola's, however, turns out to be a true-life story; but it is so good, involving as it does the outwitting of the hated tax-gathering *finanzieri*, that everyone is as keen as Franco to hear it all over again, Italian subtitled version.

It goes like this: Carlo and Nicola recently bought six horses at a bargain price from a man who was about to go bankrupt – a man who had tried to set up a riding school somewhere a few valleys away and failed miserably. Some weeks later the Finance Police, timing their arrival cunningly for suppertime when all good Italians are bound by the laws of digestion and custom to be at home at mamma's table (chorus of outrage), had appeared at Carlo and Nicola's door, upsetting their mother terribly (another chorus of outrage), to announce that the horses in question were to be sequestered to pay off the ex-owner's debts. He had had no right to sell them. The brothers might get some compensation but not until the court case was over, which could take anything up to five years. Carlo and Nicola mulled this one over as they ate. The worry disturbed their mother's digestion so badly she was hardly able to eat at all (chorus) but spurred on by her suffering her sons came up with an idea. Next morning at the crack of dawn they rode down in cavalcade to the Finance Police HQ in Diano Marina, all six of the horses in question tethered together behind them, causing much enjoyable traffic chaos on the Via Aurelia. They had been told, they said to the policeman at the reception desk, that these horses were not their property. So they had come to hand them over. They certainly weren't going to feed and care for six animals that weren't theirs: animals that now, apparently, belonged to the State, in the form of the Finance Police. The policeman panicked. Of course there are no animal-holding facilities at the Finance Police Headquarters. We should have seen his face. (Carlo does the expression of blank horror, which his audience enjoys even more the second time round.) Taken to confer with a Very Important Finance Policeman, they pointed out that evidently if the police were unable to look after their own beasts, and wanted others to take responsibility for the care and feeding of police-owned animals, it was up to them to pay for the stabling. At commercial rates. (Outbreak of *Magari!*, *Euh!* and *Ah, sì, sì* in many and various tones.) Shortly afterwards, Carlo and Nicola left for the hills triumphant, complete with the train of horses and the firm assurance that no more would be said about their ownership. Lovely! The table breaks out in assembled sighs of pleasure.

*

It will take a good half-dozen *feste*, much detailed observation of footwork and many hours of deep yearning for us to pluck up the courage to take to the dance floor for the 'smooth dancing'. As the spring wears on into summer and the serious *festa* season begins, some village or other will *festa* every single weekend; by August, a month of zero peasanting activity, they go on even during weekdays. Posters for these events are put up by the *festa*-giving village in every other village for miles around, stuck up on the officially allocated bill-sticking wall, amongst the black-bordered posters announcing local deaths and the white ones announcing recent decisions and decrees of the Comune. In our valley, we discover, *feste* are always Communist parties; while in the next-door Faraldi valley, reigned over by Christian Democrats, people still prefer the local saint's day.

At last, downing several pints of wine to deaden the nerves, we boldly lurch off into a mazurka, me with Pompeo, who just about comes up to my nose, and Lucy with Luigi. As we knew they would, our two victims have taken our disclaimers for modesty. They are unable to conceive of such a thing as a mazurka-free childhood. Both of them, once they have got over the initial shock and grasped how total is our incompetence, rise to the challenge with grace and generosity. And with a firm guiding hand-and-foot to follow, we manage not to show them up too badly. The feeling – in the bits where you are getting it right, at any rate – of being part of a huge mass of people all doing the same rhythmic thing at once is positively mystical. We are both ecstatic at the end of the dance, and certain that we now know how to mazurka. A theory utterly disproved when we try standing up together for the next one. Luckily, the floor is so crowded that our *brutta figura* passes, as far as we know, unnoticed. We are hooked: henceforth every *festa* of whatever persuasion, Communist or Christian, will find us lurking at the edges of the dance floor waiting to pounce on anyone who'll take us for a spin. We're still at it to this very day.

Check for *feste* amongst the village posters; you want the one with a luridly coloured photo of an accordion player with a sickly toothy grin. Behind whom, in these modern and liberated times, usually stands a small bevy of lightly clad young ladies with huge bouffant hairstyles. You will often find that the young ladies' features, on closer examination, bear a startling resemblance to those of the accordion player. These bands are family enterprises, and daughters and nieces will not stint when showgirl support is required.

9

Inspired by the Garden of Eden down below we are busy sickling away at our remnant of an *orto*, where Franco's bramble patch is making a vicious takeover bid, when Sergio and Lilli turn up to pay their respects and check us out. Pompeo's sickles have turned out to be a much less simple implement to wield than you might imagine, and so far Nature and her Dirt have been winning hands down. Italian brambles are a hundred times bramblier than their English relatives, and we are covered in scratches and clinging scraps of nasty prickly vegetation. Just as we are beginning, triumphantly, to get the hang of a certain flick of the wrist, something like the way you shake down the mercury in a thermometer, which sends your blade slicing through the vegetation like a knife through butter, we hear voices heading our way; people coming along our path, shouting their heads off. Nothing to worry about: Sergio and Lilli's normal conversational volume is somewhere around a hundred decibels.

They've seen our *motorini* parked at the end of the path of an evening for a while now, roars Sergio, and as our nearest neighbours and the only other people intrepid enough to live this far from the village, they've popped in with a bottle of wine to welcome us to the mountain dwellers' club. Sergio is looking very un-San Pietro again, his head hanky-free, his jeans pressed, a city-folks' T-shirt instead of a vest. Lilli is wearing something velvety black and sophisticated with a low neckline and the slinky eye make-up. Only their footwear – Lilli's a pair of broken-backed slippers, Sergio's a disgraceful pair of trainers with one toe flapping open – gives a hint of their hillside chicken-farming lifestyle. The bottle of wine Lilli now presents us with, surprisingly for mountain-folk, has a nice clean label on it and a covered cork, and has evidently been bought, for money, in a shop.

How are we liking the Wild Life of the Mountains?

Fine, we say, but it's a pity about the brambles.

Sergio takes a look at the work upon which we are engaged, which has escaped his notice till now; he sees our shredded wrists and ankles, the mess of bramble sicklings surrounding us; and goes off into a lather of outrage. Has some evil cunning peasant had the temerity to sell us this disgracefully Dirty piece of bramble-covered land? In this state?

No, most of it is Franco's, we say, as soothingly as possible.

Typical of Franco! shouts Sergio. We should complain to the Comune of San Pietro; we could get him fined.

We thought we might just ask him if he'd mind clearing it, say the wimpy Brits.

That is no way to deal with peasants, says Sergio sternly. Especially the ones here in San Pietro, who are twice as mule-headed as the rest of Liguria put together – do we know that, until poor Diano Marina put that balustrade right along the bay to stop them, they would just appear with Apes and barrows and simply remove a chunk of beach whenever they wanted a bit of building sand? They are doubly backward and benighted, and worse still have no desire to improve themselves. Look at their reaction to his mini-tractor, which he has selected after weeks of intelligent study and research as the most appropriate vehicle for farming work on this terrain. Franco wouldn't so much as read the brochure for it. They are *cretini*! It is important to show them, right from the start, that they can't take advantage! And he launches into a long and passionate description of the various unkempt-nuisance-land by-laws we might invoke in order to achieve this dubious goal.

Lilli – her husband's megawatts of moral outrage are clearly routine and water off a duck's back – decides that it is time to get on with the wine. Pitching her voice low and penetrating so we'll hear it past her husband, the way people do over the radio or the TV, she asks if we have a corkscrew and some glasses. But Sergio is on the case. Used as he is to the Wild Life of the Mountains, he carries a trusty Swiss Army bottle-opener at all times. He interrupts himself to demonstrate this, and within seconds it has done its job. Glasses are not part of the everyday accoutrements of Wild Mountain Folk, though, so I go to fetch Pompeo's beauties, which we have inherited with the house since they are old and ugly. Proving conclusively that crime does not pay.

I return to find Sergio busily outlining to a rather glazed-looking sister a letter which he proposes to write on our behalf to the Comune. Topic: unacceptable bramble-patches which impede our cultivation of a vital vegetable garden, essential to our livelihood. It is useful to have the educated city man's grasp of these matters, he explains. For example, his own house and *campagna* are right at the top of the ridge which forms the border between the Comune of San Pietro and the Comune of Faraldi in the next valley. An ignorant peasant would have no idea how to profit by this! But a man like himself can manage, by dint of sending endless streams of letters in highly competent bureaucratese, to confuse both Comuni so thoroughly that for almost two years now he has paid no rates or taxes to either!

I pass round the glasses, hoping to distract Sergio from his mission to make our lives more complicated. Sergio is now admitting to a rather more specific grudge against Frank the Knife than has so far appeared. Franco, it seems, rented them a house down in San Pietro, an empty house belonging to a recently deceased aunt, in which they stayed for almost a year while they were Adjusting their new home-and-chicken-farm. Now they have found out that he was declaring them not as tenants but as agricultural employees whose lodgings were part of their wages. And hence paying no tax at all!

Surely, I say, this is not too terrible? It sounds not dissimilar to Sergio's own tax-evasion activities.

But no, Sergio exclaims, brandishing the wine bottle, we have understood nothing! He doesn't care about Franco's tax evasion; there is nothing wrong with that. Everyone does it. But why did Franco conceal it from him? That is the question! Answer: because Sergio would have insisted on paying less rent if he had been let in on the *truffa*, the scam, that's why. Moreover, Franco was already making a fortune out of them for the building work that he was organizing – and which he was taking a suspiciously long time to finish. You rub my back, I'll rub yours. That, says Sergio, poking angrily at the air with the still unpoured bottle of wine, is the principle!

Seeing Lilli's eyes fixed with growing desperation upon his prop, I gently extricate the bottle from her husband's grasp and fill the glasses. Taking my first sip of this wine-from-a-bought-bottle I am startled to find the thought crossing my mind, unsolicited, that it may contain only-the-good-Lord-knows-what. The power exerted by peasant certainties upon a poor uprooted foreigner, cut adrift from the convictions of her own culture, is alarming. I brace myself with the memory of how many gallons of this potentially lethal stuff I have drunk in my life so far, and with no noticeable ill-effect. Not beyond the next morning, at any rate.

After a few sips Sergio turns his abundant energies from righteous anger to gloating. He still owes Franco three months' rent, he says, and has no intention whatsoever of paying it. Why should he? Who is Franco going to complain to without exposing his own dishonest dealings? He has given it to Franco *nel culo* – up the arse! he says, rising to a triumphant crescendo and finishing off with Franco's own favourite finger-under-the-eyeball gesture. There is nothing like out-cunning a cunning peasant. He laughs long and uproariously, with plenty of happy knee-slapping. Lilli does not join in: she just looks worried. She is right to worry, too, as we'll discover later.

Moreover, says Sergio once he's got over the guffaws, he has now sacked Franco and his men from the Adjusting work, which still isn't finished. They've got two habitable rooms now, and he will be doing the rest himself, with his own hands. It will be done the old way, he says, the craftsman's way: and all in stone as Ligurian building should be. Franco was using too much cement anyway. Lilli's worried look deepens.

We move on to philosophies of life. Mainly Lilli's province, it seems: she livens up immediately. The more we hear of their world-view – unimaginably avant-garde for a place like San Pietro, and probably slightly shocking even in Rome or Milan – the less surprising it seems that this pair have had to go and live up a mountain on their own. We begin to get the impression that our only neighbours are going to be rather controversial friends.

We are not married! We will never believe that true love should be constrained and imprisoned by the law and the church! Lilli announces dramatically, hands flailing, just as I'm trying to refill her glass. She flicks the spilt wine casually off the black velvet with only a momentary interruption to her flow. She is eight years older than Sergio – she does not care! What difference can years make to love? They have two children out of wedlock, aged four and seven, Alessandra and Paola. Lilli comes from Rome, from a rich, cultured and respectable family, who violently disapprove of the too-young, too-poor and (my guess) too-bumptious Sergio. They suspect him, says Lilli in tones of deepest contempt, of only wanting her for her money. They have attempted to prove this by disowning and disinheriting her. It hasn't worked. It will never work. If only her family would understand how little she and Sergio care about money! Still, they are bound to relent in the end – no one else to give their money to, says Lilli. Meanwhile, she and Sergio are spending away on their expectations. They have a small cabin cruiser anchored down at the port in Diano. It can take four adults, it is very *comodo*, has a lovely sun deck. We must come down and dine on it with them soon, out in the bay. We will sail over to Imperia for the after-dinner coffee and *digestivo*.

Great, we say, wondering if we would survive an evening stuck on a small craft with this pair, surrounded by water and unable to move away for the occasional breathing-space.

They have spent every lira of Lilli's own money on buying the *campagna* up the hill. Now they are living, they tell us, on Sergio's pension while they build up their egg business.

Pension? We look askance at Sergio, who can't be more than forty at most and looks vibrantly able-bodied. And indeed, he is only thirty-seven. But, he explains, he started work in a bank in Milan when he was fifteen. After twenty years in a bank you get an automatic right to retire on full pension if you so wish: a bank is a dangerous place, and if you've survived twenty years, you deserve a long and happy retirement.

We find this only too easy to believe. Two sub-machine-gun wielding men in wildly complicated uniforms stand outside the doors of the bank in Diano Marina at all times, while another pair lurk inside near the cash desks; every time you cross its threshold you feel distinctly that life and limb are at stake. Moreover, there are daily tales in the news of bank hold-ups, not to mention shootings and kidnappings, all over the country: the danger-money explanation of Sergio's early pension seems only too likely. (Later, with a better grasp of matters Italian, I will guess that it's just part of the complicated set-up whereby the need for a social security system is avoided, and official unemployment statistics kept down, by letting people not only in banks, but in railways, the post office, and anything at all connected with local government, retire at about forty. This system not only releases jobs early for the next generation, but also creates a comfortably privileged and conservative layer of pension-owning folk, who will devote the rest of their life to pottering about on their bit of land, cultivating their garden, doing a small bit of private enterprise maybe on the side, and generally making no trouble. In the matter of trouble-making, Sergio, though, is probably a bit of an exception.)

The manager of the very bank where Sergio worked, he says, was at one point kidnapped and held to ransom. Sergio is embarrassed to belong to a nation where this sort of thing goes on! What must we think of them! When will Italy ever reach the level of civilization of the rest of Europe?

It does, on the face of it, seem strange that kidnapping should be so popular in Italy, compared with elsewhere in Europe . . . until, that is, you've seen the regular helicopter shots on the news of the wild and desolate landscapes where the hostages are usually presumed to be being held. Anyone poor enough to consider turning to crime for money in England – or Germany or France or wherever – is unlikely to possess an isolated country retreat in which to hold prisoners: putting kidnapping pretty low on the agenda. But here in Italy, the poorer you are, the more likely you are to own some crumbling *rustico* in some godforsaken spot: a place, in fact, which is no use for anything at all, now the days of subsistence farming are gone, unless it is for holding prisoners for months on end without anyone ever noticing.

A sign of the great profitability of this kidnapping industry, unsuspected by us or by anyone else as yet, is already burgeoning on the farthest of the three ridges opposite our house. Of an evening we notice scattered lights strung out over there, along what appears to be a road. Not enough lights for a village, though, and too widely spaced anyway to be one of the higgledy-piggledy piled-on-top-of-themselves villages round here. In fact they are the first signs of a large building enterprise, the '*villaggio*' of Merea, a set of a hundred-odd holiday villas with sea views set in sumptuous gardens, being built as a Mafia-kidnap-money-laundering effort. Soon this scenario will be uncovered, and the building work held up for a decade while the Finance and other competing Police Forces unravel, at their usual snail's pace, which, if any, of the owners of the many plots of land are involved in the kidnapping and laundering, and which are the operation's innocent victims.

It has by now become evident to us why Pompeo had the habit of taking his dirty plates down to the well, rather than water up to the house. And, as a spin-off, why anyone bothered inventing plumbing. We'd never so far considered this question, but then we'd never considered the problem: water is absurdly and unimaginably heavy. You only want it for tedious and ordinary things like cleaning your teeth or wiping the table or washing the plates; and the amount of effort expended dragging it about the place seems quite ludicrously out of proportion to the importance of the task. Having to heave every drop of the stuff up from its deep underground lair in buckets on ropes, and then carry it up a hill along a steep twisty path, you find yourself becoming more and more resentful of its indispensability.

Still, we have discovered why those winding devices that tradition-ally sit on top of wells were invented. Not, as we have hitherto unthinkingly assumed, out of a twee desire to torment future genera-tions with ersatz picturesqueness. We have overturned the preju-dices of a lifetime, and now positively yearn for one. Us stone age windlass-less folk have to bend back-wrenchingly over our well, heaving our bucket up hand over hand on its rope, muscles scream-ing as we try to stop the thing banging against the sides and losing half its contents before it gets to the top. Still, working our way through the birth of civilization step by technological step as we are at the moment, we are immensely proud of our first innovation: adding a few knots to the rope. It makes all the difference, saves no end of blisters and rope burns.

Will we confound history by leaping forward into the machine age at one bound, getting a petrol-driven pump and a water tank? Will we just build ourselves a windlass? We can't decide. We have already witnessed some terrible battles with the tiny petrol-driven engines people use round here – things you wind a cord round and pull, like outboard motors on a boat. Pompeo's brushcutter spent more time in tiny oily pieces on the patio than it did actually clearing anything, and Domenico's weekly watering pump regularly does the same thing, to the accompaniment of much loud and agitated *Porca-Madonna*-ing, clearly audible from up here. It seems unwise to become dependent on one of these things unless we are planning to unravel the mysteries of the internal combustion engine and be able to fix it ourselves.

A happy fantasy where we installed an old-fashioned hand pump just outside the door and solved the problem was soon dashed. Some annoying law of physics means that these things can't raise water more than a certain number of metres; if we got one we'd have to install it two-thirds of the way up the path. So much for intermediate technology. Back to the buckets, splashing all over your feet on the way up to the house however careful you are, contaminating themselves with vast quantities of insect life and vegetable matter as you wade through the grass and floral Dirt on the path. We have mounted a ferocious sickle attack along the path to get rid of the taller seedier vegetation – only to find ourselves foiled by a plague of brown bobbly stuff falling from the olive trees into our buckets, while some type of minute and suicidal grasshopper suddenly came into season and leapt into our precious water in droves as we trailed uphill, shoulders slowly wrenching from their sockets.

At last, following Pompeo's wise example, we have abandoned the exhausting effort of moving washing water up to privacy, and instead have moved the body-cleaning zone down to the well. Our first great contribution to the house's amenities is an al fresco shower area, complete with a marble-topped wrought-iron washstand courtesy of Giacò. The water for the shower runs from a ten-gallon plastic olive barrel balanced on the rock above; this item courtesy of somebody who couldn't be bothered waiting for Domenico's rubbish lorry and threw it off the side of the mountain by our parking place, along with two broken-legged dining chairs and a bedside table. According to the legend on its side, our shower barrel, and the olives it once contained, arrived here from Greece. Sign of the times.

Our grotto down by the well now looks positively Habitat; we have even wedged some bits of marble amidst the trailing ferns and the wild irises to keep soap and shampoo on. We have also, with much effort, dragged a big flat slab of stone over for a shower base, solving the major defect that surfaced after a few uses of our fabulous new facilities: while the rest of the body got cleaner, the feet got muddier and muddier. The stone also eliminates at a stroke any fears we might have about unpleasantly large grasshoppers, the scary three-inch-long praying mantises, and their various crunchy and squiggly cousins underfoot.

Now a piece of hosepipe siphons water from the precious barrel to a tin shower head with a strange lever-like tap, bought from the hardware shop in San Pietro run by the one-eyed Mariuccia; a shop where you can buy all sorts of unimaginable things from up in the backward mountains of the *entroterra*. Not just shower heads, but also candle holders made of recycled tin cans; hand-knitted socks complete with an extra set of toes and heels to be stitched in when they wear out; shoes with uppers made out of old sacks and soles of used car tyres. Something that would have been immediately obvious to the backward mountain-folk still hasn't occurred to us sophisticated city girls: if we keep washing gallons of soapy water into the earth down here, it will eventually seep into the well itself and we will have no froth-free water supply.

Against all expectations, the day has finally dawned when we are to Do the Act. Not, as we thought when he announced it, another of Franco's innuendos: this turns out to be what exchanging contracts is officially called in Italian, '*fare l'atto*'. The lawyer is down in Diano Marina, and Franco is coming to collect us; he will be passing our place on his way back from some cow business. We are to meet Pompeo at midday at the crossroads, gateway to the town from the valleys.

Time to become clean and tidy; and at this early hour of the morning, Lucy discovers a new defect in our washing arrangements. If you take a shower before the sun has had time to warm the water in the olive barrel for an hour or two, you are first lulled into a false sense of security by the stuff which has been sitting in the tube and catching the first of the sun's warmth: then all of a sudden the breath is knocked out of your body by a deluge of freezing water straight from the still ice-cold barrel.

Lucy lets out a piercing shriek which has me haring down the path to save her life. But by now she's already wet all over, and it doesn't seem so bad. Evilly, she turns the shower head on me so I can share her experience. Now that I'm down here anyway and soaked, I may as well join her under the water for company, if not actual warmth. We splash, giggle and shriek in our ferny grot behind the veil of grapevines which protects us from any binocular wielders who may be lurking in Diano Arentino's campanile across the valley. Sunlit silver-green haziness of mountains to the right, intense blues of sea and sky to the left, luxurious froth cascading down my body . . . whence comes this strange compulsion to advertise something?

It is at this idyllic moment, of course, that we hear revving and hooting from the parking place at the end of our path, followed by shouts of *Salve!* from somewhere horribly close.

Franco has come almost an hour early. We run like the wind for the house, myriads of things with too many legs crunching under our naked feet, clutching scraps of towel and damp clothing to us; just manage to get inside the house as Franco rounds the big modesty rock which (fortunately) conceals the house from the top path.

Peeping out through the window, we see that Franco, in his natty straw hat, is carrying what looks like a large bag of cement balanced on his shoulder, his best yellow waistcoat and corduroy Mellors-the-gamekeeper outfit protected by one of his collection of old sacks.

Calce! he shouts. Lime! I've brought you a sack of lime!

Using the bench outside the door, perversely, for the lime, he carefully spreads his sack on a step, sits down on it mopping his brow, and waits courteously for us to appear at the door.

Instead of his Ape, today Franco is driving the same red lorry in which the *nipoti* usually fly up and down our hairpin bends. Once we've climbed in and taken off across the boulders, we seek information. What sort of *nipoti* are Carlo and Nicola? Are you their uncle or their grandad?

This simple question predictably unleashes an outburst of soul-baring. We are not bothered in the least; by now we are used to our role as emotional blotting paper.

The *nipoti* are the sons of his sister Silvana, the person he loves most on earth. He is closer to her, he says, than to his wife even; though (hastily) he would never dream of telling Iole that. He knows, he says, that for example if one day he was to find himself, by some desperate combination of circumstances, lying penniless and despairing in a gutter in some nameless spot – I can't remember if he actually said drunk, though that is the image I have retained of this fictional moment of high drama – Silvana would somehow sense it; she would appear, come hell or high water, to rescue him. She would not criticize him or castigate him in any way; she would just take him in her arms and comfort him with boundless loving care. That is how close they are. Like this, he says, raising the first two fingers of his right hand, tightly crossed, to show us, and allowing the lorry to lurch horribly towards the precipice as it breasts a collection of small rocks. And because of her he loves his *nipoti* as if they were his own sons.

In fact, as Franco goes on Sharing, we get the impression that the poor son is distinctly out of favour at the moment. He has, it seems, opted out of the cattle and horse business in favour of a girl's blouse of a job running the restaurant at Diano Arentino – *l'Usignolo* (the Nightingale). He is, says Franco firmly, a *deficente*.

We try asking how many antipasti you get at the Usignolo, just in case we need to go and try the place out. This, we have discovered, is the best index of good country cooking – the further up into the hills you go, the better is the food and the more plentiful the antipasti, while your bill shrinks accordingly. But Franco is not interested in the quality of the restaurant. He has never eaten there at all, he says, not once. He eats at home. He's got too much to do to waste time on such nonsense.

Poor son. Carlo and Nicola, meanwhile, good manly boys, have gone into business with their old uncle, and are the apple of his eye.

Nicola is the one all the girls fancy; the one he has told us about before, who had an English girlfriend last year. Franco is worried, he says, that this is bad for Carlo, who is becoming demoralized. Carlo is very good-looking too, and is actually more *serio* and more *simpatico* than his brother, but he never seems to get the girl. It is sad, he says, looking us both over speculatively, that Carlo can't find someone who will appreciate his finer points and not just throw themselves blindly at Nicola without giving Carlo a chance.

In fact, we know what Franco means about Nicola; but we both thought he had a bit of a 'how-fabulous-I-am' problem and preferred his brother. Can Franco have managed, in his cunning-peasant way, to detect this? Even so, we can't believe this walnut-featured farmer is actually trying to set a pair of respectable foreign women, clients of his in a manner of speaking, up with one of his nephews in this shameless way.

Anyhow, says Franco, Carlo has much the better business-head of the two; if a woman was looking to settle down, she couldn't do better than choose him. His uncle won't forget him when it comes to the inheritance, either, he adds; and checks out how this has gone down with a nifty sideways glance.

Is it, even more disturbingly, a wife rather than a night of passion that Franco is seeking for Carlo? Any embryonic designs we may have been harbouring on this pair of *nipoti* rapidly evaporate; imagine getting embroiled in Franco's family with him watching over you patriarchally, blackmailing you with olive trees or cows or whatever this inheritance may be. It is borne in upon us, rather tragically, that we must never become romantically involved with anyone from San Pietro. Imagine the awful consequences if you realized you'd made a mistake. You'd never be able to show your face here again. Still, there's the whole of the rest of the world to choose from: we will manage to go on importing our boyfriends for a good few years, until I finally fall by the wayside.

10

At the crossroads we collect Pompeo, almost unrecognizable in shirt and tie, creaking shiny shoes and hair all flattened down and hanky-free. We see, as we cross the level-crossing into Diano Marina proper, the first signs of the annual tricking-out for the tourist season – fairy lights, banners, signs to a funfair.

But the tourists, Franco says, won't start arriving in their masses for a while yet. May and June will be relatively quiet, mostly just Germans, July not too bad either until midway; it is when the big factories of Milan and Turin close down for the month that the trouble will start. August, Pompeo agrees, is a kind of siege month; there will be nowhere to park; nowhere to walk; nowhere to sit down unless you don't mind paying three times the normal rate for your refreshment. The only way to deal with it is by stockpiling necessities and staying up in San Pietro, never venturing beyond the level-crossing until the 25th, when the Enemy packs up and leaves. We won't be able to sit on the beach; Germans and people from the Pianüa book the deckchairs by the month on the private beaches; the two small public ones heave with the frying flesh of Fiat workers. We won't be able to swim, even; the bay will be jampacked with tangled bodies. Lucy and I have started to get the hang of the local predilection for doom and despair, and decide to take all this with a pinch of salt.

There are already a few lightly bronzed family groups straggling about the place now, kids sucking on ice cream cones, parents struggling under their burdens of beach gear. Pompeo glares horribly at the tall blond healthy happy well-nourished family now striding jollily past us.

Tedeschi! he spits out, *sotto voce*, as they pass.

Some new Ligurian swear word, we deduce. What does it mean?

Not a swear word. It means people from *Germania*, explains Franco. Germans. Ah.

Pompeo rants on. All full of money! *Pieni di soldi!* It's the Occupation all over again.

Aren't these Germans a bit young, though? we ask. They can't have had anything to do with the war.

That, says Pompeo, drawing himself up to his full height to wipe the smiles off our faces, just demonstrates *Nazifascista* cunning. They couldn't do it by force, but they've beaten us with the Deutschmark. *Pieni di soldi!*

Here he really does go off into dialect, having accidentally caught Franco's eye, and we are lost.

But we already know the stories from Giacò and Luigi – the villages half starved, the people living on rationed flour stretched with ground-up chestnuts, desperately grubbing about the hillsides for roots and wild greens. When they weren't getting shot in Nazi reprisals or having to take to the hills with the Partisans. The war is oddly close in history here, nothing like in our own country where it seems to belong to another world. But then, I suppose everything was simpler for the British, who only had to follow their own country's lead, blindly or not. Here, though, first under Mussolini and then under German occupation, people had to decide for themselves. First, whether to put up with Fascism; then whether to take to the hills and fight back in isolated bands with no outside support and precious little hope of winning. Heroically, the Communist valleys round here chose to fight back, and the villages went on feeding and succouring their Partisans in the teeth of horrifyingly savage reprisals. Towards the end of the war, we've been told, every dead German meant ten villagers' lives, the victims put up against a wall in the piazza and shot dead in cold blood. We've been shown the bullet marks, which are still there. Imagine living here in those times, having to watch the people who'd killed your father or mother, neighbours or cousins, people who stood for everything you hated, parading about the streets of your own town free from retribution, smug and untouchable, ordering you around. Pretty unforgettable.

Every village round here has its bullet holes, its little marble plaque in the piazza commemorating its Victims of Nazifascist Barbarism. (And, a few feet away, another plaque put up not by locals, but by the Italian State: for all the Fallen, left, right or neuter. In the interest of National Unity, no doubt. There are never any flowers under these ones, though.) The main piazza in Diano Marina is called Piazza of the Martyrs of the Liberation: a statue dedicated to the partisans and a poem about Resistance Heroes and the Fury of the *Barbaria Nazifascista* and all. Still, this is the nearest bit of the Mediterranean if you drive straight down from Germany. Probably, insulated unwittingly by language, money and BMWs, the *Tedeschi* just holiday innocently by the sea, without an inkling of what went on round here forty years ago.

People still think about the war a lot, here, don't they? I say stupidly.

Pompeo gives me a freezing look, and does his best to relieve his feelings with a stunningly long litany of insults and blasphemies – *Cazzi di Tedeschi! Porca Miseria! Putana la Madonna!* – which only stops when we collapse into giggles at the most bizarre one we've heard so far – *Lurida Vacca*, Lurid Cow.

Now we've made him lose his thread. We may laugh, says Pompeo, but look how swiftly and efficiently the ruthless German race made sure there'd be plenty of empty properties to buy up when the Occupation was over, once they'd seen how pleasant Liguria was compared to their own miserable land. Sinister, or what? . . . Not that he blames Franco for helping speed up the process, not at all . . .

Franco is posing now as a man of reason, sensible and unprejudiced, telling Pompeo that we can't blame the children for the sins of their fathers. These words don't necessarily represent his deepest feelings. A year or two from now, down at the San Pietro *festa*, we will see another side of Franco. He is standing chatting with his nephews in the piazza, where everyone is dancing, dining and drinking; he is also eyeing up a table full of jolly middle-aged German tourists enjoying a delightful evening with the simple Italian peasants. Franco looks entirely relaxed and casual, if not entirely sober: he drains the last drops from a bottle of beer, hat pushed back on his head as usual, festive yellow waistcoat unbuttoned. Now he links his hands behind his back, still holding the empty bottle. We are amazed by what happens next; thinking he is unobserved, he suddenly flick-throws the beer bottle from behind his back. It arches high into the air and crash-lands with pinpoint accuracy smack in the middle of the Germans' dinner table, covering them in pasta and wine, smashing several glasses. (Hours of practice or what? Definite signs of a misspent youth.) Panic breaks out. Now, along with everyone else, Franco rushes solicitously over to his victims.

Madonna! Who could have done such a thing? He joins everyone else in looking around for the evil culprits, his face an entirely convincing mask of shocked innocence. To everyone but us, that is.

Alberti the lawyer is a revelation, a different breed of being from anyone we've met here so far. He is straight out of Italian *Vogue*, Armani-suited, English-brogued, smooth and cultivated. Alberti's anglophilia extends well beyond his footwear; his English is good, if a little stilted, and his house is surrounded by an outlandishly smooth and unnaturally green English lawn, on which, he tells us, one has to lavish enormous amounts of care in this climate. He has an irrigation system actually built into it, under the turf: minute sprinkler-heads rise up out of it at the touch of a button, swirling a mist of water across the grass and our ankles as he demonstrates it. We seem to have wandered into another world: yet the cosmopolitan Alberti is entirely unperturbed to find himself doing business with the pair of dialect-speaking hill-billies we have brought with us. Of course they are perfectly ordinary to him, he has grown up alongside people like this, whatever his present predilections may be, and it is we English sisters who are the more disturbing presence. We horrify him with our casual attitude to lawns, our ignorance of the correct procedures; he certainly would not dream of sitting on his. And walk across it? . . . Please!

His office is on the first floor of this rococo and objets d'art-laden house in which he lives with his father and mother – normal behaviour in Italy, where nobody leaves home unless it is to marry or, if absolutely necessary, to seek better work opportunities elsewhere. To leave for any other reason implies that you don't care about your parents at all, are happy to insult and shame them publicly, in front of the rest of the family and the town. We have no idea of all this as yet, though, and add it to the list of Alberti's weirdnesses.

His office is all leather chesterfields, mahogany desks and carved cigar boxes; a good stab at an Englishman's smoking room circa 1910. He may be much too young ever to have sighted Maria's angelic English of the good old days, but Alberti seems to be infected with the same nostalgia for them. We should have got ourselves up in tweeds and hand-crafted walking shoes . . . a hint of silk at throat and hem, an understated string of pearls . . . he is clearly deeply disappointed in us as representatives of our race.

Signor Alberti's slightly obsessive cultural interests are not exclusively English, though; he is keen to point out the beautiful sixteenth-century carved stone Madonna who watches over the room from a high carved plinth; she was not made for a church, as we may have imagined, he tells us, but for a niche over the front door of a merchant's house in Genoa. He adores Italian statuettes of this period, has a small collection of them, he says, running his fingers possessively over her curves.

We sign all our bits of paper, everything in triplicate and in a legal Italian so obscure we haven't the faintest idea what it means. Pompeo agrees that it is incomprehensible, which is some consolation; Franco remains uncharacteristically silent and aloof throughout the reading and signing procedure. We are surprised to see that under 'profession' Pompeo is listed as 'Forest Guard'. We thought he just did olives. This isn't the moment to investigate, though. Alberti has risen to leave the room: strategic move for which we have been primed by Franco. He is not off to fetch a pen, as he claims, but to allow us to give Pompeo the envelope that contains the undeclared portion of the price. This, apparently, is perfectly normal procedure: no one, either buyer or seller, would dream of admitting to the true value of their property. No one expects them to. Not even the tax authorities we're defrauding.

Franco's silence, meanwhile, is covering another dark secret; later on, in one of those wine-lubricated therapy-moments, with no one else around, he will reveal that he has never learned to read, and the only thing he can write is his own name. A revelation that casts new light on his attitude to Sergio's Latest Farming Technology brochures. No wonder he agreed so readily that Alberti's documents were incomprehensible, we say.

Euh! says Franco: you don't let on about that sort of thing (finger under eye) to cunning city lawyers who might use the information in some underhand way. You don't want to go giving them any more scope to take advantage than they've already got.

Any advantage being taken on this occasion is by Franco himself, who has got his own special and equally incomprehensible 'well-reserving' document, twice as long as our own house-purchase one. Its length has something to do with Franco owning the land adjoining ours: lots of extra bureaucracy created by some wildly optimistic legislation, over a century old by now and still showing no sign of success, aimed at getting people to go and live on their land, rather than waste several hours of the working day travelling to and fro from their village homes – a tradition which some turn-of-the-century Minister for Agriculture deduced went some way to explain Italy's relatively abysmal productivity. This particular bit of legislation was designed to transform tiny scattered peasant plots into large cost-effective modern farms by giving next door neighbours extra land rights. It may have been futile as far as the original aim goes, but Franco is doing his best to turn it to some use, as we will find out later.

We finally get away from Alberti's, taking care not to step on his jewel-like lawn as we call out our last '*ciao*'s. Once we are out of earshot, Pompeo, who has begun to grasp that some of the odd things we do are done out of ignorance and not perversity (thank the Lord) – tells us we shouldn't say *ciao* except to children or people we are intimate with. Otherwise it looks like lack of respect. I cringe inwardly thinking of how many times I must have dissed old folk in San Pietro.

What about saying *salve*, the way you all do, I ask, is that OK?

Neither of our guides is quite sure if this word is dialect or Italian. But it certainly isn't disrespectful. We resolve to *salve* as much as possible in future.

What's this about your being a Forest Guard? we ask Pompeo.

We won't have noticed, he says, because at this time of year there's not a lot to do, and he only has to be *in giro* – around and about – at weekends. But come summer, he'll be gyrating the hills three days a week, on serious patrol work.

Euh! says Franco. He just drives around looking important in his jeep, getting free drinks everywhere he goes from people who hope he'll turn a blind eye when he catches them hunting out of season – that's all he has to do.

Pompeo is outraged by this misrepresentation. Come September, he says, once the forest fires start, he is often out twenty hours a day. And the rest of the year, the knowledge that he may gyrate past at any moment stops all sorts of nonsense going on. It puts people like Franco, for example, he says snappily, off shooting birds and beasts out of season, throwing old cars off the side of the mountain, dumping building rubble and old fridges in the woodlands or off hairpin bends, lighting fires in dangerous places.

We tell him about the rubbish that's been thrown off the hillside at the end of our path; he ought to drive past his own property more often. *Dispetto!* he says. Someone will have dumped stuff there out of spite, just to make him look a fool. He can guess who it was: he will sort them out. They will be sorry.

We walk along the Via Aurelia, on the way to celebrate our new homeowning status by buying a drink for our two mentors, trying out our '*Salve*' on every acquaintance we meet, much to Pompeo's gratification.

Arriving at the Bar Sito we find Mimmo, Bruno and Ciccio sitting outside with a fourth person we don't know, calling us over. We introduce Pompeo and Franco to them, amid much handshaking. It surprises us how relaxed people here are with members of other generations; Bruno is already chaffing Franco: You must be the famous Knife of San Pietro, he's saying. I worry that Franco may take offence. On the contrary, he seems flattered, and starts to tell the story of the time, in his youth, when he rode into this very bar on horseback . . .

They have got a brilliant surprise for us, say Mimmo and Ciccio; a hand-operated washing-machine! A thing you just wind round and round with a handle, a thing we can keep down by the well! When should they bring it up?

Pompeo gives us an old-fashioned look. Clearly in the mind of a good citizen of San Pietro this suggestion can only be the prelude to some kind of mass orgy. Luckily for our reputations, at this moment Mimmo's girlfriend Lorella turns up and joins us, and Pompeo's fears are allayed. She is a decent girl from Diano Arentino: he knows her father. We are safe. Lorella, now doing the shaking hands round with everybody, is big: much bigger than her tiny sinewy *fidanzato* – at least half as tall again. We have so far refrained, Britishly, from commenting on this potentially embarrassing fact. We see now that our restraint was absurdly misplaced. Franco and Pompeo both wade straight in: What a fine figure of a woman! They congratulate Mimmo heartily on having managed, in spite of his tininess, to get himself such a prize, and insist on doing some extra handshaking to celebrate the achievement. Mimmo and Lorella both beam delightedly: obviously there is nothing embarrassing about it at all. Lucky Italians. I think sadly of my various tall female friends in England who are prepared to go to enormous lengths not to seem even half an inch taller than their boyfriends, devoting their leisure moments to hunting out the flattest heels in existence. Lorella, on the contrary, is cheerfully trotting about in four-inch mules.

Ciccio introduces the unknown fair-haired man who is sitting with them; he is called Helmut, and is, oh no, a German.

Now what's going to happen? Will Pompeo spit in his face? Refuse to sit with him? To our great relief, he shakes hands like a lamb. Helmut is a very cheerful and chatty German; he is busy inviting everyone to come up to his house in Camporondo this weekend. He wants to celebrate having finished fixing his open fireplace by lighting it and eating around it in company. There is no getting away from it – Helmut is definitely one of the odious German buyers-up of empty village homes. I glance covertly at Pompeo; he still hasn't turned a hair. Helmut only looks about thirty-ish; maybe in practice Pompeo reserves his wrath for the older generation, as recommended by Franco, whatever he may say in theory?

The Diano Company are busily planning Helmut's menu for him. Heated debate about grilled fresh sardines versus spit-roasted pigling in the fireplace is going on. Helmut himself has no opinions on the matter. Wonderful! The endless Italian food-obsession can get very wearing. Whatever Pompeo may feel about him, Helmut is a great relief to us. He speaks perfect English, to start with, which is very soothing after a morning of lawyering and dialecting and all; but mostly it is the magic of talking with someone who shares our own Northern assumptions about the world.

Helmut, for example, has no problem with the idea of living in the country and not in a village. He says we have done right; he is suffering horribly from his neighbours in Camporondo, where the feuding spirit is strong. In less than a year here he has had all sorts of rows and vendettas about responsibility for falling walls and rights of way through other people's land and music after nine p.m.

Helmut's other great feature is that he too is a lover of village *feste*. We'd been sure that amongst Caterina's large collection of friends and relations there must be the odd partner-cum-trainer to help us out with our Smooth Dancing ambitions. But no. The village *festa* is practically the symbol of everything they want to escape from. Here, at last, is Helmut, a male at least, even if of the wrong nationality. He can dance a waltz, a polka, even a mazurka: all the *festa* favourites. He comes from some southern and Catholic part of Germany, he tells us, where Smooth Dancing is commonplace. Moreover, he is not, in fact, called Helmut at all, but Mario. The Diano boys have found the idea of a German with such a normal, Italian-sounding name impossible to cope with, and Helmut has accepted his re-christening with good grace.

Helmut has just got back from the *mercato dell'usato*, the flea-market, in San Remo, and we chat foreignly of strange and wonderful bargains to be found in these hills, of hunts through junkyards and second-hand shops: no part of youth culture round here, as yet.

The Diano boys leave to go back to work for the afternoon, and Helmut returns to the hills with his booty. We buy a last round for Franco and Pompeo, waiting with bated breath to hear what Pompeo will have to say about being made to socialize with Helmut.

But the horror of Helmut apparently pales into insignificance beside the scandal of Ciccio and Bruno.

So, you're hanging out with Calabresi down here, are you? says Pompeo. *State attente!* Watch out!

We don't think they're from Calabria, we say, after a pause for thought . . . in fact, we're sure they aren't – only the other day they were telling us about growing up here, all about their parents' land up in the hills . . . complaining about being dragged out of the Diano Marina games arcade by their parents, forced to learn olive-pruning, Ape-driving and vegetable-growing when they could have been using their time so much more fruitfully on the table-football game round the corner . . .

Ah, but they're *figli d'immigrati*, sons of immigrants, says Pompeo, in a tone which suggests a world of meaning behind this phrase. You can tell they're Calabresi.

Well, we can't, we say. How? They just look like Italians.

You can tell by the way they talk, says Franco.

What, they've got an accent or something? They can't have, they were born and bred here. (Their Italian is certainly clearer than Franco's, and miles better than Pompeo's, but it seems more judicious not to mention this.)

No, says Franco patiently, not Italian, it's the way they speak Ligurian – you can tell they've learnt it *in giro* – it's not the language they speak at home.

This is all news to us. What do they speak at home then?

Calabrese!! reply our true-bred Ligurians in unison. You want to watch out if you're going to hang out with Southerners. They'll get you into trouble.

But what sort of trouble? we ask.

Euh! We mustn't let ourselves be taken in. *Terroni* may be friendly, cheery and devil-may-care; they may sing, dance and make merry at the drop of a hat – but we should check out the other side of the coin. They are also lazy, spendthrift and unruly; and then there's the drink and drugs, the violence and the crime – be it just thieving, or the more sinister, organized stuff.

Really? say we. Sounds just like what people said about the Irish in our granny's day. Or the West Indians. Do Southern Italians by any chance keep pigs in the parlour and coal – or, as it were, olive logs – in the bath?

Amazingly, they do: though Pompeo can't see what this can have to do with the Irish, of whom he has heard nothing but good. In fact, they are said to be a lot more *simpatico* than the cold, snooty English . . .

OK, time to change the subject.

It seems there is only going to be a very small swimmable window between the Health Ban imposed by the green-eyeshadow lady and her supporters, and the German Invasion. We feel we'd better take advantage of it right away. Why don't Pompeo and Franco come down to the beach, too, we say, only half seriously. As we suspected they would, they laugh at the very idea. The nearest they have ever got to swimming, they say, is in the old days before bathrooms when all the village children got taken for their weekly wash to the rock pools above San Pietro. We are pleased to discover that we are not too far behind the times for these parts in our bathroomlessness. They have spent the odd day on the beach, though, they tell us; with a horse and cart, collecting building sand.

Yes, say we, and now the Dianesi have put up that promenade wall to keep you off it – the skinflints!

How right we are! Pompeo and Franco are positively bowled over by our grasp of local politics.

A beachful of the stuff at the bottom of the hill, says Pompeo, but these days you have to go to the builders' yard and pay for it. As well as the cement.

We used to mix it up with lime, in the old days, not cement, volunteers Franco.

Lime again! We are beginning to wonder whether this is just a monomania of Franco's. Can it be really the staff of life in the hills of Liguria? So far, it seems, you use it to purify your drinking water, eliminate your excreta, whitewash your house, keep insects at bay; now you make concrete with it. Absurd. Impossible. And there are thirty kilos of the stuff, as of today, taking up rather a lot of room just outside our front door. Pompeo, it is true, doesn't ever actually deny any of Franco's lime statements. But maybe he's not listening because it's in Italian. Or maybe he's just humouring his mad friend?

Pompeo doesn't seem to have been listening this time, either; inspired perhaps by the need to save us from Calabrian contamination, perhaps by the success of his *'ciao'* lesson, he has decided that it's time for a lesson in Ligurian.

Say *'Chang chaning'* he instructs us.

We do, several times. Both men go into such paroxysms of mirth that I begin to suspect ribaldry. But no. It means *Piano, piano* – slowly, slowly. Or gently, gently. It's just the usual hysteria caused by anyone who's not a Ligurian speaking their own private dialect. We now learn that Diano Marina in its own dialect is really called *'Diang Maring'*, strangely oriental this may sound; while the true name of Diano San Pietro is *'Diang San Peo'* (evidently a Vietcong hideout). And the inhabitants of Diang San Peo? Not San Pietresi at all, but, in their own tongue, *'San Peotti'*.

Say, *'Testa Janc'*, says Franco. More cackling – this turns out to mean *Testa Bianca* – White Head, and the nickname of Pompeo's elder brother. Not content with swapping pi's for ch's, Ligurians have swapped bi's for j's too.

The tale of Janc Head is now told to us with great relish by his brother, Franco simultaneously translating the tricky bits which are too exciting to be told in prissy official Italian. It illustrates beautifully the huge cultural divide between civilized Ligurians and lawless Calabrians.

Fifteen years ago, it seems, this white-headed brother employed some other villager to fix his leaking toilet roof. The workmanship was terrible. The very next time Testa Janc sat on his loo in a rainstorm, he was leaked upon anew. He called back the incompetent workman, stabbed him to death, and took to the hills, never to be seen again.

What, you've really never seen him again? we ask.

Mai più! Never again! says Franco.

Mai chü! says Pompeo proudly.

Just for a toilet roof?

Euh!

Ah, si, si!

II

It is Easter Sunday and a very small and startlingly tidy looking Domenico, combed and hanky free, appears at our door, knocking timidly, moustache newly trimmed. He has been sent by his wife, he says; people are not allowed to be alone on Easter Sunday. Two single women do not count as company for one another, and extra portions of Easter Sunday lunch have already been prepared for us by Antonietta. If we don't accept it will be the worse for him, he adds, with a sideways grin from beneath the walrus. We accept happily, ignoring the veiled insult to our sex. We wouldn't dream of turning down any offers of home cooking round here, whatever the provocation.

Chauffeured by Domenico, we Ape our way down to the village. San Pietro, now that summer is drawing near, has broken out into a wild floral extravaganza; the already larger-than-life geraniums have redoubled in strength and vitality, mixed now with the swathes of vibrant blues and purples of morning glory and hot-pink bougain-villea now festooning the houses, flowers trailing down every wall, creeping up walls and along gutters, climbers snaking up terraces among roses and lilies and jasmine. Spectacular. Though, as it happens, nothing compared to the great flood of greenery that will overwhelm the village by mid-June when the leaves finish coming out on the grapevines and all the vegetable gardens explode into business. Soon hardly a square inch of stone or earth will be visible at all. For a month or two, that is, till the desert heat of August strikes, and shrinks it all back to something more realistic.

Halfway down this flower show of a village we bump off the asphalt road down a section of muletrack so impossibly narrow that we involuntarily squeeze our elbows into our sides to help the Ape fit between the walls. Not only impossibly narrow, but also impossibly steep; and with rather noticeable steps in it. Nothing, apparently, to this Ape. Who needs an off-road vehicle, anyway?

We squeeze through a narrow archway with a millimetre to spare, and squeak to a halt in a tiny mossy courtyard full of the obligatory rusty tins of wildly blooming geraniums and buckets of gleaming aspidistra.

Antonietta appears at the top of an outside staircase leading off the yard; and we are welcomed into what must be the smallest flat in the world. It was made, they explain, by Adjusting their hayloft, no longer needed these days with only the Ape to feed, and was designed for that restful retirement they were planning to have until they found Maurizio was on the way. The living room might possibly be a reasonable size if it wasn't filled to the brim with the monstrous cupboards people here are helplessly addicted to, ceiling high and four foot thick. Not even room for the bulging three-piece suite that ought by rights to complement them. Slide back the doors of one of the cupboards, though, and there's a small bed-settee; now destined to be Maurizio's when he leaves his cot. There is just one bedroom, looking across the roofs of the village down to the sea, a tiny kitchen, and an even tinier bathroom with one of those space- and water-saving baths shaped like an armchair. In the bottom of the bath sits a small wooden cage. Inside the cage is a depressed-looking thrush. What on earth is that doing there?

For hunting, says Domenico.

Does he take it out and chase it round the yard? Not funny. Of course not; he straps it on his back, still in its cage, when he goes out with his gun; and being used to humans, and no doubt full of the joys of getting out of its bath, it sings cheerily away and lulls the other, wild birds into a false sense of security. *Boum!* says Domenico, miming the shotgun for us. Got it, thanks. Poor thrush: an unwitting Judas in a white enamel desert.

There is just about enough room here to edge carefully round the table which fills the centre of this ornament-packed room. A television is balanced on a shelf in an alcove of one of the non-bed cupboards, inches from your nose wherever you sit. Claustrophobia strikes. Luckily, outside, just across the three foot wide road and through the arch, is Antonietta's garden – not to be confused with Domenico's official *orto* up the mountain – which is where we're going to eat our lunch.

You can tell these ladies' *orti* because, apart from being closer to the home, they have flowers as well as vegetables in them. At the moment, a positive riot of flowers, as well as a selection of chickens and one of those typically Ligurian skinny angry cats. Also, against the back wall, is a beautiful beehive-shaped bread and pizza oven that Antonietta made herself, following her granny's recipe, out of hand-sized dollops of dried mud. You have to use that red kind of earth, she says. You leave the dollops to dry in the sun, then use them like bricks to build your oven over a frame of bent twigs, with more mud as mortar. Once it's dry you just light a fire inside it. The framework burns away, while the oven kilns itself into rainproofness. I resolve to make one of these as soon as I get home: how sensible to have your oven outside so you don't broil up your home with the heat. Alas, I will discover when I get back that there is no red earth round our house, only grey-brown; and that the twigs of olive and oak are short and squiggly, snap easily, not at all the right thing. You need hazel or chestnut, I suppose. I still haven't quite got round to it.

Antonietta goes back up to the flat to do something to the lunch, leaning on a walking-stick – something has gone wrong with her knee-joints since the pregnancy – and Domenico has to take us on his own to see the last, most important item: the *cantina* below the flat. Nobody lives at street level in the Diano villages, where the tiny, dusty barred windows and the ramshackle doors along the alleys give the impression that a lot more of the houses are abandoned than is really the case. On these steep slopes your lower storey is dug deep back into the hillside, making a cool, dark, even-temperatured space. Only a thriftless fool, or maybe a *straniere*, would waste such an asset by living in it. It serves a much more important purpose, as we are about to see. Domenico heaves open a pair of huge double doors big enough for a barn: amazingly, the *cantina* really is barn-sized. A huge, lofty, vaulted space. We can't believe this; why on earth have they made themselves that tiny cramped flat upstairs when they had all this vastness down below? I have to ask, though I don't put it quite like that. The answer is, I suppose, logical. You don't need much space just for eating and sleeping: but you never know how much room you may need for working and storing. We are introduced to the year's worth of olive oil, the year's worth of wine, the row upon row of glass jars of tomatoes bottled for the year's pasta sauce, the pots of mushrooms, peppers, aubergines, jams, the hanging bundles of oregano, strings of garlic and onions and dried chilli peppers; and all the equipment associated with producing this stuff, jars and bottles waiting to be recycled, cauldrons and oil-drums, the rolls of olive net, the wine-press and associated impedimenta – including the corking-machine, useless item, lying in a dusty corner covered in cobwebs – the workbench and vice, the tins of nails and screws, the hammers and sickles, spades and hoes, brushcutters, pruning-hooks and machetes, chainsaws, tomato-mincers, neat rolls of vari-sized hosepipe and siphon tubing hanging from nails in the walls, the precious new motor-driven mini-plough under its dustcloth – more vats of olives *in salamoia*, of salted anchovies . . . and, of course, a winter's worth of firewood for the stove, neatly sawn-up branches from the olive pruning. Awesome. A haven of order and plenty. All of it much more essential to life, we now see, than a few more square metres of indoor living space in a place where the weather's always fine.

It becomes evident that to Italians Easter Sunday is an extra Christmas; everyone has to gather together and stuff themselves with food. Preferably in family groups, but anything will do. Maybe we go some way to replacing Giovanni-in-Holland and Elena-in-Buffalo. We hope so. The idea of people not celebrating together at Easter is as awful to Antonietta as the idea of people being alone and isolated at Christmas would be in our own land. Hence Domenico's mission. Except that this is much better than Christmas; you eat outdoors in the sunshine, the air already warm, yet still crisp and fresh. We sit in the garden and (surprise) eat and eat, surrounded by clucking chickens and flowering rosemary bushes.

Antonietta has made the festive *tortelloni* herself, perfect crescents: one day she will show us how. The *ossobuco* which comes next is the tastiest thing I have eaten yet. It has been gently simmering all morning with wine and garlic and carrots and peas – all their own produce – and tons of their own artichokes, the latest *orto* item to come into season. They aren't at all like the globe ones we're used to; these are much smaller, and once you've sliced off the spiny tips you can eat the whole thing; none of that sucking the flesh off each individual leaf. You can make a salad out of them raw, too, sliced thinly crosswise and sprinkled with thin slivers of Parmesan under the oil and lemon. And, says Antonietta, you should never throw away the couple of inches of stalk under the head: this is as tender and tasty as the heart, once cooked, and should be saved for making a risotto later.

In the matter of the *ossobuco* the Lord is on my side – once my sister discovers that the thick delicious gravy is composed of the marrow from bones, a delicacy she is expected to pick out and eat, she can't eat any more. She has to keep surreptitiously slipping me extra bits whenever our hosts are distracted by Maurizio, who is pretending like mad to be the right sort of baby again, gurgling happily away in his Moses basket at our side. Maybe it doesn't count here, though, where there are no olive trees, only peaches.

On her next trip indoors, Antonietta gets their wedding photos to show us. Disconcertingly though, done up in their very best period gear and worn out with the strain, they look so much like some classic image – ocean liner immigrants arriving in America, maybe, or a scene from some Italian neo-realist film – that it's hard to see them as their individual selves at all.

Egged on by Antonietta, Domenico tells us the tale of their courtship. Even more like one of those films. In those days, he says, you couldn't so much as think of marrying a girl without going and formally asking her father's permission. Much less a girl from Calabria. If he wanted Antonietta, he had no choice but to go, in person, to Calabria to present himself to the family. Brought up on Ligurian tales of the violent and unruly South, he was petrified at the prospect: thirty-six hours of train through unknown and probably bandit-infested country, and an uncertain welcome at the end of it. Not only, says Domenico, was he not the rich man her parents would be hoping she'd catch for herself up in the wealthy North, but he was short, dark and ugly. Worse still, he had a secret and invisible defect which he knew, honourably speaking, meant that he should never marry any woman, far less one he really loved: a weakness in his heart from which he might drop down dead at any moment, leaving her a defenceless widow.

I've managed to keep him alive so far, though, says Antonietta, pinching his arm comfortably.

Anyway, says Domenico, he was certain that if he somehow survived the journey, if he wasn't set upon and murdered on the way by some pirate-scarfed sawn-off-shotgun-wielding desperado, or gang of ditto, the menfolk of Antonietta's family would probably do him in as soon as he revealed his designs upon her.

Still, the prospect of not marrying Antonietta was even worse than the prospect of sudden death at the hands of her male relatives. After some weeks of working up his courage, he'd come up with the solution: a weapon, as impressive as possible to make up for his lack of money, height, and sound heart. He spent all his olive-harvest savings on the train ticket and a double-barrelled shotgun. A few days' target practice on the family olive trees, and he was off on his deadly mission.

The gun, as it turned out, was not necessary for engagement purposes (of course it wasn't, says Antonietta, but it was good to know I was worth dying for). As far as Antonietta's family was concerned, any Northerner was infinitely rich by virtue of simple geography. Size was no object; he was a perfectly average height down there in the South. And the intricacies of their prospective son-in-law's health went uninvestigated. Domenico needed no other qualifications than a few dozen olive trees to please these simple *Calabresi*, who had no notion how many fewer kilos of olives you got per tree up here in the frozen North.

Permission granted. And it wasn't such a bad move to get the gun, as it turned out; many's the time it solved a cash-flow crisis in their early married life, when there would have been no meat for the pot without it.

Such crises evidently exist no longer: we go on eating all afternoon, the digestive system expanding, as usual, to fill the entire universe and more. I have to give up on the tiramisu; the evil sister uses it to fill the space which should by rights have been taken up by *ossobuco*. People burst in and out of the garden Happy Eastering, and, accompanying many of the well-known sulking faces from the bar, we meet a vast number of women we've never so much as caught sight of before, unless perhaps as part of the swirlers round the dance floor at the Colla. Once we have been officially introduced to the wives and the mothers and the daughters, we will never again be quite so unspeakable-to at the bar. The respectable-female connection has been the major missing element in our social acceptability. But by the same token we lose our mysterious therapy powers; the men of the village, with the exception of Franco, who as an outcast and rebel does not count, will henceforth be much more circumspect in their heart-pourings.

The men go off with a couple of packs of cards, leaving us ladies to our garden. Among the next arrivals, accompanying one-eyed Mariuccia from the shop, is her aged aunt: Erminia. Not so all alone in the world as she likes to make out then!

Erminia rushes over and plants a pair of kisses on my cheeks, to the amazement of the assembled guests. She even remembers that I am called Anna. I am proud to have found out, from Pompeo, the proper name of our house, too. Besta de Zago, I say, and she throws up her hands in amazement. Why didn't I tell her? There is, as I suspected all along, a perfectly good path to Besta de Zago from her place. It doesn't take more than twenty minutes. Bah. Growl.

Shamefully, my aimless walking behaviour is brought to the attention of the gathering. Or not so shamefully after all. Some of the ladies have seen interesting *Health and Your Family*-type programmes on TV, in which the presenters tell you that exercise is good for the health. A lively debate starts up on the topic. One young mother has been so impressed that she is planning to buy an exercise bike. I suggest that their hill-rushing, vegetable-digging, cheese-stirring and weed-sickling lifestyle is already packed with exercise. No. This does not count. No one except me sees any connection between these boring everyday activities and the prescriptions of the beautifully groomed ladies and leotard-clad fitness experts on the telly.

I also discover to my amazement that this tiny backwater of a village has its own fully fledged kiddies' nursery, to which Maurizio will be going in a month or two; it is open from six a.m. to six p.m., takes babies from six months onwards, and costs less per month than my friends are paying per week in London. If, that is, they can manage to find a place at all. So much for backward Catholic countries!

Notions of maternal deprivation don't trouble anyone here, either; if a child's in the village, it is as good as home as far as village mothers are concerned. I resolve to pass this information on; soon, I imagine, all those empty San Pietro houses will be full of refugee mothers from London . . . Sadly, though, this will never happen; I have forgotten what a very long way they would be from their jobs.

A major item of feminine debate this afternoon is the priest's coming visit to this *frazione* of the village, a visit paid once a year to give the Church's benediction to the homes in it. This, apparently, means that the ladies of the parish have to waste valuable time and money creating an outdoor altar of flowers, from which he will bless the general area: then, worse still, he will pop into each house individually – more work, there mustn't be a speck of dust about the place – to sprinkle a few drops of Holy Water around and bless it and its inhabitants. At this point it is obligatory to slip the priest an envelope full of cash. She for one wouldn't care, says Mariuccia from the shop, if the *sanguisuga*, the bloodsucker of a priest, dropped dead tomorrow. It would save a lot of trouble. This outrageously blasphemous remark causes much delighted cackling. But still, they all agree, there is no way out. Their neighbourhood, the Frazione Gionetti, can't be the only one to refuse to participate. What a *brutta figura* that would be! Anyway, they say, their altar is always the best.

What about just telling the priest not to bother with the coming-into-the-house part? I say. Stupid idea. The house-blessing is the only essential bit of the whole business. Who knows what bad luck you might bring on yourself and your family if you barred your door against the priest? says Antonietta. Who knows if the priest mightn't put the evil eye on you, the *malocchio*, if you didn't let him in? says Erminia.

But this is going too far. Everyone laughs at Erminia, who is practically a pagan anyway. The priest doesn't bother with Besta de' Ca' any more, and you can see why!

Now we're told of a whole litany of misfortunes that have befallen those staunchly Communist families who have refused to let the priest in. We all agree, some more doubtfully than others, that these things would probably have happened anyway. But, on balance, it's foolish to tempt fate. And so, on the principle that if you don't buy a lottery ticket, you can't win, the ladies of the parish set to working out how much of the altar they can cover for free, using wild flowers and ones they've grown themselves, and how much will have to be paid for so as not to look too stingy in the eyes of the priest. Or, more importantly, the rest of the village.

The cut-throat competitive spirit amongst the inhabitants of this valley is brought all the more sharply to our attention on the day the village of Diano Castello, till now no more than an attractive feature of our view, decides to upstage all the other Dianos by replacing the tediously old-fashioned and conventional midday tolling of its church bells – tolling which has, for the last seven or eight centuries, signalled lunchbreak to the olive growers – with a spectacularly modern thousand-odd decibel factory siren.

Diano Castello is, architecturally speaking, not a village but a small town, tiny though it may be, and is the only one of the Dianos to own a road of drivable width running through its centre – a road built as wagon access to the Castello of the medieval barons of the area, some time in the thirteenth century, and which is at least a hundred yards long. As well as its superior housing stock, carved doorways and curlicued balconies befitting a lord's retainers, there is the fact that many of its inhabitants, though long reduced to the rank of peasantry, still bear the noble name of Gastaldi. Naturally, the place has always been tarred with the brush of snobbery by the residents of other villages.

Anyway, there we are walking peacefully on this momentous Siren Day towards the Sulking Café of San Pietro. We have just come level with the church, and are busy savouring the delicious odours wafting from Maria's kitchen and bemoaning the fact that we will never taste her food again unless we somehow get organized enough to plan our lives twenty-four hours ahead, when suddenly the thing goes off. It screeches ear-splittingly out across the valley, air-raid siren-style, on the dot of twelve – just as San Pietro's own earth-shaking and eardrum-battering peals are starting up. The screaming and whooping goes on and on, reverberating round the terraces, bouncing off the hillsides, melding cacophonously with the roaring vibrating bell just above our heads . . . Is it an earthquake?

The outbreak of World War Three? . . . As we are poised to take to our heels, a bevy of agitated men comes pouring out of the café. Looking to them for a lead, we see that the expressions beneath the hankies are not those of panic or terror, as we're expecting, but of outrage. They mill and shout and gesticulate angrily, hardly audible above the racket; a whole barful of impotent fists are being shaken at the caterwauling culprit, Castello, poised smugly on its hillock above us.

Luigi, imperturbable as ever, ambles out in the frothing wake of his clientele, and since there is no point trying to speak, what with the bell still booming and the siren still wailing, rests a ham-like hand on each of our shoulders to reassure us. By the time the din is over, we have gathered that there really is no need to panic; most of his clients, over the initial shock, are now doing their best to adopt a nonchalant air, laughing scornfully, spitting on the ground, jerking their heads and saying *Euh!* and *Mah!* to one another to indicate their profound unconcern in the face of whatever folly Castello may choose to throw at them from its exalted position.

The emergency over, heated debate breaks out in dialect. A few of the more belligerent souls stay outside making menacing gestures at Castello, defying them to try saying that again. The calmer elements return to the bar to fortify themselves with their unfinished drinks while they discuss the political implications of this aural attack from above. But we can make no sense of any of it; whoever starts trying to tell us what is going on is always too excited to keep up the Italian subtitled version, and gets drawn back into shouted dialect before they've got to the end of the sentence. We can measure the gravity of the situation, though, by the fact that Luigi is doling out free glasses of his own private supply of *vino d'uva* all round.

Eventually, concerned that we should be able to participate in an informed and democratic manner in the Siren Controversy Debate, Luigi comes over to explain the scenario to us in all its complexities. Refusing, of course, as befits a man of superior wisdom, to take sides in childish inter-village rivalries. Background first: every village in the valley has always marked midday by ringing its own bell for its own peasants slowly and clearly twelve times to make sure the toilers in the olive groves didn't miss their lunch break. This has always made it necessary to stagger the peals village by village to avoid confusion.

This much we have noticed for ourselves – the good twenty minutes it takes for midday to finish happening in these parts. But of course we see only too clearly that if all the churches began to ring at the same moment, the toiling peasant might lose count and mistake midday for, say, eleven o'clock; the trickiness of the Italian digestive system could make an extra hour before lunch positively life-threatening. Equally clearly, no Diano would tempt fate so far as to trust to any other Diano's competence or good faith in such a vital matter.

As Luigi is now pointing out, logically only one village in the valley can be ringing on the official stroke of midday; everyone else has to have their church clock a few minutes out. This has not been a problem in the more casual past; but now the pressures of modernity have led, sad to say, to this distressing outbreak of one-upmanship. Nobody wants to be less than accurate. Everyone takes things personally. Is the ringing order to be based on economic importance, in which case San Pietro ought to go first – Luigi carefully resists the temptation to let any inflection of approval creep into his voice here – or should it be based on historic seniority, putting Castello in the lead? We finally grasp that it is the timing of the siren, set to go off at the same moment as San Pietro's bells, in direct competition and short-circuiting dignified democratic debate, which is so offensive to Luigi and his clients, and not the terrible blood-curdling racket itself.

Their mayor's high-handed decision to inaugurate his absurd screaming siren without consultation does nothing for Castello folk's reputation in the valley. From now on mutterings along the lines of 'Who do they think they are?' break out in bars up and down the valley each day on the officiously punctual and screamingly modern dot of twelve. Things gradually calm down as the volume is reduced once the siren's novelty has worn off. But for months any Castello native who is caught out and about by inhabitants of the other villages at siren time will be tortured with much ribald hilarity about his aristocratic provenance, addiction to expensive and ridiculous toys, and slavish timekeeping.

12

As our first Ligurian May Day is due to dawn, we find ourselves travelling, packed sardine-like into the back of a truck owned by Paletta, with a good fifteen people. We have passed the turn-off to Sergio and Lilli's house, passed the building site where the new cowshed of Franco's *nipoti* is being created, passed the wayside Madonna shrine that marks the crossroads to Franco's cowshed. If we didn't know that Franco and his *nipoti* went up and down here every day we would not have believed this abomination was even meant to be a drivable road. Huge rocks sprout in the middle of it, and our lorry skids crabwise down into deep gullies left by the winter rains, scrapes up the other side, hurling gouts of mud into the air. We have to reverse to and fro to get round ever-tighter hairpin bends, slaloming up clay cliffs as we go.

The olive trees give way to lush woodland greenness for a bit; then we are at the top of a high ridge, bare white bony rock with the odd grassy tussock and stony scree, the drop to our left stomach churning, shreds of cloud floating below us in the valley. Horribly unnatural.

Eight hundred metres here, shouts Paletta cheerfully, sticking his head out of the driver's window. I stop looking down.

Incredible though it may seem, we aren't alone in following this mad road to the bitter end. Now we catch up with a great, slow-moving convoy of cars and Apes, all stoically making their way up the mountain at zero miles an hour, joining us from all sorts of equally horrible-looking side roads from all the other Dianos. Cars jampacked with at least three generations, heads poking out of windows, shouting and cheering, people on each other's laps, suspensions being destroyed and sumps cracked on rocks as they go. Another cavalcade gradually builds up behind us to match the one in front. It is true, the whole valley really is going to the meadows. We have become part of a huge grindingly slow traffic jam prompted by only *The Golden Bough* knows what primeval stirrings of the soul to go on this awesome pilgrimage to the most unlikely place on earth.

The so-called meadows are strangely unlike my idea of a meadow – unless, maybe, the illustrations in my childhood Billy Goats Gruff story. But then we are in the foothills of the Alps, so maybe that's not too surprising. The grass is that fine, short stuff you get on cliff-tops, pocket handkerchief-sized flat bits dotted among rocks; a huge semicircle enclosing both our valley and the Faraldi one next door, the view running right down to the sea. A lot of it seems to have been terraced at some point in the distant past, and there are half-collapsed stone igloos everywhere. I suppose in the old subsistence farming days everyone who could manage it would bring a few animals up here to pasture in the summer months.

Tiny clumps of wiry mountain thyme scent the air as we trample around setting up camp, the menfolk unloading scaffolding and sheets of plastic and rolls of bamboo, while we females go off to look for wood high up on the rougher land, hunting amongst clumps of hawthorn and hazel. The hillside is a carpet of narcissi. The ones down by our house have vanished long ago, their season over, but up here where it's so much cooler they are still at maximum beauty and perfume.

Patrizia and Barbara find some plate-sized white mushrooms, which everyone gets very excited about. These are *prataioli*, it seems, delicious stuff. And as it happens we don't just have mushrooms, but also our own personal chef to deal with them: Ciccio, who recently took over the abandoned bar-restaurant in Moltedo, next village up from San Pietro, from where he is mounting a spirited challenge to Luigi and Maria's dream cuisine. Soon a mass mushroom-hunt is in progress. Ciccio snatches up the results, takes them off to the kitchen quarters he has established beside our improvised shelter, and returns them as a lovely garlicky salad to accompany our *aperitivo* of fizzy white wine. Amazing: even up here, so far from civilization, the niceties must be observed.

Mmmmm! I say appreciatively, causing the usual outburst of hilarity. Italians, for their own inscrutable reasons, don't say 'mmmmm'. They can see no connection between this sound and the appreciation of food, and every time we do it, they laugh uproariously. We are trying to control ourselves, not liking to be a laughing stock, but it's hard. Particularly when they will insist on introducing us to some new and delicious foodstuff every twenty minutes or so. They have started, annoyingly, to entertain themselves by doing pre-emptive 'mmmm's as they pass us any old item of food – crusts of bread, bits of peeled carrot. We are planning our revenge, though. One day they will come to England: we will take them out to eat in a greasy-spoon café where they will get their courses all mixed up together – how about burger, spaghetti and chips? Sausage, egg and lasagna? – and nothing but stewed tea or watery instant coffee to drink. Mmmm, we will say, loudly and often, as we watch them suffer. And none of the other customers will turn a hair.

We are having a lot of trouble remembering the names of the vast number of new people we're being introduced to up here in the wilderness. Especially the males of the company, who all have at least one nickname, sometimes two. As if all this weren't complicated enough, women don't address men, especially men of the older generation, by their nicknames: to do so is odd and laughable, not quite respectful or respectable. As females we have a double feat of memory to perform: recognize the nickname, but respond with the official baptismal name. The whole thing is a minefield, especially to foreigners who don't necessarily recognize which is a nickname and which a given one – as we discovered when looking for Pompeo and Bacalè down at Luigi's one afternoon. No, they hadn't seen Pompeo. What about Bacalè? No, they said, they hadn't seen Giuseppe. Who, we asked confusedly, was Giuseppe? Much cackling from card tables. Hours of fun unravelling the confusion. The nephew is not really called Bacalè. That is his nickname, derived – rather fittingly, it seems to me – from the word *baccalà*, dried cod. His true name is Giuseppe. So you can call him Beppe, too, if you want. Great. Thanks.

In the darkness, the whole curve of the hillside is dotted with the glowing lights of bonfires and hurricane lamps. We fall asleep under the stars sardined up under our cane and plastic shelter, listening to a mixture of distant tapes of *festa* accordions from far away, funky jazzy stuff from some closer ghetto blaster, and spooky storytelling amongst the sleeping bags.

At first light I am dragged from deep open-air sleep by the wonderful smell of coffee, the sound of a bubbling espresso pot, just in time to catch that vital May Day dawn, which, we've been told, will bring us luck for the rest of the year. The sun seems to shoot up from the sea at immense speed, the sky all frilly and pinky-yellow. Within minutes it is already turning into that dense blue that goes with big heat. Cowbells are ringing up on the higher meadows – Franco's cows – and cuckoos are cuckooing all around us. Magic.

As the morning wears on, more and more cars arrive; the meadows are filled with people, lounging about on the grass, eating, drinking, gathering wood, standing in gossiping knots, playing accordions, playing cards, making coffee on Primus stoves . . . bonfires are everywhere, ready-lit (of course) to be sure plenty of *brace*, those essential embers, are ready for lunch. Everyone wanders about visiting each others' base camps. Shelters, menus and supplies are displayed, inspected and discussed competitively, as are the lunch fires.

Really? Only oak? We always add some juniper branches to ours, you should try it, see how flavoursome it makes your pork chops! . . . Some people have actually bothered to bring supplies of olive wood all the way up here, so addicted are they to its flavour.

Small children rush to and fro squeaking and hurling balls of many and various sizes; aged grannies and grandads hobble back and forth, shaking hands ceremoniously with friends and acquaintances. On the higher slopes, teenagers show off on their *motorinos* and Vespas, doing wheelies, death-defying leaps off rocks, skidding down screes. Horrible. I'm not going to look at that. Franco and his *nipoti* are just visible in the distance, way across the meadows messing around on horseback, their steeds leaping up terraces, plunging back off, showing off just as wildly as the teenagers.

Groups playing *petanca* with those heavy silver balls are everywhere. No flat pitch, but a chase up and down terraces and screes, silver flashing in the light, shouts of triumph and despair. This, says Alberto, is how the game was originally played. You just follow the landscape; when it's your turn to throw, you try to choose a bit of terrain that fits your own best skills – backspin on slope or whatever – while making it harder for the others. He has brought a set for us, and we try it out. Addictive: we play for hours, ending up badly sunburnt – you hardly notice the sun with the fresh mountain breeze – and miles from our home-base of plastic sheeting.

We bump into Antonietta, still with her walking stick, Maurizio balanced on the other hip. By the time she's finished inspecting our lunch supplies and describing hers, Antonietta has already detected that, like herself, by no means everyone in our group is a true-bred Ligurian; she now delights those of Calabrian origin by making racy remarks in dialect which the Ligurians can't understand. Meanwhile, relaxed as everyone always is here with unknown babies, Maurizio is being passed round like a parcel, everyone cooing and gooing at him. And, relaxed as mothers always are here about other people messing with their babies, she asks if they'll look after him while she goes off for a pee.

Antonietta leans heavily on my arm as we trudge uphill seeking a good screen of bushes; she hangs on to me as she laboriously gets into peeing position and battles with her sensible knickers, making loud cackling remarks about how we're all the same down there anyway so not to worry. Once she's got herself re-arranged and upright again, she announces that we must get a bunch of narcissi each before we go back down. Good job she's here to advise me, she says, the Guardia Forestale will be about, and she doesn't just mean Pompeo. Narcissi are protected flowers these days and you can get fined for picking them. But everyone's always picked a bunch of them for luck on May Day: better to risk being arrested than risk the consequences of going home without any.

We head off arm in arm, up to the rough land where the narcissi are. No way out of this illegal flower gathering activity, then; at least, I tell myself, there are plenty of people roaming about up here to give us a bit of camouflage. But they are not roaming at all. I soon realize that every single one of these apparently innocent strollers is doing the same as us: we are all gathering narcissi. The technique is strangely un-furtive. No one even bothers to hide their booty until they have a large and – to my nervous eye at any rate –

highly visible bunch. Then they stand up and slip it half-heartedly under their jacket, holding a lapel out so as not to squash the flowers, and make their extremely obvious lumpy-fronted way back to the meadow.

When I've finally got myself and Antonietta and both our May Day bouquets – couldn't resist it, I'm afraid – back down to camp without being challenged by any plain-clothes Forest Guards or eco-warriors, I look back up at the hillside. There must be a good 150 people up there wandering to and fro amongst the broom and the juniper, all trying to look nonchalantly as if they're doing something not in the least connected with gathering narcissi.

Time for Ciccio to mastermind a banquet over a pair of bonfires. This is a highly competitive mass-eating event, and he is on his mettle. He has amalgamated everyone's provisions, and now has us all rushing around following his instructions. By the time we sit down for our extremely glamorous lunch, I am sure half the hillside must be looking on with envy. A selection of antipasti; home-made pasta, bright green with nettle-tips (a bit of a cheat, this one, he made it earlier in his restaurant) with a sauce of four melted cheeses; about fifteen varieties of grilled and marinaded meats for the second plate, and something fabulous and creamy which turns out, surprisingly, to be made of chicken gizzards. My feeble-hearted sister, deeply disturbed to discover she's eaten rather a lot of gizzards before anyone told her what they were, can't handle another course: but I'm on such good form that I can even handle Nutella pancakes next. Made by Bruno and Patrizia: Ciccio despises desserts.

One member of the party, Testone, Big-Head, also known as Nello, who has eaten hardly anything, keeps disappearing off behind the nearest clump of juniper bushes and throwing up loudly. His friends, mysteriously, seem more disapproving than supportive in this digestive crisis: they mutter angrily among themselves at each vomiting session, take it in turns to go and sit by him, speaking to him in a hectoring undertone, while he lies about in a heap with drooping eyelids, horribly pale, scratching. Monica, his girlfriend, goes and sits alone behind the shelter and cries.

Eventually Mimmo lets us into the secret. Heroin. Testone has let his friends down. The older ones, Mimmo himself, Paletta, Ciccio have mounted a major effort to help him get off the stuff: lots of people messed about with it, says Mimmo, when they were teen-agers and knew no better. They lost a good few friends to the habit; dead from overdoses or transformed into whingeing wrecks of their former selves. That is why everyone is being so stern with Testone. Last night, after a month of good behaviour, he escaped the surveil-lance of his elders and betters and disappeared for five hours. He is suspected of having driven hell-for-leather down the motorway to Genoa or Nice and bought himself a load of *roba*. He denies this hotly, but the symptoms speak for themselves.

At last: one of the famous *drogati*. But Testone is utterly unlike our image of a junkie; he is neat and tidy, looks well-fed and groomed . . . no wonder we haven't spotted any of the much-advertised heroin addicts who roam the countryside so far. Now we see the explanation: of course, living at home like everyone else here, with a mother to feed and clothe and launder you, a family to cover up for you and finance you whenever crisis threatens, how would you get yourself into the sort of filthy spotty gutter-draping state we are used to seeing in the Independent British Junkie? Poor Italian parents.

By mid-afternoon the place is beginning to look like some multi-generational music festival without the bands. Gay Pride without the outfits. A Hyde Park rally without the politics. But our focus is not a stage or a platform: it is a dense blue nothingness. Sitting on the grass, with the valleys foreshortened by height, there seems to be nothing at all beyond the green rim of the meadow but endless blue sky and immense blue sea.

I wander over to Domenico, standing right on the edge of the meadow deep in conference with Pompeo, Giacò and two other unknown men; one is another old Partisan crony of theirs called, improbably, *Bue*: Ox. The other, Epifanio, shakes my hand and tells me he spent four years in England, from 1942 to 1946; he was taken prisoner by the British in the North African desert.

You must have eaten a lot of potatoes, then, I say, bracing myself for an outpouring about the horrors of life with no *pasta asciutta*. But no. Luckiest thing that ever happened to him, he says. In those days hunger in Italy was such that regular food in sufficient quantities was all anyone would ask. He loved it. And he was proud, once

Italy had changed sides, to be requested to do some important work for the British Army.

Intelligence work? Liaising with his mates in the Ligurian Partisans? Pinpointing motorbike drops in the olive groves?

No, says Epifanio. Cooking.

Did I say no politics? I was wrong. Standing here on the edge of the *prato*, you can see below, not more than a mile away, the onion dome of Deglio Faraldi's church. Between us and Deglio, on another, lower set of meadows separated from us by a steep wilderness of juniper shrub, another huge crowd of people are junketing around another lot of bonfires: the Faraldi valley's May Day event. Our grey-headed gang, silhouetted against the endless blueness, are busy discussing Faraldi's inadequacies. No football pitch, Giacò is saying, not anywhere in the whole valley.

Pompeo shakes his head sadly. In all the fifteen years of its existence, he tells us, no team from that valley of Christian Democrat cretins has ever won the Diano San Pietro Football Trophy.

They have nowhere to practise, says Giacò.

Exactly! agrees Pompeo, perversely.

(Perhaps I have not mentioned the Diano San Pietro Football Trophy? It is held on the football pitch down beyond the cemetery, between the bar and the olive mill. In a year or two it will get itself a set of eyeball-rending Communist floodlights, and its own proper bar: and will be transformed into the Diano San Pietro Nocturnal Football Trophy, inaugurated with much pomp and splendour, to the great mortification, no doubt, of all Christian Democrats.)

An outbreak of gesticulating and *Mah!*ing from the Ox, who has been glaring downhill for some time. What is so *Mah!*-worthy now? A priest has appeared to officiate at the Faraldi event. Red rag to a bull. Christian Democrats! says Pompeo with deep scorn. Do we know that there are still people ploughing with oxen in that valley? A thing that hasn't been seen for a good twenty years in progressive Diano San Pietro! Poor saps!

Only a moment ago I was wondering why, what with how close we all are to one another, the May Day events of both valleys had not been amalgamated. Now I see that there is no point in asking. But in the interests of anthropological research, I do ask why everyone in the Diano valley is so committed to coming all the way up here on May Day, at such cost to their transport.

Because it's International Workers Day, of course, says Giacò.

Yes, I say, but why up here at the top of the mountain, up this awful road, particularly?

People have always come up here, says Pompeo.

Since before the Christian Church even existed, says Giacò, with another glare at the priestly interference down below. I suspect he's right. Surely Bormano himself once had a finger in this pie. As if to confirm the rite-of-spring theory, as the afternoon wears on to dusk and the elders, relaxed by food, wine and altitude, become less vigilant, the youth of both valleys begins sneakily commingling on the prickly slopes between Communism and Christian Democracy.

Margaret Mead would have been interested: the young of the two tribes getting to know one another, with (as she might have seen it) a view both to genetic variety and to forging new and useful social links between communities. Though it seems unlikely that Pompeo's lot would agree that any link, marital or otherwise, with the brain-dead Christian Democrats next door could be of any use whatsoever.

Still, as darkness falls and faces are no longer identifiable by the eagle-eyed relatives, the amount of canoodling going down on the slopes of no man's land suggests that the young folks have their own ideas. This will be the millennia-old equivalent of a night in the English pub. In the good old days you only got to do it once a year.

Down those twelve only-too-familiar hairpin bends we buzz, and back up another less familiar five on the other side of the valley; mounted on our trusty *motorini*, we have come to track down that nettle pasta to its source.

Outside Ciccio's restaurant, at the far end of a cobbled terrace, a pair of old men are (naturally) playing cards under a shady vine. At the near end a couple of youths watch the football on a large TV perched high under a patio roof. And in the no man's land between Youth and Age, a pair of holiday-making German couples sit foreignly in full sun, a carafe of wine on their table, waiting for their lunch. The sister and I, fence-sitters, make for a table in the dappled shade by the riverbank.

But no! no! We are guests of the house. We must come and eat indoors with Ciccio and gang, join the staff lunch. Sun-dappled terraces being a lot more to our taste than dim, echoing halls, we are not overjoyed. Still, there it is. Off we go, along with the football watchers, into the reverberating gloom where a good dozen people are already seated, talking at the top of their voices. All at once, as usual.

Considering that the four Germans outside are now the only lunch guests actually paying for the privilege, Ciccio's attitude to them is oddly hostile. He mutters under his breath whenever he has to abandon his plate to see to their needs: he sulks and glowers when they want more wine or Parmesan.

I am getting sick of all the nonsensical chauvinism in these hills. Surely Ciccio's own sufferings as a (notional) Calabrese should have alerted him to the idiocy of such stuff? What, I ask, have these poor Germans done to deserve such grumpiness?

What have they done? Is it not obvious? No Italian would dream of turning up at a restaurant at two-thirty! By now the lunch service ought to be over, the staff sitting down to their own meal in peace. Only Germans would turn up at such an ungodly hour, and not even bother to apologize!

Phew. Luckily for us, everyone has assumed that we came at this late hour specially to join the lunch for staff and friends. Should we admit the truth? No. We're too cowardly.

How horribly similar is the behaviour of Germans, now dissected in great detail by our Italian friends, to the behaviour of the English. English who have not been forewarned, that is. Firstly, they never eat a proper decent meal. Is this because they don't like spending money? Or because they don't like eating? Opinion is divided. Look how skinny they all are! Probably both, says Ciccio, certainly a fine figure of a man himself. This lot have been coming for a meal at least once a day, sometimes twice, for over a week now, and they're as tight-fisted as any Ligurian. Either just a plate of pasta, or just a *secondo*. When they have the pasta, they eat so much Parmesan with it that it costs the restaurant as much as if they'd had a main course anyway. Twice they've had the antipasti, the most troublesome course to make, a thing no Italian would dream of asking for unless they were planning to pay for a full-blown dinner – and then said they weren't hungry any more!

Here I feel there is nothing for it but to break with hypocrisy and stand up for the poor Germans – didn't we ourselves never get beyond the antipasto course for a good week? Pointless. How could anyone not understand? You can see at a glance how much work has gone into preparing all those separate titbits.

Bravely, I continue my attempt to explain the bizarre ways of ignorant foreigners. Have they considered that Germans, like my own race, might not realize that in Italy the pasta course is considered a mere preparation for the main course? In England, I say, bracing myself for the scorn I know is about to be heaped upon me, we eat pasta as a main dish – a *secondo piatto*. We put lots more sauce and meat and stuff on it than you do, that'll be why the Germans use so much cheese, not necessarily because it's free.

I get some confirmation from Ciccio here; a frequent feature of Germans' vile behaviour is the way they ask for salads with their pasta. Sometimes even cooked vegetables. A groan of horror rises from the throats of the assembled friends and relations.

Wasted breath. This generation may have broken with tradition in all sorts of ways, be stern critics of small-town hypocrisy, of mindless clinging to tradition in matters like divorce, abortion, leaving home before marriage, drug-use, and practically everything else, but notions of Proper Eating are graven in stone. The thought of people eating pasta all mixed up with stuff rightly belonging to later courses is shocking and appalling.

Now, as the hapless customers in the garden order another dose of house wine, we move on to Foreigners and Drink. Germans, says Ciccio, returning from delivering their third carafe, may not know how to eat, but they certainly have no trouble drinking. They pour wine down their necks like there is no tomorrow. Everyone joins in on this one with gusto. Germans seen getting through glass after glass of wine at seafront bars in the afternoon! Germans on the beach swigging at it from the bottle! Germans who finish eating and then sit till the small hours in restaurants drinking wine till they're legless!

Poor Germans! Here they are thinking that they're in a country where wine-drinking is practically de rigueur, where free and easiness prevails – while behind their backs all this horrified muttering is going on. Most perplexing. We are entirely certain that we've seen each and every one of our fellow eaters well over the limit on alcoholic beverages, and more than once; why are they suddenly talking like evangelizing teetotallers?

Well, say I hopefully, might it not be a natural reaction to being on holiday, and in a land famous for its wine?

Maybe, concedes Ciccio reluctantly, taking a long, thoughtful swig at his own (third? fourth?) glass . . .

At our own table, we have got through two bottles of Pinot de Pinot, delicious champagne-like dry fizzy stuff, as our *aperitivo*, and are now on a great fat bottle of red, into which everyone is tucking heartily as they munch. Still, though it may escape us entirely, there is obviously some vital qualitative difference between the drinking at our table, and the drinking being done by the Germans.

The solution to the mystery, fruit of years of diligent ethnological research, is as follows. In this part of the world civilized behaviour requires that you follow a set of very precise rules on your route to drunkenness. First and most important of them is that you regard everything you drink as, in a sense, medicinal. Before dinner (or, for that matter, lunch) you will drink an *aperitivo* – not, as you may think, a metaphorical opening to the meal, but, literally, a drink to open your stomach, to prime it for the dose of food it is about to receive (hence the terror provoked by our coffee-before-the-meal behaviour down in San Pietro). For an hour or two after six-thirty or so in the evening, or in the pre-lunch hour, it is perfectly fine to drink a glass of wine, or even two, in a bar. You are getting your stomach into starting position for the tidal wave of food that's about to hit it. Red wine is acceptable if you are an aged olive farmer, or if it's a vintage wine, but a fizzy white is best. Otherwise any of the proprietary Martini or Cinzano-type aperitifs. Or Campari. Or alcohol-free Aperol. Or there is Cynar, whose health-giving qualities are advertised on the radio by angelic voices singing the catchy little jingle '*Cynar! A base di carciofo!*' – 'It's based on articho-okes'. At these stomach-opening times of day, bars always dole out a small portion of olives or peanuts or salty biscuits with your drink to protect your delicate digestive mechanisms. You may, if your stomach is particularly firmly closed, drink not one but two *aperitivi*: your waiter will begin to look askance if you order a third glass. Best just to go to another bar if you really want one. The lunchtime *aperitivo* dispensation lasts until one-thirty-ish, the evening one till around half-past eight, when you are presumed to have eaten already. Then the snacks are withdrawn: wine ordering becomes odd and stare-worthy again.

Now you may begin your meal without fear of blockage or paralysis; and depending on the state of your digestion you may drink any amount of wine to help it along. Getting drunk is merely a by-product, fortunate or unfortunate, of the stomach's need for wine, without which it will be unable to perform its digestive functions successfully. Once you've finished eating, you will also stop drinking wine. To finish off a bottle of wine just because it's there, as do the dreadful Germans – fortunately the English are so under-represented round here that no one has any idea how disgusting our own nation's habits may be – is another indicator, along with the deceitful ordering of antipasti when you're not planning to eat another two courses, of serious lowlifery. And as for another bottle once you've finished eating . . . outlandish. In every sense of the word.

Food over, you should be drinking, along with your coffee, a lethally alcoholic *digestivo*, usually an *amaro* distilled from bitter herbs and exotic medicinal plants such as *rababaro* – rhubarb – preferably brewed by some obscure order of monks up some distant and inaccessible mountain. Perhaps you still have that not-quite-digested feeling? Not to worry – have a grappa. Country restaurants will leave the grappa bottle on your table so you can help yourself to as many as you need to keep those peristaltic waves flowing while you wait for the bill. (It won't be long till one of our own guests is led badly astray by this grappa on the table business: What, so we could drink all of it if we wanted? Well, yes, I suppose we could. Martin does his best, but can't quite manage to fit it all in. Now he goes one better than mere ill-mannered finishing of the wine: as we leave the restaurant we spot something clutched under his arm. The bottle of grappa. Extracting it from his vice-like grip we replace it firmly on the table. He is disgusted. Why can't he take it? They've given it to us, haven't they?)

There are, of course, exceptions to these rules. Aged peasants are allowed to tipple wine all afternoon; extremely aged peasants may even drink it for breakfast, too. But they are a completely different category of person, and this kind of behaviour is viewed with tolerance as the natural reward for, and perhaps consequence of, a life of hard toil on the land. Understandably, given that most holi-daying Germans (or indeed English) are evidently not aged peasants, the structurelessness of their wine-drinking is inexplicable and offensive.

13

Sergio stands with the hot sun in his eyes outside the crumbling yellow-ochre palazzo where the San Pietro Comune has its offices above the tiny post office. A dead and bloody Alsatian dog lies limp in his arms; he is hurling an impassioned soliloquy into the apparently empty square.

Will no one do anything about the peasant mafia who run everything in this village and its godforsaken hillsides? Does the Comune not give a dry fig for its duty to defend decent law-abiding citizens? Sergio's face is brick-red from his exertions, the veins standing out in his neck; still he rages on. From their usual shady stone seats in the farthest corner of the dusty sun-bleached piazza a couple of the oldest and most crumpled citizens of San Pietro look on impassive and blear-eyed; a few men in hankies lurk amongst the Apes parked round the cool side of the church, heads close together, leaning on their vehicles or their knotty walking sticks, muttering among themselves, backs turned to the appalling spectacle. There is some slight movement in the shadows behind Signor Ugo-the-grocer's fly curtain; someone, it seems, is watching from in there, too. Now, dimly visible through the dusty French windows that open on to the wrought-iron balcony above, a couple of faces appear looking down from the Comune. They quickly withdraw as Sergio turns to face the building, voice pulsating with emotion.

Why don't they come out and answer him? They are too ashamed of themselves, that's why! Is he to get no protection? He knows who has done this to his beloved dog; everyone knows. It may only be a dog this time; who knows if it won't be his children next?

There is a pause while he tenderly places the bloodied animal on the Comune steps. He turns back to face the silent square and shakes a fist in the air. *Bastardi! Figli di putana!* One day the Comune will have to face up to its responsibilities. And they can start now, by disposing of the body themselves! He storms back to his jeep and shoots off with a squeal of rubber, still shouting imprecations. The moment of high drama is only slightly spoilt by a head-on encounter with one of the larger and more implacable of the lorries from the village builders' yard round the corner, which obliges him to stop and reverse back up into the piazza.

I am watching all this with interest from the doorway of Mariuccia's hardware shop, along with Mariuccia herself: it is the latest episode in the long-running saga of Sergio's non-payment of his debt to Franco. As Mariuccia observes drily, once the jeep has disappeared in a cloud of dust down the road to Diano, all the drama would be far more effective if everyone didn't know perfectly well that Sergio had always underfed and maltreated his three poor Alsatians.

So far, the war has gone like this:

Skirmish Number One – a person unknown has strategically sawn down a tree across the road leading to Sergio's house, blocking his jeep into the driveway and causing him to have to walk all the way down to Diano to buy a chainsaw with which to saw it up and remove it. Although various Ape drivers pass him on his way down the hill, nobody stops to offer him a lift. And he is certainly not going to ask. He gets himself and the chainsaw driven back up in style in a spanking new off-road vehicle by one of his boat-owning cronies from the port. A few days later Sergio makes an unaccustomed visit to Luigi and Maria's bar where he announces in a devil-may-care manner to all and sundry that he is very pleased with life: he has efficiently got all his winter firewood ready months early.

Not long after, several *fascie* of Franco's olive trees are found to have been savaged horribly by somebody with a chainsaw. It will take them years to recover.

Skirmish Two: the tubes leading from Sergio's huge rainwater *vasca* to his domestic plumbing arrangements mysteriously come adrift, causing the *vasca* to empty itself out all down the hill and into one of Sergio's chicken-runs. His house is now toiletless until the thing refills itself in the winter rains, and he has had to move all the chickens to new premises out of the damp.

Shortly afterwards a carrier bag full of human excrement is deposited through the window of Franco's *cantina*.

What will be the retaliation for this dastardly dog shooting?

The village is agog to see the outcome of Skirmish Three. Neither Sergio nor Franco is held in great affection or esteem by the village; but Franco is ahead, just, in San Peo public opinion. His moves are certainly more classical, more in tune with the local Queensberry Rules for this type of dispute. Attacking olive trees is definitely well below the belt, and bags of shit, everyone agrees, have no place in a manly fight.

Mariuccia, like everyone else, is very interested in the lack of males in our household; and very pleased to hear that, though they may not be present, we at least own three brothers. How lucky we are! And then, of course, we have one another. She has no brothers or sisters, and she and her husband never had any children. She had a cousin, Erminia's son, who used to help her out with the men's work once she'd lost her husband, but he vanished off to Milan twenty-odd years ago, married an unknown woman there, and has hardly been heard of since. A couple of years ago they thought they might have got themselves a *maschio* about the place at last, she says: Erminia's grandson, the cousin's son, reappeared one fine day in San Pietro, now in his late teens. But as it turned out, says Mariuccia darkly, he was worse than no one.

We probe deeper into this, as we are expected to. How come?

Heroin, says Mariuccia, lowering her voice conspiratorially. The story goes like this:

Mariuccia and Erminia had only seen Giovanni a couple of times since he was a sweet little boy taking his First Communion. They welcomed him with open arms anyway, blood being thicker than water and Erminia having no one else to leave her place to. But instead of being an extra pair of hands about the yard and the *fascie*, getting himself a job, contributing something to the household, Giovanni spent most of the time lying about in bed saying he was sick; and looking, indeed, sick. When he wasn't being sick, he would disappear off on his motorbike for days on end, returning only to go back to bed and be sick again. Meanwhile the pair of them were living on Erminia's tiny widow's pension, supplemented by what Mariuccia herself could spare. Erminia had begun to look very old and tired – but then she really was getting on a bit, and even though

Mariuccia was angry with Giovanni for worrying his granny with laziness and *capricci*, she didn't suspect what was really going on. She could have kicked herself for not having spotted it. All that being sick! And the Milan connection, too . . .

Giovanni had secretly admitted to Erminia that he had a drug problem, a thing she hardly understood at all, when she'd confronted him over her gold earrings that had gone missing. He'd sworn he would reform and become a proper grandson to her, if only she wouldn't tell anyone. Erminia fell for it, kept her side of the bargain, didn't breathe a word. Silly thing to do, trust a *drogato*, but what did she know of these matters?

Mariuccia had guessed nothing until Signor Ugo kindly alerted her to the fact that her old aunt had begun to buy wine from his shop, a thing she had never done before in her life, and in surprisingly large quantities. Mariuccia had witnessed several attempts by San Pietro families to cure heroin addiction by drowning it in wine – cheap, legal, more socially acceptable. But somehow you don't expect it in your own family, do you?

Erminia was by now a sad shadow of her former self. Mariuccia faced the boy out – he'd had the nerve to come trying to borrow money from her – and told him to get out of town and leave his poor granny in peace. But *drogati*, she says, have no pity for anyone but themselves: he didn't go far, just went and camped in a *rustico* up in the hills, kept reappearing at his granny's at mealtimes asking for food. (Aha! So there really was at least one biker junkie marauder from Milan!)

Of course, once autumn arrived and the cold weather with it, Erminia gave in, couldn't be so cruel to her own flesh and blood. She let him come home and the whole business started all over again. It only ended when Giovanni got caught breaking into somebody's house right here in Diano San Pietro. On his own doorstep, *che brutta figura!* Luckily there'd been enough of this sort of trouble round here before, and no one thought any the worse of her and Erminia . . .

He was taken off to Genoa in handcuffs, in the back of a police car, never to be seen again. And good riddance too, says Mariuccia. That boy was worrying poor Erminia into an early grave. So nowadays they are a woman-only team, except when her dead husband's best mate Ettore has a moment to help them out with the heavy stuff.

Extraordinary place, this Diang San Peo. You could be living in a particularly lively edition of a British Sunday tabloid. If it wasn't for the landscape and the weather being all wrong.

June has come: in Diano Marina we stand amazed. The place is unrecognizable. Some kind of catastrophe has overwhelmed the streets with a flood of chaos and primary colours. The rather staid and classical face of the town we know has been blotted out at a stroke, the usually restrained shopfronts suddenly invisible behind wave upon wave of lurid plastic. Huge stands are crammed with tourist goodies of every kind: multicoloured toys, goggles, beachwear, flip-flops, snorkels, flags, inflatable beach mattresses, suntan lotions and everything else remotely connected with holi-daying you can think of. Tall glass-doored freezer cabinets, their shelves loaded with extravagant ice cream sundaes that bristle with paper parasols and lurid plastic swizzle-sticks, have been wheeled out and are taking up any small areas of pavement not totally inundated with gaudy knick-knacks.

The bars and cafés are obscene travesties of their former unosten-tatious selves. The two or three little round tables, which usually sit outside each one, have expanded on low wooden platforms set out in the middle of the streets; now there are hordes of frilly sun umbrellas, flowery tablecloths and swing-seats, all smothered with frou-frous and furbelows. Cars can only just squeeze past, single-file.

We weave erratically through the new-laid multicoloured obstacle course, and finally manage, dazed and disoriented, to track down the pharmacy, then turn tail and dash for the hills. No, Pompeo wasn't exaggerating after all.

Up here, too, June has arrived: and with it Apes at dawn. All around Besta de Zago the midsummer *pulizia*, the Cleaning, is starting up. From six-thirty onwards the hills are alive with the sound of the many types of tiny yet eardrum perforating internal combustion engines required for this task, buzzing and howling to one side of the house or the other, if not both at once, and dragging us stumbling and swearing out of bed and over to the coffee pot. Even people who don't bother doing anything else at all to their olive trees are now loudly and bustlingly Cleaning all round them.

Until now all has been peace and quiet apart from the gentle background racket of wildlife getting on with its business – frogs croaking down in the bottom of the valley, cicadas *skreeking* in the grass, tree crickets *krarking* in the olives, depending on the time of day. But these creatures croak, skreek or krark rhythmically and continuously and soon fade into the background. Not so this onslaught of cleaning technology, whose roarings stop and start, come and go, punctuated by sudden full-throated outbursts of cheery shouting or song from the operators when things are going well, or of black blasphemy, porky madonnas and lurid cows when the equipment fails, which it does with dramatic regularity. Voices carry beautifully in this bowl of a valley; for three mornings in a row we hear, over and over again, delivered by one invisible peasant working somewhere downhill and to the seaward of us, the same few lines of a tragic ballad concerning his great loneliness and his deep and undying affection for his horse, his only true friend.

How sad that the horses are almost all gone from this valley, I say to myself; it sounds as if the old folk miss them terribly. Remorseless repetition having burnt this fragment of nostalgic olive-farming song into my brain, I will now go around humming it off and on for months, feeling very folklorical.

How do I know that song I keep singing? asks Patrizia one day as I'm humming my way through the washing-up. How have I come to be so familiar with the signature tune of a 1960s kids' cowboy series? Can Italian TV Westerns have been worth dubbing and exporting to England? Surely not?

During this period of high concentration of knotted hankies around our home, I find I am beginning to get my eye in to the many and various knotting styles from which the modern olive farmer can choose. There are, I notice – as a whole new crop of people do their level best to get a good look at us, needing either a glass of water or a screwdriver or, to prolong the inspection, one of each – two basic designs around which you can create your own individual look. You can have four knots, one at each corner, creating the classic pudding-basin shape; or you can have two knots only, tying the corners together in pairs, one of which rests on the forehead, the other on the nape. This creates a tube-shaped head covering that funnels the breeze, when there is any, up over the knots and on to the pate below. When there is no wind, though, the loop of cloth over the forehead lies flat, forming a shady peak over the eyes. It is while I am gazing at an interesting variation on this two-knot-tube style – Lucy has gone for the screwdriver – that an amazing fact of headgear history is revealed to me. This visitor has tucked the cloth in at his nape, up under the knot, so that it hugs the back of his head, while the peak flap is left free: seen in profile this arrangement looks exactly like an ordinary English peaked cloth cap. In a blinding flash I realize that the design of the classic working-man's cap is nothing but a highly elaborated descendant of the two-knotted hanky. I envisage that first-ever cloth-cap maker gloating over his or her cunning plan to stitch the damn thing up and save all that time wasting knotting and unknotting . . . then, over the centuries, layer upon layer of reworking and refining until the original form was lost to conscious thought, veiled in the mists of history . . . Until this afternoon.

No wonder the cap never caught on in the higher echelons of society, I say to myself now that I have spotted its close kinship to an old hanky; in spite of many and complex mutations over the centuries, it was unable to escape the stigma of its lowly birth. What else could it become but the official headgear of the British working class?

Having so far managed to ignore the occasional pointed comment in dialect from beneath various knotting styles about Dirty Land and clung tenaciously to our wildflower-strewn terraces, we have given in at last. We have begun to notice, in spite of our initial aversion to the Cleaning Ideal, that whereas good tidy mowers of terraces like Domenico and our other nearest neighbour, Nino, have an attractive new growth of lush meadow-green covering their February cleaned *fascie*, you can hardly walk about on ours any more. Everything that had grown waist high by May, everything that didn't have roots more than a yard deep at any rate, has now dried out under the hot sun, shrivelled and turned to tangled knee-high prickly straw, beneath which lurks ankle-trapping dried-out undergrowth turning at earth level to murky black rot. Except for the narrow strip we keep beaten with the constant passage of feet, our path to the well has silted back up again with the dead and scratchy remnants of once exuberant plant life. As we keep finding out round here, what seems to our unpractised eyes to be a beauty of Nature is, after all, down to centuries of Nurture. The reason our terraces were so lovely when we first got here was not in spite of Cleaning, but because of it. Though we still can't really see why everyone else is so keen on keeping their land tidy, considering they're never up here and mostly don't even harvest their olives. Anyhow, we have seen the error of our ways, and have begun to Clean thoroughly. Down with Dirt.

Almost all the compulsive cleaners of this hillside seem to have the olive grower's equivalent of a Hoover, a great roaring petrol-driven strimmer and brushcutter, the *decespugliatore*, advertised by Pompeo. After our efforts with sickles among the brambles, we have decided that Pompeo is absolutely right about new technology; the horrors of the complex and delicate innards of the internal combustion engine can't be any worse than the hand-blistering back-breaking sickle horror. Sadly, though, on going down to make our bid to join the late twentieth century at the Cooperativa Agricola, we discover that they cost several hundred pounds and change our minds at the speed of light. The sooner our funds run out, the sooner we'll have to go back to England to raise more. If we want to postpone the moment of doom there is nothing for it but to mount an intensive attack with the good old-fashioned sickle, of which we have plenty thanks to Pompeo having moved on to better things. Oxen are probably a lot cheaper for ploughing than Rotavators, too, if you happen to have a couple lying about the place.

The earth is low, and we backward Faraldi-style sickle-folk soon find that due to our obsolete equipment we have great heaps and piles and bundles of hay to clear away once we have finished cutting; unlike the lazy rich strimmer owners, whose Dirt is reduced to a fine mulch that vanishes by itself in a couple of weeks. Should we get ourselves some hay-eating creature to help? A rabbit? A goat? Of course, an ox!

Will we ever make it to Peasants Professional? We console ourselves with the thought that exercise is good for us, while sickles are probably better for the rather more selective Cleaning we want to do, saving the best clumps of wild flowers.

The boring job of clearing the terraces below, the ones with the olive trees on them whose scruffiness sticks out like a sore thumb, is beginning to get us down. We've been doing a bit every day, trying to tame those eight terraces of knee-high grass and weeds. Neighbours are coming up to sort out their groves below and to either side of us. Nino is here every morning at crack of dawn, and so is Ugo with a recalcitrant ten-year-old son. Also a very grumpy and monosyllabic gentleman with a big long beard, name unknown, who owns the trees just above our parking space. All of them are setting a fine example of the correct Cleaning timetable: six-thirty prompt start, down tools at the first hoot-and-bong of midday, don't start again till four if at all. We have noticed this; we appreciate its good sense; but we are constitutionally incapable, it seems, of either starting or stopping at the right moment. We never manage to get out here till eight at the earliest, and with the summer heat building up, by ten o'clock in the morning the fierce sun is already over the ridge behind us blatting our terraces, hammering our heads, setting off those ten thousand cicadas whose *skreeking* makes you feel twice as hot instantly. By eleven, just doing the easy stuff, grasses and weeds, never mind dried-out tangled undergrowth and fierce woody prickly brambles, is almost unbearable. Twelve o'clock bongs, hoots: needless to say we grit our teeth and keep on slashing. We have to atone for the wastrel hours of coffee drinking and hanging out. Our clearing is getting more and more scruffy and incompetent. And we are fed up to the teeth with it. Depressingly, because we didn't do ours in February, even when we finally succeed in clearing all the trailing surface greenery and the dead undergrowth below it, we are left with ugly terraces of bare scrubby earth. No smooth green meadows for us unless it rains again soon. Which it shows no sign of doing. This afternoon we're finishing off the small half-a-terrace just below the house: an urgent operation inspired by a snake in the grass. This horrible thing appeared to me as I was sitting under the lemon tree over my after-lunch coffee, gazing unfocused and abstracted at the foliage below me moving gently in the sea-breeze coming up the valley. One tall stalk that seemed oddly out of rhythm with the rest gradually drew my attention; eventually it dawned on me that the off-rhythm item was not vegetable at all, but animal. Some sinister kind of long skinny snake was sitting among the tall grass, waving its top half around, cunningly camouflaged as a bit of plant life and hoping, I suppose, to catch some unwary plump insect. New light on that saying 'snake in the grass' – not just a concealed snake, as I'd always imagined it, but an actively duplicitous snake. We didn't need any of that sort of behaviour so close to home. Who knew what damage it might do to an unwary plump human? We set off a-sickling with renewed vim and mild hysteria, stamping about heavily to scare off serpent-life as we went.

And here we still are a sweaty hour later. Now, as we bend over our Dirt in the heat, our blades chop heavily and lethargically where once they flailed and slashed. Blisters blossom on our palms. Rivulets of sweat run unappealingly down our noses, trickle out from the roots of our hair to sting our eyes, as, bent double, we contemplate the lowness of the earth. What a boringly literal metaphor that's turned out to be. As if all this wasn't enough, Lucy manages in an overheated moment to embed the point of her sickle in the end of her big toe. So, when Domenico comes along the path on his way to an afternoon's Cleaning, brushcutter on shoulder, he finds us crouched on the ground inspecting a serious wound. Blood is pouring from it; the nail is threatening to come off. We couldn't have arranged things better if we'd tried.

Seeing he's here with his *decespugliatore*, he says, he may as well give us a hand with the worst bits, the stuff that's really hard to do by hand, the rest of those strangling brambles invading us from Franco's unused *orto*, for example. (Yes, there are some people so irresponsible they haven't done any *pulizia* for years. Naming no names.) And he could just as easily give a quick swipe over the rest of our land while he's at it really, there's not a lot to it . . .

But, we say hypocritically, he's got enough of his own land to clean, we can't let him do it, maybe we could just borrow the brushcutter for an afternoon, get some petrol, do our own Cleaning?

No, we couldn't. We would be much slower than him, novices as we are, and he needs to be finished here and up at Castello doing his vineyard tomorrow. Anyway, like Pompeo, he feels that we are too small and delicate to be left in charge of such a powerful machine. Have we seen the huge bundle of protective gear he's brought with him? Mask, gauntlets . . . and in any case the weight of it would break our spines. *Ah, sì, sì.* Most importantly, when it breaks down we won't know how to repair it.

Does it always break down, then? we ask.

Euh!!

The terraces below us break out into even closer than usual ear-splitting buzzings and roarings, alternating with relatively peaceful bits in which, we guess, the thing has broken down as predicted, since they are punctuated with loud mutterings, fierce metallic bangings and clangings, and, at short intervals, cries of *Porca madonna!* or *Porca miseria!* Disappointingly, the Lurid Cow does not seem to feature in Domenico's repertoire. The atmosphere of tension is too powerful for us to be able to get on with much else, while the awful knowledge that we are more likely to be a hindrance than a help keeps us from going down to share in Domenico's sufferings. We stay up by the house and mess about with our sickles, potter around our embryonic garden.

We really have managed to create something quite impressively garden-like from the wilderness. Above us, where there are no olives, only wild hillside, we have just pruned back the great yellow-flowering broom-bushes, not chopped them down to ground level like everyone else; and we've kept the best clumps of bright-pink valerian and the wild thyme with clouds of tiny mauve flowers, the trailing asparagus fronds and some pretty, round, bright-green bobbly bushes, name unknown. On the steep sloping rocky bit and terrace wall which supports our higher patio-with-cherry-tree area, we've carefully sickled away all the messy tangly trailing stuff and the long grass and left the pretty flowering things and the tiny tenacious rock plants sprouting from crevices; while on the narrow level below is a proper wildflower garden, more lacy valerian, creamy-yellow wild snapdragons, pale lilac scabious, a kind of shrubby rock-rose with a yellow heart and pale pink petals, wild sweet peas that twine up the rock, big ox-eye daisies and delicate harebells. We have left the grass high at the edges of the patio and on the next half-terrace down so as not to disturb the stunning wild lilies, now easily three feet tall, which are just beginning to open their white waxy flowers under the nearest olive trees. All rather tastefully pallid, undeniably more English country garden than Italian eye-boggler, so I have stuck cuttings of more luridly Mediterranean stuff into the ground along the edges of the pathway-terrace below the house, varicoloured ivy-leaved geraniums from Antonietta's garden, rooty bits of that violently violet-blue morning glory which spreads like a weed along the riverbed in the village, some seedlings of a three foot tall busy Lizzie-like plant called *bella di notte*, beauty by night. Hopefully all this will start to sprout as the laid-back wild flowers die down, and bring us at last into primary-colourful line with San Pietro.

After an hour or so of high-drama sound-effects from down below, we are called to the well-terrace to inspect. It is twice as large, twice as long as before. The vicious flailing nylon cord of the *decespugliatore*, aided by a fabulous rotating saw-blade attachment which Domenico now demonstrates, making us jump out of our skins, has reduced the evil jungle of waist-high brambles to a stringy mush, right down to the bare earth. Brilliant.

Unrecognizable too is the hero Domenico, who looks like something out of *Star Wars* behind a huge green-spattered protective visor (carefully arranged over the knotted hanky), his torso festooned with the machine's great criss-crossing padded straps and buckles, a long leather leg-protecting apron, huge padded gauntlets; the motor sprouts behind his right shoulder, orange handlebars and long metal proboscis dangling from their harness over his chest, sprouting curly bright-green plastic antennae at the tip. Every millimetre of which accoutrements is lightly coated in clinging damp green shreds. How can he stand it in this heat?

You'll need to start planting right away if you want to get any vegetables worth having this summer, says Domenico sternly, refusing to take any notice of our joy and excitement, or indeed of our thanks. They might still have some half-grown seedlings down at the Cooperativa Agricola, he adds. If you're not too late. And he stomps off, huge and clumsy under all the protective gear, down to finish off his own olive terraces.

At six o'clock prompt, the hour at which work must cease and the digestive system be seen to, he comes striding back up our path, heading for his Ape, brushcutter still roaring, Cleaning generously as he goes. He zigs and zags back and forth along all of our eight terraces, eliminating the last hint of scruffiness, the stuff we've lazily left along the edges of the terrace walls. Not good enough, obviously. We are a bit sad about this. We rather liked the tall frilly bits. Too late. Anyway, it's probably better for the olive trees or the walls or something.

We start to panic when he is almost at the house and he still hasn't turned the Infernal Machine off. We can't shout to him; he won't hear a word above his roaring motor. He reaches our wild-garden terrace: great swathes of our carefully preserved wildflowers fall before him, flayed to the root. Right up to our downstairs door he lays the ground bare, reducing all the vegetation around – including a great clump of the beautiful lilies – to a few damp mulchy shreds. I jump around on the terrace above, waving my arms and shouting at him to stop. But there's no way he can hear a word, or spot my desperate semaphore through that blurry sap-smeared visor.

Ecco! he shouts above the ear-hammering racket as he passes along the path below us, still strimming, mangling the baby morning glory, the next bunch of lilies and all the cuttings I've just planted. *Bello Pulito!* Lovely and clean!

We stand helpless and despairing on the patio. There's no point in complaining now; the worst has already happened. But no, it hasn't. Turning and raising the thing's flailing proboscis unexpectedly to shoulder height, as if to wave farewell with it, Domenico gives a last gay swipe-and-roar at the patch above him, just below our feet. Our lovely trailing rock-face plants, the only bit of greenery left in the wreckage, disappear damply. Domenico vanishes off cheerily round the modesty rock, full of the joys of a job well done, strimming as he goes, all the way along the path to the parking place at the hairpin bend and his Ape. Tomorrow, Castello.

Lucy and I glumly survey our almost-garden, reduced in a matter of seconds to a horribly convincing mock-up of a Scorched Earth Policy.

Next morning, though, when we step out as usual with our breakfast coffee on to our very Clean land, despair in our hearts, no more considering of lilies to be done, we realize that things aren't as bad as we thought. At least the bits round the patio and above the house are still there. And apart from the missing downstairs garden, now reduced to bare stone and earth, the rest of our land does look rather lovely. In this neatly shorn state the lines of the terraces, till now fluffy and blurry under their grasses, weeds and flowers, have been magically transformed into smooth, pure, architectural-looking horizontals and verticals, revealing the way the drystone walls follow, row upon row, the curves and contours of the hill. Beautiful after all.

Inspired, we will return proudly from our next trip to England with a small and (comparatively speaking) ladylike petrol-driven strimmer purchased for a mere eighty pounds in a catalogue salesroom. Domenico's verdict: Don't make me laugh!

And indeed, after a fortnight or so of playing up horribly over simple grass and weed, the puny plainsfolk's thing we have bought collapses terminally at the first sniff of a serious Ligurian shrub.

14

Great hollow metal objects of some unimaginably large kind – outsized oildrums? worn-out water tanks? – are rolling and crashing, bounding and rebounding, down through the oaks and the pines above the house, heading, it seems, straight for us and our suddenly fragile home. Knowing as we do the eccentricities of local rubbish disposal habits, cascading old iron seems only too likely an explanation of the outbreak of terrifying rumblings and clatterings from above. The skies turn black, blinding flashes of lightning erupt over the mountains opposite; still it takes some effort of the will to seriously believe that no human agency is responsible for the solid-sounding thudding and booming above us. The lightning zigzags wildly over the other side of the valley; each thunderclap echoes and re-echoes, crashes round the valleys for so long that the next flash comes before the sound of the first has worn itself out. The impression is of total, terrifying chaos: the house is being shaken to its very roots, every lovely new pane of glass in every lovely new window frame nerve-rackingly rattling its heart out. At last the downpour starts. Just a thunderstorm.

Off on our *motorini* once the sun's come out again, we find the whole road has turned to thick skiddy mud. The rain begins to pelt down again once we're at the Colla church. Too far down to turn back. And at least no thunder and lightning. As we negotiate the hairpin bends of San Pietro, though, our hair-products are slowly rinsed off into our eyes, blinding us so completely that we are entirely unable to distinguish between road, rock and mudbath. We have to stop and clean ourselves up at Luigi and Maria's before proceeding to Diano Marina; the sun is out again, though the sky is still rather an odd colour, by the time we leave, slightly less bedraggled. We have received much intensive advice from Maria on how to avoid the bad cold which is almost bound to be our lot after this drenching: we have turned down the grappa, but agreed to go very slowly on our bikes to avoid the *colpo d'aria*, a kind of deadly air-wallop, which will be caused by too much cool breeze on our damp clothing. But by now the asphalt is steaming again under the broiling sun, though the sky is still dark over the sea. We're soon whizzing along as fast as our tiny motors will take us, drying out and cooling down at a stroke. Not for long. Just as we arrive in Diano, the wind rises, the sky turns black, the world explodes into thunder, lightning and wild wind. The palm trees along the seafront whip to and fro as if in a hurricane; shopkeepers race to drag their stands of tourist goodies indoors; and we are now bombarded not merely by fierce bucketing rain, but by oranges flying off the trees all along the main drag.

Drenched to the bone again, we take refuge in the Bar Marabotto, whose barside experts, snug and dry on their high stools, are already deep in intense weather talk. From them we glean much useful lore which, had we but known it in advance, could have saved us this soaking. The thing to watch out for is clouds attacking from France or Spain – the south and south-west. These foreign clouds are the ones that cause the trouble. Natch. Native Italian rainclouds up in the hills to the north or east may look menacing, but will bear no consequences for us sheltered folk down on the coastline. They will just vanish harmlessly off up into the mountains to drench the people of the Pianüa, for whom we do not give a fig. Or, as we say in Italian, a dry fig. (We will all be less smug about this rain on the plain, of course, in years of late-summer drought when our *orti* and our olives are shrivelling for want of water. Now we will all sit sulking outside our parched bars, gazing at the useless north-east clouds and willing them to veer round to the south and save us, cursing those fat cats of the high plains whose pockets are filling as ours empty; their sunflowers, their corn and their cows lazily fattening through no merit of their owners.)

Confirming the Marabotto experts' prognosis, an hour later we are still, whenever we poke our heads out of the door, being bombarded by oranges. Water is still falling in sheets, great trees of lightning are crackling and crashing over the sea. We can't possibly bike home in this; the steep bits will be a torrent of mud and stones by now. No one we know well enough to blackmail into risking life, limb and suspension on our horrible road has appeared, and we are becoming desperate. Will it ever end? How many more cappuccinos can our constitutions handle?

Even when the rain does stop, our weather advisers point out, the road beyond the Colla will be part river, part quagmire for the rest of the day; we may as well abandon the *motorini* for now – we can walk down to get them tomorrow – and get the taxi from the Bar Sito to take us up. The Bar Sito's son-in-law and resident cab driver, Federico, who not only wears repellent low-cut Gucci loafers with white socks but will turn out later to be a heartless and cruel man into the bargain, is summoned in his shiny black Mercedes. For ten minutes we cruise in snug luxury, leather upholstery, bump-free suspension round the San Pietro bends, warm and dry in the teeth of the driving rain, booming thunder, crashing lightning; it's getting worse all the way. At the end of the asphalt Federico takes one look at the river of mud which at that moment passes for a road and claims not to have understood where we wanted to go. He refuses categorically to take us any further; his valuable car might be damaged by the rocks which will have been washed down on to the road, he says. Or get stuck in the mud. At the very least it will be covered in filth, and he'll have to stop work to get it cleaned.

Alas, foolish nose-cutting-off Northern folk that we are, rather than making a fuss and insisting on being taken either all the way or back down to Diano, we simply pay up in a cold and superior manner and tramp off stiff-upper-lipped through the storm, heads held high – until the enemy is out of sight, at least. Next, a very British fifteen-minute *passeggiata* through a solid wall of water only broken by the occasional terrifyingly close clap of thunder and flash of lightning. By the time we get home we are drenched to the skin again and our shoes have collected great clogs of mud that must weigh several kilos each.

We realize later, with just a bit of prompting from the Italian point of view, as represented by Franco and Iole, how senseless a piece of behaviour this was. Did we think he would feel guilty? I don't suppose Federico suffered for a moment. But thanks to Franco we discover the true identity of this evil taxi driver. None other than the very Federico who once had the nerve to try to get off with

Franco's beloved sister Silvana! We see now that he certainly was not good enough for her; and we are pleased to know that he and his family have been thoroughly humiliated for their sins by the Horseshit-in-the-Bar episode of the good old days; even if the punishment was somewhat in advance of this particular crime.

What we need of course is a covered vehicle of some kind. Preferably with four wheels, preferably free. And one comes our way: an aged Morris Minor which some friend in England is about to throw away because it has failed its MOT test miserably. Handily for us, no one in Liguria is much interested yet in such nit-picking nonsense as vehicle safety checks, so it is perfectly useable here. Heroically, our brother Rob drives it all the way across France to our very door. The Morris, as the long-suffering brother points out, is an embarrassingly hippyish sort of vehicle. Still, we refuse to look it in the mouth. Fortunately most olive farmers are unaware of the connection between Morrises and hippies – in fact, I think they were too busy, with the earth being so low and all the upheavals going on in the Communist Party at the time, to notice hippies at all.

We soon discover, though, that it is best to leave this unusual machine on the San Pietro side of the crossroads when going to Diano – whose tidy townsfolk may not have much idea of hippydom and its outmodedness either, but can certainly recognize a scruffy old banger when they see one.

In San Pietro though, people are less fussy about these things. They simply smile knowingly into their moustaches as we grind and roar our way up and down the village in our miniature tank. As well as keeping us dry, the Morris is just what we need for transporting those unwieldy objects which won't fit on a *motorino*. Thirty-kilo gas bottles, in particular, essential for our new cooking arrangements, are particularly tricky to deal with on two wheels for us novices who can't even balance a dog on our footplates. Especially when cornering. And there is a world of difference between knowing that Signor Ugo-the-grocer of San Pietro is, as our friends claim, legally obliged to bring our gas bottles up to our house, and actually having the nerve to ask him to do it. First, there is the state of our road; then, there are his well-known fearful satirical looks.

Why the gas? Till now, convinced that, apart from the bonfire, there was no other way of cooking in our far-flung outpost – how could we possibly get gas connected up here? – we have been laboriously lighting our wood-stove to cook supper, arguing about whose turn it is to go in and sweat over the thing. Our most advanced bit of technology is a wee camping gas-burner for quick tea- and coffee-making. Now we've discovered, thanks to Giacò, that mains gas is unheard of here anyway. Everyone's gas comes from gas bottles, even in downtown Diano. Not pioneers in the wild at all, then, just daft and ignorant. Giacò has brought us a strange new Italian cooking device, a little four-ring gas-hob with no oven under it, which runs off these behemoth bottles. We go on and on about how brilliant our hob is, while Giacò watches us bemused. The ovenless hob is, it turns out, a perfectly ordinary thing round here. People don't expect to have an oven at all except in winter, when they light their wood-burning stoves, with oven attached, to keep the house warm; the oven being more of a handy spin-off than a kitchen essential. Roast meats, lasagne, vegetables *al forno*, are all winter food, stuff you cook once the stove has to be alight anyway: otherwise you have those beehive-shaped outdoor ovens with just the one compartment for fire and food together, which in olden times you fired up once a week for your bread, slipping in a couple of pizzas for that night's dinner as you went; and, of course, avoiding turning your home into a Turkish bath in the process.

Giacò delivers our goods, which include four real beds – one each and two for guests – of a useable length from some secret and more modern stock than the stuff he keeps on display in his yard. He also sees and notes Pompeo's beautiful priestly marble sink and draining-board. In years to come, once his eye has been trained up to the kind of stuff that appeals to the cultured Germans who by then are beginning to move into the area in appreciable numbers, he will put huge amounts of energy into trying to buy this from us, offering us any amount of lovely modern ceramic double-sinks as part of the bargain. As yet, though, he hasn't understood any of this funny foreign stuff. He too is very worried, now he's seen where we're living, about our being so far away from humans. We have the *motorini*, only five minutes to the village on them, and now a car, too, we point out. Giacò just laughs darkly. Why don't we get ourselves a proper Ape? Where are we going to get spare parts for that thing? In this matter Giacò is prophetic. Within the year the Morris will break down, and we will have to go to enormous lengths to get a spare part from England: a spare part which, when it finally arrives, turns out to be a kind of large wooden bead with a hole in it, which causes much guffawing in the Sulking Café when Gianni the mechanic shows it around.

Next time the car gives up on us, though, a couple of years on, it will end up causing a terrible scandal in the village: no laughing matter. We push it from where it broke down – luckily on the flat road to Diano Marina – to a nice wide space behind some trees, between Luigi's bar and the olive mill, where we just leave it for several months, it being hot and summery and the *motorini* being perfectly adequate for our needs at that moment. It sits quietly waiting for our next visit to England when we will get the next lot of absurd spare parts.

By autumn, when we finally go to check what's needed, all the tyres bar one are completely flat: when I open the door I discover that the panel on the driver's side has developed a large and horribly lively wasps' nest.

When we get back, spring by now, bearing a packet of grommets or some such needment, it is only to find that the Morris has vanished completely. The good people of San Pietro have decided in our absence, after some deep debate at the Comune, naturally, that we have permanently abandoned our decrepit machine. And if we haven't abandoned it, we ought to have done, for the sake of our own health and safety, not to mention that of other road users.

Who needs MOT tests when you have a workers and peasants democracy instead? The Morris has been officially towed away into the riverbed – another favourite method of rubbish disposal of the period, and a useful spot for the larger items that are too far from the top of a mountain to be thrown off – where it sits sadly, snuggled up to a couple of old fridges and a washing machine, just visible from the road to Diano Marina between the tall waving clumps of bamboo. We are highly embarrassed at having irresponsibly left such an eyesore lying about for so long, not to mention having made the Comune go to the trouble and expense of removing it. We leave it where it is and replace it with a more sensible but almost as decrepit four-wheel-drive Fiat, found for us by Gianni the mechanic. At least, as he points out, you can get spare parts for that.

Two or three years later, the Morris is still sitting discreetly behind its screen of canes in the riverbed, along with its companion pieces. So far, no winter rains have produced a *torrente* torrential enough to dislodge it and carry it away to sea, the destiny the elected representatives of San Pietro presumably had in mind for it. We haven't given it much thought in all this time: now, though, we meet a bunch of New Age hippy Germans down in Diano Marina who are very excited about the wonderful old English car that's just lying in the riverbed near San Pietro. They want to tow it away and restore it. But being a law-abiding Germanic type of grunge person, they certainly wouldn't consider doing this without the owner's permission. We, they have spotted, are English – do we know whose it is? We admit shamefacedly that we do: it is ours. Now we are embarrassed all over again. These moral and eco-friendly youths are clearly horrified at our irresponsibility. Fancy going around carelessly throwing our old cars into other people's rivers!

Can they have it, then? they say, doing their best to keep the Green disapproval out of their voices. Of course, say we.

A couple of weeks later we are a little disturbed to see that they have unwittingly towed it back to its old home, the space between the bar and the mill. It is even more of an eyesore after its long and weedy sojourn in the riverbed. A month later, it is still there. Two months later, ditto. The youths have taken it from its resting-place in the river and then, it seems, decided it wasn't worth repairing and gone back to Germany. We are mortified. What must the Comune be thinking of us? Will they believe we didn't do this on purpose? Not unless – fingers crossed – someone spotted the German saboteurs, entirely unconnected with us, who perpetrated the awful deed.

It turns out, oddly, to be against the law to use a private car to tow another one in this otherwise carefree land, and we have to get our lorry-driving friends in to remove the Morris bodily. It makes its last journey, this time to a proper scrapyard, in style, poised elegantly on the back of Paletta's truck: and our souls are cleansed.

It may have taken San Pietro a while to catch up with the indestructibility of modern domestic materials, but once they have spotted the problem, they are very quick on the ball: at heart a deeply ecologically conscious people. In fact, river and mountain dumping made perfect sense until recently, well into the 1970s; pretty much all ordinary household stuff here was still perfectly throwable into rivers or burnable without causing any problem. An iron woodstove or bedstead was about the most un-biodegradable thing anyone was likely to own, and even that would rust away in the end, if not carried off by the *torrente* to add its dollop of harmless iron oxide to the Mediterranean deeps. Even when we first got here, shopping still came in brown paper bags or bits of newspaper, and carriers were rare and precious; while basketwork containers were more common than plastic crates and packs. Glass, of course, still isn't something to be lightly thrown away – you need all the bottles and jars you can get for the wine and the oil and the preserves.

Local eco-consciousness isn't really too surprising: after all, it's hard to find anyone in this country, even among those born and bred in the big cities, who doesn't still have family in the countryside, their own *campagna* somewhere or other supplying them with home-grown victuals – making pollution and degradation of the land much more personal matters than we landless British can imagine. Messing up the ecosystem may have an immediate practical effect on your oil and wine and whatever else you'll be getting from the country cousins this year to fill your larder.

This connection to the land has also saved Italians from the more awful excesses of mass-produced food manufacturing. Could the British sausage ever have been degraded and perverted to the meatless ground-up-gristle-and-fat state we are familiar with if everyone had had relatives in the country who occasionally sent them a pound of the real home-made thing? I think not. Could tomato producers have fobbed us off with things that may look remarkably like tomatoes but are virtually taste free? No. You need a good century of no access to the original item to reduce consumers to the sorry state of ignorance that will induce them to accept such stuff. Here, where everyone has the home-made original to compare it with, even the factory-made food is a hundred times better than our own.

Not long after the removal of the Morris to its last resting place, the Comune of San Pietro will officially recognize the fact that modern rubbish is no longer biodegradable, and the river will be cleansed, its bed cleared out with the help of a pair of large bulldozers, and clumps of flowering mimosa trees and Mediterranean pines will be planted to screen it from view. It will, necessarily, always be a bit of a weed-filled eyesore: it has to be left immensely wide to cope with the freak storms which every few years send millions of gallons of rainwater hurtling down from the hills in a matter of hours, carrying with it tons of collapsed terrace walling, along with the odd uprooted tree and whole oceans of mud and rocks – stuff that would inundate the lower-lying parts of the village if the riverbed was to be narrowed.

Now, years before any such thing is seen in England, a row of those bell-shaped green plastic recycling-domes will appear by the river where once our Morris languished: one for glass, one for paper, one for tin cans, and even one each for used batteries and medical supplies. The smoking horror at the top of the ridge will still be there for a while yet, though its worst excesses will soon be curbed. We're not too bothered by it for now – it is a useful landmark in these labyrinthine hills, a great help when we go on our foolish getting-lost-in-the-hills walking extravaganzas, and for first-time guests trying to find our house. Head for the ridge with the column of smoke coming from it: find the fire and you're almost home. Our path leads off the next hairpin bend to the right.

Franco's lime now lives in our earth closet, in one of Pompeo's galvanized buckets along with a big wooden ladle; you sprinkle it on dry, a heaped ladleful per visit, and it turns out to keep stinks at bay most impressively. Although we'd infinitely prefer a proper non-worrying water closet, it's nothing like as bad as we'd expected; and it does seem to be true that the level in the closet remains constant – maybe we'll really never have to dig another one?

Recently, official confirmation of the role of lime in local hygiene has removed our last doubts in the matter. Sitting one afternoon at the level-crossing in a great crowd of bodies and bikes, waiting with brother Rob for the Trans-Europe Express to pass by and let us back out of Diano Marina, we find, once the usual big blur of thundering train has whizzed past, that the gates remain closed. What are we waiting for now? Craning along the line, we eventually see what appears to be a Fiat 600 heading very slowly along the tracks towards us. As it draws nearer, we see that it really is a Fiat 600, one mounted on a set of train wheels. Not just someone who's lost their way, then. Its bodywork has been cut right off at the back end, and while one man in an official-looking cap drives, another stands, knotted hanky on head, shovelling white powder from a sack at his feet into a large sieve contraption protruding from the rear of the conveyance, whence it trickles gently, sprinkling the track behind. We look quizzically at our nearest companions in the crowd waiting to get across the rails.

Calce, says someone. Lime, to neutralize the danger of germs and pong from all those flying Trans-European toilets, which flush their cargoes straight on to the line as they pass through town. Ugh. Can this be true? Will it work?

Robert says it will. In the early days of our Great British Parliament, he tells us, when the River Thames was still an open sewer, the ceiling-high curtains of Westminster would be dipped in lime during the summer months to keep at bay the pollution and sickness rising from the noxious horrors which in those far-off days floated about in the waters below. Ugh again.

In view of all this pedigree, and the fact that there's still lots of Franco's sackful left, we decide to investigate its advertised paint-and-filler-type properties next. Over the months we have concluded that, beautiful though our drystone walls may be, for the inside of a house they are too uncleanable: not only does earth-dust trickle faintly from them but there are just too many cracks and crevices inside the house for Things to nest in. If what we've been told of its virtues is true, lime should solve all this in one go. Brother Robert doesn't believe a word of it: we should get some proper civilized Polyfilla and do the job well, if it's worth doing. Fine plan;

but as yet no one's felt the need for such stuff in this country, where the concept of DIY is still unknown. Everyone does things themselves – of course they do, this is a land of renaissance men, of peasants who can turn their hand to anything – but they don't expect special make-it-easy products for the non-professional. In fact, I'm not sure they know they aren't professionals. It will be a good ten years before we hear talk of DIY – or '*Fai-da-te*' – round here, before handyperson products appear in the hardware shops. For now, we have the local classics to choose from: cement mortar, limewash, or a strange crumbly white plaster called French stucco. Lime it is then.

Down in San Peo one-eyed Mariuccia, renaissance woman, shows us the right kind of glue to mix our lime with, something that's sold by the kilo, and insists that we buy an enormous and absurd-looking paintbrush, more like a soft broom with its handle cut short. We goggle at this ridiculous item which must have been made by those backward mountain folk, but buy it anyway, as well as a pair of normal English-style paintbrushes, so as not to hurt her feelings. Naturally her brush turns out to be the essential tool for applying the thick-yet-sloppy gloop we've mixed up in a bucket following her instructions. Gloop which, as predicted by Franco, really does fill and paint at the same time when applied with the right implement. The proper big flappy brush drops a great load of the stuff on to the wall at once, a pint at a go, which gets sucked into the crevices by itself as you swirl your square-foot of soft bristles about, sending myriads of unattractive creatures scuttling for cover, smoothing out the lumpy, irregular stones and filling the earthy gashes and spider-holes between them so thoroughly that the walls look almost plastered. With the more normal-looking brushes you can't pick up anything like enough of the lime. It would take you the rest of your life to finish the job. We discard the useless things in disgust after a frustrating five minutes, and now have to go all the way back down to the village to buy another pair of truncated-broom things. By the end of the day our upstairs kitchen/living room is magically transformed. Pure white and no more creepy things. Wonderful. Perfect. If only Franco was here we would hug him. How could we have doubted his wisdom, or his lime?

*

The Diano boys, like Mariuccia, also find the presence of a male in our household most comforting. In fact, they have developed an annoying tendency to address all their remarks to our brother Rob, even though he can't understand what they're saying since he doesn't speak more than two words of Italian, and we sisters have to translate it all anyway. Now, they tell us to tell him, as if it was all nothing to do with us, is the time to get on with concreting our downstairs floor, damp-proofing it as we go, and building the partition walls to create our bathroom and our two bedrooms below. Now that sweltering high summer weather is here, we have discovered that it is a good ten degrees cooler down there at night, half-built into the earth as it was by the great foresight of Pompeo's forebears, and we've moved our beds down here well away from the oven-like upstairs, which we have kindly left to the brother. Who, having as little training in such matters as he does in the language, will doubtless never guess at the superior sleeping conditions below stairs from which he is excluded. Least said . . .

Still, as everyone points out, we can't go on sleeping down there with nothing but a dirty old earthen floor. So Ciccio, Paletta, and Mimmo the master-builder sweep Rob off in a wave of manly lorry-driving camaraderie which knows no linguistic barriers, while we move our beds out under the roofed-over bit of the patio, and hang our mosquito nets for protection. Sunday morning, and a wave of wild activity begins. Wheelbarrows of gravel, sacks of cement, hillocks of sand sprout all around our home, while more and more boys and young men whose faces we only vaguely know, protégés, it appears, of Ciccio, Paletta and Mimmo, appear and heave everything along our winding path. They mix and shout all afternoon to the accompaniment of a large ghetto blaster which roars out football commentaries hour after hour. Nobody wants paying: they all, apparently, meet up anyway on a Sunday to listen to the football – there being a countrywide ban on live TV transmission of Sunday matches, aimed at keeping stadium attendances up – and they may as well have something to do while they listen, they say. Our house and lands are the ideal Sunday afternoon spot, plenty of room for everyone and no parents around to complain about noise and chaos. Of course: we'd forgotten that they all had to live at home till they got married. As the concrete goes down and we start getting to know our crowd of helpful youths, it is borne in upon us that Iron John is alive and well and living in Liguria. No shortage of role models for young males here. Paletta, Mimmo and Ciccio each have their own band of youthful followers. Paletta's collection is the largest: he was a footballing hero in his early twenties, played for the Imperia team in regional matches until he ruined a knee, and is still famous throughout the province for a string of spectacular match-saving goals. We are pleased to see that, although football may win for charisma, serious building skills (Mimmo), and cooking and jazz (Ciccio, my favourite) also attract their fair share of aficionados. Rob has attached himself to the cooking and music department, gyrating and shovelling with the foodies' gang. Perhaps there is hope for his cuisine yet.

The famous damp-proof course turns out, disturbingly, to be nothing but a giant sheet of that plastic that is also used for May Day shelters; it is simply laid on the original floor and has gallons of concrete thrown on top of it. Seems much too simple. Can this be a proper, official building technique? It takes Rob, whom we suspect of being in love with his new friends and prepared to lie and cheat on their behalf, some time to convince us that this really is what a damp-proofing course means. Even in England.

No one expects us females to do anything – not even make tea and coffee, since of course more than one coffee in an afternoon will make you *nervoso* and stop you sleeping at night, while tea is a drink for intellectuals and eccentrics. Although we are rather pleased to have nothing to do in this summer heat but lounge about, we have been brought up in feminist times and feel rather ashamed of not participating.

Eventually we go off round the back of the house to where the hammock now lives, well away from the shouting radio and the alternating roars of delight and groans of despair from our workforce, to hide our guilt and our paperbacks from view. Most satisfactory. Even our own brother, who would normally be complaining loudly about sloth and women wanting to have it all ways round, has been overcome by an attack of Italianness, laid aside his feminist (or is it anti-feminist?) training, and is keeping his mouth firmly shut.

Better still, when suppertime comes, no one trusts us to make a decent plate of pasta either. Ciccio and his cohorts, all in joyous mood because Juve has won, do that too, using a good six packets of spaghetti. The football experience has been so overwhelming that nobody seems to have noticed having done a hard afternoon's physical labour at all. While the others clatter about with saucepans, Paletta settles down to show us the amulet which, he claims, is largely responsible for Juve's great series of goals this match: it is a Mother of Vinegar, he says, handing us a shrivelled ring of leathery woody stuff, something like a very sturdy pencil sharpening, which he unthreads from the gold chain round his neck. He dried it out himself in the sun; a very delicate operation.

But what on earth is a Mother of Vinegar? It is a kind of rootless wine-eating fungus, circular and seaweed-like, six inches across in hydrated life; you pour all your lees of wine, leftovers, stuff that has gone sour, dregs from the bottom of bottles, anything, into the container in which you keep this monster, and it transforms them into a particularly tasty type of vinegar. If you are very lucky, it will reproduce; once it has made a baby, you can carefully remove the adult from its bottle and dry it out. Worn round the neck it will not only bring you good fortune, as demonstrated by this afternoon's football result, but will protect you from the Evil Eye into the bargain. Don't we have them in England? How do we make our vinegar, then?

Lucy and I are kindly allowed to make the tomato and basil salad, and do our best not to be offended by being complimented on how like a proper tomato and basil salad it is. Meanwhile our multi-talented builders, shouting, bouncing, chopping and frying, adding a bit of white wine here and some garlic and *peperoncini* there, transform our odds and ends, a small chunk of smoked bacon, a tin of peas, a couple of onions, and a tube of tomato paste, into a dish that makes the tastebuds leap. A Sicilian winter dish, they say. Fine in summer to us. Mmmmm! says Rob as he ladles his first forkful into his mouth; and is mystified when we all roar with laughter.

After dinner we go to inspect the works: our downstairs floor is smooth as a ballroom, tidy and level and with no insect potential whatsoever. We bless those wise footballing authorities who so thoughtfully keep strong young men's Sundays free with their no-TV rule. A tradition has been born. From now on we will save all heavy tasks, leave all heavy objects hopefully at the end of the path, for the Sunday afternoon football gang. They will be back in a couple of weeks, when the cement has cured, to put up the brick partition for us, says Mimmo.

Great, I say, thank you very much . . . And, says Ciccio, would we mind if he cooked everyone a fish dinner outside, *alla brace*, if they've caught a decent amount of fish that week? Maybe some mussels *alla marinara* to start, then for the *primo piatto*, *spaghetti al nero di seppie*, black with squid-ink . . . a few grilled fish . . . or maybe roasted under sea-salt . . . ?

Why not? I say, inwardly gloating. Wonderful, yes.

Then, says Paletta, when next they have some free time they ought to start helping us sort out the upstairs – get rid of these horrible old terracotta tiles and put in some nice modern kitchen units instead of that scruffy old marble sink. Concrete over the patio cobbles too, maybe, to stop all that messy grass growing up between them . . .

Lucy goes cross-eyed with horror.

Maybe, say I, noncommittally.

Great though the improvements to our home may be, the same cannot be said of Diano Marina beach, these days transformed into a kind of maritime parking lot, deckchairs in serried ranks covering every square inch of sand, a folded sun umbrella sprouting at the side of each one. Some of the umbrellas have large brown luggage labels tied to them. This, Caterina explains, means that they have already been booked by the week. Or even, maybe, the month. Agh!

So isn't there anywhere you can just sit on the sand and do what you like any more? Yes: a handkerchief-sized square halfway along; this is, it seems, the only public beach. We resolve to start a hunt for small secret coves immediately. Easy, says Caterina, just go along the *Incompiuta*: the new, flat coast road to Imperia, started forty years ago and still unfinished. It is a standing joke round here;

as you can tell by its nickname. The *Unfinished Symphony*, too, is called the '*Incompiuta*' in Italian.

We have in fact noticed the existence of this almost-road, at the bottom of a dead-end off a side-road at the far end of the bay, and wondered where it led to. Huge rusty iron gates have been put up by the Comune to prevent access to it. Ten foot enamelled notices in four languages tell you that entry is forbidden, and warn you that rocks will fall on your head if you pass the gates; and moreover that the Comune will accept no responsibility whatsoever if they do. Indeed, you can see through the gates that what appears once to have been a roadway is now strewn with huge boulders, some of which, on the tarmac sections, have sunk right through the asphalt and are beginning to sprout small rock-gardens – positively post-holocaust. Strange to discover that it has never actually been a road at all. Anyway, it hasn't entered our heads to try going along it. We have not yet learnt the machiavellian thought processes required to decipher notices from Italian town halls. Of course, our friends explain, the Comune only disclaims responsibility for insurance purposes: it knows perfectly well that everyone will use the road anyway.

Citizens of Diano have to go regularly to Imperia for work, for shopping, for matters medical and bureaucratic. It is the regional capital of our province, a real small city with a commercial shipping port and olive oil and pasta factories, as well as the region's main hospital, all the official buildings, land registers, and suchlike. It also has two market days a week instead of one, and even a genuine supermarket – only one in the province so far – with air-conditioning and shining metal trolleys. But the only drivable road to Imperia from here is a steep and wildly curving corniche, always blocked by some slow-moving vehicle or other; an Ape on its way to market, a lumbering tourist coach; and is made terrifying by the hair-raising attempts of drivers in a hurry to overtake these obstacles on blind bends. Three miles of traffic jams, wracked nerves and danger when down below there lies a flat, wide, safe mile and a half, unfinished.

Taking a closer look, we realize that this pseudo-ruin, or folly perhaps, is regularly used as a foot and bicycle path; ten minutes to Imperia instead of a likely half-hour by bus or car. The resourceful citizens of Diano have added to the gates, in one not-very-hidden corner behind a trailing clump of old man's beard, a few extra wired-on horizontal bars here, removed a spike there, and *ecco!*, a fine little ladder to elegantly overcome the annoying municipal obstacle: a ladder so well-used that its footholds positively gleam, silvery and rust-free. As we arrive, a pair of bicycles are being lifted over the top by a perfectly respectable looking middle-aged couple. The Comuni at both ends, having put up their ten foot official disclaimers, are happy to turn a blind eye to all this lawless behaviour, and the cycling couple tell us that the people of Imperia have done something similar to the gates at their end so you can get out.

As you walk along this pleasantly traffic-free coast path on the way to a peaceful swim, marvelling at the house-sized rocks that have occasionally fallen from above and sit deeply embedded in its surface at unlikely angles, you cannot help but notice that every one of the false starts has been made with seriously sub-standard materials and equipment. Bribery and corruption, we gather, with contractors and sub-contractors skimming off extra bits of profit at every level of the enterprise, have led to this state of affairs. Great broom-bushes, grass and weeds have burst right through the too-thinly-asphalted bits; the concrete bulwarks supposed to keep the hillside above in check are riddled with great cracks here, or crumbling to dust there, depending on whether the builders were trying to make savings on the metal reinforcing rods or on the cement to sand ratio. An iron handrail on the cliff side, presumably intended by the architects to stop pedestrians hurtling down a couple of hundred feet to their deaths on the rocks below, has mostly either rusted away or come entirely adrift from its moorings as the concrete in which it was once embedded has fallen away into the roaring sea. The miserable remnants of bent, rusty tubing rattle, dangle and squeak in the coast breeze.

What was once going to be the pedestrian footpath by the side of the road is bedecked with specimens of a very entertaining plant with fleshy seed pods that fly off spectacularly with a loud pop at the merest touch, bursting and landing several feet away. Hours of fun. The beaches, we discover, are rocky, and delightfully deckchair- and pay-desk-free coves way down below the road, inaccessible except by clambering down the deep and echoing shafts which once were going to be storm drains. The ingenious local beach users have overcome this one too, no problem. They have shoved makeshift wooden walkways of left-behind builders' shuttering down them, and bob's your uncle. A lovely peaceful swim.

15

We have fraternized with the enemy. Anna and Tonino, the new owners of the vineyard that should be Domenico's, have popped up to introduce themselves: we have been down to admire their Adjustment to its *rustico*. They have added an extraordinary flying roof of corrugated-iron sheets, fixed to cemented-in scaffolding. Immensely cunning, explains Tonino, a man with a powerful Roman emperor-style nose and bushy curls that make his hanky sit oddly high on his head. This way, you don't need to bother with the Comune and planning permission and all that nonsense. Luckily for us, enough olive trees grow between us and this newly towering structure to prevent its figuring in our view as more than a faint blur through the greenery.

They have heard, they say, that we have planted some strange foreign herb up here; a herb that sells for astronomical amounts in Switzerland, where it is used to make an incredibly expensive perfume. Can they have a look at it?

Magari, say we.

Evidently, at the hands of the San Peo gossip machine, Pompeo's speculations about our plans for his land have burgeoned into towering fantasy. The information we have about the so-called Sicilians isn't a lot more accurate. They have moved here, in fact, from Alassio, ten miles down the coast. The best they can do for us is a Sicilian grandparent. Oh, and they own a couple of hectares of woodland down there, supposedly, though they don't think they'll ever get to see it. Sicily's a long way away, and everyone of the grandparents' generation, anyone who might have been able to pinpoint exactly which bit of forest it was, will be long dead by now.

Upon reflection, we decide not to mention this new friendship to Domenico, who is already having some trouble getting over our wanton transformation of the downstairs space, which any right-thinking Ligurian would use for a *cantina*, into a pair of bedrooms and a bathroom. Our constant messing about Adjusting the house instead of Getting On is absurd: and this last bit of messing is not only foolish but counter-productive. Where do we think we're going to keep our year's supplies of everything? At the very least, even if we decide wastefully to buy everything else in shops, like so many of the thriftless Youth of Today, we'll still need to keep our wine and our olive oil somewhere, won't we? Or are we never going to get ourselves organized at all? And what about our olive nets, brushcutters, wine press, the chainsaw for our pruning and winter firewood? Have we thought about that? he asks us. No, we haven't! he answers on our behalf.

We are much less sure than Domenico, truth to tell, that it is one of our life's major objectives to get our groves and *orto* in full working order within the year: this, he kindly explains to us, is because we are still young and *inconsciente* – unconscious. You must look to the future! he keeps telling us, as if a Europe-wide famine was likely to break out at any moment, in which all who do not have their subsistence farming systems efficiently in place will perish miserably. Youth and unconsciousness also explain our wasteful predilection for spending time at beaches, rock pools and bars now that July is here and the heat building up. All is not lost, anyway: the thing to do, he decides, to ensure that we haven't entirely burnt our bridges by the time we achieve the full use of our wits, is to put a good stout door on to our ancient stone igloo down on the well-path. We can use that as a *cantina* instead.

We have, we are beginning to see, been adopted: America may have taken his daughter, Holland his son, but we are the living proof that staying in San Pietro really is best. Or we will be, if he can just get us organized. He's got himself something back out of the senseless chaos, the random gyration which is the modern world, at least. We, in return, have got ourselves a guardian angel. Domenico has begun to creep up on us gradually, over the months, edging inexorably towards takeover. At non-rubbish-collecting moments he is always up here on his land, beavering away with the tools and equipment of the season, tut-tutting and tugging his moustache desperately at the sight of us doing everything all wrong. He can't resist overseeing our efforts to get the *orto* going. Seeds must only be sown when the horns of the moon are pointing to the left, never to the right: the waning not the waxing moon. Our attempt at building a cane frame like his for our runner beans mysteriously transforms itself overnight into a new and infinitely more stable structure: it would never have withstood a full-strength *temporale*, he explains, so he has dismantled it and put it back up again for us. We get lessons in where to plant what, and why. Which bits of what plant to pinch out to get more crop. How to water zucchini: you flip the water horizontally out of your bucket, so it all goes under the forest of umbrella leaves without touching them. If droplets get on to the surface of the leaves, they act as magnifying glasses for the sun's rays and your plant will be scorched.

Spotting us up our trees with a handsaw, doing our best to prune, Domenico stands around looking anxious for a while until he can bear it no longer and sends us packing. A good dozen trees sorted in no time at all. Now he shows us how you use a machete to strip off the twiggy and leafy bits from the branches you've cut down. You have to burn them straight away, even in this heat, or some horrible maggoty creature which lies dormant in the young living wood will be activated as the prunings dry out, pupate and turn into a *farfalla* – a butterfly / moth – and lay millions of eggs that will infest the tree and ruin all the year's olives. The bigger wood now gets sawn up into neat logs for the winter stove. Our wood-piling technique is hopeless, so we get a quick lesson in that.

By August our vegetable garden, supervised closely by Domenico, is looking pretty impressive, and is also saving us no end of trekking back and forth carrying heavy shopping along our squiggly path. A good thing too, says Domenico. You don't want to go eating vegetables from shops. They are all smothered in *roba chimica* – chemical stuff – and may quite possibly be even worse for the health than wine not made of grapes. Domenico, rather than use pesticides, spends hours picking off by hand any insects that threaten his vegetables. Those too large to be lightly crushed between the fingertips go into an old tin mug with a small quantity of diesel fuel in the bottom of it. You don't set it on fire, he explains when we look alarmed; the stuff blocks up their air-holes and they die anyway. You can kill thousands and thousands of beetles with one cupful. But, he points out, he only goes to all this trouble for his own family; even he, if he was growing stuff for sale to *sconosciuti*, persons unknown, would use pesticides. We gather that even Signor Ugo-the-grocer himself, most of whose stuff is labelled *nostralino*, home-grown, is not above suspicion in this matter.

Aubergines turn out to have fat round purple flowers like stout drooping-headed mini-sunflowers, very fetching. They and the red peppers are coming along nicely. Amazing to find them just growing out of the earth on ordinary normal plants. Everything here grows at an amazing rate – every three or four days another foot or so of tomato plant needs to be tied back against its six-foot cane support. That granny of ours, who has fought a life-long battle under the grey skies of Scotland with troublesome tomato plants which, up there, have to be all wrapped up in greenhouses for protection, would faint for joy.

Fresh-off-the-plant snacks whenever you feel like it, just a potter down to the well; a delicious kind of baby marrow called *trombette*, little trumpets – long curly things, pale green outside, creamy and firm-fleshed within, no tendency to wateriness like the dark-green shiny things you get in England; tomato salads with basil, to which we are now heavily addicted, several times a day if required; lots of lovely green leafy stuff, mouth-watering rocket and spinach and *bietole* as well as lettuces green and red, and a square yard each of rampaging basil and flat-leafed parsley – no fear of slugs and snails in this dry climate.

And thanks to all those insistently ripening eat-me-now-or-I'll-rot vegetables we have at last understood what it is about the olive that has made it such a symbol of peace and plenty for the last couple of thousand years. The olive is magic: if you have olive oil, which we do – even though ours is for the moment bought at Ugo's and may very well be full of only the Lord knows what – you can transform virtually calorie-free greenery into nutrition-packed sustenance. Not that we ourselves need more calories at the moment. In fact, we're rather trying to lay off the olive oil. But we see how useful the principle of the thing is if, like most of the humans in the world today and throughout history, you are actually short of the calories you need to stay alive.

During the war, Domenico says, when food shortages were bad, you could live off just your *orto* – or, once you'd stripped that bare, wild greens from the hills – stuff that wouldn't keep body and soul together for any length of time at all, as long as you had your olive oil to boost it up (and as long as you had your old granny who still remembered which stuff to gather). With a good dose of olive oil and a few wild garlic heads you could transform borage, fennel, the sprouting tips of old man's beard, tiny wild broccoli or asparagus, into fine stomach-filling nutrition-packed dinners. Not, of course, that it wasn't a lot better when you could come by a spoonful of flour, an egg or two, and abandon your mashed-up *poltiglia* of greenery and oil for something classier, a *primo piatto* of borage fritters maybe – or fritters made of the flowering heads of wild garlic, even better – and a *secondo* of delicate old-man's-beard-tip *frittata*. (Inspired, we will try out both these recipes – wild garlic-flower *frisceüi* and old-man's-beard-tip omelette; both so good that we have to tell Ciccio about them. Traditional Ligurian *frisceüi* of garlic flowers are soon featuring among the antipasti up at the Moltedo restaurant. Much to the annoyance of Ciccio's mother, Francesca, who insists that there is nothing especially Ligurian about them except the silly name. She must have eaten tons of the things in her childhood in Calabria, she says.)

Of course, we ourselves haven't sunk to a state of famine yet, and probably never will, despite Domenico's anxieties. Our only problem is that we're too lazy to bother going all the way down to the shop. So, go down to the *orto* instead to see what it dictates for lunch: return with some tomatoes, a fistful of basil, a few zucchini. Boring? But cut the zucchini in strips lengthways and stick them on your griddle; when they are a bit translucent and brown-stripy, chuck them in a bowl with some garlic and olive oil, and a crumpled thyme twig. Leave a few minutes for the flavours to mix. Mmmm, as we English so ludicrously say. Or, if you're after a few more calories, grate the zucchini up and add salt; wait twenty minutes while the salt draws out their liquid. Now beat in some flour; drop spoonfuls of this batter stuff into an inch or so of sizzling-hot olive oil, fish out mouth-watering golden crunchy fritters. Next *piatto*: chop the tomatoes up (chunks, not slices, naturally), add the basil, pinch of salt, olive oil, a quick whisk, and your tomato juices, drawn out by the salt, will emulsify with the oil to produce a thick voluptuous sauce into which you can dip yesterday's dry crusts, transforming them into a gourmet's delight. Even better with a mozzarella chopped up in it, of course.

The olive not only saves your life, it makes everything taste good, too. Pondering upon this pleasing fact as we munch – we have gone for the hi-cal *frisceüi*, with the excuse of heavy painting work downstairs this afternoon – we notice that we have dealt only with the Olive and Plenty. What about the Olive and Peace nexus? Is it just that well-nourished people with full stomachs are less inclined to go to war? Very likely, we decide. At the moment, for example, well-lined with olive oil, we are feeling positively overwhelmed by a certain pacific lassitude . . . Maybe we'll save the painting till tomorrow.

Our revived *orto* is improving our diet in more ways than one. After all this time, we have still not managed to get the hang of the Byzantine complexities of local opening hours, and a surprisingly large number of our trips to the village shops are fruitless. It appears to us – although the other inhabitants of San Pietro always have some glib explanation for his erratic behaviour – that Signor Ugo-the-grocer just opens and closes as the whim takes him. He doesn't always bother to open on a Tuesday morning, for example, because it's market day in Diano Marina. Meanwhile, he often closes early for lunch on a Friday because there is no bus that day. Once the summer season has started he doesn't open for the afternoon shift till four. Or perhaps four-thirty or five if it's very hot – unless, that is, he happens to have finished lunch early because his wife's away. In which case he'll shut early. Meaning that he's already shut by five some days, others is still standing chatting at his fly-curtained doorway, happy to serve you, at eight in the evening.

True, erratic hours are quite normal round here. Shops in Diano Marina also open and shut with no identifiable rhyme or reason. But it doesn't matter so much down there in the town – if one is closed, plenty of others will be open. Here, with only the one grocer, the one hardware shop, and the one butcher, unpredictability is all very well for people who live in the heart of the village and form part of its daily exchange network of news and gossip; it is enough to drive us mountain-dwelling folk twelve hairpin bends away to distraction.

Assuming we have managed, for example, to get into Signor Ugo's shop at all, our troubles are not over. First, wait while he finishes dealing with the customers ahead of you. This does not involve merely selling them things: as well as the general gossip and trying out the merchandise, there is the in-depth debate about exactly how they are planning to cook the items they are purchasing – the relative merits of adding white wine or tomato puree to a mushroom *sugo*, the putative effects on the digestion of either, and so on. You are welcome to join in, but the conversation switches in and out of thickest Ligurian.

Once it's your turn, you still face a barrage of exhausting social complexities. Sometimes Signor Ugo will meet you with a sunny smile and include you in the in-depth gossip in progress. You will be called, intimately, '*tu*'; enquiries will be made about your health, attitude to prevailing weather conditions and so on. You may, for example, be offered various exciting new foodstuffs to try; somebody's home-baked bread, somebody else's fresh eggs that are so good you must drink one raw – eek. You may be warned of imminent dangers in the area – shown, maybe, the signs that gypsies will have left on the wall by your front door to indicate to one another your level of handout-giving or robbery-worthiness (gypsies – mostly from Montenegro – occasionally take over from junkies in the local psyche as the most likely source of anarchy and chaos in the valley).

At your next visit to the shop, you will be called a formal '*lei*', as if you'd committed some unknown offence since Signor Ugo last saw you. Just to make matters more complicated, in calling us '*tu*', he may not even mean to be intimate: persons who are older than you, or superior in some other way, may call you '*tu*' and expect to be answered with a respectful '*lei*'. So if we call him '*tu*' in return, we may be offending him with unsolicited intimacy, an unwarranted assumption of equality: if we call him '*lei*', we may be rudely rejecting a friendly move. Unnerved by the whole business, we often find ourselves inadvertently doing a bit of each. It is a minefield, and we are relieved when Caterina, rather than laughing at us for being daft foreigners as we're expecting her to do, confesses that she can't make head or tail of Signor Ugo either. Her solution to the problem is to do long circumlocutions to avoid using the word 'you' at all. Cunning. We knew the locals must have a way round it.

You might think that a non-Ligurian-speaking customer could entertain herself during the unconscionably long waits by pottering round the shop inspecting the merchandise. Wrong. Almost nothing here is on open display; no sudden shopping inspiration can strike you the way it might in a street market or supermarket. When your turn finally comes you have to ask for each item by name, wait while Signor Ugo goes and gets it from some deep dark recess of his storeroom, and then start all over again asking for the next item. All this, mark you, whilst concentrating on avoiding any formulation involving that dangerous word 'you'.

Still, Signor Ugo is, indeed, superior: certainly not a person you would address lightly as 'tu'. He is a man of education, and in some years' time, when the educated begin to be proud of their dialects rather than shunning them, will translate not a few plays from the Italian into Ligurian, and they will be put on in the piazza by the *Nui autri* circle of local dialect supporters.

It is possible that in these early days the germ of Ligurian regional patriotism is already lurking in Signor Ugo's blood, and he is not pleased with foreigners hanging out in the hills and contributing to the decay of Ligurianicity in the village; it is also possible that he feels we should support our village shop more concertedly, instead of being lured away as we often are by the gaudy charms of Diano Marina's street market or the air-conditioned marble halls and silvery trolleys of the Imperia supermarket. Apart from getting your eggs in nice rigid boxes instead of rolled up in sheets of newspaper from which you know they will never make it back to the house whole, in either of these places you won't have to deal with persons of unnervingly unstable dispositions – or rather, you need never find anything out about their dispositions at all: most soothing to us mealy-mouthed English who just want to get on with it and get home. Also, the national tradition of in-depth discussion in public of exactly how you're planning to cook whatever you're buying comes in much more handy here, since the stallholders and super-market cashiers are by no means all Ligurians, and debate is carried on in the lingua franca, Italian.

Signor Ugo will eventually become Independent non-Communist Mayor of San Pietro – though the disillusion brought on by the collapse of the Communist Bloc will hardly touch San Pietro's old-timers. Much more of a commotion will be caused by the physical collapse of the economies of the East, and the appearance of surprisingly large numbers of its inhabitants in this valley, than by the political upheavals which have made them leave in the first place. In the nineties Signor Ugo's clients won't only be fearful of junkies and gypsies, but also of Albanians.

On the twelve hairpin bends between us and Signor Ugo's you will always meet at least two huge lorries and/or an assortment of bulldozers, tractors or related large and unwieldy vehicles, so that you spend about as much time going backwards very slowly to let these monsters past without slipping off the edge of the road, as going forwards towards your (probably pointless) goal. The building instinct of their forefathers who created the village in the first place still runs strong in the blood of today's San Peotti, and seven or eight centuries later everyone is still at it, adding and improving, knocking down and putting back up the other way round: though in these modern times, rather than reusing the rather inconvenient materials nature has placed at their disposal as they did in days of yore, they understandably go for lorryloads of bricks, sacks of cement, and heavy machinery. We may have only the one grocer in San Pietro, and the DIY chains may not quite have got here yet, but we do have our very own builders' yard, the poetically named Giardino dell'Edilizia – the Garden of Eden / stroke / Garden of Building. If, by some mischance, you meet no builders on your trip to Signor Ugo's, you will instead find yourself trapped in some major cow-moving manoeuvre by Franco or his *nipoti*, the Giacom-assi boys; or get stuck behind some infuriatingly slow Ape, its truck-section weighed down with assorted petrol-driven agricultural tools, dogs, and wrinkly old men who wave cheerily at you while sniggering beneath their hankies and venerable grey moustaches every time their friend or relation at the wheel (or perhaps handle-bar) manages, with a nifty weave and wobble, to thwart yet another of your attempts to overtake. Reason enough, you may conclude, to go along with Domenico, return to self-sufficient subsistence farming, and give up shopping for ever.

Adding to the immense strides civilization is making up our hill, we have got ourselves not only bottled gas but also a fridge that runs on it, which Helmut/Mario and his girlfriend Doris have found for us. (Doris is, apparently, a trendy and attractive name amongst the *Tedeschi*.) It comes from a camper-van belonging to some other Germans, which has been badly damaged and is being sold as scrap. We and all the Diano Company are amazed by this thing – how can it work on gas? And with just the one tiny pilot light-type flame? Actually, we have no idea how an electric fridge works either: the one is not really any more amazing than the other, truth to tell. Still, we go on gazing at the thing, sitting snugly under our marble sink like a visitor from another planet, and being amazed. Until now we have been rediscovering the pre-fridge diet, living on the salami we hang from our mouse-proof hooks, on tinned and potted things, keeping leftovers edible by pressing them down hard into jars or bowls to remove any air and covering them with a layer of olive oil – another handy hint from Mariuccia – to keep them from going off. Now that we have suddenly caught up with history, we can have any amount of fresh meat, we can store vast quantities of cooked ham, mayonnaise, fresh cheeses; we can even have cold drinks with ice cubes. And at last we can start making tea again, a habit we had to give up because it was so vile with UHT milk, while it was pointless buying the fresh stuff, which would turn to yoghurt or worse five minutes after you'd bought it.

The fridge is not all. Our intensive hillside course in Great Techno-logical Achievements of the Last Few Centuries and Why We Needed Them has led to our splashing out on a water tank, a huge kingfisher-blue plastic cylinder, purchased from – where else? – the

Builders' Eden. We have noticed in our well-water a hint of perfume, a slight tendency to froth up, and have at last made the connection between this and our habit of washing vast quantities of shampoo into the ground right next to its source. The outdoor shower must go. We bump into Franco as we are paying for the tank, and he airily announces, to the great annoyance of Mr B. Eden who is in the middle of booking us an expensive delivery by lorry, that he will bring it up for us, save us the money, since he has to pass our house anyway on the way to reroof his cowshed. Of such stuff, I say to my sister, are bad reputations made. Frank the Knife is Innocent!

The tank arrives early next morning, edging its way along our path under what appears to be its own lurid-blue steam: it is in fact roped to the back of a small minion of Franco's who is bent double under it, partly to avoid the hanging olive branches, but mostly because of its weight. A boy, we see as the tank draws closer, who can't be more than fourteen, and who (we soon discover) speaks hardly any Italian. Franco himself comes strolling along behind, waving a large and beautifully whittled stick, shouting instructions in pidgin Ligurian to his porter and prodding the occasional olive frond out of the way with the stick.

We and the long-suffering boy now struggle to get the thing up to its new home a couple of terraces above the house, Franco having disappeared back to his Ape to collect something he's forgotten. Or so he says.

As we heave and grunt our way up the hill under a blazing sun, we find out that Franco's helper is not a Ligurian from some distant dialect-only outpost, as we have assumed, but, of all things, a Moroccan. We have heard, amongst the general San Peotto criticisms of Franco, that he gets his maltreated workforce from far-off places where people know no better – but still, Morocco! How would an illiterate Ligurian peasant and horse-dealer go about getting hold of a teenage Moroccan? We ask Franco, who has reappeared down the path from his lorry with a small heavy object swathed in a sack under his arm: his answer is to lay his finger along the side of his nose and wink. The object he had forgotten turns out to be a water pump he no longer needs, and which he is generously proposing to sell to us. At a bargain price, of course. No wonder he was so keen to bring the tank up. We hum and ha a bit. Why don't we all go down to the well, says the high-pressure salesman, so he can demonstrate it to us? No. The well is nowhere near as full as it might be, it not having rained more than a few drops for two months; and we still need to buy the thirty yards or so of tubing to go between well and tank. We don't want to waste gallons of water by squirting them uselessly out on to the ground just to try out a pump that's practically bound to work, at least the first time, unless Franco's completely lost his touch. We know where to find him, anyway, if we have trouble with it, says Franco with his best blue-eyed look.

A pig in a poke. But we are secretly already resigned to our fate: we know we will buy the thing. It is boiling hot, has been for weeks, and doing anything at all is an unbearable effort. This pump is already here, saving all the trouble we'd have to go to to get one from anywhere else, driving to and fro in a sticky sweaty car and being sent, no doubt, from pillar to post into the bargain . . . done. It will turn out to be the most horrible troublesome erratic pump in the world. But we will gradually get used to its little foibles, among which is the fact that you have to risk your life by unscrewing its spark-plug and adding a dash of oil-and-petrol mixture down the hole to give its feeble starter-rope mechanism that extra bit of explosive *oomph*. It is still down there at the well to this day, though, pumping away loudly and smokily for fifteen minutes once a fortnight.

I go indoors to collect cooling refreshments from the new fridge – *Euh!* says Franco, how can a fridge work on gas? – to find that the tank has completely obliterated the lovely wild rock-garden which used to be our uphill view from the window above the sink. All those various textures and colours of green, those cushions and carpets of tiny tough leaves which grew so splendidly on our mini cliff-face – and incidentally caused me to realize why anyone ever wanted to grow a rock-garden, a thing which had always eluded me – are now under or behind the monstrosity.

Lucy comes and stands gloomily next to me. There is no getting away from it, though, we'd still rather have this nightmare in blue than all those trips to the well, all that putting-off of jobs because we can't be bothered going for the water. And now we can start on our downstairs bathroom plan, get Bruno up with his plumbing gear and have water without bucketing off down the hill for it. A tap over the kitchen sink, an indoor shower at last . . . no more fear of things with too many legs coming at you when you are at your most vulnerable, naked and wall-less. We'll get another bit of root from one of those great trailing morning glories, try to grow it up the tank to hide it – if we can protect it from passing strimmers this time. Madonna-blue trumpets of flowers, thick concealing leaves. San Pietro is festooned in them, they must like the soil round here. And apart from the aesthetics, it'll stop the water heating up in the sun every day and turning to bacteria soup. Please God make it grow quickly.

Sad to say, unlike the trusty pump, this tank will not last more than a few years. Going off back to England to earn some money a few winters on, we will find, when we return in the spring, that it has vanished completely. Or not, on closer inspection, completely; a small flat bright-blue pancake, about four feet across, lies miserably up on the terrace where the tank once loudly stood. Strangely, its black plastic lid has suffered no similar metamorphosis: it is lodged surreally in the upper branches of a nearby broom-bush, still in a pristine state. And the morning glory now straggles flatly over the terrace as if there had never been anything there for it to climb on. It has somehow regenerated after the forest fire which, our neighbour Nino tells us, passed close by the house just after we'd gone, reducing our poor water tank to this sad remnant. Nino owns the dozen or so terraces above and below our path, between our parking place on the bend and our own olive-belt around the house, and he is a very dry character. The fire nearly got his olives, too, he says – he and half the village were up all night trying to put it out. Our lid must have been fired right off the body of the tank and on to a flame-free zone by the pressure building up once the heat struck.

We are lucky, says Nino, that the fire started lower down the hill among the olives trees. If it had just been in the wild scrubland above the house, no one would have bothered to come up to fight it. Our home would very likely have gone up in flames. He says this, we think, in an odd manner, almost as if he felt we deserved this terrible fate. Some time later we will discover that we are right: this is exactly how he feels.

16

We creep along in our sturdy Fiat, over rut and gulley, rock and ravine, on a mission to check out the very top of our hair-raising mountain. The so-called road finally comes to an end in a wide shallow bowl of rolling meadowy downland, dotted with ponds and criss-crossed by streams. All plant-life down below in San Pietro has withered and dried in the fierce August sun; everything is yellow and brown and shrivelled around our house now too, except for the bits we manage to water. But up here it is fresh and green, the grass thick and luscious. It's wonderfully restful on the eyes, and makes me realize I haven't opened them fully for months. They've always been screwed up against the fierce sunlight.

The occasional cow, property, presumably, of Franco and *nipoti*, wanders about the place grazing, beautiful sad-eyed cream and beige buffalo-like creatures with long legs and huge bells round their necks; nothing like the square and stocky cows you see in England. Silhouetted against the top of the ridge are small groups of distant horses. We get out and climb the steep grassy slope right to the top, wander along the ridge trying to find the spot where our muletrack joins the one that would, according to Franco, eventually take us up over the high mountain passes to the crossroad towns – Pieve di Teco, Testico, Cosio d'Arroscia; towns that were great trading centres not so long ago, in the days when the coastal strip, now bloated by tourism, was nothing but a miserable collection of negligible hand-to-mouth fishing villages.

The trading towns are these days mostly reduced to ghost towns, though you can guess at their past glories from their massive, solid medieval architecture, their slate-paved thoroughfares; for centuries the staples of peasant life, the oil of the hills, the salt from the sea and the corn of the plains – all you need to keep a decent Italian body and soul together – met up here to be bartered. The pack mules from the olive groves would have trudged their way up these muletracks, main arteries of the region's trade, to meet others carrying goods from the grain basket to the North. I see those Ligurians of ancient times – coloured hankies, I think, in those days, and maybe the odd earring, but already known for dour penny-pinchers – trudging up this very path, their beasts weighed down with salt, olives and oil, muttering bitterly to one another about the lazy good-for-nothing plainsfolk whose journey will all be on the flat, and whose crops practically grow themselves. *How* many quintals of flour for a quintal of oil? You must be joking . . .

When you get to the peak you find a cairn with a cross built on to it that takes the hilltop up to exactly a thousand metres; inside it is one of those books you sign to show you've made it up here. We do. Below us the land flows on, valley after valley, hilltop town after hilltop town, in every direction. Inland we can just make out huge peaks still snow-capped; behind us an infinity of misty sea. I have never been remotely interested in mountaineering but suddenly I can see the attraction; right up here you get an incredible sensation of power and control. But why? There isn't anything *to* control. What do I imagine I'm controlling?

Farther on, another cairn; a rough stone monument to seven Partisans killed in this spot by the *Barbaria Nazifascista* during a *rastrellamento*. We don't know what a *rastrellamento* is. But the dead were all boys in their late teens and early twenties bar one, who was thirty-five. Their names are Ardissone, Alberti, Novara – good San Pietro names. Somebody still tends the memorial; as well as the aloes and geraniums planted around it there are some fresh-cut wildflowers in a jam jar. What a terrible place to be caught and killed, on this wide bare hillside, village and home so close down below, but no way out, nowhere to hide.

A great flock of goats is grazing down below; there must be a couple of hundred of them at least, ambling slowly uphill towards us. We've never heard Frank the Knife mention having goats. But up here we are well above the point where the head of the Faraldi meets our own Diano valley. They could be Faraldi goats. The sum total of our knowledge of the Faraldi valley, apart from its fine *feste*, are the distressing facts Pompeo has shared with us: too many oxen, not enough football pitches, too many Christians. For all we know, the place may be riddled with goats.

The altitude or something has gone to my head, and a strange inspiration comes to me when finally the herd's leaders are only a few yards away. I jump to my feet, lift my arms and give a great shout at the top of my lungs in their direction. The herd with one accord turns and streams back down the green hillside; rushes on and on, leaping the low remnants of terracing, disappearing behind curves in the terrain, reappearing again in the distance, still hurrying, until they are nothing but tiny dots far below us. Wonderful; an utterly pointless sensation of power. Control at last.

Heading back down, we spot a red lorry and an Ape pulling up near our car, where the road trickles to an end. Franco and his *nipoti* arriving to attend to their beasts. We wave and jump about. Franco calls us down, and we walk right into another of those surreal Ligurian experiences.

Franco is off to take supplies to his herdsman, Ardito, he says – do we want to come and see the horses? We do. Apart from anything else we think that if we were officially introduced to this fearsome person we would find him less scary. And he might stop leering at us in that awful way.

Franco tells us that scariness is one of Ardito's most important functions – potential cattle rustlers are kept at bay by their fear that he will give them the evil eye. Carlo tells us to take no notice of his uncle, who suffers from the delusions of old age; no one believes nonsense like that these days. Franco is incensed. Cattle thieves would come from the cut-off valleys of the hinterland, the wild inland side of the mountain, of whose primitive inhabitants his molly-coddled coastal nephews know nothing. The boys throw up their hands in despair and head off for their lorry and home.

We load ourselves into the back of Franco's Ape and head off downhill and cross country, over rock and meadow, towards the Faraldi valley and an extremely huge one of those ancient stone roundhouses – triple-sized at least – which turns out to be the herdsman's HQ. He is nowhere to be seen. Hard to believe that anyone really lives in this thing. It's a man-made cave, nothing more

– the huge stones just cantilevered inwards one above the other until they meet at the top, rather than being built on the arch principle. This primitive construction method means that its walls have to be absurdly thick; five feet at least at the bottom. The doorway is practically a tunnel. An upper floor has been made by embedding four treetrunks in the walls for beams and laying thick branches followed by thinner branches followed by twigs across them. Once upon a time the thing was stabilized with some kind of mud plaster; now it is so decrepit that you can see right through it in places. This is where Ardito sleeps, clambering up to the upper floor on a rough nailed-together tripod ladder.

One of those great demijohns of wine, with a siphon tube and tap leading from its cork, stands on the earth floor just inside the door, a mug and a couple of glasses on a cracked plate next to it. Ardito doesn't even seem to have a table. A few bits of clothing hang from two of those wooden pegs built into the wall for tethering beasts, next to a contraption of sticks for holding the horses' hay. Ardito's washing facilities are a bucket and a tin bowl balanced on an old orange-box outside the door. Nearby, built on to the side of the roundhouse, is a kind of smoke-encrusted cross between a shed and a stone oven, with a wood-store below. This must be where he does his cooking. A slab of stone juts from the wall just below the fire-shelf, and on this stands a coffee-encrusted espresso pot and a battered and smoke-blackened saucepan, alongside a greasy bottle plugged with paper – olive oil, at a guess – and a food-bespattered damp and crumbling box of salt. A string of garlic hangs from a nail jammed between the rocks.

Franco is very airy about these conditions – it's what Ardito's used to, he says, as if the man had designed and built the place himself. The horses don't need to come indoors anyway, not during the summer, unless they're sick or foaling.

So he's living in a stable, really? we say.

Euh! Ardito's fine up on his branches! Nice and warm! Franco himself has lived for months on end in places just like this, and it's done him no harm.

We sit down in the warm sun on the grass outside this stone-age dwelling and wait for its inhabitant to turn up. Franco goes over to his Ape, brings back a loaf and some tomatoes. We may as well eat while we're here, he says, collecting his employee's salt and olive oil and getting out his trusty knife. He does us a slice of bread each with a bit of tomato and a lot of salt and olive oil, then nips indoors to refill his wine bottle from Ardito's demijohn. I wonder if this theft too will be blamed on the phantom *drogati*.

A few swigs later, Franco is ready for therapy. He settles in to tell us the story of his father. Or rather, his lack of a father, who we now hear died when Franco was only eleven. The father, it seems, had a huge drunken fight with his best mate; something to do with shoeing horses. In the morning when he came to his senses, he discovered that he'd broken both his friend's legs. Realizing that he had devastated the friend's life, knowing that he would be ostracized by the rest of the village and would have to support this man's family into the bargain – I suppose in those days you would have been likely to be crippled for ever with two broken legs; no way you'd be able to carry on being a cowperson at any rate – Franco's dad went straight down to the bridge over the ravine at Moltedo, just below where Ciccio's restaurant now is, and threw himself off. Franco, sister Silvana and their mother had to get along by themselves from then on; he stopped bothering with whatever schooling there was in those days, stepped straight into his father's shoes, or rather saddle, and went off up the mountain to look after the beasts.

Before we can find out more, especially what it could be about horeshoes that might cause someone to break a friend's legs, Franco, grumbling, says he has to get back down to the village. He'll just have to wait till next week to see his employee. Rooting in the back of the Ape he pulls out another three loaves of bread, five bags of pasta, a box full of tomatoes and onions, two of Iole's cheeses and another dribbly bottle of olive oil. We realize that we've been tucking in to poor Ardito's week's supplies. Last of all, Franco extracts a neat six-pack of Danone chocolate mousses from the cab. Something Iole thought Ardito needed, he explains, and dumps it on top of the pile in the doorway, in which surroundings it sits looking like some particularly glaring anachronism, a terrible mistake by the continuity person.

Is Ardito really as happy up there as Franco claims? Not at all, is the answer, in spite of the chocolate mousses, as we soon find out.

Our friend Martin is staying with us at the moment. By now, the Morris having collapsed, we are on the ancient but four-wheel drive Fiat. Franco's means of transport are off the road for various reasons, he says, and he needs to collect Ardito from his parents' house, thirty-odd miles away up into the mountains. The road is terrible; there would be no point in his borrowing a normal car to go there. Maybe, he says, Martin would enjoy a trip inland, up into the hills? Would he, perhaps, agree to take Franco in the Fiat? I imagine that Ardito has been having a well-earned holiday with his family; though I'm a bit surprised at Franco being so generous as to go and give him a ride back.

What an odd person Franco is, I say to myself, the way he takes these unexpected shines to people. I'll have to drive, though, I say, the car's not insured for anyone else. Fine by Franco; it doesn't, apparently, have to be a men-only trip. As long as Martin is coming along too. Yes, he is, don't worry, I say indulgently. Next lunchtime we set off.

On and on out of known terrain we drive, until the hairpin bends are steeper and higher than the imagination can compass, the trees unfamiliarly tall and the valleys miles below sharp, narrow abysses, mist-filled depths where the sun hardly penetrates, the occasional villages all half-abandoned stone and wood and poverty, no paint, no colours at all except mud. Out into a high moorland place where the tarmac ends and a dishevelled hamlet, more than half its houses empty ruins, crouches miserably with its back to a grey cliff.

Now that we've arrived Franco reveals, with a rather half-hearted attempt at a casual laugh, that what has really happened is that Ardito has run off without saying a word, left Franco in the lurch, and we have come all this way to get him back, make him face up to his duties.

What do you mean? I say. He doesn't have to work for you if he doesn't want to, does he?

But yes, says Franco, he does. Franco has paid for a year of Ardito's work in advance; partly in money, mostly in cheese and wine and oil. Not to Ardito himself, of course, but to his family, who have in effect rented him out. And he has broken the contract, done a runner before the full year is up.

This is stuff you read about in history books, payment in kind and by the year. You know it's bad somehow but in a general sort of way. You also know that it stopped sometime round about the end of the Middle Ages. But you are wrong. I am outraged; I certainly wouldn't have brought Franco if I'd known what was going on. You can't force a poor halfwit to live in vile conditions in the middle of nowhere against his will! And as for paying someone else for his labour, as if he was a slave . . . !

Well, says Franco with spirit, he would just have come next week when his Ape was fixed anyway, if we hadn't brought him. But he is definitely looking a bit shifty and shamefaced; and why didn't he tell us what he was really up to until we'd got here if it is so normal?

Franco has timed our arrival for the dinner-hour to be sure of catching the family in, Finance Police style. They are sitting at table eating pasta with no sauce, just a smear of olive oil on it and (judging by the perfume) a lot of garlic. A wizened bit of cheese sits on a grater between the plates. We are in a small cramped kitchen with a smoky wood-stove in one corner, on which there is no sign of the usual *secondo piatto* bubbling away. Maybe the five dropping-smeared eggs sitting on the window ledge next to a bundle of parsley are it. In the corner is a bucket of water with a jug-shaped ladle sitting in it; no sink. The one outside the door surrounded by trampled mud must be all there is.

Ardito's family consists of an aged tiny mother and two brothers who look in their late fifties, both older than him, judging by their head-of-the-family behaviour towards him. Ardito seems to be the only one with serious learning difficulties. The house is tiny, with not so much as a coat of limewash on its inside walls. Earth dribbles out of the gaps between the stones, and the floor of this upstairs area – the beasts really do live in the downstairs – is cracked and lopsided, evidently made, like the floor in Franco's awful round-house, from mud-and-lime plastered over branches and twigs. Still, though Ardito's home may not be much, it's certainly better than that place. At least he gets a plate of hot food here and some company. No wonder he's done a runner from his awful job up our hill.

Ardito just sits there saying nothing, looking dejected and guilty; the brothers rage on at him in dialect, taking Franco's side; presumably they have already eaten and drunk the payment – or wouldn't have enough to last the year if they gave it back. I suppose Ardito is just another mouth to feed. He isn't up to much more than watching dumb beasts. So they've decided to swap a year's worth of him for extra supplies. Martin and I don't know what to do. Ardito really is no better than a slave, till his year runs out at any rate. They are all shouting at him; he seems to have lied to them, told them that Franco had sent him away. Or that's the impression they want to give Franco, at any rate. I hope that secretly they were sorry for him, weren't really going to send him back if Franco didn't turn up and make a fuss. But now, with the Boss in their kitchen, they are stony-faced, telling Ardito he has to go. Franco wants him up with the beasts, and Franco has paid.

Later on, back in San Pietro, which I now see is a place of great enlightenment and modernity, I find out from Luigi that this kind of contract is in fact illegal. If we'd known, we would certainly have refused to bring Ardito back. But this, of course, is why Franco particularly wanted us two to come. Nothing to do with bad roads and four-wheel drives, but because we were ignorant foreigners who knew no better. Worse still, I suspect he was afraid Ardito's family might put up some resistance, and wanted to create the impression of a posse prepared to use force if necessary. No one from San Pietro would have come, so Martin was the ideal candidate, being large and male and having absolutely no idea what was going on.

All this sheds new light on the disapproval which Franco inspires among the respectable olive folk of San Pietro; his links to the wild hinterlands really do connect him to an ancient, backward and shameful way of life, to miserable feudal exploitation. The rest of Italy has taken basic democratic rights to its bosom and left him behind, still working by another, ancient and horrible set of rules. An intensive course of *l'Unità* would do him a world of good. Or at the very least Tom Paine and *The Rights of Man*. But first, of course, he would have to learn to read.

17

Our blue plastic pancake of a water tank – all that remained after the forest fire – is to be replaced by one that Bruno has found us. A huge, and hopefully fireproof, second-hand zinc monstrosity, now resting on the back of Paletta and Ciccio's lorry. It is even bigger than the blue plastic one. We manage to get the thing off the lorry and on to the ground, just: but what next? With only the five of us, we can hardly lift the thing. Getting it along our complicated and squiggly path is out of the question without some large reinforcement of fit and muscular persons. It weighs a ton, being solid metal, and has no handles, just a few outlet points that might give someone with unusually powerful wrist muscles a grip on its smooth flat sides. Not only is the path narrow, no more than two people wide in places, but halfway along it are those few yards where there's a ten foot drop to your left and a high terrace wall to your right. Here the path is less than four foot wide; the tank must be five or six – and it is fifteen foot long. Where do the feet of the carriers go while it's getting past the nasty bit? And if we ever get it past the precipice, there is still a tight bend round the big modesty rock, and a long steep slope up two or three six foot terrace walls to the tank's spot above the house. We all stare hopelessly at it for a while; then go up and down the path a couple of times, reconnoitring in case inspiration strikes. It doesn't. Eventually we just leave the tank on the corner where it sits immovable, taking up most of the parking space and already looking as if it's been there for a century or two.

We are now very worried that Nino may come up to work on his trees while it's there. Where will he park his Ape? Nino has only recently given us a severe ticking-off for pinching a pile of flat stones that were half-hidden in the undergrowth by the side of his *rustico* to mud-proof our path with. There are so many stones lying about these hillsides that we didn't actually perceive these particular ones as private property. But they were, in fact, Nino's ex-roof stones, which he would, of course, have let us have, he said reprovingly: but we should have asked first.

Nino makes us feel like a pair of naughty schoolgirls. Help is urgently needed before we offend him again. He's already behaved in that odd and unsympathetic way around the dead-tank-in-the-forest-fire tragedy, and has made it clear that we are not his flavour of the month.

He's very unlikely to come at this time of year, say the boys, nothing to be done to olive trees in August. But we aren't so sure. Nino is a workaholic. Nino's trees, and the *fascie* beneath them, are like textbook illustrations. He never stops doing things to them; he does more things than everyone else put together.

Fortunately the football season has begun again, and soon a good fifteen Diano boys have been recruited for the tank-moving job. The road at the end of our path looks like a parking lot, cars squeezed in every gap between olive trees and broom-bushes for a hundred yards above and below our too-small parking place. Nino, thank goodness, has not shown up.

Heavings, shoutings, *Porca-Madonna*-ings, and general tumult begin. Just as the tank arrives at the precipice section of the path, amid much uproar, it slips, almost rolling off the path and taking half a dozen youths with it. This is all too much for us – if, by any chance, the tank escapes the hands of its carriers on this bit, it will roll down a good dozen terraces on to the track below, and quite possibly on down the rest of the hill to the river if it gets up enough momentum. Taking any amount of olive trees with it. At any rate, there's no way we'll ever get it back up here again. If it takes someone with it, it's hard to see how they'd survive.

We can't possibly go on watching: Lucy and I beat a strategic retreat to get the coffee and the radio ready for when the job's done. Espresso pot on, we track back along the upper terrace by our loo-shed to watch the progress from behind the broom-bush which these days, thanks to Cleaning deficiencies, surmounts our modesty-rock. The tank has made it past the drop, and is now edging round the bottom of our stone perch, surrounded by heaving, contorted bodies, uproar and altercation. It looks strangely like some wildlife documentary: a horde of ants dragging some juicy fat maggot back to their nest. But with unusually rowdy ants.

The tank comes to a halt before our bottom door. It still has to get up the last and steepest bit, past the house and on to the rock ledge on the second terrace above. Our chain gang is exhausted, drooping on the tank, wiping the sweat from its eyes: realization is dawning that the worst is not yet over.

It is during this thoughtful pause that Sergio and Lilli drop in unexpectedly. What are all the cars doing at the end of the path? Are we having a party?

The longer Sergio and Lilli stay up in their hillside residence, the odder their dress sense seems to be getting. Lilli is at the moment wearing carpet slippers and a torn sprigged housedress with frills at the shoulders. Her eye make-up has slipped rather badly, and her hair is looped up in the most bizarrely haphazard manner, pinned vaguely in place with a huge diamante Spanish comb. Sergio has on a black T-shirt advertising a heavy-metal band, over what appear to be a pair of ladies' floral-print shorts, beige knee-socks, and brown plastic slip-on sandals. Neither of them, moreover, seems to be entirely sober. The youth of Diano Marina, who have not so far met our eccentric neighbours, are startled. This is probably exactly the sort of thing they expect to happen to people who ignore the rules history has laid down for our guidance, and go around not living in villages.

But Sergio, wild-eyed and wild-haired though he may be today, has the habit of command; and he is highly stimulated by the sight of the job in hand, not to mention the large number of young men he will be able to order about if he can manage to assert control of the operation. He is, after all, senior both by virtue of his years and of his Mountain Skills. (His house, by the way, is now finished: he gave up on the plan of 'building with his own hands out of natural stone' after a year or two, and has simply balanced a gigantic prefabricated wooden Swiss-chalet type structure on top of the original one-storey stone building, which has now become a *cantina* – as indeed many Ligurians might feel it should.)

Sergio identifies Ciccio and Paletta as the operation's leaders, and draws them aside for Important Men's consultations about the next move. A block and tackle, says Sergio: we could fix it round one of the oak trees above the house and heave, so that not all the weight would be on the boys, who will have trouble enough just finding a firm footing on the steep slope. And Sergio, as it happens, has a block and tackle up at his Swiss chalet cum chicken farm. His takeover bid has succeeded. The youths are ordered to take a rest and get their breath back while the elders organize. Fortunately we have a case of cans of Nastro Azzurro to hand: we dole out the beer. Lilli, meanwhile, vanishes indoors. She needs no help to find the wine supplies. Our leaders, all three, go off to get the equipment. But they are not reckoning on the power of marital rivalry.

As the last sips of beer go down, Lilli, in fine fettle after a few quick swigs at her glass, leaps to her feet, loops of hair sticking out at all angles, panda eyes blazing with husband-upstaging fire.

We can do it alone! she cries. We'll have it done before they get back! *Forza, ragazzi!* Come on, boys!

For a tricky moment, it looks as if the boys aren't going to accept orders from a lunatic. A female lunatic at that. But Lilli makes as if to put her own shoulder to the tank, and it's more than they can resist. Nutter or not, she's got their competitive juices flowing. They are back on the job in no time. With Lilli at their head, slippers slipping, arms flying, shouting wild exhortations – *Uno, due, tre, forza! Uno, due, tre, avanti!* The tank starts to edge its way up the stepping stones, across the steep slippery hill.

Lilli is on her last triumphant '*Andiamo, forza ragazzi!*' and the monstrous tank is just settling into its home on the uppermost terrace when Sergio, Paletta and Ciccio arrive with the block and tackle. Lilli is triumphant; Sergio crestfallen. She has made a fool of him. We suspect that Lilli's life is for some time to come not going to be too easy. And yes, Sergio suddenly notices that her eye make-up could do with some attention, and starts to throw a string of insults at her. He is hardly checked by the appalled looks our assistants are giving him. A man insulting his wife in public! And a man of that age! Lilli, though, takes no notice: she is on a roll, buzzing with her momentary ascendancy. With great dignity and a rock-steady hand, she pours herself another glass of wine and raises it to toast her accomplices.

*

The German Army was in occupation. Domenico was only fourteen. And already small for his age even then, he says. But for once his size had worked in his favour. The organizer of the Partisan raid in the offing, a certain Pompeo, had chosen him for an important mission: he was the only one who looked young and harmless enough to stand a chance of getting away with it. Domenico was handed a watch, a rare and precious object in those church-bell dependent days. He was to hide out, three nights in a row, in a dark doorway at the entrance to the Vico dello Schiavo, the alley opposite Diano Marina Station, and memorize the details of the Nazifascist Barbarians' guard on their arms store in the station: times, numbers, weapons. Times, numbers, weapons, he repeats, as if he can still hear the orders. He was not to write anything down. If he was caught, he was to drop the incriminating watch down the drain at his side and pretend he was only out breaking the curfew for a kiddies' dare. He remembers it as if it was yesterday: the blacked-out silence, the stamping feet and muttered German in the darkened station yard, the thumping heart. He spent as much time, he says, trying to devise a foolproof scheme for disobeying orders and saving the wonderful watch if the worst happened as worrying about being caught by the Nazis. Hide it in a gap in the door jamb? No, better, a piece of thread and a matchstick across the drain grille so it wouldn't fall right into the mucky water below . . . Then waiting outside the station with the others for the raid itself, over in no time. Two grunts in the darkness as the guards went down: Pompeo and Luca, Giacò's elder brother, taking one each, careful not to kill their men, the reprisals were much worse if you did. Now everybody in through the gates, running silent and barefoot through the dark . . . How many good guns, how much ammunition! *Euh! Una meraviglia!*

The *rastrellamento*, he's been telling us, the one we've seen the monument to up at the head of the valley, was the Nazifascists' response to that very arms raid. A *rastrello* is a rake; a *rastrellamento* is a raking-in, a huge military swamping manoeuvre to flush out Partisans from their hiding places up in the hillsides. Domenico had never seen so many German soldiers – thousands of them, all setting off up through the *fascie*, a pincer movement up the Diano valley

207

and the Faraldi, spread out like beaters on a hunt. And no way to warn the boys in the hills.

One of the dead boys commemorated on the stone is Luca. Another is Fabio, Domenico's cousin and childhood hero. Fabio had thick curly hair that would never lie flat whatever he did to it, and a dog he'd taught to do all sorts of tricks. He never took anything seriously, could always make you laugh fit to split your sides, and had managed, just before he was shot dead, to grow his first proper moustache. Not just fluff on the upper lip like everyone else his age. Much good it did him, says Domenico.

As usually happens when I get told these war stories, I've gone all sniffly. These cheerful matter-of-fact folk living with another, parallel vision of these safe and familiar streets and hillsides, one filled with death and danger, hunger and fear. Cautious old peasant folk who seem as solid and unchanging as their stony landscape, rooted in centuries-old tradition, but who've lived through more upheavals and earthshaking changes than I can begin to imagine, and whose stories send everything into double exposure. The Vico dello Schiavo, a high-walled leafy alley which till now has been just a useful shady bypass away from the milling mainstreet tourists of high summer, will be overlaid for ever now with a flickering image of a teenaged Domenico crouched moustacheless and scared in the dark in that last doorway, single-handedly defying Nazifascist Barbarism, yearning for a watch of his own. Over cheerful little Diano station, with its bright flowering oleanders, a jump-cut shadow of a Nazi Headquarters dealing death, a cold-blooded shooting up in the hills.

No wonder the old folk round here are all so fussily in love with the security of their daily routines, their carefully ordered meals at carefully ordered times, the endless pernickety rules and regulations about their food and drink, health and safety, the web of customs and habits, all the amulets and charms designed to ensure survival and continuity, to magically stave off any new outbreak of chaos and incomprehensibility.

This is our fourth or maybe fifth Ligurian year, and Domenico has dropped in to see if we've noticed the smoke up in the hills. So far we've survived several late-summer seasons of forest fires without any coming nearer than the next-door Imperia valley; but now a big one has started somewhere higher up in our own valley. On this side of it too. We can just see the place from the patio where we're sitting if we lean round the side of the house and look uphill along the terraces. All the men from San Peo and from Moltedo are already up there, says Domenico, they're trying to cut a firebreak between the uncultivated patch where the fire has (as usual) broken out, and the olive groves. Domenico isn't allowed to join in firefighting duties because of his heart, so he has stayed to share his fire-wisdom and a glass of wine with us. That's why we've gone back to the Partisan days when he was strong and healthy. Or at least to when he didn't know he wasn't.

On this forest fire day, another visiting brother, Jim, is down in Diano Marina checking out the beaches. It is a lot less crowded now September has come and the factories of Milan and Turin have reopened, and the seaside has started to be a pleasure again rather than a torture. Jim is lazing happily and sleepily on the sand at Diano when a pair of helicopters begin zooming and roaring to and fro over his head. Huge buckets dangle from their bellies; they hover ear-splittingly over the bay for a minute or two while these fill with sea water; then they swirl round, hurling large quantities of high-velocity sand into the sunbathers' faces, and whizz off at top speed up into the hills.

Our Jim, along with the other outraged holidaymakers, turns and gazes up into the hills, trying to make out what's going on. Alarmingly, the whole side of the valley where our house is has disappeared behind a veil of thick grey smoke. To make matters worse, as Jim is rushing for the *motorino* to come and save his sisters from charbroiling, two men in knotted-hanky-and-string gear, obviously hill-folk, appear on the hated promenade shouting agitatedly through a megaphone for volunteers to come and firefight. Our bold brother knows nothing of firefighting; but nor, he supposes, do most of the other bathers. The situation must be desperate. He rushes to volunteer, trying to explain, mostly in Spanish, that he has to go up to the fire anyway, that he has a pair of close relatives up among the flames. Handicapped by his oddly garbled speech, and by his white-blond hair, which causes everyone to think he is a

German, he is firmly rejected by the San Pietro firefighters. He leaps on to the *motorino* regardless and dashes up the hill, flying heedless over boulders and crevasses.

Lucy and I meanwhile are sitting on the patio sipping our wine with Domenico and watching the firefighting helicopters as they arrive up here from the sea and dump hissing smoking splodges of water on to the hillsides. On the ridge opposite us is a *vasca*, one of the huge round rainwater tanks people have built to collect extra water supplies, and another pilot, amazingly skilful, is hovering over this thing, dipping his dangling bucket contraption into it, and then flying off in a great arc up the valley, a curving rainbow of water drops cutting across the whole width of the sky as he loops past within feet of us and heads off up into the smoke.

The precious fresh water from the *vasca* will only be used for saving cultivated land, says Domenico, and the sea water goes on wilderness areas. Salt water will contaminate the land for seven years, so you don't want to drop it anywhere people are trying to grow things. Not unless you absolutely have to. The helicopters don't drop the water on to the heart of the fire, as we'd imagined, but round the edges to contain it while it burns itself out. If things get really bad, though, if they can't contain it, they will have to bring in the Canadians.

What Canadians? I ask. Domenico, winding me up outrageously, says that this is some extra-skilful type of pilot trained in Vietnam to incredible accuracy at salt-water bombing. I'm not entirely sure about this, not recalling any Canadian involvement in Vietnam, but before I can make further enquiries a red-faced puffing brother appears round the bend behind the rock, convinced that we ought to be evacuating the house immediately. From down by the sea it looks terrible. No, says Domenico, there's no danger yet. The fire's a good two kilometres away. The only thing we have to fear are flying sparks – they might just catch on the wild land above the house. Much better stay here so we can keep an eye, put them out straight away if they do. It's a pity, he says, that we haven't paid more attention to our Cleaning up there. Then we'd have nothing to worry about.

In a life-threatening situation, mutual understanding can make great strides. This, we suddenly see, is what has been annoying Nino. This is why he thinks we deserve to have our house burnt to the ground. Dirt is not just untidy: it is a fire hazard. Domenico, like Nino, has been hinting about all the Dirt above our house, off and on, for some years now; we have been gaily ignoring him. Worse still, we have been making mindless jokes about the local Compulsive Cleaning Disorder, the apparently senseless San Pietro hatred of all plant life that isn't edible. We never go up on the steep wild bit above the house, nothing cultivated grows there, so the idea of bothering to clear it has always seemed absurd. Just keeping the olive terraces in order is work enough, and we have so far not caught on to the idea that the Cleaning was at all connected with fire hazards.

Domenico has trouble believing we could be this thick. If one person's olives catch, so will everyone else's around. Which means, if you have to replant, fifteen years before the next decent crop. Plenty of time to go hungry. And there's a hefty fine these days, he adds, for anyone whose Dirty Land has caused other people's olives to burn.

We look nervously up at our Filth. No one's got any olive trees up above here, though, have they? we say anxiously. Just to the sides of the house and below. Domenico agrees. But, he points out helpfully, there's no reason why fire shouldn't go downhill or sideways. It's all a question of wind. And he shows us how the fire will start, first creeping low among the tangles of dried grasses, then spreading up the bushes and the clumps of broom – there are certainly plenty of those, we've never even contemplated getting rid of them, you never know when you might suddenly need a large number of tomato-ties – and on to the lower branches of the scrub oaks above the house, two of which, we see now, are actually touching the uphill side of the roof. Close to the downhill side of which, oh horror, dangle several fat branches of our two tallest olive trees. From whence, once they'd got going, the entire hillside of olives could catch fire.

We leap up, panic-stricken. We'll start sawing the branches off those oak trees straight away. And collect up all our buckets, just in case. And a hosepipe to run from our water tank – no, that won't be any use if the fire's uphill, there'll be no pressure ... Jim, wild-eyed, is already rushing about collecting anything that can hold water ... four buckets, two big bowls, a giant saucepan ...

Domenico, watching these proceedings, begins to realize the full depths of our ignorance. Haven't we ever seen a forest fire?

No, we haven't, we say, poised for action. We come from a country where it rains all the time, no olive trees, no vineyards, no forest fires. Like Holland.

Ah, sì, sì, says Domenico in his usual disbelieving way. He doesn't seem to have noticed anything about Holland except its culinary inadequacies. Maybe he went there in a heatwave or something? And he's staying infuriatingly calm.

Well, a few buckets of water aren't going to be any use to you, he says. If a living, sappy tree was to go up, the blaze would be so huge and so hot that it would catch the house anyway with just a *filo di vento*, a thread of wind. It's not a question of individual branches. We'd need to chop the nearest half-dozen trees right down.

Should we start doing that, then? we ask, raring to do something, anything, wondering if he might be persuaded to lend us his chain-saw, seeing that it's an emergency and we've got a large strong brother to hand. But we've got the whole thing arse-about-face. The point is to stop the fire getting a hold at ground level in the first place. You want it to rush past fast and low, never get enough heat going or enough height to catch a tree. Chopped-down trees lying about the place would fuel the fire, not hinder it, wouldn't they?

The dumbos stand agawp. It doesn't seem as amusing to us as it does, apparently, to Domenico.

I gaze horror-struck at the newly menacing hillside behind the house. There are enormous quantities of thick, clumpy and mostly tinder-dry grass, gorse, broom, and everything else growing thickly up the hill. It will take days to get rid of it all, I say, grabbing the sickles from their nail.

Yes, maybe, says Domenico non-committally. We are getting our come-uppance for years of laziness and Dirt, and our evil neighbour is enjoying himself like nobody's business. We scramble up the hillside and start chopping away; within minutes sweat is pouring from us in such quantities that there's no point even trying to wipe it away. The sun is unbearably intense on our heads; it has been so hot every day for the last week that it has reduced us to total lethargy from eleven in the morning to six at night. Except when totally immersed in water. On top of that, it is the mad-dog time of day, and normally only fear of death could make me, for one, step out from the cool shade of our patio roof. But fear of death – or at the very least, of homelessness and responsibility for destroying the livelihood of half of San Pietro, which is almost as bad – is exactly what's happening.

As our sweat-and-sickle torture proceeds, a roaring gale suddenly starts up at our rear, attacking from the seaward side. Not, fortunately, the Towering Inferno yet, but a smaller cousin of the bucketing helicopters, now hovering just above our heads. We stop work. Someone in a red boiler suit, holding a megaphone in one hand, leans right out of the machine and stares piercingly at us. Domenico waves; the man waves back; it flies off again.

What was that about? we ask, once we can hear ourselves speak again.

The fire-spotting helicopter, says Domenico. The water-dropping pilot, it seems, will have reported back to fire-fighting base that a bunch of apparently able-bodied people were hanging around doing nothing to help with the fire. The megaphone was to be used to tell us to get our arses into gear, and go up to join the firebreak cutters. But the pilot knows Domenico; and women and tourists are both useless for fire-fighting purposes. He has flown off to hunt for a better class of shirker.

Domenico goes off up to some of the nearest and tallest broom-bushes and cuts half-a-dozen long tufty headed branches off them, witches' broomsticks, which he stacks neatly by our door. This is not mere Cleaning: these are the best things for beating out a fire, he says, if the worst really comes to the worst.

Now, unimpressed by our technique with a sickle, he insists on joining in. This is great; all we need is for him to have a heart attack brought on by having to help clear up our ignorant foreign Dirt. He stops our wild flailing around with the sickles, puts Jim on machete duty, doing the larger bushier things, and shows us how to do the job systematically, throwing each armful of brush down on to the bare, safe patio outside the house as we go. Then he gets on silently and apparently effortlessly with the task, clearing twice as much as us in half the time.

Next to arrive at this scene of fear, sweat and self-loathing are Antonietta and Pompeo. Antonietta has got a lift up in the Guardia Forestale jeep to hunt for her husband. She lives in fear of Domenico's heart giving out one day while he's up on the land. He might lie there for hours, no one would be there to save him, and she wouldn't be any the wiser until he didn't turn up at suppertime. What if the forest fire had brought on an attack . . . ? She is very annoyed with Domenico for not coming straight down once he'd seen the fire wasn't threatening their own trees – how was she to know he was all right? And she doesn't look at all pleased to see him exerting himself so violently on our behalf. He was supposed to come back home as soon as he'd checked, give her the news and finish off some jobs around the house . . .

Pompeo nods wisely over our fire precautions. We are doing right – at last – though there's nothing to worry about really, the fire is a good way away, on the other side of a dirt-track which will act as a firebreak. Anyway, he says, if it really starts to look as though the fire is heading this way, and you haven't had time to finish clearing, you'll just have to do a controlled fire in a strip all the way round the house, and the flames will have nothing left to catch on, so the fire will hopefully go right past.

Just start our own forest fire! Great. Fighting fire with fire . . . another one of those sayings you don't bother to think about. Lucy now remembers, helpfully, that in *Little House on the Prairie* the father does just as Pompeo's suggesting; takes out the petrol can and burns a great ring around the house as fire sweeps across the wide grasslands towards his home and kiddywinks. It was all right for him, I say. If only all we had to deal with was a nice flat prairie! We, on the other hand, already melting in the heat, would be clinging to steep wobbly rocky land by our toes and fingertips. The thought of trying to start and put out fires with no hosepipe on this terrain is terrifying, however many broom branches we may have ready to hand.

There is a moment's excitement when Jim pauses long enough from his sweaty labours to recognize Pompeo as one of the men on the beach with the megaphone; while Pompeo recognizes Jim as the German speaking an unusual dialect – did he learn his Italian in Venice? – who wanted to come and fight the fire. Seeing Jim in the right company, he is now prepared to make use of him, and gets ready to load him into his Guardia Forestale jeep. Jim tries to leave the machete behind. No, you'll need that, says Pompeo. Poor Jim hasn't escaped ground-clearing then. His sisters are greatly relieved that women don't have to go and chop brush right in the teeth of forest fires, or go down in history as cowards and weaklings.

Domenico is most frustrated, though. Alone among women when all Real Men are away at the front! Even daft blond *turisti* like our brother, and people of advanced years like Pompeo. We'd never believe Pompeo was almost ten years older than him, would we? he says gloomily. We try pointing out that he's probably saved our lives, or at least our home, with his useful advice. No use. But Antonietta will have none of his nonsense; she stands him up, brushes him down, and whisks him off back home to finish mending the kitchen shutters.

As darkness descends an eerie red glow illuminates the valley inland and behind us. Jim, the returning hero, reports that the fire's more or less under control and everyone says we can rest safe in our beds tonight. It's nowhere near any of the villages: it hasn't got anyone's olive trees. So far, so good. We don't have to finish the vile perpendicular sickling job in the dark then. Or light absurdly dangerous fires round our precious home.

Moreover, after Jim's afternoon of fire-fighting, he has become a serious man-about-village: he has been adopted by the Sulking Café company, and initiated into the mysteries of *scopa*, the favourite card game down at the bar. Even Hebe and Giacinta, the two women-dressed-as-men, whose names we now know but who have still never spoken much more than a gruff 'Salve!' to us, have smiled and chatted to this brother, insisting that he must come to the *festa* this weekend at Diano Borello: if he does, they have promised to crown his glory by dancing with him.

In the middle of the night I wake up for no identifiable reason. Some unusual background noise is going on – a fridge-freezer vibrating, the central heating boiler, something like that. No. There is no electricity – ergo no central heating or fridge-freezer. The muted roaring noise has to be coming from outside.

I open the shutters. Not only is the roaring now immense, but there is a horrible lively crackling behind it. Inland, much too low for it to be the sky, much too late for it to be the sunset, all is a lurid red. I rush to wake the others and we trail out wrapped in our sheets to inspect the hillside to the landward of us. It's impossible to tell how near the fire is, though. The red glow illuminates all sorts of ridges and folds in the hillside which are never usually visible even by day because of the thick covering of fluffy olive trees. But individual treetrunks are standing out on what seems to be the nearest fold, black against the red glow: the fire is at the same level as us, and the noise is scarily loud.

As we are wondering whether to evacuate to be on the safe side – maybe it's somehow got across the firebreak-road? – we hear above the deep roar of the fire the higher-pitched sound of some large vehicle grinding through a series of gear changes at the end of our path. We run like the wind in our nightwear, sheets flapping, to find out what's going on.

There on the road, battling to get round the hairpin bend, is a real red fire engine. It is pulling a huge trailer of water with thousands of metres of hose wound round it, and having to manoeuvre back and forth to get round our tight narrow curve. The planes can't fly at night, the firemen say, and this time the olives are in serious danger. They've come from Imperia. There are already three engines up the hill, coming at the *incendio* from different directions. Although they can't be sure, the fire doesn't seem so much to have spread as to have started in another place. They fear someone has done it on purpose. There is a firebug at large.

We follow in their wake round the hairpin bend and up on to the ridge to find what looks like a scene from the Russian Revolution. Half the village is clustered on the road a little way up the hill, coats bundled on over nightwear, all outlined against the glowing red and clutching sharp glinting curved implements. Several muffled cadres wielding sickles and machetes rush up to our Jim and greet him like a long-lost brother. The weapons are waved for emphasis; you would think that not fire-fighting but vengeance was uppermost in the minds of the gathering. Fingers stab furiously; angry blades slice the air. Who can have done this, and why? Hunters wanting less cover for game once the season starts? Would-be property developers wanting to get land re-zoned? Madmen? Someone wanting to collect on their insurance?

Fire can only get a really good hold on uncleared *fascie*; there is strong feeling in this gathering against people who don't Clean at least once a year out of consideration for the lives and property of others. Even if they're not bothering to harvest their trees, they should have some sense of social responsibility. We keep our heads down. Nino seems to be looking accusingly in our direction. Oh God, he's heading this way! But he only wants to show us that you can see the lie of the land from up here, and our house is in no danger; the fire's still several folds in the hill away, much farther than it seemed. And luckily it's going uphill, towards wilderness, not down towards villages and olives. The firemen at last agree that this is so, and we trail wearily off back to our beds.

When morning comes, the scent of woodsmoke is still strong on the air. The red glow has vanished, but up at the head of the valley there are still wisps of smoke, and the hillside is no longer coloured straw-and-green, but black. All the vegetation on it has been reduced to charcoal. We decide to go down to the village for breakfast, get a brioche at Signor Ugo's and take it to Maria and Luigi's to eat with our cappuccino while we catch up on the latest news. (This is normal procedure; since they don't sell breakfast supplies in the bar, no one takes offence at you bringing your own snacks to go with their coffees.) Although the place is packed out, not one game of cards is in progress; a sign of serious agitation. Even irregulars like Sergio and Franco (at opposite ends of the bar, and studiously ignoring one another) have come down to catch up on the news.

The fire really has started in two places. Definitely a very odd coincidence. The majority verdict is for the firebug theory. And, says Maria, the Canadians are being brought in this afternoon. They don't think they can get it all under control without them. Ace pilots from Vietnam? Who told you that?

Luigi, kindly soul, does his best not to laugh at us. But Giacò, in his favourite breakfast position at the bar, immensely and loudly enjoys Domenico's joke at my expense. His many kilos still quivering with suppressed laughter, he tells us that a *canadese*, really a Canadair, is a plane which can dip its belly into the sea in mid-flight, and fill itself with thousands of gallons of water that it dumps right on the heart of the fire. For good measure he adds the tale of how a scuba diver was sucked up into one of these things as it swooped down to reload, and then dumped back out into the middle of a forest fire. Some weeks later the mysterious burnt and blackened body of a person who'd died by drowning was found halfway up a mountain. Fortunately, I've since been told this story so many times, from so many locations around the world, that I am now (almost) sure it is a complete fabrication.

At the Borello *festa*, where tripe and beans are the main attraction and Lucy is only saved from starvation by the *cundiun* and the *rostelle*, tiny crispy goat kebabs, Hebe does three consecutive dances with Jim, two mazurkas and a polka, to reward him for his heroic role in the saving of the San Pietro groves. By the end of the second mazurka, which he manages to perform rather well, the first having been a bit of a washout, he has realized that he too wants to spend the rest of his life bouncing and swirling as evening falls around a small dance floor under fairy lights beside a medieval church in lumping step with several dozen peasants. Entering into the spirit of joy and ludicrousness which has taken over now that everyone's olives are safe, Domenico has some more fun, this time at Pompeo's expense. He spends ten minutes training Jim in a relatively quiet corner round the side of the church until he can do a perfect Ligurian *Euh!*, and a passably lisping *Ah, sì, sì!*

Then, having instructed Jim to answer anything he says with either or both of these remarks, in any order, Domenico takes him to sit at one end of Pompeo's table, and has a long conversation with him about the probable identity and motives of the firebug. Jim responds to each remark with either a wise *Ah, sì, sì!* or an *Euh!*

in one of its many tonal varieties, taking his cue from Domenico's expression and tone. Pompeo is amazed. The story is soon flying round the *festa* of how our brother, who until yesterday only spoke some odd dialect from the Veneto, has mastered perfect Ligurian in no time at all. Jim and Domenico keep up this double act off and on all evening: many folk in their cups hear the rumour and come to test the amazing Englishman. The *vino d'uva* of Diano Borello being magnificent stuff, a good few of them never manage to work it out.

A week later Jim is on his way home from the beach on the trusty *motorino*, proud to have remembered all the shopping – not just the bread and milk and coffee but also the paraffin supplies for the hurricane lamps. A car has been trundling slowly up behind him for some time, but he hasn't taken much notice of it. Lots of people drive at this speed on our uncivilized road to avoid destroying their suspension. He parks the *motorino*, unhooks his carrier bag, and sets off along the path. Or tries to; the car has come to a halt behind him and four men in absurd uniforms smothered in gold braid and epaulettery – this is before the Italian police forces were redesigned by Armani and co – now jump out of it, slamming the doors, leap on him violently and inexplicably, and wrestle him to the ground.

What is he off to do in the middle of nowhere? And what is in that bag he is carrying? Paraffin! Just as they suspected. And why would anyone be taking a walk on an empty hillside with a bottle of paraffin? As they knew from the very look of him, he is the pyromaniac they were after. Moreover, he is clearly German, which makes his capture all the more gratifying.

No, says Jim, he's not a pyromaniac. Not even a German. He's on his way to a house which is just down there, he says, managing to extricate an arm with which to point along our unpromising looking path.

A house! Up here! Down there! Don't make me laugh! say the policemen. Or words to that effect.

His sisters live there, Jim insists. They are English. They have no electricity. This paraffin is for their lamps. (Jim, of course, is speaking in lightly Italianized Spanish; I am paraphrasing.)

It takes Jim, as he tells it, an extraordinary amount of time to convince them to let him get up off the ground so he can show them that there is really a house up here. He achieves this by insisting on their examining the rest of the contents of his carrier bag; they eventually agree that a packet of Lavazza, a litre of milk and a dozen rolls are unlikely accoutrements for a firebug. They allow themselves at last to be led along the path, and the results are most gratifying. The *carabinieri* see that there is indeed a house. They agree that Jim is probably not a pyromaniac, or even a German, and let go of him. They come up the steps and sit on our shady patio, accept a coffee, a grappa, and two glasses of wine respectively. And fall immediately, deeply, in love with the place.

Che posto! Che bellezza! they say, with one accord, gazing delightedly around them at the house, the *orto* and the olive groves. *Un vero paradiso!* they add, goggling at us pair of lightly clad, fair females who appear to form part of the facilities. I have wished ever since that I'd had the presence of mind to get them to sign a document to this effect. How gratifying to be the owner of a place officially designated by the *carabinieri* as a True Paradise.

18

When it's not fire in late August and early September, it's drought. This year the late tourists, the ones with most money to spend, are leaving waterless Diano Marina in droves. In theory, according to its Comune, the town's taps are being supplied with water for one hour in the morning and one in the evening. This would be bad enough for the hoteliers' trade; but in practice water often doesn't appear even at the official times. Residents are outraged: rebellion is close among what's left of the holidaymakers, who now can't even rinse the salt off their skins at the end of their day on the beach – no laughing matter at this time of year, when the seawater is so concentratedly salty that it makes you itch all night if you don't get it off. There are tales of taps accidentally left on, spouting water at three a.m. Are you supposed to stay up till dawn in case the water comes on? What kind of resort is this, anyway? Diano Marina is dry as a bone, and facing disaster. Great standing tanks of water have been put out by the Comune on every street corner, but this has not noticeably defused the situation; long queues mutter and fume at every one. Fathers of holidaying families stand waiting impatiently with sets of newly bought, sensible ten-litre containers, tapping smartly casual feet and swearing under their breath on the many and bestial variations of the Madonna, while they wait for some local black-tube-clad old lady to fill, slowly and painstakingly, dozens of carefully hoarded individual mineral-water bottles, turning the tap off so as not to waste water once each is full, while she screws on its lid, checks it for tightness, and packs it into an ancient shopping bag before unscrewing the next bottle, turning the tap back on, and starting the whole procedure all over again . . .

Bankruptcy looms for the hoteliers, the beach owners and the tourist shops. And now, to make matters worse, the town is rocked by scandal. Money allocated to building water reservoirs after the last drought has vanished: in its place has been found a mere piece of paper, a document allowing Diano Marina to share in any spare water San Remo happens to have. This arrangement has passed unnoticed for years, while San Remo did have water to spare. But now the whole Riviera is facing disaster, and San Remo is certainly not prepared to share what little it has with a no-account two-horse town like Diano. The deal was for spare water, not for a share of the water.

Our Diano friends gloat quietly; they have never been fond of the smug hotel and bar owners of their town, who are famous for never taking on enough staff for the summer season, meaning that half the youth of the town are worked to death, sixteen hours a day, seven days a week, from May to September, while the other half are out of a job. Now, those who have grown fat from tourism are sunk. And so is this Comune, already disliked for caring more about tourists than locals; having failed so miserably in this self-appointed task, it is now forced to resign.

Inland in San Pietro there's not a lot to gloat about either; the entertainment value in the downfall of Diano Marina is heavily counterbalanced by the bans here on watering your *orto* with Comune water. Only people with a *vasca* or a well are managing to keep their gardens going; others are having to sit and watch their lovingly tended vegetable plots, vital not only to their emotional well-being but often to the family budget, shrivel and die.

San Pietro's Comune, like Diano's, is in the doghouse. Its own drought-protection project, an enormously deep and expensive well which has been started somewhere up by Franco's cow meadows to avoid just such a crisis, still isn't finished. Our Comune though comes up with a positively machiavellian scheme for deflecting criticism from itself and saving its bacon. Drought instructions are posted up on the walls of the piazza as expected, giving everyone the dread news that it is forbidden to water vegetable gardens till further notice. But they go up in German as well as in Italian: the German version not only comes first, at the head of the poster, but is in slightly larger print than the Italian. It is never a hard job to foment bad feeling about German holiday-home owners, and there are certainly a lot more of them dotted around the place these days; but there still can't be more than a couple of dozen in the whole valley. The fact that the Germans don't even have vegetable gardens, only being here for a couple of summer months, and therefore certainly don't need this information, passes unnoticed. From Pompeo we hear that it's the Occupation all over again: this time, instead of killing villagers outright, the cunning *Tedeschi* have chosen the sneaky roundabout route of depriving them of their vegetables.

Meanwhile up in our mountain fastness, watering has become the main business in life. We may have our own water supply, but by now we have planted too many things for our poor well to handle in this emergency; not only all the stuff in the *orto*, but near the house a baby fig tree, two big bushes of marguerites, an oleander, a small palm tree, our big climbing plant with the salmon trumpet-flowers. Then there are the cherry and the six lemon trees, which will lose their next crop's flowers before they set into fruit if they don't get a good couple of bucketfuls twice a week; the four grapevines we're trying to persuade to grow into a shady pergola like everyone else's; and all the geraniums and flowering rock plants in the crevices of our walls. Everything, apart from the cherry and the older Pompeo-planted lemon trees, is much too young to have established a decent root system yet in this poor stony earth, and our policeman's paradise will shrivel and die for ever in this terrible heat if we can't keep up the watering till autumn comes. We are saving every drop of washing-up water, and have given up our lovely indoor shower, which drains on to the oleander and the new lemon trees outside the downstairs door. We can't allow them all the water: so we are washing our selves and our clothes in an old tin bath contributed by Antonietta so as to be able to ration it. Thank God we don't have a water closet: think what precious resources that would waste!

Until now, even in high summer, the well has always filled itself back up slowly within a week or so after we pump up a tankful; but it's not filling at all any more. It's less than a third full, and distinctly pond-flavoured. Pompeo says that in all his life he's never seen it this low. And it's turned out to be our only resource. Our other waterhole thing, which might or might not have turned out to be a well if only we'd ever got round to clearing it out, has become a shrivelled brackish pond with a cake of cracked mud at the bottom.

Our leafy salad bed is wilting horribly; our *trombette* are shrinking instead of fattening up. Domenico and Antonietta's well also contains nothing but a foot or so of smelly sludge. Nino says we can use his well if we want – he hasn't used it for years, he came by an easier, more accessible *orto* nearer home in his wife's dowry; but it's still there in a corner under the apple tree on the terrace just below ours. Antonietta and I find the spot with some difficulty, and disinter its mouth from under a pile of disintegrating mossy logs. No chance. It's as low as the others. We decide to abandon all thought of personal hygiene till the next rain comes – we may get a bit smelly, but at least, unlike our garden, we won't die.

Another ray of hope breaks through when we bump into Carlo, the nice *nipote*, who is pottering about on one of the many bits of land his family owns, just round the corner and up the hill, amidst rows and rows of half-shrivelled drought-stricken bean plants climbing up twenty foot canes. He calls us over to look at an enormous snake a good three yards long and as thick as a well-built peasant's arm, which has come down from some more drought-stricken zone and is busy lumping and slithering about in the bowels of an extremely full well in a corner of his *campagna*. We aren't sure whether the snake or the water is the more exciting discovery. The snake, although it's not dangerous – just a *bicha*, a kind of enormous bird-eating grass-snake – is still hair-raisingly horrible. The vast quantities of water in the well it is using for a swimming-pool, on the other hand, are deeply attractive.

We can use as much as we want of it, anyway, says Carlo – it is lovely and clean, his father and Franco cleared it out this spring. Great, we say, if he's sure Franco and Signor Giacomasso won't mind. Carlo's somewhat perplexing response to this is to erupt into gales of laughter. What have we done now, then?

Giacomasso, it turns out, is not, as we've thought for years, the family's surname, but the father's nickname. Once you consider the matter, which we are now doing, you can tell it means something like 'Chunk-Jack' or 'Lump-Jack'; presumably a reference to the man's impressive girth. Their real surname, Carlo now tells us to avoid further embarrassment, is Saguato. Carlo and Nicola, meanwhile, are called 'the Giacomassi' because they are the sons of

Giacomasso. Obvious. Still, it could have been worse – we might actually have addressed their father as 'Mister Lump-Jack' in some public forum.

How come your beans are all shrivelled up, we ask Carlo, when there's so much water in the well? Thereby, of course, hangs a tale . . .

His dad and Franco, says Carlo, both great bean fans, decided this spring to reactivate this bit of unused land for a family bean patch. Terrible mistake. They were utterly unable to agree on correct bean growing procedures, argued viciously for months about amounts of watering and types of fertilizer and how many shoots should be pinched out when; until eventually Franco, goaded beyond endurance, announced that he now realized he had made a terrible mistake in not opposing his sister's marriage to a man who understood nothing about beans, and should have nipped this relationship in the bud as firmly as he had put a stop to Evil Federico the taxi driver's pretensions. Brother-in-law Lump-Jack responded by telling Franco never to darken his door, or the bean patch, ever again . . . Now they are no longer on speaking terms, while the bean patch has gone to rack and ruin, both of them too proud to touch it. In fact, says Carlo, he was just wondering whether to try to salvage at least a bit of a bean harvest out of it, if there was enough water in the well, when he met the snake. Sadly, he has concluded that things are too far gone.

Even more sadly, from our standpoint, once we start thinking about how on earth we would carry any useful amount of water from here to our home, we realize that though the place may be very close as the crow flies, the trip on foot up and down terrace walls would be much harder work than the car ride to the public tap in the remnant of the outdoor public laundry in San Pietro, which is what we are doing at the moment for non-pond-flavoured water. Just to carry the canisters from car to house along the path is a killer, never mind going twice the distance over rough terrain. No use at all. So near and yet so far.

Down in the Sulking Café, everyone is waiting with bated breath for the weather to break, with chairs outside on the balcony so as not to miss a cloud, gazing in the direction of France and Spain, muttering horribly every time the sky darkens to the north, which it does regularly, to the accompaniment of many rolling oil drums. Down here, though, no water falls. The lazy good-for-nothing ignoramuses of the Pianüa get it all.

Giacò the Junkyard decides to cheer everyone up by reminding us that though the villages of the Pianüa may be stuffed with water, sunflowers, corn and meat, though its banks may be overflowing with cash, there is a dark lining to their silver clouds: the chronic woman shortage. Up on the plains, according to Giacò, all the women run away as soon as they're old enough to leave home. They can't stand the idea of spending the rest of their life up there trudging muddily to and fro across the huge damp empty spaces, hectare upon hectare of unrelieved flatness, fogbound for half the year, rainbound the rest, no life, no neighbours, no sun, no fun; you can be as rich as you like up there, he says, but you still won't find yourself a wife. Not for love nor money.

The card-players all agree. Much nodding and *Ah, sì, sì*-ing. So desperate is the plight of the Plainsmen, they tell us, that nowadays they are reduced to importing wives, mail-order, through introduction agencies and small-ads – from Eastern Europe, from the Philippines, from all sorts of distant and poverty stricken places. But as soon as these women pick up a bit of the language, realize they've got their right by marriage to a work-permit, to civilization, they won't stay on those miserable living-death farms any more than the local girls would.

Even in years gone by, pipes up one of the oldest bar-proppers, in the days before the olive net, when the women of the Pianüa used to come down here to work the olive harvest – there being nothing doing on the frozen farms of the plains in February, deepest winter still up there – their menfolk would be lucky if half of them ever went back home. *Euh!* They'd arrive here all done up in their finery, ready to scratch the local girls' eyes out, desperate to catch themselves a good Ligurian boy with a few *piante*, a decent life and a place in the sun. Nowadays, though, he explains to us kindly, women don't have to get married to leave home. They can leave anyway, whenever they want: and leave they do.

It is a terrible plight the Plainsmen find themselves in, everyone agrees, much enlivened by having shared these reflections with us. Can it all be true? No idea; but it certainly makes everyone feel better about the water situation.

I'm sick of it. Why don't we just give up this stupid place for good? Something's always going wrong, it's just too hard to survive up here . . . I'm seriously demoralized by the no-water situation. Could we somehow deepen the well? No. You couldn't get the machinery along our horrible path to do it, and even if you could Domenico and Pompeo both agree that we might cause a catastrophe, maybe lose the whole thing, by breaking through the rock-base of the well. They both keep on and on telling me that this has never happened before, probably never will again, but I don't care. Besta de Zago just isn't liveable-in. I'm giving in, I say, it was a silly idea anyway, trying to make a home in a vile parched hovel on an eyeball-searing desert of a mountain.

In the nick of time Caterina and the Diano *compagnia* step in: they are taking us off for a cooling and cheering weekend trip to the mountain lakes above Triora. So serious is the heat and drought situation down here that, unusually for our tribe of Diano hunters and gatherers, there is no food-collecting subtext to this outing. Nothing to collect anyway, they say; much too hot and dry. They just want to escape the water shortage, the sweaty itchy heat, the packed greasy bodies on the coast. They will show us a place where, though it is a mere thirty miles inland, all is coolness and greenness and space, and there is never any shortage of water. Extraordinarily hard to believe under present shrivelling conditions. Despite my grumpy scepticism, though, it turns out to be true. Three-quarters of an hour of slow uphill hairpin bends here doesn't just change landscape but apparently season too. As we drive up the narrow green gorge of the valley of the Argentino river, four valleys along towards France, it is like going from high summer in the Sahara to a pleasantly warm, green, shady springtime in the Black Forest. How sensible these Italians are. Or at least, how well they know their landscape.

Arriving at Molini di Triora, we stop at the village to shop for camp supplies: not as simple as you might think, not with a bunch of Italians. Still, at least there's a cool breeze up here. Our friends spend a good half-hour communing with the village butcher whose fine meat from his own herds in the high meadows is renowned throughout the area (knew there had to be a food subtext in here somewhere); when we manage to drag Ciccio away from his blood-brother the butcher (Patrizia says we've done well – he was in there for over an hour last time), it is only to go and do the same thing at the baker's. Mills of Triora: of course, we are at the home of the famous bread-that-never-goes-stale. A mile up the hill is Triora itself, a tiny town with a peculiar mini tourist industry based on it being the location of the last witch-burning in Italy. The sister and I do our best not to stamp and snort in our impatient hot-foreigner manner, while everyone buys in their stock of the flat round loaves of Triora, a transaction which inevitably takes another half-hour, what with the low quality of modern yeast and the need to discuss in great depth the problem of getting decent flour these days.

At last we are back in our small fleet of cars, heading for open country. Park and walk for twenty minutes along a shady path, tall green-leafy chestnut trees over us, hazels in among them, rich dark humus underfoot, ferns and wild strawberry leaves: and way below us, at the bottom of the steep banks to our right, yes, the sound of a river, a loud full-bodied healthy river, no trickling shrunken coastal *torrente*. The path runs level, clings to the side of the ravine, heading to meet the river at the high pools. If only we weren't loaded down with absurd numbers of carrier bags it would be perfect. Suddenly we are there, precious roaring rushing water, thousands of gallons of it, clear freezing mountain-spring stuff pouring down a dozen silver channels through the rocky hillside into a great blue mirror of a limestone lake. We put down our burdens and marvel.

Clothes off and into the water, splash about for hours, dust-free at last, clean and damp, ferns and verdure all around, dappled sunlight instead of the shimmering white heat of the coast. Up here with your feet in the cool ripples of shallow downstream pools, tiny trout slipping through your fingers, it's hard even to imagine our sad mudhole of a well, the tragic shrivelled hay which is all that's left of our once-luscious green terraces, our taplessness and bath-roomlessness.

One of Paletta's ingenious shelters is already going up in a clearing under the chestnuts, and we mess about making benches out of hazel saplings, wander about the woods, up and down ravines, finding new pools and tributaries to the main river and splashing in and out of them, full of unaccustomed energy now the heat can't get us. Lucy and I realize that this is our chance to collect the bendy twigs we need for our Antonietta-pizza-oven, and get ourselves a lovely big bundle.

We have brought an SAS survival guide with us, a present from a recent English guest who couldn't tell the difference between Liguria and the Mato Grosso: following its instructions, infected by the local hunting-and-gathering ethos in spite of ourselves, we make a very serious-looking fish-trap out of woven hazel wands, which so impresses Anna and Patrizia that they do one, too. We put them, as directed by the SAS, in a fast-flowing bit between two rocks, where everyone keeps prodding and poking at them all afternoon, much to Anna's despair, rattling them around and alarming any fish stupid enough to be poking its nose into the things. Unsurprisingly, we catch nothing. No one cares: Italians don't think river fish are really worth eating anyway, not even trout. We grill some of the several tons of meat we've brought instead. As dusk falls a billion damp green frogs start to croak sexily on all sides of us, and we have to add lots of green-leafy stuff to our bonfire to smoke the midges away.

By lunchtime next day one of those usual large crowds of friends and relations has gathered up here, bearing vast quantities of loaves and fishes (proper sea fish, that is), meat and vegetables, and even the only missing item for a home from home, a great cast-iron grill. Also a pair of four- and five-year-old girls, Marila and Miki, who are as overwhelmed as us by the wetness and coolness of the place, not having been here before either. Miki and Marila speak Italian to about the same standard as us, even make the same mistakes; and all the humorous allusions of the grown-ups to Italian popular music and TV series of the last decade pass them by, too. Lovely not to be linguistically and culturally handicapped for a change. We bond immediately.

Soon an eating orgy is, as usual, under way. After weeks of stomach-shrinking heat and no appetite worth speaking of, after weeks of doing the absolute minimum to avoid melting into a puddle of sweat, we find that all the unaccustomed activity in this cool green place has left us famished. We have no trouble at all keeping up. But alas, after lunch our infant friends are forbidden to go in the water. Not for at least three hours, their anxious parents tell them. Kiddies cry; foreign females save the day. We bravely enter negotiations on their behalf; English children, we say, do not die from paddling after lunch. Can Italian kids be so much more fragile? Eventually, once we've promised under no circumstances to let the *bambine* get wet above the knees, we are permitted to leave together for the shallow pools down river to hunt for minnows. We find we have so much in common that we hang out together for the rest of the visit, to the exclusion of the adult company.

Time to go: misery. Time to face not only the dry despair on the coast, but the very irritating travelling behaviour of our friends. They are obsessed, for inexplicable Italian reasons, with travelling in close convoy. Nobody knows why, but it is vital that we all travel and arrive simultaneously: we often, or so it seems to me, spend as much time waiting by the side of the road as at our official destination. A market day in some hilltown, a concert, an asparagus hunt: it makes no difference. We are always in at least half-a-dozen cars, and have to keep stopping every ten minutes, waiting for the rest of the bunch to catch up, doubling back on our tracks to hunt for lost or straying members of the band who have stopped to use a loo or get a bottle of water or a snack or a coffee or do a spot of hunting and gathering or pop in to visit an old auntie or whatever.

Huge rows break out every time we are held up by someone vanishing, but this doesn't stop it happening: it just means that as well as the fifteen stops, there will be fifteen outbursts of rage. Of course this is all very healthy, you'll be saying. Latins are famous for doing it, steam is let off and soon all is joy again and you've saved all that money you would otherwise have had to spend on psychotherapists. Fine, in theory. We'd like to be able to do it ourselves, even. But you have to be brought up on it. We weren't, and the rowing sends us into stress-alert panic every time, neck muscles tied into anxious knots. And we can't get anyone simply to arrange to meet at the end of the journey, rather than trying to keep one another in sight all the way.

Don't the others know where we're going though? we ask plaintively.

Of course they do.

Why can't we just meet there, then?

Nobody knows why: we just can't, that's all. We are gazed at as if we were saying something incomprehensibly absurd and outlandish. Or made to suffer rude jokes about the unsociability of the English. And we really are unsociable compared to our Italian friends. They never seem to need to be alone. They find a group of less than half a dozen positively uncomfortable: if by some mischance you find that you're alone with just three or four of them – ideal for foreigners like us, who lose track of what's going on when groups get too big – they will wander restlessly around bars and telephones until they have added another few to the band. This doesn't mean they necessarily chat the whole time; any of them may decide to read a book for a bit, or have a nap, listen to their Walkman, play patience in a corner. But we haven't learnt to do this either; ignoring people we're with is just as unsettling to us as having to be constantly in company.

In years to come, we will learn to reduce the cross-cultural travelling discomfort to a minimum by insisting eccentrically – all right, Englishly – on being shown on the map exactly where our destination is, and going in our own transport so as to have only one wait, in the place we're aiming for, rather than twenty pointless hangings around and shouting matches on empty brain-boilingly hot mountain roadsides or hair-raisingly busy crossroads. But for now we are still learning: and after gorging ourselves on coolness, dampness, and billions of gallons of pure mountain water, we face the ardours of the trip back with all these extra Sunday lunchtime visitors and the usual incompetent military manoeuvre-style travelling behaviour. As we expected, it takes for ever just to get ourselves and all our luggage, including the massive grill, back along the path to the cars. Adding insult to injury, we are made to leave our bundle of twigs behind in case the Guardia Forestale stops us. Surely they won't care about a bundle of twigs, we ask, if they don't bother about bonfires and benches? Not to mention great hordes of people gathering forbidden narcissi?

You never know, says Alberto, whose car we are travelling in. Best not to give them any excuse to harass you.

As we travel gently downhill following the rushing water below in the gorges of the Argentino, heading for drought again, we begin to wonder where all this water goes to. Why can't the combined Comuni of these valleys just build a reservoir on this river, have all this stuff to hand when it's needed, instead of doing dodgy deals with San Remo and running low on water every summer? But of course, we are not the first to have thought of this. There have been several attempts, we are told, to build a dam across one of the high, wet valleys; our friends point out three of these false starts as we drive down, enormous concatenations of abandoned concrete pillars and blocks on the steep tree-clad sides of the Argentino's high banks, already half vanished into the undergrowth. But the problem is that no damable valley exists, which does not have fifteen or twenty villages dotted about lower down, below where the reservoir would be. Each time work gets started, the inhabitants of these places notice that, were the dam to burst, they and their homes and lands and olive trees would very likely be washed away in the flood.

They agitate against the scheme: work is halted while litigation goes on. And litigation taking the decades it does here means in practice that the dam is abandoned for good. Easier to look for another site.

I say something thoughtless and superior about the resistance of aged country folk to modernity and change. Mimmo, Alberto and Anna leap down my throat. Do I not remember the flat road to Imperia from Diano Marina? Indeed I do: the *Incompiuta*. And yes, now I see what they mean. If a dam was to be built to those standards of workmanship – and what innocent villager living in its shadow could tell how well-built it was until it was too late? – no one below it would ever get a wink of sleep. I put my silly foreign attitudes away immediately.

OK. We'll just have to wait for it to rain then. And, amazingly, as we travel down towards the sea – oh joy! – the sky suddenly darkens. Over towards France, too, no less. And yes, as we arrive at the coast and hit the Via Aurelia, it begins to rain. Rain! Next time we stop to wait for some lost car or other, we ring Diano: is it raining there as well? Yes, it is. And it goes on all night too, and all the next day. By the end of the week our well has begun, slowly but surely, to fill back up. We are saved.

19

I wander cheerfully down to the well to give a drink to the long-suffering *bietole* and tomatoes, humming a happy ditty. Not too much water after the thirst they've been through, though, or the tomatoes' skins will all split, say the experts. Hard to follow this instruction – the temptation to bung an extra bucket of kindness to a sad, shrivelled plant, a plant that has treated me so well, provided me with so many lovely lunches, is extreme. I lift the lovely anti-snail-and-dog lid, beautifully carpentered by myself – and behold! The well is bone dry! Not a drop of water in it! I let out a shriek of horror. Has it sprung a leak? Can wells leak? How can we have got through that whole drought without running out completely, only to have it all suddenly disappear now, just when it was refilling so nicely?

The trusty Domenico, who is down below checking out what he's managed to salvage of his own vegetable patch, hears my scream and comes rushing up. What is it? Soundlessly I point down the well.

Domenico is as horror-stricken as I am. We both stand and stare, aghast. Someone has pumped it dry, he says.

On the face of it this makes more sense than my leak theory; and yet, who could it be? And why? And where would they have pumped it to? I sit down on the ex-shower stone by the side of the well and burst into childish tears. The drought has been horribly stressful, I am only too aware of how impossible it would be to survive up here without water, and now it seems we have a secret enemy bent upon our destruction. Someone who wants to drive us out . . . and they won't have to keep this up for long to succeed. It would cost thousands of pounds, which we haven't got, to get water piped up here from the village. It's this little well, with its fortnight's worth of water at a pumping, or nothing. I'm sick of it all, I say. I'm going back to nice green wet England and giving this hopeless place up for good.

Domenico will have none of it. At least, he says, this will give you a chance to get down there on a ladder and scrape out a few decades' worth of mud from the bottom of the well while you're waiting for it to fill up. The thought, strangely, does not fill me with joy. We were just going to pump our tank full for the first time in almost a month, have showers, do proper washing-up instead of the version we've been condemned to for so long – using a teaspoonful of mineral water. Maybe even mop the floor . . . I was looking forward to getting thoroughly clean at last, to seeing our *orto* green and pleasant again, our garden happy and un-wilted. Now, it seems, I'm supposed to be pleased at the idea of going down a deep dark scary hole to get covered in slimy mud instead. Why didn't we do our pumping yesterday? And more to the point, why bother? Why not just give up? How can we survive up here if whenever there isn't a drought, which there usually is, people are going to come and steal our water? I sit paralysed with despair on the edge of the useless well, moping and snivelling.

But Domenico, Partisan hero, is not content to sit and wait. Moping and snivelling are not part of his repertoire. And he has no intention of allowing us to abandon San Pietro in despair. He sets off on patrol, stamping to and fro, up and down the terraces, looking for signs of water-thievery. Eventually, having quartered every *terreno* on this side, he crosses the dirt-track to the so-called Sicilians' land. And lets out a cry of triumph. Here it is!

I totter down to see what he's found. A pair of large fibreglass water tanks, which were certainly not there last week, are sitting outside their flying-roofed *rustico*, inexplicably brimful of water. The evidence seems overwhelming. But why on earth would Anna and Tonino steal our water? And why would they do it in such an obvious way? Grim-faced and pale beneath his eternal tan, Domenico tells me not to worry; he will sort this out. He storms off back to his Ape; I hear the poor creature screaming in agony as he pushes it to its downhill limit over the bumps and ruts towards San Pietro.

As dusk falls, there is still no sign of him. We haven't done any well-cleaning – somehow it seems pointless. We have a wash in the usual two teacupsful of San Pietro water in the bottom of a salad-bowl, and set off to hunt for news. There's no one in Luigi's bar –

not very surprising, it's official dinner time – and Luigi hasn't seen either Domenico or Pompeo all afternoon. Should we go round to see Tonino and Anna? We decide we can't do that. We are not entirely convinced that there is no other explanation for the full tanks outside Tonino's: we certainly don't want to go accusing neighbours face-to-face when they may turn out to be entirely innocent.

Next morning Domenico and Pompeo appear, fuming. They have had no qualms about going round to Tonino, who has admitted freely to draining the well: though, he claims, he had no idea it was ours. Frank the Knife, he says, offered to sell him a well right near his land, one that never dried up completely even in the hottest summer. Franco explained where the miracle well was, told Tonino to go and check it out. Tonino went and had a look; the land around it was all Dirty (oh God, that again. Though it is true that now we only pump every fortnight or so the well has got a bit overgrown, no daily trampling feet to keep the path clear) so he hadn't guessed it was in use at all. He thought our own well must be up nearer the house. (*Magari*: we should be so lucky.) And, as any sensible peasant would, Tonino had not merely looked, but had pumped the thing dry to make sure it refilled again and wasn't just a hole in the ground full of rainwater. What with Franco having a certain reputation, this had seemed a wise precaution to take before entering negotiations. And since it would have been stupid to just throw the water away under present droughty conditions, he'd emptied it into the two *vasche*.

This sounds very convincing to me. Especially the bit about sensible peasants emptying a well to make sure it really still functioned. We, of course, hadn't thought of any such thing when we were buying it. Our minds turn to Franco's well-reserving document: what did he reserve the right to, exactly? Are we dealing, not with water-thieving, which would be bad enough, but with an actual legal competitor for our precious water supplies? Pompeo, like us, thought he was reserving the other well, the muddy hole, since Franco was talking about watering beasts; but none of us recalls any very specific description being made at the *notaio* Alberti's. And we all know how slippery the law is, says Domenico. Not to mention how slippery Franco is, says Pompeo.

Domenico is still not entirely sure Tonino isn't lying through his teeth. Franco may be a devil: but on the other hand, water stealing is just the sort of behaviour you'd expect from Sicilians. Or, as it were, people from Alassio. Especially ones with no qualms about buying up vineyards to which they knew perfectly well other people have a moral right. Knowing that he had only two defenceless foreign females to deal with, Tonino could easily have made up this Franco story to cover himself . . .

The two of them put their heads together and confer privately in impenetrable dialect. We can detect only the name of Franco, repeated in tones of ever deeper outrage. Eventually we get the translation. Franco is probably just trying it on. Probably he wants to sell his rights, but not necessarily to Tonino at all. More likely, we are his targets. He's realized, what with the drought, that we would probably pay the earth to secure our water supply. And Tonino just happened to be there, useful as competition. More power to Franco's arm, up the price and panic us. Wait and see if he doesn't come and offer to sell you your own well soon, now he's softened you up.

No, we say, that can't be right.

Yes it can, says Pompeo. That's Franco for you. Low cunning, and let the weak go to the wall.

Let's ask him, I say, maybe he just meant the water-hole and Tonino misunderstood – or maybe he really has got another well down on his bramble terrace, and it was all a mistake . . .

Pompeo and Domenico aren't listening. They are off, tight-lipped, on a mission. They will be back later.

Lucy and I sit there dismally contemplating all the horrible possibilities. Truth to tell, we've already had nightmares about that well-reserving clause, especially since we were reduced in the drought to using the mud-hole as well as the proper one to water the vegetables. We certainly need both of them. And by now, if experience wasn't enough, we've seen *Jean de Florette*: we've watched Gérard Depardieu, in a very similar setting to this, being driven to despair, madness and eventually death by the machinations of a cunning peasant – who, as chance would have it, looked remarkably like Franco – over his water supply. How lightly, how ignorantly did we sign that document!

Some hours later, Pompeo pops back alone, looking mightily pleased with himself. It's all sorted, he says. We will hear in a day or two that Tonino is no longer interested in buying the well, nor Franco in selling it. Nothing to worry about. And, apart from a few obscure remarks about Franco, double-dealing, and irresponsibility, he will say no more.

A few days later, Tonino comes up to apologize, and to offer us a demijohn of this year's wine to make up for the trouble. He really, really didn't know it was ours. His own well has been dry as a bone since July, he's had to give up on his *orto* for this year, leave everything he'd planted to die a miserable shrivelled death, Franco's offer seemed like a gift from heaven . . .

We forgive him immediately. Now he tells us a very strange story. Someone has come in the middle of the night and emptied all the water out of his two *vasche*, every drop just poured out on to the ground: not only this, but they have also pumped his own well, which was beginning to fill up again, completely dry. There are footprints everywhere in the mud around the *vasche*, it looks as if a good half-dozen men were in on the attack. Someone, he says, looking at us out of the corner of his eye, does not want Franco to succeed in selling his well.

Tonino, distant though his Sicilian connections may be, is only too able to recognize this kind of hint. Faced with such odds, he has no intention of buying such a troublesome item, whoever it may legally belong to. He will just build a bigger *vasca* and replant his *orto* next year, he says, resigned. Thanks to our own profound lack of Italian training, we do not grasp the finer points of what has happened for some time. Then we realize that we have not only been saved from the immediate danger of Tonino buying the well, but that our powerful and unknown protectors have scared Franco off ever trying to sell it to any other neighbours, who in any case wouldn't buy it for fear of meeting the same fate as Tonino. Our water supplies are permanently secured. Partisan heroes indeed.

Up at Moltedo Ciccio and his partner Franchino have been suffering the torments of drought, too. The water from the Moltedo standing tanks, according to Ciccio, makes his pasta taste vile, and he insists on going to collect buckets of mountain water from the little cascades that feed the rock pools above the village instead. Franchino, desperately worried about what could happen if the health inspectors find out, did his best to convince his partner to use bottled mineral water instead, even if it would bankrupt them. But the bulging and temperamental artist of the pasta machine refused. He had tried this in the past, he said, and mineral water has no bite, makes a limp and insipid pasta as bad as the brackish standing-tank version. Upshot: Ciccio won, and for several weeks a bucket party has set off from the restaurant at dawn for the waterfalls, Franchino lurking, twitching, at the restaurant windows until the pasta is made up and the danger of detection over.

Franchino's anxiety about the forces of law and order is understandable – scandal has hit the restaurant. Franchino was, to his eternal shame, caught smoking a spliff on the beach at San Remo: the news was plastered all over the local papers. The restaurant proprietors were well known, of course, to be 'sons of immigrants'; that, if the food was good, could be coped with. But as far as the dinner-going citizens of Diano were concerned, a drug connection on top of the *Calabresi* connection was the last straw. The cooking might be excellent, but who knew what went on behind the scenes? Might you not get caught up in some drug-dealers' shoot-out, hit by flying bullets as you worked your way through the antipasti? Might they not lace their *sugo* with Class-A drugs so you would become hopelessly addicted, unable to function without a daily dose of Moltedo pasta?

Their friends, us included, were rather surprised by the calm and relaxed way Ciccio and colleague took this undoubtedly heavy blow. Nobody left to cater for but Plainsfolk and Germans now. Oddly, they seemed almost pleased by it. Eventually they came clean. Did respectable Diano but know it, this petty drug scandal, by attracting police attention in however small a way to their restaurant, saved them from a genuine and serious attempt to get them involved in organized crime. This too, of course, based on their Southern origins. Franchino wishes he'd thought the thing up intentionally – it couldn't have worked out better if they'd planned it.

For some time a mysterious men-only group of unknown Sou-therners had been booking their whole restaurant up once a month: men in expensive formal suits and rather exclusive jewellery, men who did not live anywhere local and yet who expressed the heartfelt wish to go on holding their regular grand reunions in tiny lost-in-the-hills Moltedo.

Was it the excellence of the cuisine? Ciccio and Franchino had indeed provided on request – booked well in advance, naturally – an array of luxurious twenty-course themed dinners: seafood, wild mountain game, Ligurian specialities, all washed down with oceans of high-class wines, seas of grappa. They were hugged and slapped and kissed by these unusual and slightly scary customers, compli-mented largely on the food, and several times left enormous tips which amounted to even more than the already princely bills for these sumptuous meals. After the first few visits, the approach they had been beginning to expect was made: a dinner of Southern Italian dishes was requested, and much was made of the 'brothers from our own land' aspect of things. Once the company was on its *digestivi*, a simple proposition was put to them. Their turnover might gradually, and over a period of some months so as to avoid suspicion, be made to grow to double what it really was. They would pay taxes on these earnings; everything would be above board; except that a large percentage of the extra money would be regularly returned to the kind investors who had supplied it. Ciccio and Franchino sweated blood over this one. If they got involved at all, might they get dragged in deeper, blackmailed into doing jobs less simple and possibly more distasteful than mere money laundering? Might something nasty happen to them, though, if they refused? What about the Finance Police, who were quite capable of coming and parking outside the restaurant for weeks on end if they felt like it, monitoring the true numbers of clients in the place and comparing this with what was being declared on their tax-forms?

In spite of the proud to be *Calabresi* bravado that Ciccio and Franchino have (perforce) adopted so as to be able to hold their heads high, the fact is that the intricacies of Mafia manners are as much a mystery to them as to their Ligurian cousins. Should they take at face value their new friends' protestations that this was entirely a matter of free will and their own good judgement? Would some relative of Al Pacino appear a week or two later if they turned down the offer, and firebomb the place?

Now, thanks to Franchino's well-timed drug-arrest, the problem is solved. There will be no more approaches of this kind. Once you have blotted your copybook with the police, you have lost the essential qualification for the job.

Our part of the hillside becomes a hive of activity again once the heat of summer finally begins to die down. There are people putting out olive nets early, grape- and tomato-harvesters, people sawing up the logs saved from their olive pruning into stove-sized pieces, loading them up into their Apes and carrying them home for the winter; also snail gatherers, mushroom hunters, and men in splendid hunting outfits, all belts and straps, getting their dogs into training for the opening of the hunting season in a few weeks. A whole new wave of passers-by find some excuse to pass close by and inspect us and our doings; some so far behind in the gossip that they seem to be checking down by the well for signs of our mystery Swiss Herb crop.

Lilli becomes one of our most prominent poppers-in as this September wears on; appearing several times a week on foot, desperate, it seems, for company. After a while an ulterior motive is revealed. There is a wine famine up at her house. The chicken business is not going as well as it could be, probably due to Sergio's amazing ability to offend and enrage the local populace; he blames San Pietro in general, the Evil Franco in particular, and endlessly plots revenge. Lilli feels that wine is an essential nerve tonic under these stressful conditions, but Sergio has decided she's drinking too much. He has won the argument by main force; just refuses to keep any wine in the house. This, in an Italian home, is an unheard-of state of affairs, and Lilli is understandably outraged. She has never learned to drive – Sergio has always interpreted her requests for driving lessons as a slight on his manhood: why should she need to drive when she has him to look after her? – so she can't go down herself. Or rather, she can go down all right, on foot, but she certainly couldn't carry enough supplies back uphill to make the trip worth while.

Sergio himself goes out for a soothing digestive drink most days – not, of course, to San Pietro among the benighted peasants, but to Diano, to the classy yachtsmen's bar down by the port. He even takes his daughters to play with the other kids on the promenade while he sups; but he refuses categorically to take Lilli. So we find ourselves providing both wine and company. Pray God we don't become Sergio's next targets. Judging by the amount of wine Lilli gets through, though, and we're talking wine drunk without so much as an olive to justify it, Sergio is not entirely wrong to be worried about his wife and alcohol. Still, try though she may, Lilli has hardly made a dent in our wine supplies. We have Tonino's water-ransom, delivered good as his word and already decanted into fifty-five one-litre bottles, stashed away in our stone roundhouse. Proving, as Domenico points out, that he was right about our needing a *cantina*.

Moreover, *vendemmia* – grape harvest – time has come, and with Domenico's help we'll soon be making our own year's worth. The crossroads on this side of Diano, before the level-crossing, are jam-packed every morning with grape-laden lorries from all over the country; from Tuscany and the Piedmont where the nobler grapes are bred, from the South where they're cheaper and sweeter. If you don't grow enough for your year's supplies – and many people don't – you buy them in now, in September, by the lorryload or the *quintale*, the hundred kilos. Lorries lurk in every patch of shade while their drivers wait for a good offer; the ones to go for, says Domenico, are the lorries with the most insects buzzing around them. Only fools – people from Diano Marina, for example – prefer the more sanitary looking and fly-free loads. An ounce of sense will tell you that these have either had Chemical Stuff sprayed on them, or are so low in sugar you wouldn't get a decent strength of wine out of them anyway. The lorries are surrounded by swarms of three-wheeled Bees too, whose owners, thoughtful men in hankies, knowledgeably squeeze, bite and sniff at the wares, seeking just the right qualities to blend with their own year's grape harvest for the perfect *vino d'uva*. The roads are full of them, trundling slowly and noisily homewards to the Diano villages loaded down with the year's selection, grape-juice dribbling from their truckbeds.

Domenico should have known better than to try to have a serious wine discussion with us. We have vaguely heard of the varieties of grape he's talking about – Ormeasco, Dolcetto, Sangiovese. The cheapest is Nostralino, which is just the local 'bastard' grape; the most expensive, nearly three times the price per *quintale*, is Brunello, which is used to make high-class wines like Margaux. If we want to make some white, too, we could get Lumassino, Vermentino, Pigato.

Domenico expects us not only to know what all these taste like, but to have some idea of how we'd like to mix them up and in what ratios. He retires frustrated. We will just have to have the same as him: Nostralino with a touch of Dolcetto. Though of course ours won't be as good as it could be, he says pointedly, with hardly any grapes of our own to add.

Yes, we've let Domenico down again. We still haven't got to grips with the lowness of the earth, and though we've managed to quell most of the old man's beard that was threatening to overrun the vines, we haven't pruned them properly – you're supposed to prune them right back practically to stumps, to get a decent crop. *Pazienza*.

Back in San Pietro, just to walk down the central muletrack makes you feel drunk. Heady fumes from the fermenting grapes crushed into the great wooden vats in the murky depths of everyone's *cantine* fill the air, trapped in the village's narrow passageways. Giacò invites us in to have a look at his *cantina* – not the one beneath his home near Patrucco's, which he uses for tools and olive equipment only, but another one he happens to own halfway down the village, for reasons connected with the complex system of interrelationships and inheritances hereabouts. A good wine eats fire, he says, shepherding us into the warm spicy gloom, did you know that? We didn't. We are busy putting our ears to his row of head-high vats, amazed at how loud are the gurglings and simmerings going on in their bowels. Giacò steps up showman-style on to a stool, lights a match and brandishes it, burning brightly, in front of our eyes. Watch! he says, and slowly he moves the flame towards the mouth of the reeking barrel. The second it meets the fumes from the grape-broth, it is killed stone dead. He lets us have a few tries just to prove there is no trick. There isn't. It really does eat fire.

Our wine supply may be well in hand, but the same cannot be said for our water. We're not short of the stuff any more, but the whiff of rancid pond down our well is getting even stronger. Something needs to be done, urgently. We decide to boldly go for the lime down the well project.

So, a bucket of lime; add water, stir well. The stuff is horrible to mix, fills the air with choking dust instead of sinking in; suddenly goes soggy, does a strange lumpy fizzing. You beat the lumps to pieces with a stick and throw your bucketful of unpromising-looking thick white soup into the well: *Butta! Butta!* shout our advisers – Chuck it in! – and you are amazed. The whole well seems to boil up, frothing and bubbling. The water goes pure opaque white and stays that way for hours. Once the stuff has settled, a day or two later, there is a beautiful snowy-white coating all over the inside of the well, any organic detritus has vanished without trace under a nice antiseptic coating beneath which it can no longer rot or breed bacteria, and the water is clear and fresh; not a hint of pond-perfume in it. Brilliant. Sadly, you've now added your own limescale to what once was soft water, and your kettle furs up abominably. Still, that's nothing compared to rancid pondwater.

The lime saga continues thus: some time later we go on a trip to Rome with visiting English friends. They have brought a guide book written by a fine woman who tells you all sorts of fascinating anecdotes about the city. We love her and her book, shower her with praise. Until, that is, our friends read out to us a passage dealing with the enormous destruction wrought on Roman remains over the centuries by the Italians (who are unconnected, it seems with the Romans, as if there had been some total genetic and cultural discontinuity the day the Empire fell) who have, she tells us, dragged tons of marble away over the centuries – columns, architraves, whole buildings – 'for no better reason than to burn it in lime-kilns'.

Lime! Not a good reason! Lucy joins me in a chorus of outrage. Does this woman, who until now has seemed such a kindred spirit, not realize the importance of lime to civilization? We have no doubt, we tell our friends heatedly, that the people who had the nous to burn chunks of Roman masonry will have been the most advanced and progressive section of the populace. We would never, we add with great feeling, blame any inhabitant of medieval Rome for preferring a cleansing, life-enhancing sack of lime to a useless old marble column! The real vandals will have been ones who sat gazing nostalgically at the ruins of their lost greatness while their water grew pond-stink and pollution, their walls seethed with vermin, their shit lay around spreading disease, and people dropped like flies around them from cholera.

We have startled ourselves almost as much as our poor innocent friends with this passionate limelovers' outburst. Unusual to find yourself in such total agreement with Frank the Knife.

With the Boots Home Wine Making Kit the actual wine-making procedure takes all of three minutes. You mix a tin of concentrated grape juice with a lot of water and a bag of sugar: easy. But first you will have spent an age obsessively scrubbing out anything that's going to come into contact with your wine, steeping it in swimming-pool-flavoured Bottle Sterilizing Fluid. Twenty minutes per object, *or else*.

This truly British experience is all I have to draw upon; and although I am used enough to Liguria by now not to be expecting much Bottle Sterilizing Fluid, I had imagined that up here in Domenico and Antonietta's wine-making zone, which turns out to be in their other olive grove overlooking Diano Castello, we'd at least be doing quite a bit of cleaning work. Not so. As I sat on one of those handy rocks washing my feet under the outdoor tap, preparing for my first-ever chance to stamp luxuriously about in a great pile of grapes, I found the bar of soap rudely snatched from my grasp by Domenico. No, no! No soap allowed; just wash with water. The principle being that whatever's naturally and organically on your feet is less likely to be inimical to the well-being of your wine than soapy perfumy *roba chimica*.

No doubt true, but disturbing to the Boots-trained novice. The trampling job was done, sad to say, in a rather unromantic large galvanized bathtub. Domenico is not keen on people stamping around inside his great-grandad's wooden vats the way you used to in the good old days; they might get ruined, and these days decent wooden vats are hard to come by. No one makes them any more.

So you stamp in the bath, then lift each bathful, heaving and groaning, shoulder-high and tip it into the vat. Our personal contribution, four carrier bags of Besta de Zago's silly Americano grapes, strawberry flavoured, got squashed in quarantine in a separate bucket for fear of it contaminating other people's serious supplies.

Today, too, we have simply rinsed out our equipment, several old plastic buckets, two big tin funnels, and ten glass demijohns, under the outdoor tap and thrown ourselves and everything else about on dusty tarpaulins and muddy grape-juicy ground. No sterilizing, scrubbing or any such pernicketyness so far, not even so much as a drop of washing-up liquid. The tap is set into an upright rock in the terrace wall below a long, low *rustico* with a lichen-covered terracotta roof; in here stands the row of fat towering vats in which the squashed grapes have been sitting for the regulation four days. Now it is time to decant the wine from the fermenting vats, wringing it out of the grapeskins which have finished doing their job and must be removed. Then the fizzling purple *mosto* will go into the demijohns for a forty days' rest.

This place is higher than our house and over the other side of the valley the view downhill is all sea and sky. Besta de Zago ought to be visible somewhere over to our right; needless to say it isn't. Nothing but wave upon wave of olive trees. On the wide terrace to the seaward side of the building Domenico is hard at work at the grape-wringer, aided by a man even smaller and sinewier than himself, a man whose unusual name, I have gathered, is Compare Gianni: Gianni Appears. Like a stage instruction. And he does just this: appears like magic to help out whenever there is a big wine or oil job on hand. At the moment Compare Gianni and Domenico, vests rolled up to their armpits, are busy heaving, sweating and straining round and round the barrel-like wine-press which is bolted to a purple-stained concrete slab set in the dusty ground so it won't tip over under the strain.

At every grunt and heave on the six foot windlass, a dollop of wine-to-be squirts from the spout at the bottom of the press into a lightly rinsed old plastic bucket: the handle edges its way half a turn down the great wooden screw at the centre. *Forza!* Every now and then they stop their winding and straining while one of them goes indoors to empty the full buckets down the funnel into the *damigiani* – demijohns – sitting ready on a raised dais in their plaited straw paddings, and then to refill them with more wine and grape broth from the hissing gurgling vats. The other unwinds a few turns of the *torchio* to release the pressure, adds some more wooden blocks to take the crushing-plate down to the new level. The *mosto* goes in, and they start their winding again. The men are in full sun, covered in sweat and sweet grape juice. Flies are attacking them from every side, and there are still another two full vats to go. How pleasant to be female and be able to do your job under a shady broad-leafed *nespolo* tree.

Antonietta and I (Lucy is off earning money in the Land of Beer) have got the fire lit in the outdoor oven round the other side of the building, another of those beehive-shaped things like the one in her *orto* down in the village. We have a sackful of beetroot to go in it to roast in their skins once the wood burns down. Later we'll get the fire going under the iron grill that is cemented in to some rocks beside it, so the *brace* will be ready for lunch. But the main women's business is over here on the big tarpaulin in the shade, sorting grape twigs.

Every dozen or so bucketsful, when the wine-press gets too full up with solid remnants to take any more *mosto*, the men undo its four big wing-nuts, heave out a two-foot thick round damp mat of heavily crushed grape twigs and skins from the bottom of the device, and chuck it over to us. We shake out and unravel the tangly matted things, pulling out as much of the damp twiggy innards of the grape bunches as we can and throwing them away on to the olive tree *fascia* below us, where they will quietly biodegrade over the winter. The rest, mostly grape skins, we keep in a big wine-reeking pile to one side. They will go back through the press again when the first pressing's over. Not only is there lots of wine left in there, say the experts, but it's the skins that give the wine its colour and perfume.

Considering what shy and elusive creatures they usually are in this hot and sunny land, I am surprised, as I shake out my grape mats, at the rather large number of crunchy crushed snails in among the crushed grapes. I wonder whether I'm supposed to pick them out as well. Obviously not: Antonietta's ignoring hers. Snails are just part of the recipe. And since they've already been sitting fermenting away in the wine vats all week, I don't suppose there's much point in not squeezing every last drop out of them now. Still, I can't resist mentioning it. *Vino d'uva e lumaccha*, I say, wine of grapes and snails. Antonietta, predictably, cackles happily and says it all adds to the flavour. If you eat snails anyway, I suppose there's no reason why their presence should bother you. And if your word for what wine does when it's fermenting happens to be 'bollire', which also means 'boil', then I daresay you do feel that in four days they've been thoroughly cooked. I am not so sure.

Antonietta keeps calling this place a *taverna*. I am confused. Did someone once sell wine in this unlikely looking spot? No: of course they didn't! Whatever gave me such a silly idea? A *taverna* is just a *cantina* that also contains a table and seating space in it, a few cooking facilities; a place not just used for storing but also for producing (and, of course, consuming as you go) the family's food and drink supplies. This one does indeed contain not one but two tables: a gigantic square oak one with irregular turned legs standing in the middle of the room, big enough to seat four a side easily, and a long thin marble-topped one up against the wall being used as a work surface with one of those little gas hobs sitting on it. I tell Antonietta how lovely they are, hoping she may be dying to get rid of them. Not lovely, she says, old and ugly, but they have sentimental value – they belonged to Domenico's granny. Anyway, they're extremely useful. Sigh.

We have taken a break from our labours to come in and look for an important missing item: a special device for sucking the oil off the top of the demijohn before you start to siphon the wine into the bottles, a kind of mini-suction pump, I gather. We don't need it just yet, but we will do in forty days' time, and its disappearance has been bothering Antonietta. I am actually only pretending to look for it, since I haven't got the faintest idea what it looks like. She eventually roots it out of a dusty pile in a corner: it is a proper official factory-made Demijohn Olive Oil Removal Pump, neatly packed away in its box. They really haven't just invented this olive oil corking business themselves, then.

Of course not! Some people use food-grade liquid vaseline, which you can buy in the Consorzio Agrario, says Antonietta, but its very name smacks suspiciously of *roba chimica*, and she and Domenico steer well clear of it.

Now we have to go and check out the old litre and a half bottles which are lying in a dusty heap in the other room of the *taverna*, make sure there are enough of them. These are what we'll be decanting the wine into in forty days' time. Antonietta explains that you only bother with small bottles and real corks if it's such a good vintage that you're going to keep it for years. Which this apparently isn't.

How can you tell? I ask. By the grapes, says she, giving me one of those 'how brainless can you get' looks. I probe no further. In any case, this being a mysteriously undeserving brew, we will be reusing the old screw tops, double-sealing, just in case, with a drop of the olive oil we will have recycled from the demijohn pump, wasting not and wanting not.

Does everyone just rinse their stuff in water, I ask, or do some people sterilize their equipment? In our country, I say tentatively, we think the wine will go off if you don't. Antonietta's never heard of such a thing. Anyway, as she points out, it's no wonder people have funny ideas about wine making in a land without grapes. She probably wouldn't be able to make beer if she tried, either, she adds, generously. So, Mr Boot, we won't be bothering to sterilize the bottles either. Just a good rinse under the tap. Or, if they've got a bit of residue in the bottom, chuck in a few pebbles with the water, rattle them around; that soon gets them nice and clean.

I decide to say no more about my experience of British wine making: best not to mention the tins of concentrated grape juice and bags of sugar hidden in my murky past. I haven't got enough energy left to really enjoy the outbreak of horror it would be bound to provoke.

On this side of the *rustico/taverna* is an extraordinarily ramshackle and haphazard-looking chicken run in which half a dozen fowl scrabble and cluck; also a great open-topped cement-rendered tank, which Domenico built a few years ago to make the grape squashing easier, but which they no longer use – still, at least it comes in handy as a rainwater butt. The idea was that you could get right inside it and trample around with no fear either of spillages or of breaking the planking on the vats: it has a tap built in at the bottom to let the juice out, like the vats, but would hold six times as much. It would have saved all the effort of heaving bathful after bathful of squashed grapes shoulder high to decant the contents into the vats. A brilliant plan, say we.

Yes, says Domenico wistfully, gazing at his defective brainchild, you wouldn't have needed to bother with the vats at all, just cover the tank for four days. But the cement, he says, somehow sucked all the flavour out of the grapes. After two years' unsatisfactory vintages, he went back to using the vat and old galvanized bath. That's why, these days, he's so protective of his vats.

Twenty demijohns at fifty-something litres each. We will have made, amazingly, nearly a thousand litres of the stuff. But, of course, they calculate a couple of litres a day easily for a household of two. Not that they necessarily drink that much, but you use a lot of it in your cooking round here, and then there's family and friends popping round for dinner, not to mention having to keep your voracious Mother of Vinegar fed. Five demijohns for us, and our Americano brew, which has been mixed half-and-half with the proper *mosto* and put in its own mini-demijohn, to the accompaniment of horrible faces from Domenico. Fifteen for him and Antonietta.

What about you, Compare Gianni? I ask. Don't you drink wine? I am answered by an outburst of uproarious laughter from all concerned. '*Compare*' they keep repeating, and collapsing with mirth again. I am used to this sort of thing, and wait in a quiet and dignified manner for them to get over it and explain. I discover that not only have I spoken in the dialect of Calabria, a thing highly laughable in itself, but I have just, in effect, claimed to be a native of the place: '*Compare*' is what, if you're a Southerner, you call someone from the same village as you. Or more literally, the godfather of your child.

Gianni is from Antonietta's birthplace; he is also Maurizio's godfather. So, of course, she calls him *compare*. (Nothing to do with *appearing*, then. Pity.) And Domenico's connection by marriage with the place allows him courtesy *compare*ship. I, on the other hand, should just say Gianni.

The answer to my question, though, is that Gianni Appears will be doing his own wine next week: we will be going up to his *campagna* to help him in return. Ah. Until now I have been toying, as I rattled my mats, with the idea of working out how much I have saved, or not, by making this wine instead of buying it. This new information ruins all my calculations. There are a horribly large number of imponderables to deal with anyway – would I for instance base my sums on the price of wine in England, or in Italy? Work out my hourly rate as if it was an office job? Or lower because it's agricultural labour? Or higher because it's more tiring? Or at nothing at all because I would much rather be doing this anyway and it's a kind of holiday entertainment, which some people might even pay to do? Then, is the wine more valuable because it is made of grapes to my own personal knowledge? Or less valuable because it is crude peasant stuff, maybe? I am already in deep waters when this new variable, another day's work up at Compare Gianni's as part of the bargain, is introduced. It is more than my overloaded brain can bear. I give up the attempt. Shepherd's Bush and Diano San Pietro are just incommensurable, that's all. And a year's worth of wine is a year's worth of wine.

The last bucket of the morning goes into its demijohn in the cool of the *taverna* and we stop for lunch. Our pile of steaming roast beetroot already awaits us, cooling on the ground in the shade. Today the *orto* dictates that for the *primo piatto* we fry up a big pile of those tasty green pointy peppers with just a bit of onion, no tomato, because Domenico says that ruins their flavour; for our *primo* we boil a potful of just-lifted new potatoes which we cut up and dress with the pepper stuff, as if they were pasta. A pile of *bistecche* and lamb-chops sizzles on the grill, cooking into delicious stripiness as we baste them from a cup of salted olive oil with thyme crumbled into it, using a rosemary stick as a busting-brush. We peel the ashy skins off the warm beetroot, slice them up and dress them with olive oil, lemon and a big handful of parsley from the patch. Domenico and Gianni bring out a jug of the *mosto* to wash it all down with. Lovely, halfway between wine and fizzy grape juice:

but no more than one glass, says everyone, or you'll get a terrific headache.

Now, at last, relaxing over the coffee, there is time for the experts to deal in depth with the question of spoilt wine and how to avoid it. Sterilizing does not come into it. Everyone agrees that the only absolutely essential thing with wine, apart of course from rinsing everything thoroughly with plain water, is never to perform the vats-to-demijohns operation, the one we are doing now, at the full moon. This is always fatal. The moon can be waxing, the moon can be waning, it doesn't matter; but a full moon will surely turn your wine to vinegar.

Seeking information from the Diano company about exactly what conditions we'll be facing once winter sets in, we hear that it pours with rain and is bone-achingly cold the whole time. Enquiring among the denizens of Luigi's bar, we discover that the younger generation have been absurdly optimistic: it rains even more than that, and is twice as cold. We know that, comparatively speaking, these tales of Siberian weather conditions can't be true: otherwise why would anyone ever have bothered with Wintering on the Riviera? Only Ciccio, with a Wintering in Denmark experience under his belt, agrees tentatively that from some standpoints it could possibly be considered rather mild here.

Everyone is busy wrapping themselves up anyway in this pleasantly warm weather to fend off the *colpo d'aria*, that Hit of Air which may strike an Italian down at any moment once August is over; something, we imagine, like the draughts that used so to preoccupy our grandparents when we were young. Not draughts though, which Mimmo tells us are called *spifferi*, lovely word. The *colpo d'aria* is something much more menacing and all-embracing than a *spiffero*. A chill, perhaps? In deference to local custom, we too have started to take a jacket or a pullover with us when we go out of an evening. Sometimes we even go so far as actually to put it on. By day, we remain fearless as far as air-hitting is concerned, going around in our mad foreign short sleeves even though October is heading this way.

The worst thing about the house, we decide when we try to

imagine, say, a whole week of rain and cold, or possibly even snow, will be our steep little path with stepping stones, the only way of getting between our two storeys. It already turns, like the road, into a mud-slide whenever a *temporale* strikes. We can face the idea of having to keep umbrellas strategically placed at all times; but underfoot, it seems to us, a solid stairway, even if it still has to be an outside one, will be essential. We are soon consumed with the idea that, like everyone else in this valley, we can Do It Ourselves.

You look, for example, out of Luigi's window at one of those old outdoor drystone staircases, built over an arch with a useful winter woodstore below, and you can just imagine some Sanpeotto waking up inspired one morning a century or three ago, or maybe it was only thirty years, and saying to himself, ah, I know, if I just built a bit on at the side here between my house and Bacì's, and a wee archway there to support it, I'd get an extra balcony and wood-store at the same time, and he could use the other side of the arch for a stair down to his chicken-run . . . Or was it Bacì who wanted the stair, and thought the wood-store would come in handy for his neighbour? Who can say? Anyway, none of it seems to fall down; all of it looks beautiful. And as I've mentioned they're still at it, all over the place, to this very day, even if in a more rectangular and concretey way. We have become more and more convinced that professional builders are not, as we once assumed, essential to building works. Architects even less.

We wonder whether to suggest a staircase project to our football-listeners for their Sunday-afternoon *divertissement*. But on second thoughts, no. We have ended up tiling the new floor downstairs ourselves because our kind-hearted helpers were too appalled by the scruffy old second-hand hexagonal slate tiles from Giacò's yard that we were going to use, and kept telling us to wait until they found us some nice new ones to make a decent job of it. You can't very well ask people to do jobs for free and then start nit-picking about exactly how you'd like the work done – especially not if you want something odd and old-fashioned that goes against all the local modernizing instincts. We will have to do the staircase ourselves if we want it to be even faintly curvaceous and stony. And we've done all right on the tiling considering we'd never mixed a bucket of cement before in our lives. The bedroom and bathroom floors have ended up slightly irregular, but then the rest of the house is slightly irregular too, so it all looks fine. We can surely do a slightly irregular staircase ourselves.

We have told our most recent guests from England of this plan, and thanks to them and the Intermediate Technology Bookshop in Holborn we are now the proud owners of the best building manual in the world. Some time in the late forties a certain practically minded priest, the Reverend Harold K. Dancy, noticed that a would-be spreader of the Word looked a bit of an idiot arriving in some Third World spot, where even the most benighted know how to build their own homes, claiming to represent some superior culture and world-view yet not having the faintest idea how to build his own shelter, superior or otherwise. If you want to convince your parishioners that you know something they don't, you must, reasons Harold K., be able to supervise in all its detail the building of a full-blown mission house, and a small church to acompany it.

After poring over the book for some days, we conclude that the thing to do, to make up for our lack of muscle and the difficult terrain, is to abandon drystone arches (just for the moment) and build our staircase with a nice modern heart of concrete and steel reinforcing rods, with only the visible bit, the treads and risers – as we professionals call them – made of stone.

We proceed to expend much sweat and blood on this staircase, and give many hours of entertainment to the staff of the Giardino dell'Edilizia builders' yard. Thanks, perhaps, to the disgraceful history of women in the Garden of Eden, it is, if anything, slightly harder to extract information about building materials, techniques and products from these men's men than to actually make the stairway. If it wasn't for the Reverend, whose advice allows us at least to give a semblance of having some idea of what we are about, the natives would have had us beaten into submission in no time.

Once we have the system worked out, and great piles of gravel and sand, sacks of cement and reinforcing rods are finally sitting at the end of our path, it is all just hard slog – endless amounts of nasty heavy stuff to be carried along our hundred yards of up-and-down-hill path. By hand, too. A wheelbarrow lent by Helmut/Mario, our only sympathizer in the matter of weird old-fashioned home improvements, turns out to be worse than useless on this terrain as far as we are concerned. Downhill it runs away with us, uphill it grinds to a halt and then rolls back on top of us; worst of all, on curvy bits it tries its damnedest to tip over sideways and dump its contents irretrievably on to whichever olive terrace is below at the time. Ruining Nino's nets into the bargain. We don't have enough biceps to control it; we are wasting huge amounts of energy for nothing.

In the end we break the sacks of cement in half, load the horrible itchy powdery stuff into carrier bags – not buckets, which wear out those hardly existent biceps twice as quickly – and drag ourselves along the path with it as if it was particularly heavy shopping. Ditto the *misto*, the sand and gravel mixture. Interesting sidelight here on why those milkmaids of yore used wooden yokes to dangle their buckets from – if your shoulders aren't wider than your hips, you can't simply hang the weight of a bucket neatly from the shoulder the way men do. You waste lots of arm power on holding the things out away from your body to stop them banging against your legs at every step. Fortunately, thanks to the inventor of the carrier bag, we don't have to waste time carving ourselves a pair of yokes.

Faced with the impossibility of getting a cement-mixer down the stupid path, we devise a superb girl's blouse of a cement-mixer out of a large square of that thick building plastic. You chuck all the ingredients on to it, hold two corners each, and then take turns at heaving, right arm, left arm, bit of a flip-over from the foot beneath the plastic . . . saves any amount of wasted energy manfully lifting wet sand about on the end of an already absurdly heavy shovel. Even if football fans do chortle annoyingly at the sight of it.

Five curving quarter-circle steps are at the bottom of our staircase, fitting neatly round the corner of the house at one side and resting on a rock at the other, so you can choose whether to head right for your bedroom or left for your *motorino*; and six straight ones continue on to the upstairs door. The most we can manage to build without killing ourselves is a step a day, what with the unexpectedly huge volume of concrete that goes to back-filling the hidden support-raft on its steel rods. We have got the biggest two, the bottom curvaceous ones, done already, and they look perfect. We are about to begin number three when, with all the ingredients mixed and ready to go, I am suddenly seized with a powerful notion that something is horribly wrong with our design.

I don't know what the matter is, I say, but we can't go on till I've worked it out. I stare and stare at the space where the step is meant to go. Ten minutes later I am still staring, and Lucy is starting to get annoyed. According to the Reverend, she reminds me snittily, all concrete should be in place within an hour of being mixed. Forty minutes to go. Could I just try to explain what I'm worrying about?

No, I couldn't. So much for not needing an architect: I wish one would materialize at my side right now. Without the words, the concepts to give form to my unease I can't even think about it properly, never mind say it. I am groping blind at the Intangible. The sister, sick of being lumbered with a ditherer, and one with Speaking Difficulties into the bargain, storms off to sit on a nearby hillock, where she snaps on a pair of impenetrably black sunglasses and boycotts me, muttering crossly.

Just as I too am beginning to think I must be mad, revelation strikes. What we have done wrong is to take the corner of the house for the centre of our curve; if we go on symmetrically, step number five will be at vanishing-point. Our staircase will come to an abrupt end halfway up the house. We should have measured out in mid-air the width of an as-yet non-existent step and taken its (invisible) centre as our mid-point. I manage to express this – at last – in words, and the sister forgives all, solves the problem with a rapid on-the-spot redesign: steps three and four will not be symmetrically placed over steps one and two after all, but will each shift artistically a foot or so to the right.

Once we have finished this lopsided creation, it turns out to look more like the local architecture that inspired us than our original plan did. We congratulate one another; evidently we are not the first people to have changed plan mid-staircase in these parts. Just one of the everyday hazards of architect-free building.

Finished! No more the mountain goat. We walk sedately up and down, down and up, marvelling at how much more often you can be bothered going downstairs to your bedroom to fetch something you've forgotten when the terrain is so regular. We marvel still to this day, as we endlessly stumble, spill coffee, and curse on arriving at the bottom step, at how right our priestly helper was to insist on the immense importance of every step being exactly the same height. One of the marvels of the human brain, Harold K. points out, is its capacity to adjust itself instantaneously, without need for conscious thought, to even a completely unknown set of steps; an adjustment entirely based on the notion that every step will be equal. For reasons we can no longer remember, connected either with mathematical incompetence or the drooping terrain down below, we built the bottom step half-an-inch higher than all the others. And though the staircase is by no means unknown to us after all this time, that extra half-inch goes on baffling our marvellous human brains.

20

This year's rules and regulations for the hunting season have appeared at Luigi and Maria's: a large notice – black on white to show it's Comune business, immensely long and complicated, in tiny print like something off the back of an insurance policy. Another decorates the poster wall in the piazza. We are surprised to see that to hunt a wild boar you have to go in a party of at least twenty. Opinion at Luigi's is divided as to whether this is a measure to protect humans from wild boar, which will shred you limb from limb with their razor-sharp tusks given half a chance, or vice versa, to protect the *cinghiali* from being devoured down to the last boarlet by humans. Probably the latter, though, since everyone agrees there are no *cinghiali* left in this valley. You have to go right up into the mountains, they say, twenty or thirty kilometres, maybe even as far as the Piedmont, to find a wild boar these days. There are hardly any hares left either; the only thing left moving are the birds. But not for long.

A series of loud pops from somewhere uphill: and Franco the Knife appears from the wild land above us, wearing a mysterious bulge down the front of his vest and looking very pleased with himself. He insists on giving us a quick and furtive look down his cleavage. Yes: a collection of very small, very dead and very bloody birds.

Are those tiny things worth all the trouble to cook and eat? we ask incredulously. Of course they are; you just crunch them up, bones and all. Delicious. Iole will be cooking them tonight, if we fancy popping in to try some . . . The hunting season isn't due to start officially till tomorrow, but Franco couldn't resist going out just the one day early. That's why his dinner is down his vest. It's hard to believe that any Forest Guard he happened to meet along the way would fail to spot the strange excrescence above his belt as easily as we did; or indeed the large something-in-an-old-sack whose form is oddly reminiscent of a shotgun. Still, going by experience so far, Forest Guards round here are blind as bats. Who could imagine Pompeo arresting Franco, anyway?

We now find that the pathway over which we have built our fabulous staircase forms part of some kind of hunters' right-of-way for getting round the back of our house and up into the wilderness. Or have our hunting neighbours just made this up? Every day more and more hobnail-booted men trudge up our virgin steps and right past our door, handkerchiefs swapped for camouflage caps, corduroy jackets protecting them from the dangerous autumn *aria*, dogs leaping excitedly around them, their owners festooned with belts and cartridges and yards of webbing. And, often as not, small caged birds on their backs.

Signor Ugo turns up with a lovely dog that looks, to our ignorant eyes, like a mongrel, a spaniel crossed with a retriever maybe. He is most offended. It is a pedigree English setter; the Rolls-Royce of hunting dogs. We are, it seems, casting aspersions on its breeding by being English and not recognizing it. As the hunting season wears on, we will see more and more of them: soon I can spot one at thirty paces.

The solidity and stylishness of our new staircase naturally comes in for a good deal of praise from these gun-toting English-setter owners. But the one-off appearance by Helmut with the wheelbarrow has been blown up out of all proportion by the gossipmongers of San Pietro. Helmut, as far as the village is concerned, built the thing: the compliments are all aimed at him. Fancy a wee skinny runt of a city-bred German being so proficient at staircase building! say our staircase admirers. Or words to that effect.

Naturally we huff and puff and insist that we did it all by ourselves. But far from complimenting us in Helmut's stead as we expect them to – only more so, you'd think, since we are novices and women into the bargain – Nino, Ulisse, Mr Beard, Signor Ugo, just look uncomfortable and change the subject when we insist that it was us, not Helmut, who did all the work. Finally we get it. Our do-it-yourself-ing is not something to be proud of; on the contrary, it is a tragic admission of our failure as women: of our inability to get ourselves a man to do the job.

Soon Domenico too arrives in hanky-free Official Hunting Mode, a small felt hat covering his head against the potentially violent air instead. That poor thrush is strapped to his back in its cage, chirping away for joy at being out of the bath. Doesn't he think it's a bit mean, using it to innocently lead its relatives to their deaths? Domenico will have none of this nonsense. Do we know what you use to trap robins with at Christmas? he asks. No, we don't.

A tomato! And do we feel sorry for a tomato? Do we think the tomato is bad? No, we don't.

Against our own better judgement, we are intrigued. Is it a joke? What do you do with a tomato?

You build a trap, or just use a cage with a nice wide entrance. You put it in a place where there are plenty of robins – a bit higher up near the Giacomassi cowshed is a good place. You put the tomato inside – best to use a round *tondo liscio*, not a plum tomato or a *cuore di bue*. Now you just wait. Robins are such warlike creatures that they'll do anything to get at your tomato, which looks to them like another male robin insolently displaying its breast, claiming territory. In the heat of the moment they will completely overlook your trap or cage. You grab your robin. You wring its neck, chuck it in your sack (or down your vest) and wait for the next customer. Simple.

Domenico is wearing his wooing-shotgun slung over his shoulder on a leather strap, gleaming in the sun: a beautiful thing. He gives us a hold of it. The action, all engraved scrolls and curlicues, has 'Sheffield' stamped on it. Sheffield!

Of course, says Domenico, all decent shotguns are made in *Seffyelda*. He is amazed to discover that *Seffyelda* is in England. The stock is Italian though. Would we like to take a potshot? Of course we would. Then, says Domenico, snatching it out of my hands and slinging it on his back again, we must come to the Hunters' Festa in a couple of weeks, up on the Gascio, the scrubby pastureland just above Sergio and Lilli's. But, he warns us, no music, no dancing. The Hunters' Festa is serious business. He sets off serious and businesslike up the hillside.

There may be a wild boar shortage now, but in a few years' time things will have changed so dramatically that I will personally meet one: not in the Piedmont, but just outside our own house, where it is masquerading (or so it seems at the time) as a workman from the Electricity Board. I will say in its favour that although it gave me a nasty shock, considering I had heard so much about wild boar ferocity and was expecting it to be a human anyway, it seemed to be a relatively peaceable, if quite scarily ugly, creature. Luckily the encounter took place at the crack of dawn, before I was awake enough to be thoroughly alert to my peril. I certainly did not have another nineteen people to hand if the worst came to the worst. There was only Lucy and her boyfriend Tom, not at all the boar-hunting damsel-defending type.

The day before this boar encounter, I had been rudely awoken early in the morning by the sound of much shouting and carrying-on just above the house. I am quite used to being awoken by shouting and carrying-on: but usually from below the house where there are vineyards, vegetable patches and olive groves to saw and strim and blaspheme and rev your motor in. At this time of year the goats, our only likely visitors from above, are far away up in the hills. And they don't shout anyway.

Dragging on a dressing gown I go out to investigate. Once I've succeeded in focusing, I spot two men in tidy bright-blue boiler suits in the scrub oaks beyond the water tank, busy grappling with an unwieldy tripod thing. They are shouting because it won't balance properly on the steep and rocky slope. It looks as though they are trying to triangulate something. Unnerving: we've never been sure where exactly our land ends in the uphill direction. Surely nobody could be planning to build something just above our house, and on an 8-in-1 slope, when they have the whole of the rest of the hillside to play with?

I speak: and once they've got over the shock of meeting a foreign female in a dressing gown in this place where only men in hankies ought to be, they explain that they are from the ENEL, the Electricity Board, and are marking places where concrete footings need to be built so that electricity poles can be erected. This is unnerving too. We've never asked for an electricity supply, what with our gas fridge and our generator and our solar panel plan which is being hatched round about now: and the fact that we've been told we'd have to pay the cost of putting in the pylons ourselves.

We don't need electricity, I say. We already have our own, thank you. We haven't asked for it, even.

Don't worry, say the ENEL men. They have been told to say, if anyone asks, that it will be at least three years before anything happens. But, they tell me privately as one human to another, I can rest assured that this will be an optimistic estimate, designed to defuse the rage of customers who actually want electricity. Realistically speaking, we will not be pestered by unwanted electricity for five or six years, if ever. And perhaps it's only supposed to go straight past here anyway, down to some Germans who have just bought and started to do up one of the small clump of *rustici* further down the hill (estate agent, a certain Franco). I stomp off back to bed, to dream fitfully of a small Disneyland opening just above the water tank.

So, next morning when I am awoken by more rumpus up the hill, I shoot out of the door.

Buon giorno! I cry, squinting up the hill with the sun in my eyes. I wonder if . . . ? I break off. There is something very odd about this workman. Is he lying down? What has happened to his blue boiler suit? And his mate? A moment or two of focusing work later, I am appalled to discover that the blur above me is not even human. There is a large brown hairy pig-thing staring at me from the spot where the workmen were yesterday. A dark ridge of bristles along its back is erect with rage . . . or does it, perhaps, always look like that? Its face is hugely bristly too, its lips drawn back in a horrible sneer. Its head and shoulders are much too big for its body, which trails off to nothingness at the hindquarters. The abomination stares on, evidently as appalled by me as I am by it. It wags its head slowly from side to side. It flicks its strange stubby tail over its back, lifts a foot and paws the ground . . .

After a long moment of open-mouthed paralysis, I decide it is best not to wait to find out what its intentions are, and hare indoors to wake Lucy and Tom to come and look. By the time I get back out again it has disappeared, probably to warn its own family, *au contraire*, to avoid coming to look at us. Lucy, too closely related to me for respect, refuses to believe that there ever was a boar here at all. By the end of the week, though, complaints about *orti* being dug up, reports of other boar sightings, are coming so thick and fast that even she no longer dares deny my sanity.

A week later a party of twenty men is to be seen tramping grimly off up the track, bristling with guns, on its way to eliminate the deadly creature. They manage, we hear, to catch a *cinghiale*; but there must have been more than one. Since then either it or one of its relations has been back several years running, snorting, rooting and trampling in the early mornings, digging deep holes under the olive trees.

Our bit of mountain is officially called Monte Quaglia, Mount of Quails; still, we have only recently seen our first quail. Not one, in the end, but a whole troupe of the things running along the road in front of our car, too daft to turn aside into the undergrowth. We have eaten one recently, too, in our antipasti at Sergio and Lilli's. Sergio was cock-a-hoop about his quail; though it was not the hunting season, he had managed to run it over accidentally – and who could complain if you accidentally killed a quail on the road out of season, and why shouldn't you eat it? What were you supposed to do, leave it lying there to rot? The thing to do was to leap out of your jeep and snatch it up quickly before anyone saw you. By the time we met it, Lilli had transformed it into a tiny pâté of an elegance undreamt of, surely, by any crude Ligurian peasant.

In the darkness a line of men wearing camouflaged hunting-jackets, shotguns cradled in their arms, stand in a small clearing in the oak trees on the edge of a high ridge, casting enormous shadows in the greenish glare of a pair of huge searchlights that rake the tree-clad valley and light up the night sky ahead of them. Giant mountain moths, big meaty creatures four inches long, attracted by the lights, flap around scarily, crash loudly into the searchlights, into the silent men with the guns; and, hair-raisingly, into us as we crouch nearby, watching and waiting under a stand of young oaks. The man at the right of the line raises his gun to his shoulder, sights down it, and roars a meaningless guttural sound into the darkness, echoing down the valley. *Uuhh!* A luminous yellow plate hurtles out from the bowels of the hillside below him and spins across the starry skies. The gun leaps back against his shoulder. Missed. Another bang and leap, and the plate shatters into hundreds of tiny luminous yellow shards that scatter their way down to vanish in the pitch darkness below. Now, in unison, each of the men takes a step to the right: while the one who has just fired leaves the line, slinging his gun over his shoulder and walking silently round behind the others and back to the end. The next gunman steps up, sights. *Uhh!* Another plate skims out over the valley. Bang! Bang! All step to the right, except for the last shooter, who leaves the line . . .

This is the Gascio, and the Hunters' Festa is under way. We are watching phase one of the *tiro al piattello* competition: plate shooting, or as we English eccentrically call it, clay-pigeon shooting. As Domenico has warned us, this is no frivolous night out. It will go on for three days; over in a clearing under the trees is a makeshift stand on which are arrayed the fifteen or twenty elaborate Hunters' Cups for the winners.

At the back of the clearing under some pine trees a kitchen has been set up. Iole is helping with the cooking; they've had to buy in the rabbit and boar from further up in the *entroterra*, she says. Not like the old days: the whole point of the *festa* was that these were the heartlands of the hare and the boar. It isn't seven o'clock yet, but the tables under the trees are already packed with hungry hunters and their families. Crunchy deep-fried ravioli for starters, wild mushroom sauce on the pasta, roasted rabbit or wild boar *alla Ligure*, with lashings of red wine, thyme and the mottled Taggiasca olives.

Further inland, in another clearing along a broad and surprisingly well-kept cobbled track, is the *tiro alla cartolina*, the target-shooting competition. Luigi is over here, in the lead by several dozen points. He is in two minds whether to be proud of his prowess or ashamed of it; being a man who keeps abreast of his times, he is well aware of the criticisms being aimed at hunters by the eco-lobby; he has not failed to notice the disappearance of the wild creatures that were once so plentiful in these hills. He can't help being good at shooting, he says hastily, he learnt when he was just a kid. Nowadays he would never dream of shooting at anything except a bit of cardboard, or a flying plate.

We go off down a side-track on which a bunch of small children are squeaking over the scary, suicidal giant moths, terminally wounded from hurling themselves into lights. The kids are collecting them up into empty cartridge-boxes to take home. All around us in the darkness those *woo-hoo-hoo-hooooo*ing owls have started calling. Down here, in a long narrow clearing, we find Pompeo refereeing the Moving Target event, in charge of a piece of machinery that would surely have delighted the heart of Heath Robinson. A *motorino* motor operates a concatenation of old wheels of various sizes, meshed into a bicycle chain-operated gear mechanism which in turn is hooked up to an immense length of wire cable, its far end just visible among the low-lit branches at the other end of the clearing. Pompeo attaches a printed cardboard target to the wire; the marksman gets himself and his gun ready; Pompeo shifts a lever, and the target heaves clanking slowly off into the distance. Once it has got about twenty yards away, it gives a great jerk and suddenly changes direction, whisks horizontally across our line of vision: a rather convincing impression of some startled wild creature hurtling panic-stricken out of a clump of trees. At this point the competitor gets a few seconds to take a potshot or two at it; the target changes direction again, comes lumbering and squeaking back along the other side of the clearing towards us, ending up back here with Pompeo and the Heath-Robinson machine from whence it started. Only this time, the marksman hopes, Pompeo will find it full of holes.

When friends come visiting these days, keen to get jollily off their heads trying out the local vintages, we tend to take them travelling, hairpinning up and down the valleys, lurching to and fro along the coast – a seaside bar here, a far-flung hanky-headed mountain gambling den there, an accordion-swirl around some village *festa*, tourist-guiding them up hill and down dale around the many and various orders of local nightlife. Not entirely from generosity: we like to spread ourselves so thinly that the local gossip machine will be unable to collate our outing into the night of scandalous behaviour it really was.

How much easier and more discreet it would be, we catch ourselves thinking, if our guests really must go out and get tiddly, if we could just take them to the so-called pub, where nobody – nobody who counts, that is – would ever get to hear about it.

No! How have we sunk so low? This awful degeneration is, we have to face it, the flipside of the coin of Belonging: the horrible pay-off for integration – even if, in our case, only part-time and honorary – into local life and community. Driven to yearning for the privacy of the English pub. No chance, though. No one is going to come all this way to see the charms of peasant Italy, only to spend the night in a place called Excalibur, a place where they sell pints of bitter on tap. Even if it has got vaulted arches; even if you don't pay till you leave, the Italians still not having got their heads round the barbaric notion of making you pay drink by drink.

Zoe and Christina have walked down to San Pietro bra-less in string vests, drunk vast quantities of spritzers – or rather white wine with fizzy water, which was the best Maria could do for them – and thumbed a lift to Diano Marina. Nine out of ten Ape-drivers, they say, slowed down to two miles an hour, boggled at them, and drove on past, craning round once the danger of being accosted was over to have another look and make sure they weren't just imagining it. Horrible, disgusting old men.

Poor old San Peotti. Our hearts sink. What San Pietro ladies do when they want a lift is get themselves to the official waiting-for-a-ride spot, the stone seat where the road passes the church: here they sit sedately, clutching their empty shopping bags to their bosoms, and raise a majestic hand when any suitable vehicle passes Diano Marina-wards. Of course anyone who goes past is bound to know who they are, be it a friend or relation or acquaintance of an acquaintance, so it's a perfectly ordinary favour to ask. Round here, that thumbing a lift action is unknown, something only seen on foreign TV shows: the very sight of it will suggest to our Ape-driving neighbours that the hitchhiker is either a maniac killer or a loose woman out for some wild sex. Or both, maybe. What respectable *contadino* would take all that on board? Even a daring mould-breaker like Frank the Knife, or a kind-hearted Domenico, would hardly dare pick up a pair of strolling wild-haired thumb-wavers with the eyes of the village upon them: they would never hear the end of it.

Our friends agree, provisionally and doubtfully, to try the whole-hand church-seat system out. They are amazed. Every person they hail stops immediately. And they are all really sweet.

The string vest question is harder to resolve. Zoe and Christina feel that it is good for olive-farming communities to face up to modern post-feminist realities. Why should women have to cover their bodies when men don't?

Men do, though, I say: the rolled-up vest is the height of nipple-concealing modesty. But, say our friends, the beaches at Diano are full of topless bathers, and people from San Pietro go there every day. It's not even two miles away! Not just two mutually incomprehensible cultures, but three to explain – starting with the Olive Curtain between San Pietro and Diano Marina. In the village our friends are creating an effect of calculated rudeness, not unlike walking into someone's living room and baring your bum at them. How will anyone know it's meant to be a political statement? Unless, maybe, we print a manifesto for the poster wall: *Why We Insist on Behaving as if We Were in Central London*. Though, come to think of it, I don't recall many scenes of mass toplessness there either.

We are by now – as you may detect – caught up willy-nilly in the web of obligation and respect that local culture imposes on its citizens. Any bad behaviour on our part – from causing fire hazards through lack of Cleaning to drinking an unseemly amount of wine at a *festa*, never mind being responsible for semi-naked Jezebels swilling litres of the stuff in mid-afternoon – will, we are horribly aware, not only be reported on and discussed in much detail all over the valley but, here's the rub, will reflect badly on any local person who has adopted us as friends, embarrassing them deeply and casting doubt upon their judgement in associating with us in the first place.

Trapped. On the positive side of the Belonging business, whenever anything goes wrong, someone we know, or someone who knows someone who knows us, is always there to help. If our car breaks down or our bike won't start, half a dozen people will help us to fix it, or take us round to their mate Bacì who knows all about these matters and will give us a nestful of fresh eggs from his chickens round the back while we wait. Someone else will give us a lift home if it won't be ready till tomorrow. If we've run out of cash and need a loaf of bread or a gas-bottle, we can always get it on tick. When we lose (as we have done recently) a pair of non-Italian speaking teenagers down on the coast, can't find them anywhere and are worried sick – it's nearly midnight and they're riding *motorini* for the first time in their lives; have they had an accident, fallen off a corniche road into the sea, decided to go for a joyride on the motorway? – within twenty minutes of asking at the Bar Marabotto if anyone's seen them we have a full report on all their movements over the last five hours. They have had several beers and a pizza at La Briciola; a game of pool and more beers at the Bowling di Diano; and were last seen leaving the Sito with even more beer, hair wet as if they'd been for a night-time swim. We will track them down within the hour to a corner of the public beach, where they are lying in a drunken heap. Meanwhile a clever second-string posse has found the *motorini*, driverless, and knowing that these youths are in no condition to ride them, fearing that they may take off again before we catch them, has chained the things together for us with a lock from one of their own bikes – key thoughtfully left in nearest bar – to prevent accidents. Very pleasing to their parents, our guests, and a fine story for all to tell. Still, what a level of surveillance! You could certainly never manage to die and not be found till you were black and flyblown the way people so regularly do in England: but you might be driven to suicide anyway by the relentless pressure. Or be driven to escaping to Milan, Turin, or heroin.

There is no denying that all this weighs more heavily on the female sex. Oppression lurks horribly unreconstructed amongst all the cheerful nosey-neighbourliness. Men's duties may involve a lot of spanners-by-the-side-of-the-road camaraderie, and the carrying of many back-breakingly heavy objects: women's are much simpler. Do nothing worth remarking upon, ever. And, remember, hardly anything round here isn't worth remarking upon.

The behaviour of Zoe and Christina, alas, is extremely remarkable. Antonietta soon takes up the cudgels on our behalf over them. She has seen those *Ones* we've got staying, she tells us one afternoon down at the *orto*, keeping her voice low in case they've crept back and are eavesdropping from the terraces above. Every time she comes along the path to her *campagna*, she sees them lounging around reading books on the terrace and trying to get a suntan at a time of year when they ought to be wearing their woollen underwear. If, that is, they aren't out gyrating, still seriously underdressed. She has noted their long fingernails, their weird purple nail varnish. Evidently they can be of no use to us round the house: they couldn't even wash the dishes with nails like that, never mind help with the cooking or the *orto* or the laundry in their fancy outfits. How long are we going to let them stay? We are too kind. We shouldn't let people take advantage of us like this.

We have got used to Domenico taking offence at the laziness and incompetence of the various male friends who come and stay; why do they not get on with the Men's Work that needs doing about the place, a bit of pruning or Cleaning or putting back up bits of terrace wall that have fallen down? (Useless to say that they are on holiday: Domenico and Antonietta's only holiday ever was that one to Holland, and doubtless they drove their son and daughter-in-law mad by getting on with helpful things all the time they were there.) Only our concreting, fire-fighting brothers have so far found favour in Domenico's eyes. But who would have guessed how easy it was to spot that our female guests, too, are lacking in the domestic virtues proper to womankind? Nobody even needs to actually come inside your home to find out: they just need to take one look at their fingernails to Know All.

No, no, we say feebly, as we do about the limp-wristed men we invite here: they do help, honestly they do. And anyway we've invited them here to have a holiday in the sun, hang out, go for walks on the beach . . .

Antonietta gives us one of her long, sharp looks: she doesn't believe a word. It is obvious to her that we are being taken for a ride, a pair of gutless Cinderellas battened upon not just by useless parasitic men but now by these dolled-up Lazy Sisters too.

The respectability question will come to a head over the matter of my Two Husbands. On the second year of our sojourn in these hills I have done a very foolish thing and introduced my first official visiting boyfriend, who shall remain nameless, as my '*marito*', my husband. Or rather, Domenico and Antonietta have presumed he is a husband: and, with some vague idea of not shocking them by denying it, I have gone along with the idea. They only meet him this once; we split up within the year. But, used to the impermanence of London, the constantly shifting populations of friends and acquaintances in a big city, I have not yet grasped that in a place like San Pietro, a word once spoken stays with you for ever, graven in stone. Or, if you're unlucky, multiplies and is fruitful, and grows into a great tower of San Peotto fantasy, as it will in this case.

Domenico and Antonietta, understandably, have seriously believed that Man Number One was my husband. They've concluded, from the way I never mention him these days, the way he's never turned up here again, that we must be separated, and that the subject is a painful one. Some years on, I have forgotten all about this husband episode; I have arrived, planning to stay for the rest of the year, with the current man in my life. When we meet Domenico and Antonietta, with, I suppose, the same vague idea as before, that they may be shocked at the idea of my cohabiting without being married, I introduce him as my *marito*.

Out of consideration for my feelings, they have kindly refrained from asking me anything about my earlier *marito*; but of course they remember his features perfectly well. They are startled when I claim that this completely different person is him. Do I really think they can't tell the difference? But, in the best traditions of *omertà* – silence – they say nothing. They don't want to embarrass me in front of this husband by mentioning the last one. And I, stupidly, don't even notice that anything's wrong. We go down to eat a gargantuan dinner in the smallest flat in the world, together with Domenico, Antonietta and Maurizio, who by now is seven or so and, along with his comprehensive collection of plastic Master of the Universe models, makes the place seem, if possible, even smaller. We eat, we drink, we chat, we inspect the Masters of the Universe, Antonietta's *orto* and the *cantina*; and not a word is spoken about my dubious marital status.

But a few days later, Antonietta comes up alone during Maurizio's morning school hours, stumping along our path with her stick to get me alone for a serious talk. Do I seriously think, she asks, that she and Domenico can't tell the difference between a tall, fair *marito* and a short, dark one? She is not a fool; she understands about things like divorce, even though round here they don't get talked about much. She understands that I don't want to discuss it in front of Domenico: it isn't men's business anyway. But I can be frank with her. I am the same age as her daughter in America. And although she would never mention such a thing to anyone in the village, this daughter is divorced too. That is why she's guessed at my secret. But I must be more circumspect with the rest of San Pietro; I would do much better to introduce this person as yet another of my vast collection of brothers. Or just to say nothing. And I certainly mustn't go presenting him as my husband down at Luigi and Maria's, for example, where everyone is still speculating about the last one.

Are they? Oh God.

Kind Antonietta. I am mortified. Why didn't I just tell the truth in the first place, instead of putting good people like her in invidious positions? After all, unmarried folk cohabit all over Italian television screens every night: and this is much more serious stuff than the right to display your nipples or to get pissed. They will have to get used to it in three dimensions sometime, stop having to go around never mentioning their daughters, for example – poor Antonietta! Someone has to break the ground, and Sergio and Lilli, who managed to put everyone's backs up almost as soon as they arrived, and these days have almost no truck at all with the village, are certainly not the positive role models San Pietro needs. Nor am I, I daresay, but still, I should have owned up openly to my naughty city behaviour. Now, if it comes out, it will reflect badly on Antonietta.

Or so I think. Meanwhile, though, Domenico is secretly taking a much more frivolous attitude to all this potential scandal; some time later I will hear, at a *festa* in Diano Borganzo, about the other Englishwoman – supposed to be utterly mad, but perhaps I know her anyway? – who lives far away up in the hills in some isolated ruin and is rumoured to have two husbands. This Englishwoman, my aged informant seems to recall, does some men's job for a living – some kind of construction work, is it? And the husbands just stay at home and don't lift a finger except to look after the house, leave all the men's work to her.

No, I don't, I say, trying hard to visualize this unusual ménage, which even by depraved English standards sounds rather unlikely. Does she perhaps mean the only other Englishwoman I've heard about round here, one who's recently moved into the Colla, an ex-alcoholic who used to be married to an Italian ship's captain and has now found God? I've heard she's pretty peculiar, and have been doing my best to avoid meeting her . . .

No, no! That's Sheila, says my interlocutor, I know her very well. (Oh God, what have I said?) No, this other woman, she continues, keen to jog my memory, hangs out, people say, in the old bar-and-restaurant in Moltedo, the one that is nowadays run by a bunch of Southern Mafiosi drug-dealers . . .

Ah. In spite of my by now long familiarity with the Diano valley's gossip and scandal machine, I have been a bit slow off the mark here. The identity of the mystery Englishwoman is obvious. It is me. I'm friends with Ciccio and Franchino: I once built a staircase: Englishmen (or, at least, the ones I know) know nothing of Ligurian agricultural procedures: and Domenico, at some point, has done some serious blabbing about my love life.

21

Once October has brought the occasional shower, mushroom fever strikes these valleys. With Caterina and Anna we drive up almost to the Piedmont to look for *funghi porcini* in the steep pine and oak forests here. We only find half a dozen; stopping in a bar on the way home, we meet an aged couple with a whole basketful. I get us all a bad *brutta figura* by insistently asking where they found them.

Euh, impossible to explain, they answer. But here, say I, is a handy paper napkin and a pen – just draw us a quick map . . . Volley of incredulous glowers: how can I be so thick-skinned? Caterina has to draw me aside: of course they're not going to tell me!

Next, twenty-odd of us go in weekend cavalcade after *Gambe Secche*, those Dry Leg mushrooms in the hills above Cervo; much more successful except that Lucy and I don't know that when you're sun-drying mushrooms you have to bring them indoors at night or the dew makes them go mouldy. So our Dry Legs go mouldy. Next, with Iole, we collect a load of tiny button mushrooms up on Franco's high pastures – ones whose stalks go bright yellow when you cut them with a knife, poisonous according to our English mushroom guide. Rubbish, says Iole, they have to be pickled by boiling in vinegar and water, then potted in olive oil. It is true you wouldn't eat them raw like *porcini*, or plain fried, they would upset your stomach. But they are delicious *sott'aceto*. This solves one mushroom mystery for us – we haven't been able to understand why people round here desecrate what seem to be normal button mushrooms in this way, potting them all vinegary and nasty. We give ours away to Fabio, whose dad loves potting and bottling things. Who finds it so hard to believe we don't like them that he pots them and sends us three jars back anyway.

Eventually, going for an autumn wander above our house, we discover that there was no need for all that wandering far afield; there are dozens of mushrooms of every variety right here at home, bursting from tree roots and rock crevices, nestling in the grassy patches. Although we know lots of them must be edible, we have no advisers to hand. And in spite of, or maybe because of, our miserable failures so far, we too have become obsessed. Left to our own devices, we're only absolutely sure of the *gallette*, chanterelles, so brightly coloured and oddly shaped that they're unmistakable. Even something we're sure must be a *porcino* isn't: the cap changes from yellow to bright cyanide-blue in seconds when we break a bit off it. Worse, the only poisonous ones we can definitely detect are the deadly snow-white *amanita*.

Can we bear to just leave all this plenty lying about the hillside, though? What we'll do, we decide, is to pick everything that even looks as if it might be edible, drive the whole lot down to Luigi and Maria's at *aperitivo*-time and get the advice of the assembled pundits of the Sulking Café on their edibility or otherwise.

When we roll into the bar with our carrier of *funghi* – a good three or four pounds of mushroom, poisonous or not – the game of competitive mushroom expertise proves even more popular than *scopa*, and several card tables suspend operations while they come to inspect our haul. We soon have the whole lot spread out over several tables while woollen-vest-clad patriarchs pronounce upon them. Two different kinds of *porcino*, both very tasty – good news, we had thought there was only one edible kind, and the other must be poisonous – and in such good condition, young and juicy, that everyone agrees we should eat them raw as an antipasto, sliced as thin as possible, dressed with a drop of olive oil. And maybe some flakes of Parmesan.

The star of our collection, though, turns out to be the most unlikely looking thing, a bright yellow *fungo* as big as your hand and shaped like it, though with too many fingers; called a *dieta* by some, a *manina* by others; no one has seen such a decent-sized one for years. They are so good that our informant has to kiss his knuckles – you don't do fingertip kissing round here – and call Maria away from her kitchens to come and look. Maria's recipe: fry lightly in olive oil with a couple of cloves of finely chopped garlic, then add (in this order) a big handful of chopped flat-leaf parsley and a glass of white wine. Simmer for a few minutes till the wine has evaporated away. Perfect as a pasta sauce. Warning: add no Parmesan – this will ruin the flavour.

Giacò and Luigi can't agree whether the three big white puffball things we've brought are called *farinelle* or *ovuli*: one name is Italian, one dialect, but which is which? Whatever they're called, they are pronounced delicious by everyone – slice them thick and fry them up like steaks with maybe a hint of onion or garlic. This will complete our mushroom meal perfectly.

Extraordinary. In this country Nature herself, it seems, wishes you to divide your meals into *antipasto*, *primo piatto*, and *secondo*: in just the one collection of funghi she has provided us with the basis for a fine respectable three-course dinner.

Now for the rest of our bag, the more small and insignificant items. Disturbingly, heated arguments begin to break out in various corners of the bar over the edibility of a good half of what's left. Our advisers examine them minutely, turning them round and round, prodding and squeezing delicately at them with big callused fingers, taking them over to the window for a better light, *Euh*-ing away. But a mushroom which to one card-player is edible but doesn't taste good enough to bother with, to another is poisonous; another will come over to see what *fungo* is under debate and tell the other two they're insane, this is a particularly delicious little number, his family's favourite. The others snort and puff and tell us to take no notice, throw those ones away, you'll end up with a stomach-ache, if not in Imperia Hospital.

In the end, the pile of questionable items is somewhat larger than the definite yes's and no's. Can we trust anything they say? How come they are all still alive when they do so much wild-mushroom eating and yet have such a surprisingly minimal grasp of which ones are actually edible? Is it really their wives and mothers, maybe, who collect the things for them, and all this knowledgeability is just a sham?

Eventually the answer dawns on us: each family must always have gone off and collected its own *funghi* in its own private top-secret places. And each family will, naturally, only collect the ones they have been taught by their parents are absolutely safe. Who have been taught by their grandparents, and so on. Probably with each passing generation a few species have got lost to the table of each family, species that by some mischance happened not to be around during their childhood training. We have unknowingly created what is probably the first San Pietro forum for the public pooling of mushroom information in centuries. Brilliantly deduced! When would they ever have found themselves all in one place, sharing their mushroom expertise? And why? They might likely eat one another's mushrooms, but once cooked or potted, one *fungo* looks much like another. This means, we conclude triumphantly, that any mushroom any one person says for sure is edible, really is edible. On reflection, we decide to go for any two people, in case there is the odd ignoramus or homicidal maniac among our advisers. All the hitherto debatable items now go into the carrier along with the definites, to the delight of their supporters and the despair of their critics. We set off with our haul for the hills, cries of '*buon appetito*' following us from the open windows of the bar. Hopefully not with ironic intent. And all goes well. We cook: we savour: we live.

As soon as mushroom fever dies down, chestnut hunting takes over. Round here, we discover, the chestnut is surrounded by a nostalgic miasma compounded in almost equal parts of pleasure and pain. On the one hand it conjures up all the pleasures of autumn, the end of the ferocious dry dusty heat of summer and the coming of mists and mellow fruitfulness; on the other it is redolent of hard times in the not-so-distant past, of scarce flour having to be stretched with ground-up chestnuts to make enough bread, of some horrible kind of chestnut polenta or porridge which had to take the place of wheat pasta during the worst bits of the war. The old folks remember only too clearly a time when they heartily wished never to see another chestnut – but still, in the end it is a good friend, always there when you're desperate. And so, to be celebrated. Time to go up to Testico for the yearly chestnut *festa*.

Testico is one of those ancient muletrain trading towns placed strategically between the olive valleys and the grain plains, once so busy and prosperous, now half-deserted. As the crow flies, it is only fifteen miles away from us, directly inland. From the top of our small mountain on a clear day you can see it perched there on the promontory of one of the high inland ridges. There is, or was, a muletrack which took you directly there, a continuation of ours. But by road you must go, perversely, right down to the coast, along the Via Aurelia for ten miles to the town of Andora, and set off back inland again, taking the predictable vast numbers of hairpin bends till you're back just above where you started from. We hear the tweedling accordions drifting down the terraces miles before we can see the place, as we zig and zag our way up to it. We arrive in Testico's main piazza as dusk is falling; a triangle perched on the pointed end of a ridge with two bars and a village spring, and low stone walls all round for gossiping on. A few merchants' houses, too, places that must have been very glamorous in the early Middle Ages, with massive carved doors and bevelled slate frames, oddly literal-looking Lambs of God carved into their lintels. On the inland side is a wide cloudy view across an unfamiliar type of valley, smooth and furry with pine trees in the half-light, hilltops pointy and Alpine, and on up to the high peaks far inland already snow-tipped; on the seaward side the bright green of chestnut woods are close below, rolling on down to the familiar rounded hills of home, grey-green with mist and olive trees, a faint smudge of sea beyond. At the far end of the piazza stands a crumbling Romanesque church inside which, we happen to know (Testico is famous not only for its Chestnut Festa, but also for its yearly Animal Fair, which we have dutifully checked out already) hangs a piece of parchment written in near-illegible medieval Latin, promising the reader some large number of decades off any sojourn in Purgatory they may be due, if they will only say a certain number of Hail Marys in this church on one particular day of the year. Which just happens to be the day of the Fair. Come to Testico for your yearly shop! Not just a bargain in this life, but in the next too!

Can the fact that this commercial enterprise is still going strong after eight centuries be at all connected with this barefaced advertising sponsorship direct from Heaven? The parchment, we concluded, must be one of those famous and expensive Indulgences that caused such outcries about corruption and money-grubbing in the medieval church; scandals that ended in Martin Luther, Wittenberg, and

Protestantism. A chain of events that led, more or less directly, to our never being taught to say a Hail Mary: and hence, alas, to our being unable to take advantage of the Special Offer.

Tonight we follow the narrow cobbled roads, which are, unusually, just wide enough for an Ape – evidently the place was once so busy with commerce that whole carts needed to be got down its streets, not just the odd mule – down towards the music. The alley turns towards the *festa* at last and the scene we are heading for is laid out before us. Three levels, one above the other. At the top the church looms enormous, high and dark on the skyline, outlined black against the stars. Below us a bright harlequin dance floor heaves with cheerful galloping dancers. But what is going on in the shadowy space between the two, level with our eyeline, too far and dark to decipher clearly?

Arriving at dance floor level we are dazzled: eye-boggling colour and chaos. The bandstand vibrates with saxophones and accordions, frilly shirts gleam under the spotlights, the stage is outlined in festoons of fairy lights. The packed dance space in front of it is paved with wildly assorted brightly coloured tiles left over from everyone's home Adjustings, and lit up with strings of multicoloured lightbulbs slung on cables from the encircling trees; to the side of the dance floor are rows of trestle tables busy with laughing, shouting, gesticulating roast-chestnut eaters and wine swillers.

It's still hard to decipher that darkened strip between the starry heaven with its silhouetted church and the bright sinful gallivantings below. The red glow in the darkness, the bent figures scurrying back and forth engaged in some great labour: heavings and shovellings, smoke and dark flame, metallic bangings and grindings . . . a dark satanic mill, the sufferings of the damned? Heaven, Hell and Purgatory maybe? A subtle reminder to us feckless partygoers that we would be well advised not to miss the next Animal Fair Day?

Some kind of smoke-blackened infernal machine, tubular and gigantic, looms on its pivots among a great heap of glowing embers . . . one of the souls in torment bends to its gaping, smoking maw, shovel in hand, outlined against the red; a group of sweat- and smut-smeared sinners labours half-hidden in the smoke to wind a monstrous handle welded to one end of the device, turning the thing endlessly round and round, over and over, choking and swearing as the fire cracks and spits around them. Meanwhile a chain gang of bent figures groaning under the weight of their burdens, huge blackened buckets with steaming, flesh-searing contents, trudges up and down the steep path that separates the gay lights of the innocent festivities from the hellish fire-terrace.

Nothing to worry about: just mass chestnut roasting in progress. Arriving at the Palace of Sin below, spitting on their singed fingers, the bucket bearers tip great steaming ash-covered piles of chestnuts on to the massive platters which stand on the trestles amongst the revellers below. We rush to join the heaving throng.

Not just roast chestnuts, but *castagnaccia*, a thick heavy chestnut cake; chestnut polenta, chestnut bread, chestnut tart, sweets made of chestnut purée, whole chestnuts boiled in syrup. We gallop the night away with the residents of Testico and their guests from the valleys around – we can do a rather competent Ligurian-style polka these days – pausing from our labours only occasionally to swill some more wine and stuff some more food. By the time we leave Testico, we have done the chestnut thorough homage.

In the last few days rolls of olive nets have appeared everywhere, lying along the roadsides. Apes rush up and down the hairpin bends, humans dash up and down the terraces, anxious to protect their next year's supply of oil. Big storms have been forecast over the weekend, and there is a rush on – the olives are starting to ripen and the nets must be laid before half the crop gets knocked netless to the ground and goes to waste.

Pompeo, true to his word, has brought some nets up for us – but he has no time to show us what you do with them, he says, we may just have to wait till next year. Next year! Can't he just explain how you do it? But of course, he can't. Older men like Pompeo and Domenico quickly lose patience with all our hows and whys and wherefores. Everything they do seems perfectly obvious to them: they half-believe they were just born knowing all about olive nurturing, vegetable growing, wine making. Anyway, none of it has ever been expressed in words. You have to wait to be shown, and that's it. We go clambering up to Nino's land – naturally his nets have been out for weeks – to examine the job, see how complicated it looks. Not at all complicated, really: a bit like fitting a dress to a body. Only the size of the elements involved is different – three-inch nails for pins, the cloth in unwieldy forty-foot long, fifteen-foot wide lengths, and the body you're fitting much too big to take in in one eyeful – hill-sized, in fact. And with limbs poking out of it in rather unorthodox places.

On our morning bread-run to the village, we pop in to Mariuccia's shop to check whether there are any hints and tips we need to know before we start. Women for some reason have much less trouble imagining that in spite of being relatively sane, we may just not know some things which seem incredibly obvious to them and that a quick description in words, requiring hardly any muscle power and no bulky equipment of any kind, could easily remedy this defect. Mariuccia as always is deeply informative. Never just pin two raw edges of your net flat together, she says; you must roll them over double, french-seam style, or else when you roll the olives down-terrace to be bagged up for the mill, half of them will vanish through the gaps. And check your terrain for the longest straight downhill stretches so you can angle your net correctly as you unroll – it's hard to change angle a few terraces down, you'll have too much weight on the ground by then, easy to rip the net if you have to drag it. But as it happens, she is off to help Aunt Erminia lay hers as soon as she shuts up shop for lunch – maybe we'd like to come and help, it's a big job for only the two of them anyway, and then we'll see everything?

Do women often do the nets on their own, then, we ask? No, they don't – but Mariuccia's family is very short of menfolk, as we know. Soon we are bouncing our way up towards Erminia and Besta de' Ca' in Mariuccia's clanking Renault.

A lot of those roadside rolls of olive netting waiting to be laid have pieces of paper pinned to them, a number or a letter drawn on them. What's all that about? They show the laying order, which bit of hillside each roll has been cut to fit. People with an awful lot of *piante*, or with especially intricately shaped gaps between their trees, do the bits-of-paper trick as they roll each net back up and put it away, to save time and confusion next time round.

Erminia is extremely pleased to see us, insists that we must stay to lunch once we've finished the job – there's plenty of rabbit in the pot, she says. Rabbit? Surprise. We know the path between the two Bestas well by now, and have heard the story of Giovanni and his drug addiction many times. Still I find it hard to connect twentieth-century junkie hell with Erminia's positively medieval lifestyle – just another thing to cope with, heroin addiction among the olive groves and the soap vats.

We scramble about in a half-loft above the rabbit zone, throwing the nets down and dragging them out, great dusty unwieldy things full of bits of plant and straw from last year's outing, and piling them on to the olive terraces by the side of the house. Erminia of course doesn't have hers labelled – she can remember where they go perfectly, she says, doesn't need such nonsense. Doesn't she just. We waste a good sweaty half-hour laboriously unrolling the first couple of nets, scrambling down very dodgy walls while trying not to get tangled up in the netting, only to discover our bit has a great slit cut in the end of it in the wrong place, designed to fit round a tree that isn't here. Back uphill, re-rolling, while Erminia tries to work out which tree is four terraces down and three feet to the left of a join . . . eventually, hot and irritable, we have the things all laid out in the right places and are ready to start pinning. We have learnt something already: we will certainly be numbering our nets. We may even make Erminia a set of labels, too, once this is over.

Erminia vanishes off into the house with Mariuccia to get the pinning equipment; my sister and I wait out here in the yard on the stone seat above the dodgy arch. The ladies return bearing four dishcloths, some string, and a carrier bag with several hundred rusty nails in it. As is our wont, Lucy and I gaze hopelessly at this collection of objects, waiting for a lead. We know about the nails, but where do the dishcloths and string come into it?

Simple: you tie a knot in each end of your dishcloth, then use the string to hang this improvised bag round your waist to keep the nails in. Eat your hearts out, bumbag manufacturers. Now we begin, absurdly, to do french seams all down a hillside; roll, tuck and pin, roll, tuck and pin. It would be a lot easier if the nails weren't rusty, though. As we'd imagined, the activity is strangely reminiscent of dressmaking on a gigantic scale; every now and then you need to fold, nip and tuck round a large rock, or pin a great ten-foot dart into your netting so it will drape snugly up walls or round curves and bulges in the terrain. I wonder idly whether Christo the artist has any Ligurian blood: it would be but a small step from this hill-couture to curtaining off the Grand Canyon or wrapping Sydney Opera House.

We're doing all right, we're told, except for a tendency to stretch our net too tightly. Don't forget you have to walk about on it in a few months when it's time to beat the trees, and if it's strained or taut it will rip. With four of us at the job, the terraces round the house are almost done when a lot of bongs and a long-drawn-out ear-splitting wail announce lunchtime. We aren't desperately hungry yet, we say, we could easily finish off first if they'd rather. No, they wouldn't. Outlandish suggestion; didn't we hear The Midday? Later when we have completed our digestion, and not before, we'll go back and sort out the rest.

For now we're back inside in the deliciously dark cool kitchen with the pasta pot on and the rabbit bubbling away. We sip at Erminia's red wine as we wait for the water to boil – we're still on her last year's vintage, she says, and it is wonderful, smooth and full bodied, nothing like her sulphurous white stuff. I'm sure it would cure me of heroin addiction, no trouble.

On the hotplate of Erminia's great square cast-iron woodstove our rabbit-in-sauce has been simmering away while we were working. The rabbit juices will be the sauce for the pasta. Nobody here, with the exception of restaurants, makes a separate sauce: you cook the day's meat long and slow in a potful of whatever there's a lot of in the *orto* at the moment. Lift it out and what's left in the pot is the sauce for the pasta; then serve the meat for the *secondo* with a salad or some other vegetable dish – today Erminia has a load of wild salad, rocket and some kind of dandelion, to mix with her red lettuce, *lollo rosso*. Lightly crush a couple of garlic cloves with the heel of a nearby coffee cup, douse the lot with olive oil. The perfect rabbit accompaniment.

Erminia, whose home is by no means packed with mod cons, has, above her sink, one of the ingenious dish-cupboards we have begun to yearn for. Everyone in this country has them: except, of course, us. They hang on the wall directly above the washing-up area and have doors but no bottom to them. Instead of shelves inside, there are draining-racks. Your dishes, knives and forks get washed up straight into here – which is also where you actually keep them. Washing-up, drying-up, and putting-away in one fell swoop. And it certainly isn't new technology. Erminia's is made of wood, the racks of dowelling, and it looks a good century old. How long have Italians had these things? And why has no one in our own backward country ever noticed? Have no other English people but us ever managed to get into Italian kitchens? Or is it just that historically speaking most travellers have been men with no grasp of the intricacies of housekeeping?

Our hostesses have by now noticed our bizarre interest in this perfectly ordinary item: I try explaining that we don't have them in England, describe the vast amounts of unnecessary labour performed by British housewives every day. But it is beyond them. Why don't these English women just go get a carpenter to make them a proper washing-up cupboard? It wouldn't cost very much. Ah, say I, but they don't know they need one. I get a most disbelieving pair of looks, and give up. I'm not sure I really want to publicize the fact that my whole nation is mentally defective. We return to the more comprehensible topic of olives.

Why, I ask as we chomp, do people all seem to put their nets out at different times? Our neighbour Nino, for example, already had his out weeks ago. And why do they need to be put out so long before the harvest anyway? – won't any olives that fall just go off if they're left sitting there for months?

No. Think how it takes forty days to soften up an olive even with the help of a vat of brine, says Erminia between mouthfuls. The net keeps them off the earth, and that's enough. You can put your nets out whenever you want; if you do it too early though you'll maybe save a few quintals of olives you might have lost if there was a big storm, but you also risk having a load of Dirt grow up through the mesh – then it's a work of the Madonna to get them up without ripping them.

Mariuccia doesn't agree with her aunt about this eternal olive business. The oil doesn't really taste so good if the olives have been lying about for months – it's much better if you can manage to collect them up and get them down to the mill straight away if there's a decent amount of them – if there's been a big storm or something and a lot have been knocked off.

But, I ask, won't they be unripe anyway if they've fallen off so early? No. Ripeness in an olive is, it seems, all a matter of taste: the oil's already there long before the olive is ready to fall off the tree. It's just the flavour that changes. Early olives make a much greener oil with a hint of bitterness. Some people like it better, especially for salads, and do an early beating to get it: then when the olives are properly ripe, another one for cooking. In Tuscany, says Mariuccia, she's heard that they start their harvesting as early as October, get all their olives in well before Christmas.

Euh! says her aunt, several times in several different tones of voice ranging between horror, amazement and disbelief, and then makes her niece repeat it in dialect just to be sure she's heard right. Before Christmas? She has never heard of this outlandish behaviour by the *Toscani* before. The olives won't be ripe! What on earth can their oil taste like? Why would they want all their olive oil to taste bitter? Or do they just leave it for months to settle before they use it, never eat it fresh?

Mariuccia doesn't know: but it's a different variety of tree they have down there, anyway. The olives aren't mottled brown-and-green like our Taggiasca ones. She's not heard that this Tuscan oil is bitter: just that it doesn't taste of very much at all.

Erminia is not at all soothed by this information, and now as she adds another gill or two of her own properly matured oil to the vegetables on her plate, she makes horrible sucked-a-lemon faces to herself and goes on muttering, 'Before Christmas! *Euh!'*

Anyway, Mariuccia says, addressing us alone since her aunt naturally knows it already, Ligurian oil is not only much more tasty, but generally better for you than Tuscan. She hasn't actually tried the Tuscan stuff, but it stands to reason that whatever type of tree it is, olives should not be harvested before they're ripe. No wonder Tuscan oil is not good for the *digestione*.

Later I will hear the Tuscan version of the timing of the olive-oil harvest controversy; my Tuscan informant tells me that Ligurians, penny-pinchers as ever, only leave the olives on their trees to full maturity because they weigh more when they're ready to fall of their own accord. This, he says, is a pointless exercise since the extra weight is not oil but other olive juices. Olives should not be left on the trees till they are ready to fall of their own accord. Needless to say, Tuscan oil is lighter and more digestible than Ligurian. I leave this debate to the cognoscenti.

The tale of our own first-ever home-grown olive oil does not end well or redound to my credit. We get our nets spread rather competently, impressing Domenico as planned: he turns up to find us pinning our very last row all by ourselves, ethnically bedizened with dishcloths and string. He isn't at all impressed by our nail-pouches, though, of which we're very proud. He just thinks they're normal.

He is also most deeply unimpressed by our never turning up at all for the harvest, immersed in various London money-earning schemes as we are. I get back alone in the middle of March, hoping they'll still be millable, only to find that he has been unable to bear the sight of our wastefulness and has got them in himself, taken them to the mill with his own. We have got nearly six kilos of oil per tree, he reckons, which is doing very well for people who have hardly looked after them at all.

I didn't know you measured oil in kilos, I say humbly – what does that mean in litres?

A kilo of oil is a litre plus a wineglass, he says severely. I can see I'll have to work it out for myself as punishment. He has also, in case I wondered where they'd got to, taken up Pompeo's nets and put them away in our roundhouse. So they haven't been ruined by the Dirt growing up through them, as I probably thought they would have been, he adds reprovingly.

Oh, the guilt. All right, I'll never leave San Pietro ever again.

A pair of precious first-ever demijohns of our very own cold-pressed unfiltered extra-virgin olive oil is waiting for me in his *cantina*: a hundred-odd litres of the stuff, another two hundred in a huge stainless steel vat against the wall, and I've not lifted a finger. We couldn't possibly need more than a litre a week for the year, says Domenico, but he couldn't bear to sell the rest on to the miller. Even though, surprisingly, the price of olive oil has begun to creep up to something worth having again . . . Still, he thought we'd want it for family or friends. In any case, we'll have to leave the second demijohn where it is. One's enough to carry along that *miseria* of a path.

Why don't I just decant it into bottles, say I, and save the trouble? I can just take it up a few bottles at a time. But of course I can't. If I don't siphon it out into another container and throw away the sediment every couple of months, it'll go off, won't it? And if I'd bottled it, I'd have to siphon out each individual bottle over and over again, wouldn't I? Which would be stupid as well as leading to a lot more wastage, wouldn't it?

I see what he means.

The demijohn is so heavy that Domenico and Pompeo now strain every muscle in their bodies to get it along our annoying path on a wheelbarrow padded with several dozen filthy old sacks and crumpled newspapers, one pulling it from in front with a rope, the other heaving from behind. There's no point me trying to join in – I know from our staircase-building labours that I can't handle a wheelbarrow along this path. Anyway it would just be taken for ungraciousness.

Oh, even more guilt. Once we've lugged it into the house, I get new sediment-decanting advice from Pompeo. The stuff you scrape out from the bottom of the vat, far from being thrown away, must be saved: it makes a particularly delicious type of *focaccia*, slightly bitter yet very tasty, called *fogason* in dialect. He will tell me more when I have some ready to use.

But I never will. In no time at all, with my ignorant Northern ways, I manage to destroy the whole lot before we so much as find out whether it would have lasted a year, as projected by Domenico, or not. I never even make it to the first siphoning.

Since we are foolhardily using our *cantina* as a pair of bedrooms, the demijohn is living upstairs in the kitchen/living room; where, being a good three feet high and ditto wide, it is highly visible. And since the beauty of the giant green glass bottle is completely hidden by a horrid grey greasy plastic replica of the traditional plaited straw container, it is a most unattractive addition to the living space. But I see, when I go to decant some, that the top half of the repellent cover can just be lifted off. So, assuming this protection was only needed while the demijohn was bouncing up rocky roads, on and off Apes and wheelbarrows, I remove it, clean the oily grime off the bottle, and cleverly create an object of beauty where once there was only a dismal plastic encumbrance.

How could I know that some law of physics states that where there is a huge weight of olive oil in a very large and relatively thin glass container, the smallest tap on the glass will cause it to split open like an egg? It does this two months later at the merest touch from a passing handbag buckle, wasting what must be a good hundred pounds' worth of oil and causing a terrible slithery mess which (although it will eventually turn out to have improved the look of our terracotta tiles no end) will take days to clear up. Or so I hear. Lucy has to do the cleaning. I am packing, about to leave; that's why I was flapping bag-buckles about in the kitchen in the first place. My flight to England is this very afternoon.

Antonietta, who has popped in to say goodbye, is horrified at the sight of the gallons of olive oil all over the floor, the broken fragments of demijohn. Surely I'm not seriously proposing to go and get on an aeroplane after I've just spilt a whole *damigiana* of oil? Have I lost my wits?

I don't immediately grasp the connection between olive oil and aeroplanes: does she mean that it is unsisterly of me to leave all that cleaning to Lucy? No. Hereabouts, spilling olive oil is like breaking mirrors. Just to waste a litre or so, when your bottle slips from your hand as you dress your salad or some such thing, will bring you seven years' bad luck. But a whole *damigiana*! There is no way that plane is going to survive, according to Antonietta, who as we know has her doubts about air travel at the best of times. I will never reach London in one piece. I should cancel my ticket immediately.

Iole, next up to say goodbye, is equally appalled by my plan to travel in spite of the catastrophe. Ciccio and Paletta are due to come and give me a lift to Nice airport: I am not too surprised when Paletta, seeing the mess of glass and oil all over the floor, decides not to come after all.

I think myself, however, that the seven years' bad luck attached itself not to my travel plans but to my olive-oil plans. Every year so far we have sworn we'd stay here right through the winter, get in those long walks – the all-day ones, to Testico, to Triora, much too long and steep to contemplate except in the cool of winter – and a good dose of wood-stove-snuggling in the evenings; be poised, rested and ready for the olive harvest. It goes on not happening.

It really will be years till we finally manage to get ourselves and our olives down to the mill in good order: till then, we'll end up relying on Domenico, who comes up with a proposition. Recently the medical opinions which once were so opposed to fatty substances of any kind, which recommended nothing but the oil of the dreaded sunflower, have been muted, and new priests of olive oil are on the road. The sophisticated city folk have begun to realign themselves with the crusty old peasants – in the nick of time, as far as our Ligurian neighbours are concerned – and olive oil is sellable once more, at a surprisingly decent price. Since last year, Domenico has been renting another plot of olives, near his Castello one, to take advantage of this fact. Now he has, inconveniently, four separate sites to travel between: his vineyard, his olive groves one and two, and his *orto* with olives. (Ah, how right was that land-consolidation legislation!) Moreover, he hates working on the rented trees. The land was practically derelict when he took it over, he says, and he had to bring the plants back from death's door. Now the owner, a fat rich *stronzo* (a turd) who owns a hotel down in Diano Marina, has decided to put the rent up this year. Because the price of oil has risen, and because, now the trees are better kept, they're producing more! Domenico is supposed to pay the *stronzo* extra for the privilege of having improved his property! And he is beginning to get problems with the *digestione* from dwelling on the injustice of it all.

He would infinitely prefer to take charge of our *piante* up here, seeing we don't seem to be much good at it ourselves . . . (pause for knowing moustache-twiddling grin) . . . He could dump the rented land, and seeing we come and go like grasshoppers, it would be to our advantage to have someone looking after our land properly for us. And to his, because our trees are next door to his own ones.

Instead of rent, he will go on giving us a couple of demijohns a year of our oil, till we get ourselves sorted out and are ready to take over; meanwhile, he'll keep the profits if there are any. Brilliant plan. Domenico is pleased as punch when we agree. Thus will the *stronzo* get it *nel culo*! And, he says, it's a fine bargain for him, because there's no chance of a brainless pair like us without so much as a proper place to store our tools (is this a reference to our bedrooms and bathroom?) managing to take over in anything less than a decade. Thanks, Domenico.

By the time we finally manage to break the mould and get here for the olive harvest, mighty changes are taking place in this country as it gears up to join the New Europe. First item on the modernizing agenda: a cunning plan concocted by the Italian State to eliminate vast swathes of that great national hobby, tax-evasion, at a stroke. Or rather, not at a stroke, but region by region. In a mere six months' time, every shop, bar, hotel, garage, restaurant in Liguria will be obliged by law to use a Fiscal Till, which will instantaneously register every transaction on to a regional Tax Computer. Pairs of plainclothes Finance Policemen will lurk outside business premises, accosting customers, demanding to see their receipts. No receipt? Swingeing fines for both enterprise and client. Your old and trusted customers will become, willy-nilly, unofficial police agents.

Understandably, the small-business folk of the area are appalled at this wanton attack on all the traditions they hold most dear. Social relations are about to be overturned, pitting man against man; Ligurian pockets will be badly hit. What is to be done?

After much agitated debate, the whole of Liguria has decided to go on an eight-day general strike in protest against this dastardly Roman plot which will doubtless bring to an end civilization as we know it. But, world-shaking though these events may be, no news service in England has thought them worthy of note. The sister and I arrive at Nice Airport this February day, day two of the strike, heads full of olive nets and oil-mills, utterly unsuspecting. The first train leaving for Italy is a fast one to Genoa that only stops at Imperia and leaves out Diano Marina. Never mind, we'll catch it anyway, get supplies in before we go up to the house. The blue bus will take us the last three miles to the waiting Fiat in Diano. We'll do some shopping in Imperia first.

But no, we won't. Every enterprise in the town is firmly shut and barricaded. Affixed to their doors or their plate-glass windows are long and close-printed posters protesting in great detail about Injustice and Unwarranted State Interference and the Death of Liberty.

An aged passer-by sees the dismay on our faces as we fight our way through the complex bureaucratic Italian of this awesome pronouncement. He stops and cackles. Eight days! he says cheerfully. No shops till next Monday! *Ah, sì sì!*

We know that, we've read the poster, thanks. We'll go and sit in a bar, get a coffee while we think over what to do next. But no, we won't do that either. The bars are all emphatically closed and shuttered too, every last one of them. By now we are in Imperia's Piazza Dante, usually a positive obstacle-course of bar tables and chairs; its imposing colonnades look strangely naked and archaeological today without the café furniture. A fountain usually plays soothingly in the centre of the piazza: that is switched off too. Gloom and desolation.

We put our bags down and lean miserably against a bare stucco wall instead. We can't go up to the house. How will we weather eight days of strike without food, drink, loo paper, candles, and all the other stuff that makes life liveable? Worse still, as far as we can remember we have used up all the firewood, and without a new gas-bottle at least, if not a chainsaw and a skilled pruning operative, we will freeze. February here may be bright and blue and warm by day, but as soon as the sun goes down it gets extremely nippy.

We heave our bags back on to our shoulders and wander disconsolate under the draughty arcades by the fishing port looking for passers-by to accost. Usually it's hard to move a step in this country without half-a-dozen helpful bystanders doing a running commentary. Today, nobody. Of course; there's nothing to go out of the house for. It takes a good five minutes for the customary knot of advisers to gather around us. When they do, their verdict is unanimous. No hope. Waste of time to look for anything around here: the strike is solid in Imperia, a town known for its militancy. But, the knot points out, in Diano Marina, where greed is often known to get the better of principle, and solidarity means nothing, we may well find the odd strike-breaker.

Quelling as best we can the shame of our association with a town so famous for its blacklegging treachery, we leap on to the next bus. At least the buses aren't on strike. Forward to Diano.

As we lurch loopily down towards the bay, as Diano finally heaves into sight, an awful thought occurs to me. Would you call the desire to evade taxes a principle? No. Or at least, if it is a principle, it is one so closely allied to greed and self-interest that even the most apolitical, or indeed right-wing, of Diano's blackleg types would likely be keen as mustard to support it. There is no reason why, in this matter, they shouldn't be in complete agreement with the Left on the Oppressive Role of the State. Hope fades. Sure enough, the bus wheezes to a halt in a dead town, empty streets festooned with posters. The *commercianti* of Diano have become militants to a man. Now what are we going to do? Could we scrounge necessities off everyone, an item here, an item there? Exhausting thought; it's late and we're tired. Think how much socializing it would all involve. Can't face it. We are, after all, English.

Next idea: stay, for tonight at least, at Luigi and Maria's. They will have been forewarned, and hopefully forearmed with victuals, against this shopless week. Unless, horror of horrors, they're on strike too?

But no, a quick phonecall establishes that they aren't. A quick detour to the Bar Sito to dig out Federico the cab driver, whose version of the strike turns out to be a sit-in in the back bar, and in no time at all we are dragging our baggage joyfully up the stairs towards those once-reviled hammocky chainmail beds.

Down at the bar, Luigi explains to anyone who cares to listen – mostly just us two, everyone else knows it already – that all this tax-rationalizing business is really down to the end of the Cold War. The only reason this pathetic, inefficient and ramshackle Italian State, run by bloodsucking criminals, has managed to limp along for the last few decades, he says, is that the United States has stuffed money into its pockets to keep it going. Loans, subsidies, billions of dollars, anything to fend off the Soviet threat. But now the days of the corrupt are numbered; now there's no reason to shore them up. They're a bulwark against nothing, and honest democracy's got a chance at last in Italy.

Great, we say, we're pleased to hear it. Is this why he hasn't joined the strike?

It is easy, he says, ignoring the question and fixing us with an accusing eye, to go on about the Americans. But we British are just as much to blame as the USA for the sad state of his country. Did we know that?

No, not really, we say. Looks like we're in for one of Luigi's lessons. Here it comes.

Who, he asks, did our Allied Command put in charge of the liberated areas as we fought our way up Italy in 1944 booting the Germans out? Do we know that?

We admit, humbly, to having no idea. But Luigi is not going to tell us. Not yet.

We probably imagine, don't we, that we would have chosen our allies, the Partisans? Firm democrats, people who had been risking their lives for years fighting the Fascists?

We might very well have thought that: something tells us we would have been wrong.

Mafiosi, that's who. Corrupt local bigwigs with their bands of arse-lickers. People who had never lifted a finger against the Fascists; who had collaborated, even. Gave the bastards a leg-up when they'd been all but swept away. So obsessed with the Communist Threat that we preferred to re-install corruption and feudalism all over his country.

Not a good feeling, suddenly to find yourself responsible for the post-war renaissance of the Italian Mafia. Even if you weren't actually around at the time.

Luigi takes pity on us. It doesn't matter any more, he says. Now, at last, rational capitalism is on its way. Luigi, of course, does not like capitalism: but if he has to have it, he prefers the clean rational kind to the corrupt inefficient kind. That, of course, is why he didn't join the strike of the Vile Petty-Bourgeois.

22

Inspired by the renaissance of the olive, and by the EEC money available for the regeneration of agriculture in decaying mountain regions, or some such thing, a course entitled New Techniques in Oliviculture is about to start, organized by the Comune, down at the Town Hall in Diano – a series of five talks from experts and a lovely fat illustrated handbook to go with it.

On the first night a good fifty people have turned up, among them a pretty healthy contingent of under-forties. Some have even managed to drag their aged parents along: Ciccio is a few rows away from us with a gloweringly reluctant Salvatore. He's thinking of giving up his share in the restaurant and turning *agricoltore* along with his old dad, now you can make a decent living out of the land at last. No worries about taxes and Mafiosi and the discrepancies in taste between Germans and Italians. And he could work when he felt like it for a change. No you couldn't, says Salvatore: *la terra e bassa* – the earth is low.

One of those beardy red T-shirty men – Ligurian Regional Pride styling – appears to start the class and nip family feuding in the bud. He has come right from the other end of Liguria – rumour has it, from somewhere past Genoa – to set us on the road to olive riches.

The Beard From Beyond Genoa begins by lulling us into a false sense of security by telling us no end of interesting facts, such as that the olive is not really a tree, but technically speaking a bush since it will sprout branches all the way up its trunk if humans don't stop it. (I suppose that's why everyone round here calls it a plant, not a tree: probably not much of a surprise to them.) Then, having established his expertise, and gained everyone's deep interest by telling us that by the end of the course we'll be able to make twice as much olive oil with half the labour, he launches a swingeing attack on the Good Old Ways.

The terraces in this area have been planted too thickly with olive trees, he says; our grandfathers, good Ligurians (speak for yourself, says Salvatore *sotto voce*) couldn't resist squeezing an extra plant in wherever there was a bit of space. But this means too many trees have to share what nutriment and water there is. We will find we actually get more *quintali* of olives, says our Beard, if we simply eliminate every second or third tree. A wave of horrified muttering goes round the room. He'll lose his audience in no time if he goes on like this. Sacrilege! Destroying olive trees is not a subject to be lightly bandied about this valley. Your man is clearly from some spendthrift wastrel type of a place, even if it is notionally in Liguria.

Moreover, says the vandal, the trees round here have been left to grow excessively tall, and thereby waste a lot of olive-producing energy. Being too close together to start with, they compete point-lessly to get the most out of the available sun. The local pruning technique – maximum height, maximum width and openness – may be ancient and customary, but it is wrong.

Rebellious muttering breaks out again: the lecturer presses inexor-ably on with his revolutionary thesis, ignoring all.

Tall, wide trees may have been fine in the days when people could count on a big extended family at harvest time to clamber about up ladders beating at endless high branches: these days, though, when a lot of family members have other jobs, you want to reduce the essential workforce to just one or two people. He will be showing us how to do this and at the same time get more, not less, oil from our trees. (Good job he keeps emphasizing this: it seems to have a calming effect.)

He will, he says, show us a series of slides to introduce us to the main point of the course: the *taglio drastico*, drastic cut. We are plunged into darkness, and the show begins.

Slide One: its owner stands proudly by a huge and noble-looking tree, wide and spreading and tall as a house. There is a small outbreak of excitement: someone recognizes the man.

Yes, says the lecturer, this is in the Imperia valley; he and his team have (cunningly) been trying out their new techniques on a terrace or two in each of the Provinces of Liguria, so people can go and see the improvement for themselves; you don't have to take the word of a *sconosciuto*, an unknown, for it . . .

Slide Two: the owner poses, wooden-faced now, with his chainsaw next to a tragic-looking stump. His prize tree is now only a foot or so taller than him, with a few sad little tufts of skinny young branches left popping out at the top and sides. It looks utterly ridiculous. A deathly silence falls.

Slide Three: later that summer, and the tree has recovered a bit, trailing tufts of new green growth all over the place, which do indeed seem healthier than the original version, springier and sappier and bursting with fruit . . . but alas – *Next Slide*: the poor tree has been pruned drastically again. Only downward-pointing young branches must be left, we are told sternly. Ones that point upwards don't bear fruit and just waste energy. The victim is looking terrible again, the fat gnarled trunk totally out of proportion to weedy dangling fronds. The older members of his audience are suffering terribly – it is more than they can stand to see such treatment of their beloved olive. Ciccio is practically holding Salvatore down in his seat; much *Euh*-ing is going on, hushed yet appalled, among the true-bred Ligurians. Miraculously, by year three the poor tree – or rather, bush – has become a wildly energetic-looking dark-green weeping willow, every dangling twiglet positively bursting with fat healthy olives. And, says our lecturer triumphantly, it has produced six kilos of oil – as much as it did in the last year of its former incarnation, when it was ten times bigger.

The class comes to an end amidst much discussion: the man who recognized the owner of this tree, a man called Orlando Bellicoso (really), insists that Bellicoso is such an incompetent that practically anybody, including bearded ignoramuses, could have made it produce more oil than he did.

Anyway, says another of the old guard, they will have paid him to let them experiment on his *campagna*, won't they, so he's bound to stick by their story: he's not going to let on if it doesn't really work, is he?

Nearby the lecturer's political allegiances are being debated. Maybe he was owed a favour by the Left Alliance, under whose auspices he has come here, and they had to let him come, no matter what nonsense he was going to spout? Some of the older men decide to have no more truck with these politically motivated classes.

Never mind the supposed alliance of the Left under the Olive Branch symbol; this is clearly a crafty Socialist plot to ruin good Communist olive plants. Others look at the question from another, perhaps more Freudian, standpoint: the bigger your tree is, the better it must be. Everyone knows that: and there's an end to the matter.

In lesson two we move on to harvesting techniques, where we are told not to batter our trees with sticks the way we always have done. It damages the bark and makes them more liable to fungal attack. Instead we should buy an extremely expensive rattling machine, or at the very least a kind of vibrating comb contraption, to get the olives off the branches and into our nets. This will also mean less bruising to the fruits themselves, and a higher quality oil. Several of the few remaining members of the older generation in the class conclude that our teacher is in the pay of some agricultural-equipment manufacturer, and propound this theory with much passion at the end of class. An American multinational – or maybe a Tuscan consortium? Someone has heard that in Tuscany they use these absurd contraptions . . .

Not too surprisingly, by lesson three, there are only three members of the older generation left in the class to keep us younger folk company as we hear the latest in the battle against fungal infections and parasites; pesticides versus organic solutions. Ciccio's father has refused categorically to come and listen to arrant nonsense for a whole hour and a half after dinner, when he could be using his time more fruitfully and profitably playing *petanca* with his mates on the esplanade as usual. But his second-eldest daughter Rosi has come in his place. She was so annoyed by her father's Luddite attitudes, she says, that she decided to come herself to show him. She has just bought herself a piece of land a few valleys along, with vineyards and olives on it and half a *rustico*, and she wants to know all there is to know even if her father's determined to stay ignorant.

We are following with interest the fortunes of the Anglo-Saxon concept of country living, which seems to be slowly making some headway in this land. Is she going to build herself a house on it? She doesn't know. Maybe. It's right near Civezza, a lovely little walled town along the coast a bit. The place is beautiful, has a tiny river full of fish running through it, and if she didn't buy it she knew some Plainsman or German would. That, really, was the only reason. A bit childish, she says with a grin. She will wait and see.

In lesson four, called The Market and Financial Incentives, a new and dynamically besuited person explains to us very longwindedly that The Family down here on the coast is admirably placed for Economic Diversification, able simultaneously to take advantage of the full-time employment of the summer tourist season, and of their traditional links to the Land. We knew that already, thanks.

Not only this, but new legislation allows us to band together in cooperatives as long as there are at least twelve landowners among us; we will get EEC grants too if our cooperative can rake together more than some huge number of hectares. (Aha! I spot yet another attempt to consolidate this absurdly sub-divided land!) He waves a leaflet at us; we should pick it up at the end of the class. It explains everything.

In the last lesson Mr Suit gets very excited about the new Public Relations initiatives being taken. The world's attention is to be drawn to the fact that olive oil, like wine, has a myriad of different flavours and styles. Hopefully, there will soon be an outbreak of olive oil connoisseurship, just as in the world of wines; the public image of olive oil will go upmarket and stay there, and we, a couple of dozen sons of hanky folk, one daughter of ditto, and a pair of foreign females will reap the benefit.

To celebrate this, and the end of the course, we take Rosi and her brother for a mostly-female-olive-owners' coffee, where we pore over our Financial Incentives leaflet. We are all much inspired by the Future of the Olive, and Rosi is cock-a-hoop to find that she has made a wise business investment in her bit of land, and not just a childish up-yours gesture to putative holiday-home owners. She wants to go over there as soon as she can with Ciccio and his chainsaw and get on with some drastic pruning. Should we try to form a cooperative? Twelve people with bits of land shouldn't be too hard to find. Her family plus us two already makes nine. But would Salvatore come in on it? There's no chance he'll let anyone drastically prune his trees, though. Far too much of a dyed-in-the-wool old-timer.

*

When Ciccio's father won't (as predicted) let him do any drastic pruning on his own land – certainly not, have you taken leave of your senses? – he goes with Rosi to do hers and then, with the passion of a new convert, demands to be allowed to come up with his chainsaw to do ours as well. Fine, we say, as long as Domenico doesn't hate the idea – we'd have to ask him first, out of respect. Domenico, who refused even to consider coming to the course, proves surprisingly open-minded on the matter. Is there, he asks with a meaningful wink, more than meets the eye to Ciccio's interest in the welfare of our groves? I am, as it happens, rather fond of Ciccio. But I'm certainly not letting on to Domenico – not after the two-husbands outrage. In any case, Domenico is intrigued to see the outcome of these newfangled ideas. As long as we don't touch his own trees, that is. You never know with these university intellectuals and their mad experiments: remember Mussolini and his grapeless wine?

The results on our landscape of the full drastic attack are not, it has to be said, immediately inspiring. Where once our trees stretched elegant fingers right up to the height of the house, veiling roof and sky in shimmering silvery leaves, there are now ugly bald stumpy things with only a few downward dangling branches left, looking stupidly out of proportion to their great twisted trunks. Is it really worth it just to earn a few bob? Worse, will the trees ever recover from this savage treatment enough to make earning a few bob at all likely? The slides on the course showed beautiful healthy weeping-willow trees on the third year, but the fools haven't put the photo in their handbook for us to show Domenico; he can't believe any good will come from such a massacre. We'll be lucky if we see another crop in less than a decade, never mind the year after next, he says. Even Pompeo the modernizer – who was very disappointed that Bacalè, to whom he's now handed over most of his olives, didn't bother to go on the course, and has been making us tell him all about each lesson in great detail – is seriously taken aback when he sees what his ex-trees have been reduced to. Are we sure Ciccio's done it right? He wasn't just after an extra few winters' worth of firewood, was he? Guffaw.

But by the end of the summer, they do look as if they'll recover; they've each grown a round head of fluffy stalky branches, which at least conceals the havoc we have wrought, even if their new pom-pom tops still look ludicrously out of place at the top of those noble trunks.

Alas, when spring comes, we have to cut almost all of them off again: we are only allowed to leave the downward-hanging ones, the man said. We almost rebel in the interests of aesthetics; but pride, and so many interested parties, makes us stick to our guns. By the end of the second year, the difference is stunning. The one tree we've left in its old shape to shade the back terrace from the sun now looks like the sickly cousin of the rest, which are bursting with health and energy, trailing fat green branches so loaded with fruit they almost touch the ground.

Pompeo, irritatingly, claims to have known it would be a success all along. Domenico refuses to be impressed: he's not sure whether losing two years' harvest is really worth it. He'll know when he sees whether the crop goes on being this good next year. And the year after.

But alas, he will not live to find out. This autumn a black-edged card arrives in London. Domenico's dodgy heart has finally given up the struggle, to Antonietta's overwhelming grief. He was only sixty-four. They had just got their first phone installed: mainly because Antonietta feared something like this. But the instrument was useless, it was all over in a matter of seconds. No time to call an ambulance. At least, she tells us when we ring her on it, the long-awaited tragedy came while he was sitting peacefully at home with her and Maurizio, watching the evening news on the telly. He'd just got back from putting the nets out with Compare Gianni; they were going to do ours next day. It was always Antonietta's great fear that he would be left lying suffering and alone up on the land: thanks to the Lord it didn't happen like that. And he was universally loved. The whole of the valley turned out for his funeral to prove it.

On Domenico's grave in the walled cemetery in San Pietro you will find, high above your head, a little oval enamelled photo of him, moustache brushed and bristling, hair neatly parted and slicked back, looking most ill-at-ease and un-Domenico-like in a tidy jacket and tie; something he can't have worn more than half a dozen times in his life. His poor thrush lives on in the bath in his memory. It always lived there while Domenico was alive, says Antonietta: she can't free it now. It will stay there in its white enamel coffin, no more yearly outings, until it too gives up the ghost.

As if the loss of Domenico wasn't enough, the Grim Reaper now cuts a swathe right through the Diano valley. The first hint we get is when we hear that Erminia's junkie grandson has returned home: not as a reformed character come to work the groves and support her at last in her old age, as everyone hoped, but to die in Imperia hospital, much to her distress, of a mystery disease. Soon others begin to be diagnosed HIV positive – people who experimented with heroin in their late teens and early twenties, some in the big cities, some right here among the olives, gaily sharing their needles. I find it hard to imagine any of these people, reliable and lucid since I've known them, ever having stuck needles in their arms: but stick them they did. Just a bit of teenage-rebellion fun. Now, all these years later, the thing has come back to haunt them.

Anna and Tonino lose their eldest son, who's been in Turin for the last five years, within months of Giovanni; then Paletta's big brother Batista is diagnosed positive too; he is married with a two-year-old. His wife and child are negative, at least. And, one by one, a whole collection of people I only know vaguely, sons and daughters of respectable village folk, friends and relations of the Diano company, people who've left to work away in the big cities, fall victim. Every couple of months there is another whispered name to add to the list. Our friends are distraught.

But how come? Why here? I ask. Why should such a senseless plague be visited upon a small quiet valley in Liguria? But of course, it's not just here: I should read the newspapers. It's happening all over Italy.

Their nation's leaders may be aiming these days for clean-cut rationalizing modernity, but our neighbours Sergio and Lilli are heading resolutely in the opposite direction: they have moved into a positively Gothic phase. We are warned by Carlo and Nicola, who stop their cow-lorry for a chat once we've reversed round two hairpin bends to let them past, to steer well clear of our neighbours if we don't want to get embroiled: things are looking bad.

Just before we arrived, the brothers tell us, there were a few snowstorms which, higher up, actually settled on the ground. At crack of dawn Carlo and Nicola were driving up in their lorry to check on their beasts when, passing the end of Sergio and Lilli's track, they saw a figure lying, apparently unconscious, under a tree in the snow well away from the roadside. Had there been an accident? Stopping to investigate, they found Lilli, rolled up in a wet duvet with a small overnight bag at her side, claiming to have left home because her husband was treating her cruelly. Lilli did not seem entirely sober, and had no very definite idea about any alternative destination: just kept insisting regally that they drive her to Rome, where they would be well rewarded for their pains. We would never have stopped if we'd realized what was going on, says Carlo: *fra moglie e marito/non metter' mai il dito* – between husband and wife/never put your finger. But there was nothing for it now; and finally they persuaded her to go home instead. Home to a pale tense Sergio who thanked them in a studiously casual manner, as if losing wives in the snow was an ordinary everyday occurrence up here, while looking daggers at Lilli whenever he thought they wouldn't notice. Then he offered them a choice of half a dozen malt whiskies from a selection on the sideboard, as if this was some kind of social occasion. Before breakfast! says Nicola, shuddering at the memory. They wondered whether they oughtn't to stay in case Sergio murdered her as soon as they left, says Carlo. But it would just as likely be them who got it in the neck for having witnessed his *brutta figura*.

Sergio and Lilli's two daughters, Paola and Alessandra, now at the brink of teenagerhood, have severely shaken any conviction I may ever have had about the importance of parental influence in child-rearing. There is no way you would ever guess what a pair of nutters had brought them up. Sergio does all he can to draw both girls into sniggering conspiracy against their mother: how hopelessly incompetent she is, how pointless her beauty routines. Lilli meekly puts up with this, stays slightly drunk if possible so as not to notice. Alessandra, tall with long wavy blonde hair, was the apple of her father's eye until she reached puberty, when he began to call her *testa di merluzzo* – cod features – especially when there was company around – and complain that she wasn't pretty any more. Now he swapped to Paola, small, dark and intense, for Best Girl. Recipe for mental illness and general derangement in later life, you'd think. But the girls are cheerful and outgoing, the best of friends in spite of Sergio, and gently indulgent to their batty parents.

Now they appear at our house on their pair of large motocross bikes to tell us that their mother has disappeared again: this time she's made it out of the valley. They have just heard from her, from a nunnery some way along the coast, in Savona, where she has taken refuge. She refuses to return.

A nunnery?!

His wife's escape to the Bosom of Christ combines with his nation's battle for probity to have a most unfortunate effect on Sergio, never the most stable of neighbours. He appears, seriously manic, some time later to tell us that he has abandoned chicken farming for ever. Everyone has ganged up to ruin him, his wife, the benighted peasantry of Liguria, and the State, the whole lot of them. Someone in Castello has started a rival egg business, and since Ligurians all stick together like glue he now has hardly any customers left. He's virtually bankrupt anyway, and if he's going to have to pay taxes the game isn't worth the candle. His aged mother, says Sergio, can only just manage the girls, chicken rearing is beyond her, and Lillì refuses to return from her nunnery for at least six months. By which time he will definitely be ruined.

Next time we see him, things are at crisis point. Sergio is positively wild-eyed. Lilli is still refusing to come home, and the State bandits in Rome, not content with destroying his egg business, are conspiring to spoil his leisure time as well. They're after his boat now! Ironic that it should be a Roman who has ruined his home-life too: why didn't he do as his mother said and marry a nice steady Northern girl? He doesn't care about the death of the chicken farm – he's decided to go into gold, anyway, he says enigmatically – but this boat business is going too far. Even comradeship is being undermined by Roman decree! Now corrupt Rome wants him to pay up in hard currency for his berth!

(Thanks to comradeship, we discover, Sergio has for years just handed over a small consideration in kind every now and then to some mate in the *Capitaneria* of the Port, the harbour master's office, to pay for his mooring-place in Diano Marina harbour – chickens perhaps, or eggs. Or even, who knows, gold. Comradeship, of course, is entirely unconnected with nepotism and corruption.)

This time they have gone too far! What use will the State make of all this money it's extracting from innocent citizens like himself? It will end up lining Roman pockets! Or be sent to the South, supposedly to rebuild its economy or help earthquake victims or some such thing, straight into the coffers of the Mafia! Who are in cahoots with government anyway!

They may attack Sergio, as he has mentioned, from all sides, but they will not defeat him. He is planning a heroic last stand at sea. We must come down to the port tomorrow afternoon, when his mooring-rent is due to be paid, and we will see him give it to them up the *culo*!

I am sorry to say that, not realizing quite how spectacular Sergio's last action as captain of his ship is to be, we don't make a note of this appointment. In fact we only remember it at all when, in mid-shopping, we spot an unusually large number of people leaning on the wall between the Via Aurelia and the harbour, commenting animatedly on something that's going on down below in the port.

Squeezing between them we see Sergio standing shouting on the quayside, wearing a bright green shirt and surrounded by a gaggle of spectators. Next to him is the empty space where his boat once was: an empty space from whose depths huge bubbles gurgle to the surface every now and then. The bystanders, keen to share the experience with us, say that Sergio has made a lengthy and impassioned speech from the rear deck of his boat on the topic of the government embezzlers in Rome who don't care if they grind the small man into the dust. He has emphasized each salient point, and there were many, by bringing a large crowbar smashing down into his fibreglass hull, so that the boat slowly sank under him as he orated, the seawater rising up to his knees, up to his thighs; till he had to climb on to the cabin roof for his closing remarks, making his final leap to safety on the dock at the last moment as his ship finally disappeared heaving, frothing and groaning beneath the waves.

Our informant and his cronies, however, suspect that Sergio had secretly removed a bung or something from his boat before he began the spectacle: it couldn't have sunk that quickly, not with just those few holes he made in it . . . They find these practicalities much more gripping than Sergio's actual motive for destroying his boat, and we make our way to the hero of the hour, who luckily for us latecomers is still orating, brandishing the crowbar.

Any Italian up here in the North who shows the smallest sign of industry or initiative will be destroyed, taxed dry, he shouts, while the feckless South won't lift a finger to help itself. Or to root out dishonesty from the body politic! Down with crooked Rome! Independence for the honest North! They won't get a lira in mooring fees out of him!

Some time later, we will discover that Sergio didn't necessarily think up this inspiring speech all by himself. (Except, perhaps, the bit about the mooring fees.) His outpourings bear all the hallmarks of the rabble-rousing set-pieces of a certain renegade ex-MP, Umberto Bossi, who is at present gathering around him a Movement of disaffected Northerners. A movement whose preferred shirt colour is bright green; and whose insignia is a Nordic warrior of the Heroic Period brandishing a huge broadsword: a figure modelled, maybe – who knows? – upon Sergio and his crowbar. Soon Mr Bossi will be calling for regional autonomy for the prosperous North, for Milan, Turin and the surrounding fertile plains, the Pianura Padana. A new Plainsfolk-only paradise will be created, to be named, naturally, Padania. Degenerate Rome will be left behind to stew in its own juice, along with its rotten progeny, the poverty-stricken crime-ridden South. And, of course, all those backward, work-shy, short, dark *terroni*.

Less scarily, we will also discover, eventually, what Sergio meant by his mysterious remarks about dealing in gold: he has become a sales representative for a company that specializes in supplying gold to dentists.

*

Various of our Diano friends are unexpectedly, thanks to the reverse in the fortunes of the olive, beginning to fulfil their parents' long-abandoned dreams and going back to the land. The family *terreni* are no longer useless encumbrances, oppressive parental emotional baggage, but a worthwhile job. Much respectable home-making and settling down and even a bit of reproducing is under way among the Diano company. The family olive groves are at last being nurtured and the *orti* cultivated. Fathers glow as their advice is sought at last, mothers finally get the chance to pass on their *cantina*-filling lore, *motorino*-ing up and down the villages demonstrating the once-dying skills of potting and bottling, jam-making, tomato drying, anchovy salting. The future seems not only settled and assured, but likely to be everything the long-suffering parents of San Pietro could have wished. They will see their grandchildren grow up after all, in the empty houses that are now (yes, even more builders' lorries on our narrow hairpin bends) being Adjusted up and down the hillsides. True Ligurians find bits of neglected family property to reactivate, house prices in Diano being way out of the league of locals these days. Mulesheds and haylofts are transformed into kitchens and bathrooms, crumbling drystone walls reinforced and neatened with a nice dollop of rendering, drooping roofs are straightened out; not for holiday-home Germans and weekender Plainsfolk, but for another generation of olive farmers. A dream fulfilled; a cosy return to the past but with modern conveniences added.

23

We've escaped from the English Christmas hysteria. We're going to lurk peacefully up in the hills, with calm and quiet and big wide views, blue skies and crisp winter air. Instead of last-minute present-buying panics, canned *jingle-bells* everywhere, days of stuffing ourselves with oceans of food and drink we don't really want, we'll get a bit of healthy exercise putting the nets out, and a quiet time working on the house and sorting out the vegetable garden, while waiting for the olives to finish their fattening-up for harvest. Fantastic.

We arrive in San Pietro to find that the Hand of Nature – or rather, the Hand of Human Intervention in Nature – has decorated the village most dramatically for Christmas. Whatever Nordic-mythological explanations we may have heard about the origins of the Christmas tree, we see at once that the splendour of winter citrus trees covered in these improbable-looking golden fruits must be what really lies behind our Northern bright-bauble-decorated trees: a tragic yearning for the warm abundant lands abandoned by our idiot forefathers at the dawn of history. Everything deciduous is faded and gone, the vines bare, a lot of brown naked earth and branches showing: but this just throws into three-dimensional relief the explosion of deep shiny luscious colours on the orange and lemon trees, the intense Day-Glo fruit bursting from every terrace between sea level and hilltop, every leaf gleaming an impossibly perfect green. Imagine the poor benighted travellers of yore heading for the warm South, the traders and pilgrims, thieving crusaders and what have you, trekking down from the cold colourless industrious climes they'd been lumbered with, seeing for the first time the Christmas orange and lemon trees around the Mediterranean. Their folk memories, assuming they had such a thing, must have lurched and buzzed at the splendour of it. They must have been gobsmacked. So are we.

Why, though, did we fantasize peace, quiet and solitude at Christmas in this land of compulsive sociability? I have no idea. We find that we are honour-bound, unless we want to offend everyone mortally, to go and stuff ourselves for days on end with everyone we know. We have escaped two days of force-feeding in the bosom of our own family only to find ourselves doing a whole week of it here. Moreover, at this time of year, filling in any small gaps between your full-time eating engagements, you meet the ubiquitous *panettone*. This thing, something like a huge and exceptionally fluffy Chelsea bun, the Italian equivalent of a Christmas cake, is the focus of an absurd ritual cake-exchanging extravaganza which now begins to take over our lives. Everybody has to visit everybody at this time of year: and no one is allowed to do so without bringing a gift of one of these things, which come in a huge cardboard box a couple of feet tall and take up half your kitchen once you've got a dozen of them lined up on the sideboard in various stages of eatenness. Neither of us likes *panettone* that much anyway – a small slice is OK for breakfast toasted with your coffee, but try munching your way through great dry chunks of the stuff in the middle of the afternoon, or, worse, after a voluptuous and many-coursed Christmas meal.

I don't know about the rest of Italy – I hear it's different in the South – but here people seem to have used up all their culinary inspiration on the savouries and have none left over for the sweet stuff. The favourite local pastry, over which our friends here go into delirium, is a thing called the *crostata*, a close relative of the jam tart, but rather more like the bits of leftover pastry our granny used to spread thinly with jam and bung into the bottom of the oven for us kids so it wouldn't go to waste. I daresay if this is all you're used to in the way of baked sweetmeats, *panettone* isn't too bad. Maybe, but we can't keep up with the steady influx of the things, and by the sixth or seventh day of Christmas the boxes of half-eaten *panettone* sitting about the place have begun to mount up disturbingly. Even more annoyingly, since you can't go to anyone's house without one, we keep having to go and buy more of the things into the bargain. In desperation we come up with a cunning plan: we'll recycle them. As each new one arrives, we pop it, still in its huge box, on to the shelf with its friends and relations, and offer chunks from an earlier one instead. Now we can take the unopened ones with us on our own calls, dramatically reducing the backlog and concealing our ungratefulness at a stroke. Clever.

Or perhaps not so clever after all: we soon find out that we are not alone in thinking up this solution to the overwhelmed-by-*panettone* period. One of our own recycled items reappears upon our kitchen table a week later, recognizable by a bit of my scribbling on its box. We can't remember who originally gave it to us, or who we passed it on to, there being so many of the things flying about at the moment, but with the help of the shamefaced culprits Mimmo and Lorella we work out that it has visited at least four homes on its Christmas circuit without ever being opened so far: must have done, because it was given to them by someone we hardly know and can't possibly have given it to. Food for thought. Can the whole *panettone* business be an enormous confidence trick? Are we the only people foolish enough to actually eat the things?

At every one of our Christmas eating marathons, the hot topic is the EEC. Will Italy be let in as a fully paid-up member on the latest European Economic Initiative? Is the country irredeemably backward, corrupt and debt-laden, or can it participate as an honourable, reliable and solvent member of the industrialized modern nations?

Antonietta is finding some consolation in the thought that if only it all works out there will be jobs for everyone here like there are in Germany or England, and Maurizio's future will be safe: he won't need to go and leave San Pietro.

Maurizio, a big boy now, sits glued manfully to the television screen, dauntless among the looming cupboards, while we three women squeeze into the tiny kitchen, where Antonietta kneads and chops and stirs and talks about Domenico and cries and cries. Maurizio has found a crackly old audio cassette we all made on a decrepit ghetto blaster one summer afternoon years ago while we were making lunch up under the olive trees, chopping salad and cooking sausages over our bonfire. We put it on while we sit over this sad winter's meal – Antonietta insisting everyone else eat, not touching a thing herself – and listen to ourselves chatting, to

Domenico teaching us to sing a silly song in Ligurian, in the days when our Italian was a joke in itself: *Caterina sull' articiocca, che non ne posso ciü* . . . 'Caterina's sat on the artichoke, can't stand it any more . . .' Lots of laughter from Antonietta and Maurizio as we mess up the dialect bits, Domenico correcting us: no, *'carciofo'* is Italian, you have to say *articiocca* in Ligurian.

Maurizio listens to his five-year-old self demanding to sit on his dad's lap while he eats his lunch – Domenico asking how he's supposed to eat his with a great boy on his knees – and can't handle being manful any longer. He leaps up to shut himself away in his parents' bedroom where he can sob in peace. Us women sit around the table telling our best Domenico stories. The time he strimmed our garden out of existence . . . his hand-in-marriage trip to Calabria . . .

Domenico, says Antonietta, was sure the EEC would bring him a brand-new crusher lorry instead of the old tip-up truck: there was talk in the Comune meetings of a modern wheely-bin system, a proper rubbish deposit in line with the advanced North, where apparently we would burn our garbage neatly in huge furnaces instead of untidily in the open air. He thought there was a chance of subsidies for olive farming – loans to help get your fallen terrace walls put back up, maybe, or a nice new Rotavator that doesn't break down every five minutes. That would have been great. But without Domenico . . . ? Do we think a woman can officially be an *olivicultore*?

Of course you can, says her son, who has reappeared and plonked himself in front of the TV again, giving every appearance of not listening. We agree: EEC equal rights legislation, we say. She doesn't look very convinced. Anyway, she says, giving him a big squeeze from behind, it won't be long now till Maurizio's big enough to take over, will it? Maurizio pats her hand but gives no reply, just goes on staring intently and adolescently at the telly.

Will he? Won't he? Nothing much seems to have changed since he was three months old: everyone's still on tenterhooks about his Attitude to Olives.

Sergio, on the other hand, is very annoyed about the Europe thing. As Lilli, back from her nunnery and being the perfect house-wife again, rushes to and fro with course after course, we hear that in a desperate last fling to balance its books, to look economically viable in the eyes of the EEC, the Italian State has been pestering Sergio for several years of back tax payments, even threatening him with legal action. He is, naturally, outraged.

He is also outraged, as it happens, at the way Lilli has done the chestnuts. They are no good at all done in the oven like this, but his wife is too lazy to light a fire outdoors and cook them over the *brace* so they get that essential smoky flavour. She just can't find the time. Even though there are no chickens to look after any more, thanks to her going off for her nice long holiday with the nuns. Lilli flutters and giggles, doing her best to make out that this is just jolly banter. Alessandra and Paola roll their eyes.

Sergio has actually had the Finance Police up here demanding to look at his books, he says, wanting him to prove where he gets his money from! Never happened before, and still wouldn't, according to Sergio, if it wasn't for Europe. But, he says, he doesn't blame Europe alone. If it wasn't for the South, for the Roman Mafia, the country would be perfectly solvent. One day the North will have to break away; there's no other answer. *Viva Padania!*

A groan of despair rises from all our throats. Not that again!

Sergio fixes us with a baleful glare. What's the point of trying to talk reason to a gaggle of ignorant females?

At Ciccio's house we hear from Salvatore, who has been working hard at the wine bottle over the first half-dozen courses, that this United Europe business is all a load of nonsense. Don't his offspring realize that the whole world's run by the USA already? The thing's a farce. Europeans all hate one another anyway: what's the point of them trying to unite? Look at the English and the French. Or at the Germans and the Italians. Salvatore once did a spell as a migrant worker in Germany. In this tiny *buco-del-culo* arsehole town where he was based, there was a notice on the bar door saying 'No Dogs, No Italians'. United Europe! Pah!

Uproar breaks out round the table. Salvatore's son and all four daughters, his two sons-in-law and his two eldest granddaughters, all talk, or rather shout, at once. His three grandsons are too small to care about Europe, but they are already deep in noisy disagreement about whose turn it is on the Gameboy. It is unbearably loud in this small packed room. The daughters, we gather, are all keen Euro-enthusiasts. Rosi can't see why the rest of Europe should want to take on Italy's stupid problems though. Nothing has changed, in spite of all the Mani Puliti, anti-Mafia, judges and the anti-corruption campaigns. She should know; her work is split between France, Germany, and Italy. This country is the only one where backhanders are still the norm. A disgrace.

Ivo, husband of Rosi's sister Giusi, and the only real Northerner round the table, has a better solution to that problem. It is, sad to say, one we have heard before. The North, he explains, should simply expel from the body politic the feckless Mafioso South. There is an unbridgeable cultural difference between the two: Separate Development, old South Africa style, is the only answer. Ivo has not chosen quite the right audience for this speech – he seems momentarily to have forgotten that he has married into a family of Southern origin. The response is spectacular. Giovanni, husband of third sister Grazia, and a Sicilian to boot, goes wild, struggling to his feet, shouting so hard he goes purple, and sticking his face right up to Ivo's across the Christmas fare. Grazia, too, leaps up, trying to calm her husband before his blood pressure goes through the ceiling. The volume rises to an impossible crescendo, menacing fingers jab at Ivo from all around the table, angry forearms slice the air around him as the decibel count goes off the Richter scale.

The point being made by the participants in this uninterrupted interruption is, we gather, that the North's much-vaunted prosperity is all down to the labour of poor migrants from the South anyway. Mamma Francesca appears with a bubbling-hot oven-tray of lasagne, weaving nimbly through the flailing limbs, signing to us to ignore her family and get on with eating.

By now Ciccio is on his feet, too, shaking his napkin and loudly threatening to leave: he is not putting up with this. Why should he have to listen to a snake of a racist *coglione* in the bosom of his own family? Why doesn't Ivo come straight out with it and just call them *terroni*? In the nick of time, his wily mother slaps a plateful of fragrant lasagne on to the table before her only son, pressing a fork into his hand. He subsides, muttering evilly. Giusi, flicking her hair contemptuously, dissociates herself from her husband and edges round towards our side of the table, squeezing between the heaving bodies and her mother's many cupboards (which almost outdo Antonietta's for size and cumbersomeness) to apologize for her husband's lunatic outpourings.

A dozen or so courses later – each of the four daughters has cooked and brought enough food for the whole family, just in case the others failed in their duty – there is an unexpected audibility gap. We seem to have got off politics at last; and Grazia is telling the tale of a parking ticket she got recently. For some reason she's managing to do it without being interrupted. Everyone's busy digesting, probably.

She arrived as the traffic cop was starting to write out the ticket, she is saying, and naturally couldn't help but mention that her husband was himself in the traffic police – 'uno del mestiere', 'one of the trade', as she puts it. Ah, said your man, putting his pad away, OK then: no fines, of course, for wives of the mestiere.

We English take this to be an illustration of the corrupt old-Italy style behaviour she was criticizing earlier, and nod encouragingly. Did she tear him off a strip? Send him away with a flea in his ear?

No. We have completely missed the point. A week later, says Grazia, lo and behold, the demand for payment of the fine arrived in the post anyway! He hadn't annulled it at all! What is the point of being a married to a policeman? There is no sense of brotherhood left in the Polizia Stradale these days!

The whole table is shocked at such a betrayal of professional honour, and poor Giovanni is red with shame. Rosi doesn't seem at all comforted by this evidence of modern incorruptibility either. I look expectantly over at Ivo: he, at least, is bound to seize the chance to accuse his Southern kin of shameful backward attitudes, support the non-corrupt parking-ticket-man . . . No, he too is nodding away in outrage, in perfect agreement with the Calabrian branch of the family. No unbridgeable cultural difference on this one, then.

As the meal draws to an end, ominous references to panettone begin to surface in the hubbub. We are not afraid: we have a defence against panettone attack – a delicious gingerbread cake we have made ourselves to our granny's recipe. (Though we've had to use honey instead of the golden syrup and treacle, which no one has ever heard of in this backward and corrupt land.) I open the tin in which I have carried the cake down the mountain with a flourish, put it proudly on the table, and slice it up: the sister hands it round. Oddly, though, gingerbread turns out to be about as appealing to our hosts as *panettone* is to us, and after a polite tasting session and rather a lot of bits left on the sides of plates, the *panettone* gets brought out anyway.

We are rescued from yet more food – eating is due to start up again as soon as the family gets back from a stomach-clearing walk along the seafront, and we are being insistently invited to stay – by Ciccio and his youngest sister, Marisa. They are, they announce boldly, going to take us off to a party instead.

Francesca is deeply perturbed by this madcap scheme, her usual puzzled look turning to one of downright anxiety. What, no Christmas supper?

Her offspring point out that we have been sitting at table for almost four hours so far today and give her a series of simultaneous lectures on healthy eating. Francesca's worried look deepens by the second. Eventually she manages to get a word in: there is still tons of food to be got through. Are we absolutely certain we don't want to take the other trayful of lasagne to protect us against Night Starvation?

Lucy and I are thinking longingly of a quiet place up a mountain, a place where people only speak one at a time, and in English. We need to rest our reeling brains. But it is not to be. Either more food, or more drink. Francesca is only reconciled to the idea of our leaving for a food-free zone when Ciccio, inspired, claims to be fearful of a *panettone*-shortage at the party. Perhaps she's got a spare one we can take?

She certainly has. We get three of the things for good measure – who knows how many people may want some? We might, as Francesca points out, be left with none for ourselves if we only took one. Maternal honour satisfied, at last we make our escape into the quiet darkness of the street, dragging our giant boxes. Which, as soon as we've got round the corner, Ciccio and Marisa insist on loading into the boot of our car: of course we won't need them at the party, which is bound to be heaving with the things.

Yet more *panettone*. There also turn out to be yet more days of Christmas business here in Italy: first the *festa* of Santo Stefano, St Stephen, and then just when you think it's all over, the day when the *Befana*, a sort of white witch, delivers presents to the kids. Even more presents. Or, supposedly, a lump of coal if they've been bad. We stoutly maintain that we've never heard of either of these personages, ever, until we remember whose feast it was the day Good King Wenceslas Looked Out. And discover that the *Befana* is just a corruption of the Epiphany.

We manage to escape to the hills anyway to celebrate Saint Stephen and the Epiphany quietly, by dint of confusing everyone into thinking we're at someone else's place. It is wonderful and peaceful up here: the sun shines, the sky is blue, birds twitter wildly everywhere now that what hunters there are left are busy being force-fed *panettone*, unable to get out and about. The temperature is just right for wandering about up muletracks to use up a few of those million extra calories we've consumed recently, or along terraces to do a comparative study of olive crops. Our drastically cut ones aren't quite as good as Domenico's yet, nowhere near the obsessive Nino's, but rather a lot better than the more laid-back Ugo's. We can hold our heads high in San Pietro.

Evening draws in early and we go indoors to light the wood-stove. We won't need to bother cooking for weeks, while the Christmas fare works its way through our systems. The *panettone* collection alone will last a month at least. Toasted on the stove top, it's not bad at all. We settle down snug and smug with a bottle of last year's grape wine. At last, the Christmas we've been imagining.

A week or so later, we are still breakfasting, lunching and occasionally even dining on *panettone*. Venturing downtown now the festive season is safely over, we bump into Francesca who tells us, diplomatic as everyone always is round here, that she has given the rest of our gingerbread to the chickens because no one would eat it. So much for a United Europe.

24

Everyone has already forgotten the days when half the hillsides were abandoned, left to the encroaching wilderness. Now they feel about unloved and uncultivated olive groves the way you might feel about watching someone absent-mindedly shredding a bundle of ten-pound notes. Bad feeling is beginning to grow over the now-multitudinous German-owned olive trees in the area, which still go unpruned and unharvested, as they have done for years. To the holiday home owners they are just part of their gardens. Often they have very large gardens, because another bit of that wishful land-consolidation legislation says that the more land you own, the more you are allowed to add to your house. Instead of attracting olive farmers to gather large holdings and go and live on their land, as it was intended to do, this has just meant that holiday-home buyers with no interest whatsoever in farming buy up as much land as they can so as to be allowed to enlarge the house. An awful lot of terraces have ended up lying terminally derelict: and now hanky-headed peasant and designer-clad Diano son alike glower and *Porca-Miseria* away at the sight of all those olives going to waste.

Why don't the *Tedeschi* just offer a deal whereby the trees are pruned in exchange for firewood, like any local would, and an arrangement to give oil in exchange for help with the harvest, like we'd done with Domenico, if they can't be bothered doing it themselves? *Magari!* They are so perverse they would rather see their trees go to rack and ruin than give someone a load of free firewood. And so rich and selfish that they don't care. Why don't they let someone collect the olives at least, instead of just leaving them to fall off the trees and rot?

We know that, like us in earlier times, the Germans see the olive trees simply as a bit of romantic woodland that happens to come with the house. They're psychotherapists and graphic designers and suchlike: why would they know anything about olives? We're sure they'd be happy to let some local have the firewood, we say, and probably the crop too, if anyone went and actually spoke to them instead of just muttering away behind their backs. They don't know, for example, that everyone uses olive wood for their stoves, that the wood's worth enough to cover the cost of the pruning work. They're bound to think they'd have to pay someone to do it. And to harvest the crop. And they're as paranoid about being ripped off by some cunning peasant as you lot are about Germans. So they just do nothing.

Euh! says Pompeo in his most disbelieving tones. This is (more or less) the response we've had every time we've made this speech to anyone. How come you know so much, then? he asks, looking round at our neatly spread olive nets, evidently having completely forgotten his own part in our learning process. If it took us years to get to this point, we say, when we're here for a good half of the year and speak Italian, what hope has a six-weeks-a-year non-Italian speaker got? Why don't you try explaining it to them instead of just fulminating under your hanky?

But of course this sensible suggestion flies in the face of all received peasant wisdom: what fool would tell someone they were sitting on a gold mine if they hadn't noticed it for themselves?

The German Olives Situation reaches a crescendo of absurdity when the manoeuvrings of cunning peasants lead to the destruction of the home of poor Uli, the newest German arrival, an excitable Beethoven-haired red-faced music journalist who is hardly ever to be seen entirely sober. Just as his new upper storey, which is, naturally, being put up by our old friend and enemy Franco, is almost finished and ready to be plastered, the official decree comes through. No ifs, no buts: it must be demolished forthwith.

Uli's tiny bothy is not even one up, one down – the lower storey is only half a room, a cave-*cantina* built into the side of the small cliff which forms the foundation for the large upstairs room. But it comes with an enormous piece of land, on which stand a couple of hundred olive trees, under one of which Uli sat happily and inno-cently all summer at a small plastic table with matching chairs in tasteful and apt olive-green, with a large bottle of wine and a lap-top computer, looking down hopefully on the building-site which would one day be his home, practising his Italian on Franco, banging out articles on the Nice Jazz Festival and suchlike. We have befriended Uli, who is a sweetheart, and have helped him find someone to clear the land around his house, which is choked up with waist-high brambly stuff. Mimmo and Paletta have agreed to do the job for nothing, in exchange for the olives, which won't be a lot because the trees are a bit neglected, but still two or three hundred pounds' worth, decent pay for a few days' work. They will also, after the harvest, do the pruning in exchange for the firewood. I am very proud of this achievement – at last one step has been made towards international harmony: one German will not be seen as a money-bagging wastrel.

Antonio, the ex-owner of the land, is the wild card that causes the catastrophe. He is annoyed with Franco, who he feels, probably rightly, has made a lot more out of the deal than he has. He is angry that he sold the land just as the price of olives was on the turn, and now, we gather, wishes he hadn't. Antonio has already been seriously put out by Franco leaving piles of building stuff all over the place, blocking the access road to what's left of his own land several times, once for over a fortnight, and forcing him to carry his olive nets on foot the last hundred yards. And when nets appear spread out under his ex-trees he concludes that this too is Franco's handiwork. Being as convinced as everyone else round here that no German would never agree to anyone working their olives, he is now certain that, adding insult to injury, Franco is unlawfully appropriating olives which, if they are to be harvested at all, ought by rights to be Antonio's own.

How to punish Franco? Antonio decides to denounce Uli's building as 'abusivo' – unauthorized. He only wants to inconvenience Franco, get the building work halted for a few months. If you take the cellar-cave as ground level – and why not, on a terraced hillside? – then the building is now three storeys high. Houses restored and Adjusted in these hills must not be more than two storeys high. The Comune has another look at the paperwork: Antonio is as surprised as everyone else when things get seriously out of hand, and the order goes through to demolish the top storey.

Uli, who knows nothing of the olive wars raging around his

property, is even more surprised than Antonio at this news, and hotfoots it back from Frankfurt. But there is nothing to be done. His new storey is knocked down – by Franco himself, who charges him almost as much for demolishing it as he did for putting it up – and he has to wait till next year to have it approved again and rebuilt. By which time the once-beautiful land around his house is a rubble-strewn wasteland. And it is Franco who puts it back up again: Antonio's revenge has backfired, and Franco has got three times the work for nothing. Driven to distraction, Antonio, who belongs to the Oliveculture Classes are a Socialist Conspiracy clique, now manages to convince Uli that Mimmo and Paletta's pruning – semi-drastic only, for efficiency combined with beauty – is the work of lunatics and incompetents. All my international harmony work utterly undone.

We clamber about in the trees, rattling at their loaded branches with canes and broomsticks to get the olives to fall; nobody has got round to getting one of those sissy Tuscan electric combers-and-shakers yet, so we are all trying to be delicate, now we know about the fungal diseases we might be exposing the poor trees to. All except Paletta, that is, who refuses to believe a word of it and whacks away with a seasoned olivewood shillelagh and all his might. Now we heave at the nets, roll the olives down terrace after terrace. Tiring business: you have to get right under the nets half the time, bent double, for a good rolling position. Then shovel it all up, with wide-mouth rubbery builders' buckets so as not to rip the nets.

We are working mob-handed, with the help of Patrizia, Mimmo, Lorella, Caterina, Alberto, Anna, Dario the baker, Testone (apparently heroin-free these days), and of course the Two Cousins Ciccio and Paletta; and we are doing Antonietta's olives first, along with Compare Gianni and Maurizio. This plan, at least, has worked; Maurizio, finding that strong young men – including ex-football heroes – are happy to be peasanting about up here, is joining in with a will. Suddenly it seems a skill worth having. Antonietta is overjoyed.

We get their crop into Compare Gianni's Ape and arrange to meet them next week to do the Castello olives, which aren't as ripe as on this side of the valley. Eventually our own fifteen lovely big sackfuls, after much painful wheelbarrowing to and fro along the evil path, repose on the back of Paletta's lorry. Even with these impressive results from our drastic cut, though, there is still plenty of space left on our oversized transport. We wonder whether to round up our quintal quotient, since we're overflowing with manpower, by stopping on the way down the hill to collect some abandoned German olives.

With just a small detour we will pass the lands of a pair of amiable gay doctors who haven't shown up at all, to our certain knowledge, for a good four summers. Sure though I am that if the owners by some unlikely mischance were to turn up unexpectedly on this particular February evening they would be positively charmed to find us industriously making sure that their olives don't go to waste, I can't convince my accomplices of this. As far as they are concerned, we are launching a daring raid on German terrain: stealing, in fact. It makes no difference that the olives would only go to waste if we didn't take them. Maybe they're right to worry: perhaps the doctors would not give a bunch of unknown locals a rapturous reception if they were unaccompanied by known and respectable English neighbours. Still, here we are, respectable English neighbours. We insist.

We throw our nets down any old how under the Germans' trees – not so easy on overgrown land that hasn't been Cleaned for years – and as the sun begins to go down behind the ridge opposite, doing one of its over-the-top orange- and purple-stripe performances, we start rolling and heaving: much harder work when your nets aren't stitched together and you have to do each tree individually, but we've soon got another five sacks loaded up.

Now, though, our fellow olive thieves refuse point-blank to go with our haul to either of the mills down in San Pietro in the morning. We are too well known there, they say; we will have to go to the *frantoio* – oil mill – in the Faraldi valley, the one in San Bartolomeo, where the owner's son is a friend of theirs. And where people won't be sure how many olive trees we own.

Are they seriously telling us that if we went to a *frantoio* in San Pietro our fellow customers there would be so well-informed about the exact number of trees we've got, the amount of olives they're likely to have produced, that they will actually spot half a dozen extra sacks and suspect us of misdoings?

Yes, that is precisely what they're saying. I realize how far I still have to go before I plumb the computer-like depths of the olive-farming mind. And, points out Patrizia, you can't very well stand about in the mill saying, don't worry, we didn't nick the olives off a Sanpeotto, just off some Germans, can you? You'd be under suspicion of olive thieving in the village for the rest of your days. Steal from one, steal from all, they'd say. Your names would be mud . . .

Moreover, says Paletta, coming at the thing from the supernatural angle as usual, stolen olives are known to bring *sfiga*. Someone in my position shouldn't tempt fate.

What does he mean, my position?

Have I forgotten the Curse of the Broken Demijohn, which may come upon me even now?

The lorry gets settled down for the night well away from prying eyes, lurking – very noticeably in my opinion – on the bend at the end of our path. Its owners get a lift home in Dario's car, while we stomp off to bed muttering about how absurdly complicated life in this country is, and how deranged its inhabitants.

Our drivers arrive by Vespa at dawn, keen to get moving before other olive harvesters start Aping nosily past the lorry counting our sacks. Paranoia is such that Ciccio takes the bike down separately, while Paletta drives our dodgy load not along the normal road through San Pietro and along the Via Aurelia, but by a series of long, slow and hair-raising detours over dirt-tracks as yet unknown to us in spite of our intensive explorings over the years. We follow in our latest vehicle, a perfectly ordinary looking Fiat Uno whose plain and simple exterior conceals a highly exotic defect. For inscrutable Italian reasons, it was made in Brazil and then re-exported here. This means that all its components measure just a millimetre or so more, or occasionally less, than the Italian version, and finding spare parts for it is almost impossible. This annoying machine has recently begun to develop a thing called (the experts tell us) 'windscreen cancer', a strange bubbling effect in the glass as if someone had been sticking sheets of clingfilm on to it. But the bubbles are actually sandwiched, by some fabulous Brazilian process, right inside the glass, and they do not improve visibility. Quite the contrary, they make Paletta's secret route to the mill even more hair-raising than it really is. Naturally, the windscreen, too, is a couple of millimetres out, so we can't buy a new one; while along with the rest of the interference in people's private lives engendered by this modernization of Italy business, there are now MOT requirements here, too. Gianni the mechanic is scouring the scrapyards of Liguria for another Brazilian-sized windscreen: if he hasn't found one by June, our car is dead.

Our convoy arrives just as the San Bartolomeo mill is opening – and we find great commotion at its gates. An ambulance is pulling out of the yard, and Apes full of olives stand about at odd angles, knots of hanky-headed men and bescarfed women deep in agitated conversation. Paletta's fears of *sfiga* have come true; someone, we are told, has tried unsuccessfully to commit suicide, and is being taken off to hospital with a broken arm and leg.

Paletta climbs down from his lorry and nudges me in the ribs: see? That broken demijohn. Very likely there will be no milling this morning.

But who could have tried to kill themselves, and why first thing in the morning? In an olive-oil mill of all places? How would you go about killing yourself in an oil mill? Head under the millstone? Is it the miller perhaps?

No: the miller comes out of his buildings now to join the onlookers, all in one piece, if a little pale and shaken, ready and willing to tell the tale all over again.

Arriving half an hour ago to start up the machinery, he says, he heard strange groaning noises coming from the back of the building where he parks his lorries – one an open-bed lorry for hauling away the *sansa*, the greasy sawdust-like remnants of ground-up olive stones left after the milling, the other an oil-tanker (new take on oil-tankers here; never thought of an olive-oil version). Going to investigate, he saw a big chunk of rooftiles smashed in, then heard groaning coming from inside the *sansa* lorry. And there was this man lying half-buried in the *sansa*. Serves you right, said the miller, convinced he had caught a thief who had slipped and fallen while trying to break in through the roof. There's nothing in here to steal anyway.

But the man, dazed and semi-conscious, managed to say that he was not stealing; he had jumped off the motorway above, trying to kill himself. The worst of it, says the miller penitently, is that I didn't believe a word.

Motorway? Is there a motorway above? Squinting upwards into the sun, we see that indeed there is; we are right down in the bottom of the valley, in the river bed, and the motorway is so far up on its immense viaduct, its supporting concrete stilts fading off into the distant skies above, that you don't even notice it. How could anyone survive a fall from right up there?

Amazingly, the would-be suicide managed to hit the roof bang in the centre of one of the three-foot gaps between the beams; we all troop in to look at the hole where the sky shows blue through the shattered terracotta tiles. Having miraculously evaded being smashed to pieces on a beam, he now needed only to avoid hitting the stone flags below to survive. Which he did by landing in the lorry full of *sansa* that cushioned his fall and saved his life.

Euh! says everybody, including us.

But there is more to the miracle even than this, says the miller. The driver usually parks the lorry a few feet back from where it is now. He shows us, to a great chorus of incredulous *Euh!*s, *Porca-Madonna*s and *Porca-Miseria*s, the iron spikes which stick vertically up just behind its cab, on which the would-be suicide would have impaled himself if it wasn't for the inexplicable forces that made the driver park that bit forward last night.

Everybody crosses themselves and mutters more *Porca-Madonna*s and *Miseria*s. And we all stand around agreeing, *Ah, si, si*, that when it's not your time to go, it's not your time to go. *Euh!* Nothing to be done about it. *Niente da fare!*

Is there no end to the versatility of the olive? What, I wonder aloud as we stand about in the yard waiting to get our turn on the wind-machine and blow the leaves and rubbish out of our crop, is the story behind this life-saving *sansa* stuff? We've heard about the second pressing no one admits to doing, but we didn't know you got oil out of the stones as well.

Of course you do: you crush whatever's left over after that, pulp, stones and kernels, mix it up with some kind of acid to dissolve the *olio di sansa* out. Why do we think people make such a fuss about cold-pressed extra-virgin oil? The oil from inside the stone, *olio di sansa*, also counts as olive oil, and cheap olive oil is very likely to have this chemically recovered stuff mixed in with it. The *sansa*, drained of its oil, gets used for fertilizer next; though some people have specially designed heating systems that run on it. *Frantoiani*, millers, mostly.

Paletta decides to tell us yet another use of the olive, one that he thinks I may need to try. In the hands of an expert, he says, olive oil can remove the *malocchio*, the evil eye. Adepts in matters mystical – he is thinking of a particular old man in Diano Borello, though there is a woman they say is OK down in Diano Serreta – will float a layer of virgin oil on clear spring water in a glass. You will kiss the glass. The expert will murmur certain words, make certain mystic passes over it, while you concentrate with all your power on the oil and water chalice. If the *malocchio*-removal charm works, you will see the oil suddenly break up on the surface of the water and fly dramatically apart into globules. You are free at last from the *sfiga*.

Sounds like a drop of washing-up liquid on the fingertip to me, I say. I bet I could do that. Paletta is disgusted. Why does he waste his breath on me? Later, I will demonstrate this trick to him, mystic passes and all, without managing to shake his faith in the old man from Borello one jot.

Fortunately, I don't have to go all the way to Borello to get my luck restored for now. Healthy roaring noises are coming from within the mill, and *malocchio* or not our olives will be pressed today. We finally get our turn on the olive-cleaning machine: a sort of mini conveyor-belt with a huge fan blowing up from beneath it. Ciccio and Paletta are not at all pleased to discover that in this neat concreted yard you have to sweep up all your own twiggy bits and remove them, leaving the yard clear for the next customers. In San Pietro you just leave them lying about to biodegrade into the cobbles. A lesson to us all, I point out smugly, not to go foolishly cementing over cobblestones.

The boys stomp off for a chat with their mate the miller's son – another run-through of the suicide story, no doubt, but with more genealogical detail – while Lucy and I carry on a-shovelling, a-winnowing and a-sweeping up. And so it happens that when a big fat shiny so-called off-road vehicle pulls in alongside us bearing a Milan numberplate, complete with cow-rails and rows of spare petrol canisters and all the survival gear, we alone are in charge. A pair of sleek Plainsmen sit in the front – fully macho Outdoor Wear-ed up – their Barbour-clad wives in the back. The driver, in emerald-green Arran-knit – is it a political green, Northern League, or does he just like the colour? – addresses us in a most patronizing 'my good woman' manner.

Is this, he wants to know, a traditional stone-grinding mill?

Yes, it is, we say.

Then, says he in a conspiratorial hiss as if he was after some Class-A drug, will we sell him some of our oil?

The marketing-plan of the bearded olive adviser and his besuited colleague has begun to work: these are tourists of a new breed, olive-oil tourists, who these days will travel hundreds of kilometres along the *terroni*-built motorways down from the North, now well-worn, to be sure of getting the real thing. Make a holiday of it, visit some lovely old hill-villages, try out the country restaurants, explore the rugged hairpin-bending tracks in your safari mobile, grab yourself a bunch of wild mountain thyme as you go, and pick up a selection of olive oils, a taste from each valley. Directly from the mills to be sure of what you're getting.

There have been rumours (probably untrue, of course) of Greek, Spanish, North African olive-oil tankers creeping stealthily by night into the port at Imperia, full to the gunwales with oil from those dry and overheated climates, oil whose acidity level is all wrong; which cargo they pump under cover of darkness straight into the town's oil-processing plants to be used to water down, or is it oil up, the genuine Taggiasca. There is a lot less danger of that sort of thing if you go straight to a mill in the *entroterra*, where the locals get their own oil pressed: a place, moreover, where there is no seaport, only a dry torrent along which dubious foreign olive-oil tankers could never penetrate. Unless, that is, they sat and waited for a chance *temporale* in the hills.

These *Milanesi* have gone a step further: they don't even trust the country miller. You never know, explains the putative Greenshirt, what millers may slip into the bottles they make up to sell to *stranieri*. How would you know if it's fresh? If it's really stone ground? If it's been adulterated with second-pressing? With *olio di sansa* even? We, on the other hand, look like good honest folk. Will our husbands sell him a few litres?

Are we flattered to blend in so well with the surroundings these days? Or annoyed by the assumption that our own personal olives are the property of some invisible male? Will we just laugh at your man for a paranoid nutter? Anyone can tell if oil's fresh: it's all green and cloudy. And if he asked the *frantoiano* nicely, instead of creeping about cunningly out here in the yard, he could stand right there in the mill and watch it trickle straight out of the press and into his bottle.

Still, maybe a Plainsman in this steep and hilly land is right not to trust the miller. Or anyone else. I remember Pompeo's friend Fabio, one of the last few fishermen still working out of Diano Marina harbour, telling us with great glee how, during the tourist season, he always stows a fridgeful of frozen items away in his hold before leaving for his night's work: you don't know how bad your catch may be at sea, but on land for sure, as you roll back into port at breakfast time, you'll hook a bunch of soft-in-the-head Torinesi and Milanesi queuing up to buy your just-caught fresh fish at a premium. A quick dip in the sea and the *gente de Pianüa* never know the difference.

Blameless though this man may be, I can't help it: I have taken a dislike to him. I am horribly prejudiced against the weekend driving owners of these squeaky clean off-road vehicles, which creep along our road at a snail's pace, trying not to spoil their nice new suspension and carrying on as if they were on some particularly perilous Himalayan goat-trail, so busy with their Great Adventure that they don't notice the Brazilian Uno behind them, chafing at the bit. Why don't they get off the road, then, if it's a darned off-road vehicle?

I've taken to hooting childishly long and rude at them, overtaking them with as much dramatic roaring as I can get from my scruffy tropically deformed machine, smothering them, where possible, in a cloud of genuine Ligurian mountain dust.

Not to worry: the trusty sister has devised the ultimate humiliation for our would-be client. She turns to me and, laughing gaily, addresses me in fluent English. Your man is mortified: he has been addressing another Superior Northern being like himself as if she were nothing but a lowly Ligurian peasant.

A few weeks later we hear the latest news on the would-be olive-mill suicide. Returning from hospital, the grapevine tells us, he found in his post a hefty fine from the Traffic Police. He had, in the heat of the moment, Abandoned his Vehicle on a Motorway. He went straight off and hanged himself – from an olive tree of course. And this time he succeeded in his mission.

25

When we first arrived here, the countryside was strangely silent; only in early spring did you hear birdsong in the trees. Now feathery things *tweet*, *meep* and *krark* all year round. As the numbers of hunters shrink, the numbers of the huntable have built up to levels unseen, I daresay, since the invention of the shotgun. We've seen not just boar and quails, but pheasants and badgers, pine martens and hoopoes, and even, further up in the hills, a couple of chamois. Some kind of eagle has reappeared from the high mountain fastnesses to take advantage of the newly snack-packed hillsides, gliding and swooping above our valley, *screeeeee*ing through the sky all summer long, snatching, ripping and guzzling the small birds and mammals now left in peace by humans. The Hunters' Festa has gone for good now: you will find only the odd blackened ring of stones in the grass up at the Gascio, bonfires built by lonesome hunters with no place to go.

Nowadays, with Saints, Communists and Hunters all fallen by the wayside, only food is left as the excuse for a village *festa*. Still, that will do just as well. You hold a *sagra*, these days, of some particular foodstuff. Luigi, his moustache now iron-grey, insists that the *sagra* is more ancient even than Christianity: a remnant, he says, of Primitive Communism. When a village had an extra-large harvest of something or other, more than it could possibly eat, dry, bottle, or preserve, rather than throw the stuff away, it would invite the other villages around to come and share in Nature's bounty. Thus was the *sagra* born.

In these modern times of plenty, though, a village can *sagra* anything it fancies, however unlikely. We have attended a dried cod party, *sagra del baccalà*, at tiny Villa Faraldi up at the head of the next valley – a place whose connections with the Atlantic cod-fishing industry must surely be rather tenuous. We have participated heroically in Moltedo's *sagra delle rane ed anguille*, frog and eel party, which took place, somewhat alarmingly, on an improvised dance floor in the middle of the torrent-prone riverbed. Borganzo's *sagra* was held in honour of the snail, a delicious creature as long as there's enough garlic in the sauce and you can manage not to think about what it once was.

The women of Diano Borello pride themselves on their fresh cheese-filled *ravioli al pesto*; we recently *sagra*'d an abundance of that in their lovely piazza under the Romanesque church, to the accompaniment of an extraordinarily loud and literal-minded band which called itself Rosa dei Venti, Rose of the Winds, and blew great blasts of some supposedly rose-flavoured perfume at us from a wind-machine as we ate. Until, that is, agitation and heated debate broke out in the cooking zone. The chefs had rebelled. No politics, no religion, OK; but at least some respect for the food. How could anyone appreciate the subtleties of the cooking against such competition? The *sindaco*, the mayor, was called over. Although he had personally booked this band, to whose members he was (naturally) distantly related, the palate comes first: the winds were turned off, not to rise again until dinner was over.

These days a *sagra*, if you can come up with an excuse to hold one during the summer season, will attract large numbers of visitors from the coast, sometimes as many *stranieri* as villagers. A fine way to fill the village coffers, money to spend on asphalt or on fixing those eternally crumbling terrace walls, and nobody much minds this, apart from a few hidebound traditionalists. Even Pompeo, soon to hit ninety but still going strong, has come round to the notion that if you can't keep the Deutschmarks at bay, you may as well do your best to grab a share of them.

The inhabitants of Diano Marina, meanwhile, are becoming ever more overweening. We have recently been obliged, along with many other right-thinking people, to abandon the Bar Sito, once a favourite *aperitivo* spot, for ever, in protest against a disgraceful attempt by its proprietors to turn the May Day up-the-mountain festivities into a California ranch-style barbecue party. Right there in the middle of the meadow – on the wide flat bit where everyone usually potters about and plays *petanca* and socializes, a kind of Bar Sito compound mushroomed up at crack of dawn, a dining table for thirty-odd topped with a great frilly shade canopy, which took up twice as much space again, along with hordes of folding chairs and sunbeds. This swish seating area was fenced off from us lower mortals with an array of off-road vehicles and a selection of immensely sophisticated and expensive-looking cooking equipment. Among which was a red and silver rotating eye-level barbecue bulging with gyrating chickens and rabbits, running off a whole array of gas-bottles and operated with pride by Franco's old enemy, Federico the cab-driver, kitted out for the occasion in a cashmere designer jumper. The womenfolk of the clan set off the scene perfectly in sequin-butterfly-appliqué tops and yards of make-up. The centre of the *prato* was thus out of bounds to everyone else for the rest of the day, while the poor old Bar Sito dad, aged innocent, sat in his folding armchair in a corner of the canopy looking bewildered. Wondering, I dare say, what had happened to May Day. Rumour has it that the boycott has worked: the Bar Sito folk have repented of their sins. We'll see next May Day: till then, we can be found taking our *aperitivi* at the Bar Nelson instead.

Orti covered not in vegetables but in roses are a surprising new feature of our landscape. The EEC is not doing so well by olive farming as it is by cows and flowers, and you need an enormous number of trees to get help with modernizing and upgrading – enough for your olive farming to count as a full-time job. Roses being more labour-intensive than olives, it is easier to get support for floriculture. As you can tell from Patrucco's empire, which now takes up a good square mile of the riverbed lands and boasts a whole fleet of refrigerated lorries bearing his name and the legend '*Rose d'Autore*', which translates roughly as 'Roses by Design'. Not to mention the evidence of the new rooftop swimming pool. So, we are told, the thing to do is plant these EEC roses – you have to do that, they come to inspect them, but you can always root them up after a year or two – and then use the money for stuff that is also handy for your olive farming, new mini-ploughs, fertilizer, winter-proof reinforced terrace walls; or some of those status-symbol olive nets, bright orange ones that cost a fortune but are twice as strong as the old white ones and don't start biodegrading after a few years. Then there's that wonderful new invention, the hand-held sewing machine for stitching your nets together *in situ*, saving hours of fiddling with dishcloths, string and nails. This, you can claim, is vital floricultural equipment: how else can you protect your budding roses from the ravening flocks of birds that have returned to the hills?

Chomping their way down towards us from the top of the ridge, gigantic against the blue horizon, have come a clutch of startlingly huge and lop-sided bulldozing machines, Mad Max post-holocaust transports. They have dug their way over mountain and valley a thousand miles and more, leaving a massive three-metre deep scar of a trench behind them; straight as the crow flies across rock and scree, olive grove and wilderness, up and down almost vertical hillsides, bringing piped gas to Italian homes. One day there will at last be an end to the dragging of heavy gas bottles to and fro, in and out, up and down staircases, shop to home and back again . . .

The trench passes just twenty yards from the end of our path, slowly crunching its way downhill, flinging great grey rocks carelessly hither and thither. One of the drivers, alerted to our presence by the large collection of transport on our bend, pops along to visit us. Four men have died on the job so far, he says; the machines occasionally topple over and off into gorges and abysses, in spite of being designed supposedly to do no such thing. Heroic deaths in the interest of progress, these days, get hushed up rather than noised abroad. Not like in the days of the Roman Empire, when you'd get a statue put up to you where you fell. No indeed.

Sympathetic though we may be to the plight of bulldozer drivers lumbered with dodgy technology, we cut this conversation short: we have learnt that this sort of remark about the Roman Empire more often than not leads inexorably on to how Mussolini wasn't all that bad and Fascism did a lot for the Italian people . . . This driver, like the *carabinieri* before him, greatly appreciates our lovely shack and lands, and stays for a tour of our *orto* and a cup of coffee.

Down in San Pietro many hanky folk are cheerfully awaiting their compensation cheques for olive-tree disturbance, and debate has been raging in the bar about these earthshaking machines. Have they, as some assert, ground their way up from Sicily to bring us gas from the deserts of Algeria in a pipe under the sea? Or from Russia, to bring it from Siberian wastes across the frozen Caucasus? Here, we think, is a source of hard information at last. But the driver doesn't know either. He only took over somewhere in Umbria. Moreover he doesn't really care. This job, he says, is worse than his last one, which was in the middle of the Saudi Arabian desert. There, you were rescued from desert solitude by a helicopter that came to whisk you off on a Friday night to the fleshpots of some big city for the weekend; here in Italy, since the operators are presumed to be somewhere civilized already, they are left to get what entertainment they can in miserable mountain villages, places where the nightlife consists of one bar and a bunch of old men in hankies playing cards. We know what he means.

The next time we try to walk down to San Pietro, we find that the trench cuts straight through the muletrack; scaling it utterly ruins our tidy going-to-Diano outfits. We curse and sulk. Of course nobody will ever put our lovely path back together again, what with how it isn't vital to anyone's economy any more. But we are wrong; heritage awareness in this land has grown so dramatically over the last decade that the pipeline company has been contracted to put everything neatly back together again just as it was. A month later, there is the muletrack neatly cobbled again, the terrace walls replaced – although with huge inhuman-sized rocks shifted by bulldozer. We will find, next spring, that wild broccoli love nothing better than freshly turned earth. We, and everyone else in San Pietro, eat our fill; there are still enough flower-heads left to cut a great yellow swathe downhill and up again, once summer comes, right across the valley.

I, meanwhile, far from being modernized, have recently found myself being put through a typically Italian trauma of which, with my Anglo-Saxon background, I could never have dreamed: I have transmuted, inexplicably yet inexorably, from a *signorina* to a *signora*.

Unprepared mentally for this event, which has no equivalent in my own culture, I have found this rather hard to handle. I have always been a *signorina*: I have accepted this word as somehow defining my identity. Then, from one day to the next, as it seems, I have been allocated, by a mysterious collective decision in which I have no say, a completely new definition. I am now a *signora*. Everyone in the world except me has apparently detected some huge change in my being which requires this adjustment. There is nothing for it but to embrace this unsettling transformation foisted upon you by unanimous public agreement.

The *signora* newly emerged from her chrysalis spends, I find, an awful lot of time in front of various mirrors in various bars trying to work out what it is exactly that has changed so drastically. Nothing, you say to yourself, I look exactly the same as I did a few months ago: and yet, here too, I have just been called *signora*. Is the change, perhaps, not in the outward aspect, but in the very essence? Traumatic, anyway: I wouldn't be surprised to hear that more than one woman on the brink, having her identity suddenly snatched and swapped like this, has ended up on the analyst's couch – if not in the clutches of Paletta's Old Man from Borello.

Caterina tells me that *signora*-ing is only intended as a mark of respect, a courtesy title. You ought to be married by your age, and it would be rude to draw attention to the fact if you aren't. Really! Join the twentieth century.

Patrizia tries another tack: feminists in this country, she says, of whom there are by now enough to be faintly noticeable, have been campaigning for all females to be called *signora* from puberty onward. A sudden overwhelming public response to this demand may have caused my overnight precipitation into *signora*-hood.

I mull this over hopefully, but in the end find it hard to believe. Sanpeotti, avid readers of *l'Unità* though they may still be, are unlikely to be much influenced in their daily lives by modern feminist theory. In Diano Marina, meanwhile, where most of these *signora*-ing outrages are taking place, the *Gazzetta dello Sport* is the only paper regularly perused. The Dianesi will never have heard of such a thing.

★

Luigi and Maria's bar has moved upstairs to what was once the first floor, and these days you enter it from the bridge over the muletrack. The old downstairs bar, at muletrack level, has been transformed by an enterprising cousin of Antonietta's, who rents it from Luigi and Maria, into a Saturday-only disco – a club which has become so popular amongst Italian under-twenties that, rather than opening for the tourist season, it keeps its doors firmly shut all through the summer, and only opens once the chaos is over. The strange habit of travelling hundreds of kilometres for a night's partying is firmly established among the youth of this land, and as autumn weekends arrive and the tourists leave the coast, streams of teenagers from all over Italy converge on the Sulking Café for a night out in San Pietro. If the wind is in the right direction (and if we've managed to get home at all through the tidal waves of cars in which the convoys of youth travel) we can just hear a distant muffled thumping, a faint echo of the well-known Insistent Repetitive Beat, throbbing out through the valley till the place closes at four a.m. At which point its energetic habitués drive off another few hundred kilometres to some distant after-hours venue, in Pisa or Genoa, where they will keep on going till the early afternoon.

The once-a-week close encounter with the strange behaviour of modern youth has combined with the removal of the threat to their livelihood to broaden the horizons of the hanky folk out of all recognition. These days a good proportion of the denizens of Luigi's bar are ready to chat cheerfully of matters agricultural and meteorological to all comers, in Italian, too, as if there was no reason necessarily to suppose that *stranieri* are off another planet, even when wearing outrageously revealing outfits. Stefano keeps the bar open till one o'clock on these nights, a thing previously unheard-of in early-to-bed, early-to-rise San Peo. The youth assembles up here before going downstairs to business: plumping up the fiscal till no end by consuming oceans of Coca-Cola, coffee and ice-cream. Stefano makes the fresh-fruit ice-creams and sorbets himself, so good they've made the bar an obligatory stop-off for gastronomic tourists.

I am still asked occasionally, at some distant *festa*, whether I know the other Englishwoman, the Mad Builder in the Hills with her two oppressed house-husbands and no proper toilet, who is probably a drug fiend into the bargain. This bogey of old folks' legend, cunningly wrought out of a couple of decades of intricate gossip and calumny, will clearly live for ever, although the mentality that created her is, fingers crossed, rapidly vanishing.

What with the extra business from the ice-cream, the clubbers and the olive-oil tourists, and with their regulars' disposable income having risen comfortably, Luigi, Maria and Stefano naturally feel no temptation whatsoever to open their restaurant to the public. It remains a private, bookings-only affair.

Patrucco and the miller between them now keep a small fleet of two-, three- and four-wheeled vehicles cluttering up the space between the *frantoio* and the bar, very much annoying Luigi, who needs the parking for his regulars. They too, thanks to the renaissance of the olive, have gleaming new conveyances to show off. In spite of the parking problem, glowering, once a full-time occupation in the bar, has tailed off to virtually nothing. Everyone's too busy up in the hills to bother. The sad songs of wasted lives, abandoned land, and evil lifeblood-sucking cities are sung in San Pietro these days, when they are sung at all, with a cheerful gusto that rather undermines their tragic lyrics.

The Lord's great foresight in the matter of the dozen tight hairpin bends that carry the asphalt road criss-crossing through the heart of the village is now clear for all to see. Here in San Pietro there are hardly any houses you can't reach within twenty-odd yards on wheels. No one in their right mind would choose to rebuild and refurbish in a place where they had to carry all their shopping up and down a long steeply stepped pathway. (Except, that is, for romantically minded German holiday-home owners, who are at last getting the praise they deserve for preserving the old housing stock so meticulously.) But refurbishing your old family home, one of the ancient houses that cluster round the muletrack, is perfectly feasible here, unlike many of the other villages in these hills, whose old central alleyways are being left to slowly biodegrade. Here in San Pietro there is no need to leave it all to fall down. Not that there isn't quite a bit of building on the periphery too, with all the returning

Lost Generation; square chunky villas, faintly 1930s looking, have appeared on every hairpin bend, squeezed in among the old barns and vaulted *cantine*. But the tastes of the San Pietro young are not too different from those of their parents, and the new buildings are smothered in such an array of twisting and twining plant life that they are hardly distinguishable from the rest. Just leave the road and go off up the steep track which is still the heart of the village, and you find the old folk sitting and gossiping under the ancient archways of an evening as they did when we first met the place, as they have done for centuries. Nowadays, there are children playing noisily on the terraces above and below them, football nets strung between the olive trees. Hope for the future: infinitely better than picturesque decrepitude.

These kids have appeared in such numbers that a big new primary school, a chunky oblong in ice-cream stripes, has been built between the village and Patrucco's rosebeds, thanks to Mayor Ugo-from-the-shop; a school to serve all the newly repopulated hillside Dianos, and preserve the youth of the valleys for as long as possible from contamination by degenerate Diano Marina. Signor Ugo has also had a lovely new enamelled road sign put up at the entrance to San Pietro, with a map of all the townships in the valley – excluding, naturally, Diano Marina – and the bold Legend 'Communita Montana dell' Ulivo': Mountain Community of the Olive. Just in case you couldn't guess.

The San Pietro riverbed is these days festooned with 'No Dumping' signs, and has been dredged clear of all old ironmongery. Giacò has retired, his chaotic bit of riverbed cleared and ploughed smooth, abandoned to the tall waving clumps of wild canes: he still asks after my marble sink-and-drainer whenever I bump into him. Several families of ducks have taken over the newly clean riverbanks. This year there is even a pair of large and elegant swans with a fluffy young family, whose choice of San Pietro as home has caused some hard feeling in Diano Marina. They were purchased last year by Diano's Comune to beautify their river and entertain the tourists, but almost immediately left to entertain the unkempt peasantry of San Pietro instead. Even more entertainingly, this summer a huge and spectacular *temporale* filled the *torrente* to maximum capacity, drowning several hundred vehicles and rather a lot of stock in the basement stores of Diano's shop owners whilst leaving San Pietro unscathed. Guffaw. The money-grubbers of Diano Marina had caused the catastrophe themselves by gradually cementing bits of the riverbed over to get more space for their tourists. Worse still, during the exciting flood-event the Mayor of Diano Marina sent a carload of *carabinieri* to remove a pair of children to whom he was related from the new San Pietro school, which is right next to the riverbed, for fear the flood might get them. Righteously outraged by this appalling piece of behaviour – either all the kids were in danger, or none of them were; and San Pietro is quite capable of taking care of its own, thank you, and wouldn't be so stupid as to block the *torrente* – Signor Ugo is now punishing his rival Mayor by taking him to court for Misuse of Public Servants.

The Comune of San Pietro has at last got itself the crusher lorry Domenico dreamed of, official recognition that the good old days when all rubbish was either burnable or biodegradable have long gone; and the horrible smoking eyesore on the side of the mountain is no more. A pair of those big wheely rubbish bins has appeared on each of the village's hairpin bends, and Domenico's replacement whizzes to and fro emptying them into a fabulous modern rubbish-compacting purpose-built jobbie by automatic grabber. Out of respect for his father, Maurizio, now a tall gangling youth, has been told that a job in rubbish collection is his for the asking as soon as he gets his driving licence. He is not sure about this. He is training at Dario's dad's place to be a baker. We can see at last, too late, alas, for Domenico, that Maurizio was the right sort of baby after all: not only has he not left San Pietro, but he is often to be seen Aping his way uphill at Antonietta's side, off to help with the *campagna*. Better still, with his very first wages he bought his mother that last word in oliviculture gadgetry, the hand-held net-sewing machine. When Maurizio is not available for peasanting work, being too busy at the baker's, a certain courteous and behankied gentleman named Ettore is to be seen accompanying Antonietta up to her *campagna* in his own Ape. A suitor, we suspect, judging by his immensely solicitous behaviour.

Sergio and Lilli, sadly, no longer live up past our place: their chalet-balanced-on-a-*rustico* has been sequestered by the Finance Police for non-payment of debts. Alessandra and Paola are rather pleased with this outcome: the family have found themselves in a civilized little flat in downtown Imperia at just the right age for all that essential teenage socializing and clubbing, and the girls can gyrate happily with their *compagnie* of friends without worrying about the dozen hairpin bends to home. We often bump into them outside the bar in San Pietro of a Saturday night, looking very cool. Lilli is no longer Sergio's isolated prisoner; not being able to drive makes no difference in Imperia, where you just step out of the door to find great flocking masses of humans. And of course, great flocking masses of bars and supermarkets laden with alcoholic beverages. Alessandra says that this sociability and availability treatment has worked wonders on Lilli's alcohol problem, which now hardly exists. Oddly – or perhaps predictably? – it is now their father, no longer lord of all he surveys, who has the alcohol problem. Sergio, we have been told at Luigi's, amid much snickering, has been visiting San Pietro a lot recently for the purposes of litigation. He has unearthed some ancient San Pietro by-law according to which the Comune is supposed to contribute to supporting its indigent citizens, and is doing his best to prove that he is owed a monthly dole. He has managed to get about fifty thousand lire out of them, we hear: twenty pounds or so. The case will no doubt drag on for years.

Meanwhile Franco is now reconciled with his son, who has produced a granddaughter, the apple of Franco's eye. With the help of his *nipoti* and the EEC, he has succeeded in conquering his aversion to new technology, and expanded his activities to take account of the explosion in world demand for pesto: the land to the hillward side of his house in the village, where his old wooden basil-greenhouses once stood, their glass whitewashed (or was it limewashed?) against the sun, has been re-terraced into much wider and higher-walled *fascie*, on which proudly stand a whole series of modern steel-framed greenhouses, all automated air-flaps and humidity controllers. Eat your heart out, Patrucco. Here, instead of the small amounts he and Iole used to grow for local shops, are great green forests of basil, collected weekly by some factory above

Imperia to be made into potted pesto for export. He has not, of course, thrown away the old wood-frame sections of his earlier low-tech greenhouses: they live in a pile on his bean terraces up above our house, just in case.

Franco is busy these days doing up an old cowshed high in the hills, near Sergio and Lilli's chalet. This place is, he says, going to be his retirement home: we know, don't we, he adds, fixing us with that bright-blue gaze, that like us he is happier away up in the hills than down in San Pietro. This is certainly true at the moment: he is banned from Luigi's for the rest of the year for having caused great chaos and destruction when he decided, in his cups, to repeat one of the triumphs of his youth and ride his horse into the bar. Stefano's ice-cream counter required major repairs. We aren't sure we believe the retirement-house story: would Iole stand for isolated country dwelling? Is Franco capable of retiring? More likely, we think, under cover of the special building dispensations for Adjusting your own home, Franco is secretly planning yet another coup among the *stranieri*, a last property speculating fling. We will wait and see. Only time will tell.

Ciccio meantime still hasn't decided whether to dump the restaurant and devote himself to the olive groves. Salvatore, worn out by modernity, has offered to pass on the family lands to his son; but only on condition that he finds himself a good woman to settle down with – a woman who will of course contribute a respectable number of her own trees as dowry. I am seriously considering the proposition.

Nowadays in the nineties our once-isolated retreat among the olive groves is at the heart of a hive of industry. The hills are alive with the sound of the myriad tiny petrol-driven agricultural implements without which these narrow strips of terraced land would never have been worth bringing back into cultivation. Up and down the valley cement mixers rumble as the crumbling terrace walls are rebuilt with (thanks to the roses) a nice dollop of concrete concealed at their core wherever possible; one more never-ending, back-breaking job eliminated. The valleys resonate to clangings, roarings, strimmings, sawings and blasphemous calls upon the Madonna from dawn till the twelve o'clock bongs and hoot from three in the afternoon till seven on the dot, when the rush-hour down the hairpin bends to the village begins – praise the Lord for the delicacy of the peasant digestive system, which still requires pasta at seven-thirty sharp, or else – and all is peace again.

Everywhere around us the wilderness is being reclaimed. Mankind has returned to the trees. And our illiterate impresario neighbour, evidently not so close to retiring as he led us to think, has just offered to buy up our house and groves for many times what we paid. We know him well now, and of course there's a catch somewhere. We wouldn't dream of it anyway. We like it here.